SW 8340 & SW 8350

APPLICATIONS OF COGNITIVE BEHAVIOR THEORIES TO INTERPERSONAL PRACTICE I & II

Course Readings

Edited by
Antonio González-Prendes
Paul Koonter
William Vanderwill

School of Social Work
Wayne State University

WILEY

CUSTOM SERVICES

To order books or for customer service, please call 1(800)-CALL-WILEY (225-5945).

Printed in the United States of America.

ISBN 978-0-471-78185-1

10 9 8 7 6 5

Table of Contents

Reading 8
Iwamsa, G. Y. (1997). Behavior therapy and a culturally diverse society: Forging an alliance. *Behavior therapy*, 28, pp. 347-358.
Course pack page: 195

Reading 9
Lantz, J. (1996). Cognitive theory and social work treatment. In F. J. Turner (Ed.). *Interlocking theoretical approaches in Social Work Treatment*, (pp. 94-115). New York: Free Press. ISBN: 0-684-82994-0
Course pack page: 205

Reading 10
Segal, Z. V. and Shaw, B. F. (1988). Cognitive assessment: Issues and methods. In Dobson, K. S. (1988*). Handbook of cognitive-behavioral therapies*. New York: Guilford Press (pp. 39-84) ISBN: 0-89862-704-4
Course pack page: 229

Reading 11
Sperry, L (1999). *Cognitive therapy of DSM-IV personality disorders*. Philadelphia: Brunner/Mazel. Chapter 2: Character and schema change (pp. 20-32).
ISBN: 0-87630-900-7
Course pack page: 275

Reading 12
Thomlison, B. and Thomlison, R. (1996). Behavior theory and social work treatment. In F. J. Turner (Ed.). *Interlocking theoretical approaches-Social work Treatment* (pp. 39-68). New York: Free Press. ISBN: 0-684-82994-0
Course pack page: 285

Reading 13
Wenar, C. and Kerig, P (1999). *Developmental psychopathology*. Boston: Allyn Bacon. Chapter 9: Conduct disorders and the development of antisocial behavior (pp. 189-212). ISBN: 0-07-069617-9
Course pack page: 317

Reading 14
Sperry, L. (1999). *Cognitive therapy of DSM-IV personality disorders*. Philadelphia: Brunner/Mazel. Chapter 3: Temperament and style change (pp. 33-58).
ISBN: 0-87630-900-7
Course pack page: 343

Reading 15
Mattison, M. (2000). Ethical decision-making: The person in the process. *Social Work Journal*, 45, 201-212.
Course pack page: 359

Reading 1
The Paradoxes of Depression

The Paradoxes of Depression

Lying awake, calculating the future,
Trying to unweave, unwind, unravel
And piece together the past and the future,
Between midnight and dawn, when the past is
    all deception,
The future futureless. . . . —T. S. Eliot

A scientist, shortly after assuming the presidency of a prestigious scientific group, gradually became morose and confided to a friend that he had an overwhelming urge to leave his career and become a hobo.

A devoted mother who had always felt strong love for her children started to neglect them and formulated a serious plan to destroy them and then herself.

An epicurean who relished eating beyond all other satisfactions developed an aversion to food and stopped eating.

A woman, upon hearing of the sudden death of a close friend, emitted the first smile in several weeks.

These strange actions, completely inconsistent with the individual's previous behavior and values, are all expressions of the same underlying condition—depres-

sion. By what perversity does depression mock the most hallowed notions of human nature and biology?

The instinct for self-preservation and the maternal instincts appear to vanish. Basic biological drives such as hunger and sexual urge are extinguished. Sleep, the easer of all woes, is thwarted. "Social instincts," such as attraction to other people, love, and affection evaporate. The pleasure principle and reality principle, the goals of maximizing pleasure and minimizing pain, are turned around. Not only is the capacity for enjoyment stifled, but the victims of this odd malady appear driven to behave in ways that enhance their suffering. The depressed person's capacity to respond with mirth to humorous situations or with anger to situations that would ordinarily infuriate him seems lost.

At one time, this strange affliction was ascribed to demons that allegedly took possession of the victim. Theories advanced since that time have not yet provided a durable solution to the problem of depression. We are still encumbered by a psychological disorder that seems to discredit the most firmly entrenched concepts of the nature of man. Paradoxically, the anomalies of depression may provide clues for understanding this mysterious condition.

The complete reversal in the depressed patient's behavior seems, initially, to defy explanation. During his depression, the patient's manifest personality is far more like that of other depressives than his own previous personality. Feelings of pleasure and joy are replaced by sadness and apathy; the broad range of spontaneous desires and involvement in activities are eclipsed by passivity and desires to escape; hunger and sexual drive are replaced by revulsion toward food and sex; interest and involvement in usual activities are converted into avoidance and withdrawal. Finally, the desire to live is switched off and replaced by the wish to die.

As an initial step in understanding depression, we can attempt to arrange the various phenomena into some kind of understandable sequence. Various writers have assigned primacy to one of the following: intense sadness, wishes to "hibernate," self-destructive wishes, or physiological disturbance.

Is the painful emotion the catalytic agent? If depression is a primary affective disorder, it should be possible to account for the other symptoms on the basis of the emotional state. However, the unpleasant subjective state in itself does not appear to be an adequate stimulus for the other depressive symptoms. Other states of suffering such as physical pain, nausea, dizziness, shortness of breath, or anxiety rarely lead to symptoms typical of depression such as renunciation of major objectives in life, obliteration of affectionate feelings, or the wish to die. On the contrary, people suffering physical pain seem to treasure more than ever those aspects of life they have found meaningful. Moreover, the state of sadness does not have qualities we would expect to produce the self-castigations, distortions in thinking, and loss of drive for gratifications characteristic of depression.

Similar problems are raised in assigning primacy to other aspects of depression. Some writers have latched onto the passivity and withdrawal of attachments to other people to advance the notion that depression results from an atavistic wish to hibernate. If the goal of depression is to conserve energy, however, why is the patient driven to castigate himself and engage in continuous, aimless activities when agitated? Why does he seek to destroy himself—the source of energy?

Ascribing the primary role to the physiological symptoms such as disturbances in sleep, appetite, and sexuality also poses problems. It is difficult to understand the sequence by which these physiological disturbances lead to such varied phenomena as self-criticisms, the negative view of the world, and loss of the anger and mirth responses. Certainly, physiological responses such as loss of appetite and sleep resulting from an acute physical illness do not lead to other components of the depressive constellation.

THE CLUE: THE SENSE OF LOSS

The task of sorting the phenomena of depression into an understandable sequence may be simplified by asking the patient what he feels sad about and by encouraging him to express his repetitive ideas. Depressed patients generally provide essential information in spontaneous statements such as: "I'm sad because I'm worthless"; "I have no future"; "I've lost everything"; "My family is gone"; "I have nobody"; "Life has nothing for me." It is relatively easy to detect the dominant theme in the statements of the moderately or severely depressed patient. *He regards himself as lacking some element or a tribute that he considers essential for his happiness:* competence in attaining his goals, attractiveness to other people, closeness to family or friends, tangible possessions, good health, status or position. Such self-appraisals reflect the way the depressed patient perceives his life situation.

In exploring the theme of loss, we find that the psychological disorder revolves around a cognitive problem. The depressed patient shows specific distortions. He has a negative view of his world, a negative concept of himself, and a negative appraisal of his future: the *cognitive triad.*

The distorted evaluations concern shrinkage of his domain, and lead to sadness (Chapter 3). The depressive's conception of his valued attributes, relationships, and achievements is saturated with the notion of loss—past, present, and future. When he considers his present position, he sees a barren world; he feels pressed to the wall by external demands that cheat him of his meager resources and keep him from attaining what he wants.

The term "loser" captures the flavor of the depressive's appraisal of himself and his experience. He agonizes over the notion that he has experienced significant losses, such as his friends, his health, his prized possessions. He also regards himself as a "loser" in the colloquial sense: He is a misfit—an inferior and an inadequate being who is unable to meet his responsibilities and attain his goals. If he undertakes a project or seeks some gratification, he expects to be defeated or disappointed. He finds no respite during sleep. He has repetitive dreams in which he is a misfit, a failure.

In considering the concept of loss, we should be sensitive to the crucial importance of meanings and connotations. What represents a painful loss for one person may be regarded as trivial by another. It is important to recognize that the depressed patient dwells on hypothetical losses and pseudo losses. When he thinks about a potential loss, he regards the possibility as though it were an accomplished fact. A depressed man, for example, characteristically reacted to his wife's tardiness in meeting him with the thought, "She might have died on the way." He then construed the hypothetical loss as an actual event and became forlorn. Pseudo loss refers to

the incorrect labeling of any event as a loss; for example, a change in status that may in actuality be a gain. A depressed patient who sold some shares of stock at a large profit experienced a prolonged sense of deprivation over eliminating the securities from his portfolio; he ruminated over the notion that the sale had impoverished him.

Granted that the perception of loss produces feelings of sadness, how does this sense of loss engender other symptoms of depression: pessimism, self-criticism, escape-avoidance-giving up, suicidal wishes, and physiological disorders?

In order to answer this question, it would be useful to explore the chronology of depression, the onset and full development of symptoms. This sequence is most clearly demonstrated in cases of "reactive depression," that is, depression in which there is a clear-cut precipitating factor. Other cases of depression, in which the onset is more insidious, show similar (although more subtle) patterns.

DEVELOPMENT OF DEPRESSION

In the course of his development, the depression-prone person may become sensitized by certain unfavorable types of life situations, such as the loss of a parent or chronic rejection by his peers. Other unfavorable conditions of a less obvious nature may similarly produce vulnerability to depression. These traumatic experiences predispose the person to overreact to analogous conditions later in life. He has a tendency to make extreme, absolute judgments when such situations occur. A loss is viewed as irrevocable; indifference, as total rejection.

Other depression-prone people set rigid, perfectionistic goals for themselves during childhood, so that their universe collapses when they confront inevitable disappointments later in life.[1]

The stresses responsible for adult depressions impinge on the person's specific vulnerability. Numerous clinical and research reports agree on the following types of precipitating events: the disruption of a relationship with a person to whom the patient is attached; failure to attain an important goal; loss of a job; financial reverses; unexpected physical disability; and loss of social status or reputation. If such an event is appraised as a total, irreversible depletion of one's personal domain, it may trigger a depression.

To justify the label, "precipitating event," the experience of loss must have substantial significance to the patient. The precipitating factor, however, is not always a discrete event; insidious stresses such as the gradual withdrawal of affection by a spouse or a chronic discrepancy between goals and achievements may also erode the personal domain sufficiently to set the stage for a depression. The individual, for example, may be continually dissatisfied with his or her performance as a parent, housewife, income producer, student, or creative artist. Moreover, the repeated recognition of a gap between what a person expects and what he receives from an important interpersonal relationship, from his career, or from other activities may topple him into a depression. In brief, the sense of loss may be the result of unrealistically high goals and grandiose expectations.

[1]For a more comprehensive account of the predisposition to depression, see Beck (1967).

Experiences just prior to the onset of depression are often no more severe than those reported by those who do not become depressed. The depression-prone differ in the way they construe a particular deprivation. They attach overgeneralized or extravagant meanings to the loss.

The manner in which traumatic circumstances involving a loss lead to the constellation of depression may be delineated by an illustrative case: a man whose wife has deserted him unexpectedly. The effect of the desertion on the husband may not be predictable. Obviously, not every person deserted by a spouse becomes depressed. Even though he may experience the desertion as a painful loss, he may have other sources of satisfaction—family members and friends—to help fill the void. If the problem were simply a new hiatus in his life, we would expect that, in the course of time, he would be able to sustain his loss without becoming clinically depressed. Nonetheless, we know that certain vulnerable individuals respond to such a loss with a profound psychological disturbance.

The impact of the loss depends, in part, on the kind and intensity of the meanings attached to the key person. The deserting wife has been the hub of shared experiences, fantasies, and expectations. The deserted husband in our example has built a network of positive ideas around his wife, such as "she is part of me"; "she is everything to me"; "I enjoy life because of her"; "she is my mainstay"; "she comforts me when I am down." These positive associations range from realistic to extremely unrealistic or imaginary. The more extreme and rigid these positive concepts, the greater the impact of the loss on the domain.

If the damage to the domain is great enough, it sets off a chain reaction. The positive assets represented by his wife are totally wiped out. The deprivation of such valued attributes as "the only person who can make me happy" or "the essence of my existence" magnifies the impact of the loss and generates further sadness. Consequently, the deserted husband draws extreme, negative conclusions that parallel the extreme positive associations to his wife. He interprets the consequences of the loss as: "I am nothing without her; I can never be happy again"; "I can't go on without her."

The further reverberations of the desertion lead the husband to question his worth: "If I had been a better person, she wouldn't have left me." Further, he foresees other negative consequences of the break-up of the marriage. "All of our friends will go over to her side"; "The children will want to live with her, not me"; "I will go broke trying to maintain two households."

As the chain reaction progresses to a full-blown depression, his self-doubts and gloomy predictions expand into negative generalizations about himself, his world, and his future. He starts to see himself as permanently impoverished in terms of emotional satisfactions, as well as financially. In addition, he exacerbates his suffering by overly dramatizing the event: "It is too much for a person to bear" or, "This is a terrible disaster." Such ideas undermine his ability and motivation to absorb the shock.

The husband divorces himself from activities and goals that formerly gave him satisfaction. He may withdraw his investment in his career goals ("because they are meaningless without my wife"). He is not motivated to work or even to take care of himself ("because it isn't worth the effort"). His distress is aggravated by the

physiological concomitants of depression, such as loss of appetite and sleep disturbances. Finally, he thinks of suicide as an escape ("because life is too painful").

Since the chain reaction is circular, the depression becomes progressively worse. The various symptoms—sadness, decreased physical activity, sleep disturbance—feed back into the psychological system. Hence, as he experiences sadness, his pessimism leads him to conclude, "I shall always be sad." This ideation leads to more sadness, which is further interpreted in a negative way. Similarly, he thinks, "I shall never be able to eat again or to sleep again," and concludes that he is deteriorating physically. As he observes the various manifestations of his disorder (decreased productivity, avoidance of responsibility, withdrawal from other people), he becomes increasingly critical of himself. His self-criticisms lead to further sadness; thus, we see a continuing vicious cycle.

The anecdote of a man deserted by his wife illustrates the impact and reverberations of a loss in a vulnerable individual. We can now depart from the particular case in order to establish generalizations about the development of depression. The depressive chain reaction may be triggered by other kinds of losses such as failure at school or on a job. More chronic deprivations, such as disturbance in key interpersonal relations, may also be triggers.

The concept of the depressive chain reaction can be expanded to provide answers to the following problems: Why does the depressed patient have such low self-esteem? Why is he pervasively pessimistic? Why does he berate himself so viciously? Why does he give up? Why does he believe no one can help him?

LOW SELF-ESTEEM AND SELF-CRITICISMS

As the depressed patient reflects about adverse events (such as a separation, rejection, defeat, not measuring up to his expectations), he ponders over what these experiences tell him about himself. He is likely to assign the cause of the adverse event to an heinous defect in himself. The deserted husband concludes, "I have lost her because I am unlovable." This conclusion, of course, is only one of a number of possible explanations, such as basic incompatibility of their personalities, the wife's own problems, or her desire for an adventure related more to thrill-seeking than to a change in her feelings for her husband.

When the patient attributes the cause of the loss to himself, the rift in his domain becomes a chasm: He suffers not only the loss itself but he "discovers" a deficiency in himself. He tends to view this presumed deficiency in greatly exaggerated terms. A woman reacted to desertion by her lover with the thought, "I'm getting old and ugly . . . I must be repulsive-looking." A man who lost his job due to a general decline in the economy thought, "I'm inept . . . I'm too weak to make a living."

By viewing the desertion in terms of his own deficiency, the patient experiences additional morbid symptoms. His conviction of his presumed defects becomes so imperative that it infiltrates his every thought about himself. In the course of time, his picture of his negative attributes expands to the point that it takes over his self-image. When asked to describe himself, he can think only of his "bad" traits. He has great difficulty in shifting his attention to his abilities and achievements and he glosses

over or discounts attributes he may have valued highly in the past.

The patient's preoccupation with his presumed deficiency assumes many forms. He appraises each experience in terms of the deficiency. He interprets ambiguous or slightly negatively toned experiences as evidence of this deficiency. For instance, following an argument with her brother, a mildly depressed woman concluded, "I am incapable of being loved and of giving love," and she became more depressed. In reality, she had a number of intimate friends and a loving husband and children. When a friend was too busy to chat with her on the phone, she thought, "She doesn't want to talk to me any more." If her husband came home late from the office, she decided that he was staying away in order to avoid her. When her children were crabby at dinner, she thought, "I have failed them." In reality, there were more plausible explanations for these events, but the patient had difficulty in even considering explanations that did not reflect badly on her.

The tendency to compare oneself with others further lowers self-esteem. Every encounter with another may be turned into a negative self-evaluation. Thus, when talking to other people, the depressed patient thinks, "I'm not a good conversationalist . . . I'm not as interesting as the other people." As he walks down the street, he thinks, "Those people look attractive, but I am unattractive." "I have bad posture and bad breath." He sees a mother with a child and thinks, "She's a much better parent than I am." He observes another patient working industriously in the hospital and thinks, "He's a hard worker; I'm lazy and helpless."

The harshness and inappropriateness of self-reproaches in depression have either been ignored by writers or have stimulated very abstract speculations. Freud postulated that the bereaved patient has a pool of unconscious hostility toward the deceased loved object. Since he cannot allow himself to experience this hostility, the patient directs the anger toward himself and accuses himself of faults that actually are characteristics of the loved object. The concept of inverted rage has remained firmly entrenched in many theories of depression. The convoluted pathway proposed by Freud is so removed from information obtained from patients that it is difficult to test it.

A careful examination of the patient's statements provides a more parsimonious explanation of the self-reproaches. A clue to the genesis of the self-criticisms is found in the observation that many depressed patients are critical of attributes they previously had valued highly. For example, a woman who had enjoyed looking at herself in the mirror berated herself with indignities such as "I'm getting old and ugly." Another acutely depressed woman who had always traded on her conversational ability and had enjoyed the resulting attention castigated herself with the thought, "I've lost my ability to interest people . . . I can't even carry on a decent conversation." In both cases, the depression had been precipitated by disruption of a close interpersonal relationship.

In reviewing the histories of depressed patients, we often find that the patient has counted on the attribute that he now debases for balancing the usual stresses of life, mastering new problems, and attaining important objectives. When he reaches the conclusion (often erroneously) that he is unable to master a serious problem, attain a goal, or forestall a loss, he downgrades the asset.

As this attribute appears to fade, he begins to believe that he cannot get satisfaction out of life and that all he can expect is pain and suffering. The depressed patient proceeds from disappointment to self-blame to pessimism.

To illustrate the mechanism of self-blame, we might consider the sequence in which the average person blames and punishes somebody who has offended him. First, he tries to find some bad trait in the offender to account for his noxious behavior—insensitivity, selfishness, etc. He then generalizes this characteristic flaw to encompass his total image of the offender—"He's a selfish person"; "he's bad." After such a moral judgment, he may consider ways to punish the offender. He not only downgrades the other person, but, given the opportunity, he may strike at some sensitive point in order to hurt him. Finally, because the offender has brought him pain, he may want to sever the relationship, to reject the other person totally.

The self-castigating depressed patient reacts similarly to his own presumed deficiency and makes himself the target of attack. He regards himself at fault and deserving of blame. He goes beyond the Biblical injunction, "If thine eye offends thee, pluck it out." His moral condemnation spreads from the particular trait to the totality of his self-concept, and is often accompanied by feelings of self-revulsion. The ultimate of his self-condemnation is total self-rejection—just as though he were discarding another person.

Consider the effects of self-criticism, self-condemnation, and self-rejection. The patient reacts to his own onslaughts as if they were directed at him by another person: he feels hurt, sad, humiliated.

Freud and many more recent writers have attributed

the sadness to a transformation of anger turned inwards. By a kind of "alchemy," retroflected anger is supposedly converted into depressed feelings. A simpler explanation is that the sadness is the result of the self-instigated lowering of self-esteem. Suppose I inform a student that his performance is inferior and that he accepts the assessment as fair. Even though I communicate my evaluation without anger and may, in fact, express regret or empathy, he is likely to feel sad. The lowering of his self-esteem suffices to make him sad. Similarly, if the student makes a negative evaluation of himself, he feels sad. The depressed patient is like the self-devaluing student; he feels sad because he lowers his sense of worth by his negative evaluations.

When a depressed patient makes a negative evaluation of himself, he generally does not feel angry with himself; in his frame of reference he is simply making an objective judgment. Similarly, he reacts with sadness when he believes that somebody else is devaluating him.

PESSIMISM

Pessimism sweeps like a tidal wave into the thought content of depressed patients. To some degree, we all tend to "live in the future." We interpret experience not only in terms of what the event means right now, but also in terms of its possible consequences. A young man who had just received a compliment from his girl friend looks forward to receiving more compliments; he might think, "she really likes me," and he foresees a more intimate relationship with her. But, if he is disappointed or rejected, he is likely to anticipate a repetition of this type of unpleasant experience.

Depressed patients have a special penchant for expecting future adversities and experiencing them as though they were happening in the present or had already occurred. For example, a man who suffered a mild business reversal began to think in terms of ultimate bankruptcy. As he dwelt on the theme of bankruptcy, he began to regard himself as already bankrupt. Consequently, he started to feel the same degree of sadness as though he had already suffered bankruptcy.

The predictions of depressed patients tend to be overgeneralized and extreme. Since the patients regard the future as an extension of the present, they expect a deprivation or defeat to continue permanently. If a patient feels miserable now, it means he will always feel miserable. The absolute, global pessimism is expressed in statements such as "things won't ever work out for me"; "life is meaningless ... It's never going to be any different." The depressed patient judges that, since he cannot achieve a major goal now, he never will. He cannot see the possibility of substituting other rewarding goals. Moreover, if a problem appears insoluble now, he assumes he will never be able to find a way of working it out or somehow bypassing it.

Another stream leading to pessimism arises from the patient's negative self-concept. We have noted that the trauma of a loss is especially damaging because it implies to the patient that he is defective in some way. Since he considers the presumed deficiency an integral part of himself, he is likely to regard it as permanent. Nobody else can help restore a lost talent or attribute. Moreover, his pessimistic view leads him to expect his "flaw" to become progressively worse.

Such pessimism is especially likely to strike a person

who generally considers himself instrumental in reaching his major life goals. He characteristically relies on his own ability, personal attractiveness, or vigor to attain his objectives. A depressed writer, for instance, did not receive the degree of praise for one of his works that he had expected. His failure to live up to his expectations led him to two conclusions: first, his writing ability was deteriorating; second, since creative ability is intrinsic, his loss could not be salvaged by anybody else. The loss was, therefore, irreversible.

A similar reaction was reported by a student who was unsuccessful in a competition for an award in mathematics. His reaction was, "I've lost my mathematical ability...I'm never going to do well in a competitive situation." Since not winning was tantamount (for him) to complete failure, this meant that his whole life, past, present, and future was a failure.

An energetic career woman who developed transitory back trouble and had to be confined to bed, became depressed. She concluded that she would always be bedridden. She incorrectly regarded her temporary disability as permanent and irremediable.

As pessimism envelops the patient's total failure orientation, his thinking is dominated by ideas such as, "The game is over...I don't have a second chance. Life has passed me by...It's too late to do anything about it." His losses seem irrevocable; his problems, unsolvable.

Pessimism not only engulfs the distant future, but permeates every wish and every task that the patient undertakes. A housewife, who was listing her domestic duties, automatically predicted before starting each new activity that she would be unable to do it. A depressed physician expected, prior to seeing each new patient, that he would be unable to make a diagnosis.

The negative expectations are so strong that even though the patient may be successful in a specific task (for example, the doctor's making the diagnosis), he expects to fail the very next time. He evidently screens out, or fails to integrate, successful experiences that contradict his negative view of himself.

SNOWBALLING OF SADNESS AND APATHY

Although the onset of depression may be sudden, its full development spreads over a period of days or weeks. The patient experiences a gradual increase in intensity of sadness and of other symptoms until he "hits bottom." Each repetition of the idea of loss is so strong that it constitutes a fresh experience of loss which is added to the previous inventory of perceived losses. With each successive "loss," further sadness is generated.

As described previously (Chapter 4) any psychopathological condition is characterized by sensitivity to particular types of experiences. The depressed person tends to extract elements suggestive of loss and to gloss over other features that are not consonant with, or are contradictory to, this interpretation. As a result of such "selective abstraction," the patient overinterprets daily events in terms of loss and is oblivious to more positive interpretations; he is hypersensitive to stimuli suggestive of loss and is blind to stimuli representing gain. He shows the same type of selectivity in recalling past experiences. He is facile in recalling unpleasant experiences, but may "draw a blank" when questioned about positive experiences. This selectivity in memory has been demonstrated experimentally by Lishman (1972).

As a result of this "tunnel vision," the patient becomes impermeable to stimuli that can arouse pleasant emotions. Although he may be able to acknowledge that certain events are favorable, his attitudes block any happy feelings: "I don't deserve to be happy." "I'm different from other people, and I can't feel happy over the things that make them happy." "How can I be happy when everything else is bad?" Similarly, comical situations do not strike him as funny because of his negative set and his tendency toward self-reference: "There is nothing funny about my life." He has difficulty in experiencing anger because he views himself as responsible for and deserving of any rude or insulting actions of other people.

The tendency to think in absolute terms contributes to the cumulative arousal of sadness. He tends to dwell increasingly on extreme ideas such as "Life is meaningless"; "Nobody loves me"; "I'm totally inadequate"; "I have nothing left."

By downgrading qualities that are closely linked with gratification, the patient takes away gratification from himself. In depreciating his attractiveness, a depressed patient is, in effect, saying, "I no longer can enjoy my physical appearance, or compliments I receive for it, or the friendships that it helped me to form and maintain." The loss of gratification evidently trips a mechanism that reverses the direction of affect arousal—from happiness to sadness. The prevailing tide of pessimism maintains the continual state of sadness.

While the usual consequence of loss is sadness, the passive resignation shown by some depressives may lead to a different emotional state. When the depressed patient regards himself as totally defeated and consequently gives up his goals, he is apt to feel apathetic. Since apathy often is experienced as an absence of feeling, the patient

may interpret this state as a sign that he is incapable of emotion, that he is "dead inside."

MOTIVATIONAL CHANGES

The reversals in major objectives are among the most puzzling characteristics of the seriously depressed patient. He not only desires to avoid experiences that formerly gratified him or represented the mainstream of his life, but he is drawn toward a state of inactivity. He even seeks to withdraw from life completely via suicide.

To understand the link between the changes in motivation and the patient's perception of loss, it is valuable to consider the ways in which he has "given up." He no longer feels attracted to the kinds of enterprises he ordinarily would undertake spontaneously. In fact, he finds that he has to force himself to engage in his usual activities. He goes through the motions of attending to his ordinary affairs because he believes he should, or because he knows it is "the right thing to do," because others urge him to do it—but not because he wants to. He finds he has to work against a powerful inner resistance, as though he were trying to drive an automobile with the brakes on or to swim upstream.

In the most extreme cases, the patient experiences "paralysis of the will": He is devoid of spontaneous desire to do anything except to remain in a state of inertia. Nor can he mobilize "will power" to force himself to do what he believes he ought to do.

From this description of the motivational changes, one might surmise that, perhaps, some physically depleting disease has overwhelmed the patient so that he does not have the strength or resources to make even a minimal exertion. An acute or debilitating illness such as pneumonia or advanced cancer would conceivably re-duce a person to such a state of immobility. The physical-depletion notion, however, is contradicted by the pa-tient's own observation that he feels a strong drive to *avoid* "constructive" or "normal" activities: His inertia is deceptive in that it is derived not only from a desire to be passive, but also from a less obvious desire to shrink from any situation he regards as unpleasant. He may feel re-pelled by the thought of performing even elementary functions such as getting out of bed, dressing himself, and attending to personal needs. A retarded, depressed woman would rapidly dive under the bed-covers whenever I entered the room. She would become exceptionally aroused and even energetic in her attempt to escape from an activity that she was pressed to engage in. In contrast, the physically ill person generally wants to be active. It is often necessary to enforce bedrest in order to keep him from taxing himself. The depressed patient's desire to avoid activity and to escape from his current environment are the consequences of his peculiar constructions: the negative view of his future, his environment, and himself.

Everyday experiences—as well as a number of well-designed experiments—demonstrate that when a person believes he cannot succeed at a task, he is likely to give up. He adopts the attitude, "there's no use trying," and does not feel any spontaneous drive to work at it. Moreover, the belief that the task is pointless and that even successful completion is meaningless, minimizes his motivation.

Since the depressed patient expects negative out-comes, he does not experience any internal stimulation to make an effort; he sees no point in trying because he

believes the goals are meaningless. People generally try to avoid situations they expect to be painful; because the depressed patient perceives most situations as onerous, boring, or painful, he desires to avoid even the usual amenities of living. These avoidance desires are powerful enough to override any tendencies toward constructive, goal-directed activity.

The setting for the patient's powerful desire to seek a passive state is illustrated by this sequence of thoughts: "I'm too fatigued and sad to do anything. If I am active I shall only feel worse. But if I lie down, I can conserve my strength and my bad feelings will go away." Unfortunate-ly, this attempt to escape from the unpleasant feeling by being passive does not work; if anything, it enhances the dysphoria. The patient finds that far from obtaining any respite from his unpleasant thoughts and feelings, he becomes more preoccupied with them.

SUICIDAL BEHAVIOR

Suicidal wishes and suicide attempts may be regard-ed as the ultimate expression of the desire to escape. The depressed patient sees his future as filled with suffering. He cannot visualize any way of improving his lot; he does not believe he will get better. On the basis of these premises, suicide seems to be a rational course of action. It not only promises an end to his own misery but presumably will relieve his family of a burden. Once the patient regards death as more desirable than life, he feels attracted to suicide. The more hopeless and painful his life seems, the stronger his desire to end his life.

The wish to find surcease through suicide is illustrat-ed in the lament of a depressed woman who had been rejected by her lover. "There's no sense in living. There's nothing here for me. I need love and I don't have it anymore. I can't be happy without love—only miserable. It will just be the same misery, day in and day out. It's senseless to go on."

The desire to escape from the apparent futility of existence is illustrated by the stream of thought of another depressed patient. "Life means just going through another day. It doesn't make any sense. There's nothing that can give me any satisfaction. The future isn't there—I just don't want life anymore. I want to get out of here...It's stupid just to go on living."

Another premise underlying the suicidal wishes is the belief that everybody would be better off if he were dead. Since he regards himself as worthless and as a burden, arguments that his family would be hurt if he died seem hollow to him. How can they be injured by losing a burden? One patient envisioned suicide as doing her parents a favor. She would not only end her own pain, but would relieve them of psychological and financial burdens. "I'm just taking money from my parents. They would use it to better advantage. They wouldn't have to support me. My father wouldn't have to work so hard, and they could travel. I'm unhappy taking their money, and they could be happy with it."

EXPERIMENTAL STUDIES OF DEPRESSION

Although the preceding formulations of depression were derived primarily from clinical observations and reports by depressed patients, it has been possible to subject these hypotheses to a series of correlational and

experimental studies. These studies support the model of depression I have presented in this chapter.

DREAMS AND OTHER IDEATIONAL MATERIAL

I observed that depressed patients in psychotherapy showed a higher proportion of dreams with negative outcomes than did a matched group of nondepressed psychiatric patients. A typical dream of a depressed patient showed this content: The dreamer was portrayed as a "loser"; he suffered deprivation of some tangible object, loss of self-esteem, or loss of a person to whom he was attached. Other themes in dreams included the dreamer's being portrayed as inept, repulsive, defective, or thwarted in attempting to reach a goal. This observation was borne out in a systematic study (Beck and Hurvich, 1959).

The theme of deprivation and thwarting are apparent in the following typical dreams of depressed patients: The dreamer desperately wanted to call his wife. He inserted his only coin into a pay telephone. He got the wrong number; since he had wasted his only coin, he was unable to reach his wife and felt sad. Another patient dreamed he was very thirsty. He ordered a glass of beer at a bar. He was served a drink containing a mixture of beer and scotch! He felt disappointed and helpless.

The finding of typical negative themes was validated in a second, more refined study of the most recent dreams of 228 depressed and nondepressed psychiatric patients (Beck and Ward, 1961).

Another approach to the thinking patterns in depression was based on the administration of the Focussed

Fantasy Test. The materials consisted of a set of cards; each card contained four frames depicting a continuous sequence of events involving a set of identical twins. The plot was similar to that observed in dreams of depressed patients; namely, one of the twins loses something of value, is rejected, or punished. Depressed patients were much more likely than nondepressed patients to identify with the twin who was the "loser" in each sequence.

In the long-term clinical study previously noted (Beck, 1963), I analyzed the verbatim recorded verbal productions of 81 depressed and nondepressed patients in psychotherapy. I found that depressed patients distorted their experiences in an idiosyncratic way. They misinterpreted events in terms of deprivation, personal failure, or rejection; or they exaggerated the significance of events that seemed to reflect badly on them. They also perseverated in making indiscriminate, negative predictions. The distorted appraisals of reality showed a similarity to the content of the dreams.

Our research group has conducted a series of correlational studies to test these clinical findings. We found significant correlations between the depth of depression and the degree of pessimism and negative self-evaluations. After recovery from depression, the patients showed a remarkable improvement in their outlook and self-appraisals (Beck, 1972b). These findings lent strong support to the thesis that depression is associated with a negative view of the self and the future. The high correlation between measures of negative view of the future and negative view of the self supported the concept of the cognitive triad in depression.

The relation between negative view of the future and suicidal wishes has been supported by a number of

studies. The most crucial study attempted to determine what psychological factor contributed most strongly to the seriousness of a suicide attempt. We found that hopelessness was the best indicator of how serious the person was about terminating his life (Minkoff, Bergman, Beck, and Beck, 1973; Beck, Kovacs, and Weissman, 1975).

Another way to test the primacy of the negative attitudes in depression is to attempt to modify them and observe the effects. If we ameliorate the depressed patient's unrealistically low concept of his capabilities and of his future, then we would expect the secondary symptoms of depression, such as low mood and loss of constructive motivation, to improve accordingly.

When presented with a simple card-sorting task, depressed patients in the psychiatric clinic were significantly more pessimistic about their chances of success than a matched control group of nondepressed patients. In actuality, the depressed patients performed as well as the nondepressed patients. The depressed patients who succeeded in reaching their stated goals were much more optimistic on a second task. Moreover, their performance on the second task was better than that of the nondepressed group (Loeb, Beck, and Diggory, 1971). We repeated this study with depressed and nondepressed patients who had been hospitalized because of their illness. We found that following a successful experience, the depressed patients showed an increase in self-esteem and optimism that spread to attributes not related to the test. Thus, they were more positive about their personal attractiveness, ability to communicate, and social interests; they also saw their future as brighter and had higher expectations of achieving their major objectives in life.

This change in self-appraisal was paralleled by a lifting of their mood (Beck, 1974).

A similar study of 15 depressed inpatients focused on the depressed patients' difficulty in expressing themselves verbally. They were given a graded series of assignments proceeding in a progression from the simplest step (reading a paragraph aloud) to the most difficult. The final assignment, which all the patients were able to master, consisted of improvising a short talk on a selected subject and trying to convince the experimenter of their point of view. Again we found that the successful completion of these assignments led to significant improvements in their general appraisals of themselves and their future. Their mood also improved.

Our finding that the depressed patient is especially sensitive to tangible evidence of successful performance has important implications for psychotherapy. The meaning of the experimental situation, in which the subject receives positive feedback from the experimenter, obviously has a powerful effect on the depressed patient. This tendency to exaggerate the evaluative aspects of situations and to overgeneralize in a *positive* direction after "success" provides guidelines for the therapeutic management of depression.

A SYNTHESIS OF DEPRESSION

We have analyzed the development of depression in terms of a chain reaction initiated by experience connoting loss to the patient. We have noted how the sense of loss pervades the person's view of himself, his world, and his future, and leads to the other phenomena of depression.

The typical losses triggering depression may be obvious and dramatic, such as loss of a spouse, or a series—of experiences the patient interprets as diminishing him in a significant way. More subtle kinds of deprivations result from the patient's failure to negotiate a reasonable balance between the emotional investments he makes and the return on the investments. The imbalance may stem from a relative deficiency between the gratifications he receives in proportion to what he gives to others, or from a discrepancy between the demands he makes on himself and what he attains. In short, he experiences an upset in his "give-get balance" (Saul, 1947).

After experiencing loss (either as the result of an actual, obvious event or insidious deprivations) the depression-prone person begins to appraise his experiences in a negative way. He overinterprets his experiences in terms of defeat or deprivation. He regards himself as deficient, inadequate, unworthy, and is prone to attribute unpleasant occurrences to a deficiency in himself. As he looks ahead, he anticipates that his present difficulties or suffering will continue indefinitely. He foresees a life of unremitting hardship, frustration, and deprivation. Since he attributes his difficulties to his own defects, he blames himself and becomes increasingly self-critical. The patient's experiences in living thus activate cognitive patterns revolving around the theme of loss. The various emotional, motivational, behavioral, and vegetative phenomena of depression flow from these negative self-evaluations.

The patient's sadness is an inevitable consequence of his sense of deprivation, pessimism, and self-criticism. Apathy results from giving up completely. His loss of spontaneity, his escapist and avoidance wishes, and his suicidal wishes similarly stem from the way he appraises his life. His hopelessness leads to loss of motivation: Because he expects a negative outcome from any course of action, he loses the internal stimulation to engage in any constructive activity. Moreover, this pessimism leads him ultimately to suicidal wishes.

The various behavioral manifestations of depression, such as inertia, fatigability, agitation, are similarly the outcomes of the negative cognitions. Inertia and passivity are expressions of the patient's loss of spontaneous motivation. His easy fatigability results from his continuous expectations of negative outcomes from whatever he undertakes. Similarly, agitation is related to the thought content. Unlike the retarded patient who passively resigns himself to his "fate," the agitated patient fights desperately to find a way out of his predicament. Since he is unable to grasp a solution, he is driven into frantic motor activity, such as pacing the floor or scratching various parts of his body.

The vegetative signs of depression—loss of appetite, loss of libido, sleep disturbance—appear to be the physiological concomitants of the particular psychological disturbance in depression. The physiological signs of depression may be regarded as analogous to the autonomic nervous system manifestations of anxiety. The specific psychological arousal in depression affects, in particular, appetite, sleep, and sexual drive.

The continuous downward course in depression may be explained in terms of the feedback model. As a result of his negative attitudes, the patient interprets his dysphoria, sense of loss, and physical symptoms in a negative way. His conclusion that he is defective and cannot improve reinforces his negative expectations and negative

self-image. Consequently, he feels sadder and more impelled to avoid the "demands" of his environment. Thus, the vicious cycle is perpetrated.

Experimental studies of depression provide leads for therapeutic intervention. By helping the patient to recognize how he consistently distorts his experiences, the therapist may help to alleviate his self-criticalness and pessimism. When these key links in the chain are loosened, the inexorable cycle of depression is interrupted and normal feelings and desires re-emerge. As we shall see in the discussion of other emotional disturbances, the major thrust towards health is achieved by reshaping the patient's erroneous beliefs.

Reading 2
Generalized Anxiety Disorder and Panic Disorder

Generalized Anxiety Disorder and Panic Disorder

Incidence

The statistics regarding the incidence and the prevalence of anxiety disorders vary considerably. According to some reports, those with anxiety disorders form a significant proportion (6 percent to 27 percent) of all psychiatric patients (Marks and Lader 1973). I. Marks and M. Lader found a good deal of agreement among five population studies conducted in the United States, the United Kingdom, and Sweden between 1943 and 1946. They reported a prevalence rate of from 2 to 4.7 per 100 population and found that the condition was more prevalent in women, particularly between the ages of sixteen and forty. S. Agras, D. Sylvester, and D. Oliveau (1969) reported annual community rates of phobia in the range of 7 to 8 per 100. C. G. Costello (1982) reported very high annual rates of phobias of all types in women (19.4 percent). In a 1975 survey in New Haven, M. M. Weissman, J. K. Myers, and P. S. Harding (1978) reported the rate of anxiety disorders of all types as 4.3 percent with a substantial overlap within the anxiety disorders group. Over 80 percent of the people with generalized anxiety disorder had had panic disorder and/or phobia at some time in their lives. Thirty percent of those with phobias reported having had panic disorders.

General View of the Etiology of Anxiety Disorders

It is probably counterproductive to speak of "The Cause" of the anxiety disorders, as there is a wide variety of possible *predisposing factors*. These include: (1) hereditary predisposition, (2) physical diseases leading to persistent neurochemical abnormalities (hyperthyroidism) or producing continual fears of impending disaster (mitral valve prolapse), (3) developmental traumas leading to specific vulnerabilities, (4) inadequate personal experiences or identifications to provide appropriate coping mechanisms, (5) counterproductive cognitive patterns, unrealistic goals, unreasonable values, assumptions, or imperatives learned from significant others.

Similarly, there is a vast array of possible *precipitating factors*. Some examples of these are: (1) physical disease and/or toxic substances, (2) severe external stress (for example, a series of exposures to physical or psychological danger), (3) chronic insidious external stress (for example, continuous, subtle disapproval from significant others), (4) specific external stress impinging on specific emotional vulnerability (for example, the imposition of strict military discipline on an autonomous individual).

A particular case of anxiety disorder may have any combination of the preceding factors. One case, for instance, may show an extreme amount of genetic predisposition with minimal environmental stress; another, no hereditary factors but an unusual degree of environmental danger. The "cause" of these psychological disorders may be found to reside in no specific factor but is best viewed as a composite of many interacting factors —genetic, developmental, environmental, and psychological.

BIOLOGICAL STUDIES

Some preliminary evidence of a familial pattern in anxiety disorders is presented in a number of articles. R. R. Crowe et al. (1983) found a high incidence of anxiety disorders of all types among the relatives of patients with panic disorder. Another study by S. Torgersen (1983) studied monozygotic and dyzygotic twins with anxiety disorders. He concluded that, for generalized anxiety disorder, genetic factors were not evident. However, they did appear to influence the development of other anxiety disorders, especially panic disorder and agoraphobia with panic attacks. Thus, there seems to be evidence that panic disorder is related to genetic mechanisms, but the role of hereditary in generalized anxiety disorder still needs to be clarified.

In a series of studies, a group of investigators have presented evidence that panic disorder can be induced by biochemical infusions and can be relieved through pharmacotherapy. F. N. Pitts, Jr., and J. N. McClure, Jr., (1967) reported the precipitation of anxiety after an infusion of sodium lactate. H. J. Grosz and B. B. Farmer (1972) challenged their conclusions on the following grounds: (1) Unless exercised, anxiety neurotics do not as a rule have elevated blood-lactate levels even when acutely anxious. Although they may bring about some elevation in the blood-lactate level by hyperventilating, normal subjects can do so too. (2) Anxiety neurosis is not typically present in patients with lactic acidaemia—that is, with very marked and chronic blood-lactate elevations. (3) With neither the sodium lactate nor the sodium bicarbonate infusion is the onset of symptoms associated with significant blood-lactate elevations.

Since that time new reports tend to lend some support to the findings of Pitts and McClure. Panic attacks have been precipitated through the infusion of sodium lactate (Appleby, Klein, Sachar, and Levitt 1981). Similarly, Klein and his associates found that the administration of imipramine as well as other "antidepressants" serves to ameliorate this disorder (Gorman, Levy, Liebowitz, McGrath, Appleby, Dillon, Davies and Klein 1983). These findings, which are being subjected to further clarification at other centers, may cast some light on the biochemical mechanisms in this disorder. However in view of the strong evidence of cognitive and other psychological factors in this disorder as well as behavioral methods for relieving it, it seems premature to make a commitment to an exclusive organic etiology.

PRECIPITATING PSYCHOLOGICAL FACTORS

1. *Increased demands:* A variety of factors appear to be involved in the precipitation of generalized anxiety disorder (GAD). These seem to involve an increased threat to important values and a depletion of coping resources. An individual typically has greater expectations, increased responsibilities, and an overall increase in energy output. The result is that he becomes more concerned about failure. If he strongly believes that his intrinsic value is based on his level of performance, the threat of failure is aggravated. Examples are the new type of demand imposed on a parent after the birth of a child. Similarly, a job promotion that increases responsibilities, expectations, and work load can precipitate this disorder.

2. *Increased amount of threat in a life situation:* A person's circumstances may change in a way that poses a serious threat to him. For example, an ambitious young physician moved into a new position under the supervi-

sion of a hostile chief. He felt continuously "under the gun" and believed that at any time he could commit a catastrophic error that would cost him his job. Similarly, a new mother was faced with an infant that was susceptible to various infections. The mother became increasingly concerned that she would not take proper care of the child (for example, the child might suffocate if the mother did not hear her cry).

3. *Stressful events that undermine confidence:* A person may have a number of moderate reversals or a major reversal that makes him believe that he may not be able to achieve an important objective. For example, a young lawyer failed an examination to qualify for admission to the bar. He was faced with the immediate problem of not being accepted by the firm that had hired him. At the same time, his girlfriend had informed him that she did not love him. The overall impact was to make him fear that he could never be happy on his job and, even worse, that he would never be able to have a loving wife and a family. Each of these notions contributed to a chronic state of anxiety. His two major sources of satisfaction were threatened.

INTERACTION OF PRECIPITATING FACTORS WITH PREVIOUS PROBLEMS

In cases of GAD, we often see that the problems reported by the patient did not start with the precipitating events but actually extended far back into the developmental period. The precipitating stressors are potent only insofar as they strike at a person's specific vulnerabilities. The mother who was chronically anxious after the birth of her child had experienced longstanding "feelings" of inadequacy. However, the problem now was: Her inadequacy could risk the baby's life and thus became a source of danger. A person faced with the threat of failure in his career now thinks seriously for the first time, "I may not be successful in my career and thus I can never be happy." The young lawyer had always believed that he lacked personal charm, but now he was faced with the problem that he might never find an acceptable mate who would accept him.

DO COGNITIONS CAUSE ANXIETY DISORDERS?

Many statements have been made in the literature and elsewhere to the effect that cognitions cause depression or anxiety disorders. We believe that this conception is misleading. We consider that the primary pathology or dysfunction during a depression or an anxiety disorder is in the cognitive apparatus. However, that is quite different from the notion that cognition *causes* these syndromes—a notion that is just as illogical as an assertion that hallucinations cause schizophrenia.

What, then, is the relationship between cognition and anxiety disorders? We propose that an upset in the regulatory functions of the cognitive system leads one indiscriminately to interpret environmental events as dangers. Ordinarily there is a reasonable balance among the modes (chapter 4) relevant to danger, threat, enhancement, and loss, so that when one of them has been hypervalent for a prolonged period, an opposing mode is activated. Thus, during a period of elation, an individual becomes sensitized to negative feedback, and the self-deflation mode may be activated by a disappointing experience. Similarly, hostility is generally counterbalanced by anxiety. These cognitive appraisals of a situation influence affect and behavior. Although the usual appraisals probably do not deviate drastically from reality, it sometimes happens that one mode becomes so dominant—say, the self-enhancement mode—that the integration of corrective feedback is blocked. Thus, for a time, experiences are overinterpreted exclusively in self-inflating ways. This imbalance is generally corrected eventually, and the individual does not remain in a state of elation and inactivity. However, in psychopathology, there seems to be interference with the turn-off of the dominant mode, which progresses to a level of hyperactivity for a prolonged period. The results are systematically biased interpretations of positive information (in mania) and of danger (in anxiety disorders) and consequent excessive mobilization of the somatic and the autonomic nervous systems. This overmobilization itself can produce secondary symptoms, such as gastrointestinal dysfunctions.

What factors are responsible for the failure of the hyperactive cognitive system to "turn off"? It is possible that fatigue may interfere with the action of the rational cognitive system to exert a corrective influence by producing more realistic interpretations. However, why the opponent mode remains relatively inactive and thus cannot contribute to a more balanced view of reality is obscure at this time. It could be speculated that certain neurochemical disturbances either stimulate an overactivity of the danger schemas and prevent their habituation to danger, or else interfere with the activation of the "security" mode.

In essence, far from being a cause of anxiety disorders, cognitive processes constitute a major mechanism by which the organism adapts itself to the environment. When a variety of factors interfere with the organism's smooth operation, it becomes the mechanism through which anxiety disorders or other disorders are produced.

Generalized Anxiety Disorder

SYMPTOMATOLOGY

The symptoms in anxiety disorders reflect overactivity of the cognitive, affective, and behavioral systems. The affective and somatic symptoms are found in table 6.1; the cognitive-behavioral symptoms in table 6.2. The most common symptom—inability to relax—found in 96.6 percent of 100 cases, appears to represent an overmobilization of all the systems and incorporates anxious feelings and mind racing. The rest of the affective-somatic symptoms reflect anxious affect (frightened, terrified), motoric mobilization (tense, jumpy), and activation of the sympathetic nervous system (hands perspiring, heart racing) or of the parasympathetic system (sweating all over, difficulty catching breath, urgent desire to urinate, nausea, diarrhea, or faint feeling). There are also signs of the "collapse" of the motor systems (feeling wobbly and weak all over).

The most common symptom of cognitive impairment is difficulty in concentration (86.2 percent). The high frequency of confusion, mind blur-

TABLE 6.1

*Frequency of Affective and Somatic Symptoms in
Generalized Anxiety Disorder*

Symptom	Frequency (%)
Unable to relax	96.6
Tense	86.2
Frightened	79.3
Jumpy	72.4
Unsteady	62.1
Weakness all over	58.6
Only hands perspiring	51.7
Terrified	51.7
Heart racing	48.3
Face flushed	48.3
Wobbly	44.8
Sweating all over	37.9
Difficulty catching breath	34.5
Urgent desire to urinate	34.5
Nausea	31.0
Diarrhea	31.0
Faint or dizzy feeling	27.6
Face is pale	24.1
Feeling of choking	13.8
Actual fainting	3.4

ring, and inability to control thinking indicates that "cognitive impairment" is an important aspect of GAD. The most common symptom referable to the theme of danger is the fear of losing control which occurs in 75.9 percent and thus is an unexpectedly important feature of GAD. The fear of being rejected (72.4 percent) is almost as common.

Difficulty in communicating (for example, blocking, broken sentences) occurs in a significant proportion of the cases and thus must be considered a salient feature. Similarly, certain symptoms of uncontrolled motor activity (trembling, shaking, swaying) constitute a significant minority. In sum, the symptomatology taken as a whole suggests a composite of the activity of the various systems.

TYPES OF GENERALIZED ANXIETY DISORDER

There are two general types of cognitive content in generalized anxiety disorder. In the first, there has been a traumatic event, involving actual injury or threat of injury or a threat to an interpersonal relationship. The most dramatic expression of this type of disorder is the "combat neurosis" characterized by perseverative ideation relevant to catastrophic events in battle. A similar reaction is seen in less dramatic ways in civilian life and may be precipitated by a frightening event such as a surgical operation or observing injury to another person. These traumatic reactions are found

TABLE 6.2

*Frequency of Cognitive and Behavioral Symptoms in
Generalized Anxiety Disorder*

Symptom	Frequency (%)
Difficulty in concentration	86.2
Fear of losing control	75.9
Fear of being rejected	72.4
Inability to control thinking	72.4
Confusion	69.0
Mind blurred	65.5
Inability to recall important things	55.2
Sentences broken or disconnected	44.8
Blocking in speech	44.8
Fear of being attacked	34.5
Fear of dying	34.5
Hands trembling	31.0
Body swaying	31.0
Body shaking	27.0
Stuttering	24.1

most commonly in acute anxiety states. The second form of generalized anxiety disorder seems to be an extension—and aggravation—of fears that a person has experienced during his early development, and takes a more chronic form.

Acute Anxiety State. The acute anxiety syndrome occurs in situations that are considered to constitute a serious threat to an individual's physical or psychological survival. This syndrome is generally associated with actually being *in* the danger situation or having images of the danger that are so vivid that the individual believes, at least partly, that his life is threatened. The acute anxiety syndrome consists of total mobilization for immediate action. There is an activation of reflexive behavior (for example, flight, freeze), of the subjective experience of anxiety, and of the autonomic nervous system (palpitations, rapid breathing, profuse perspiration). Because of the intense somatic and affective feelings, this state can escalate into panic attacks.

When the danger is not perceived as immediate, anxiety and partial motor and autonomic mobilization may occur. At this point, the mobilization involves primarily sympathetic innervation. As the individual enters the danger situation, there may be a switch from preparation for action to generalized inhibition (interference with spontaneous activity and fluency of thought and speech). Moreover, certain susceptible people (blood or injury phobics) will experience a switch from mobilization of the sympathetic system to an atonic (weak, wobbly), parasympathetic (faint or actual fainting) reaction.

The acute syndrome will be discussed in terms of the type of traumatic event that precipitated it: namely, events producing a serious threat to life or limb (mutilation), and events presenting a serious danger to a crucial interpersonal relationship.

Traumatic Event Involving Physical Danger. The first major class of generalized anxiety disorders could be labeled "traumatic anxiety disorders." This condition has been included in the DSM category of "posttraumatic stress disorder." In this disorder, the major problem generally involves a perceived threat to the individual's health or life. In our experience, we have found that a frightening incident, such as a surgical operation or an accident, may have such a powerful impact on a person that he is not able to assimilate the experience; it remains in the background of his thinking, easily activated by any relevant stimulus. The features of the experience—for example, its life-threatening nature and the patient's helplessness—undermine his belief that he can cope with such a situation, and thus he cannot dismiss the fantasy. Many cases of acute anxiety—lasting a few days to a few weeks before a person sought help—had an acute onset following an experience that was directly or indirectly threatening.

Autonomous Images.   A bus driver, for example, had repeated fantasies of getting into an accident while driving his bus. Each fantasy had generated anxiety, which had become so intense that he had taken a leave of absence from his job. This disorder occurred following his observing a fatal bus accident. Even after he left his job, his anxiety continued. Another patient, whose acute anxiety followed an automobile accident, continually "relived" the accident in fantasy. A third patient, after learning that her best friend had cancer, began to have continual images of dying of cancer and experienced continuous anxiety. In each of these cases, the images appeared to be producing the unpleasant anxiety.

Autonomous or "uncontrolled" images are activated in these cases and tend to persist without the patient's being able to stop them (Beck 1970). We have found that the fantasies in these acute syndromes have the following features: First, they are not under volitional control. A person experiences them despite his attempts to stop them. They may be evoked regularly by relevant stimuli, such as hearing about someone else having an accident or a fatal illness. However, they often occur without any particular external stimulus. Once an image has started, the person cannot "turn it off." It continues or repeats itself until he is distracted or goes to sleep. Secondly, the person who is having the image experiences it as though the traumatic episode were actually occurring *in the present:* that is, he cannot discriminate between the image and present reality. It is as though the past has encroached on the present. Finally, the terror and anxiety wax and wane predictably according to the sequence of events in the fantasy.

The core problem in the traumatic neuroses may be explained as follows: The normal person is able to determine fairly rapidly whether a stimulus is a signal of a real danger. As he is able to label the stimulus an insignificant sound or scene rather than a danger signal, his anxiety dissolves. In contrast, the anxious patient does not discriminate between safe and unsafe and continues to label the sound as a danger signal. His thinking is dominated by a concept of danger. Once a stimulus has been tagged as a danger signal, the association between the stimulus and the concept "danger" becomes fixed.

Traumatic Psychosocial Event.   This disorder usually starts with an identifiable precipitating "cause," such as a traumatic event (say, a threatened break-up of a relationship), a sudden increase in demands and expectations (say, the birth of a child or a new, more demanding job), or an increase in the threatening components in a situation. The effect of the event is to jeopardize certain valued functions, such as maintaining a relationship or performing adequately at home or at work.

The *automatic response* to these threats is the mobilization for self-protection leading to a kind of spastic interference with one's goal-oriented performance. A person's arms are tight, and he is clumsy in performing vital functions. He is taut and tongue-tied in the presence of the person who may reject or depreciate him, such as his lover or boss. When not in the threatening situation, the person fears what might happen in the next confrontation. He has images of being abandoned or fired or making a fatal mistake. He not only has continuous anticipatory anxiety but, after a "test" of his abilities or desirability, fears that he may have alienated his lover or made a serious error on the job which will lead to disaster.

Another consequence of the acute anxiety reaction is the development of a range of physical symptoms, such as headache, gastrointestinal disturbances, chest pain, palpitations. These physical symptoms, in turn, trigger fears of a serious physical disorder and catch the individual in the web of increasing fears, leading to increased symptoms which reinforce the sense of vulnerability and undermine efficacy. The vicious cycle helps to explain why the anxiety state escalates instead of subsides.

Chronic Anxiety Disorder. Anticipatory anxiety is most important in chronic anxiety disorder, as in the following examples: (1) A college student worried and felt anxious throughout a school year because he believed he would perform poorly (according to his own standards). He was apprehensive when he was studying; before going to class; after class; before, during, and after exams—in short, all the time. (2) A young psychiatrist was concerned whenever he heard the telephone ring that he might hear a patient of his had relapsed or committed suicide. At other times, he feared that he was not treating his patients adequately, that his patients and supervisor might disapprove of his performance, and that his patients might get worse. (3) A newspaper reporter had chronic anxiety in her work situation: she feared that the people she interviewed would consider her an inept interviewer, that her editor would reject the typed copy, and that the readers would disapprove of the printed story. When working in the newsroom, she was concerned that the other staff people were judging every move she made.

In all of these cases, the anxiety seemed to be an extension of problems the patients had experienced throughout most of their lives. It appeared that the most common feature of these chronically anxious patients was the continuation into adulthood of fears originating in the developmental period.

The areas relevant to developmental fears can be condensed into (1) the problems revolving around relations with other people (sociality), and (2) those relevant to identity, mastery, autonomy, and health (individuality). An individual's survival, satisfactions, and attainment of goals are to some degree dependent on the support of other people and to some degree on his own competence in eliciting the support of others, in protecting himself from various dangers, and in implementing his goals. The psychosocial fears, thus, revolve around the threat of losing caregivers and consequently being vulnerable to injury or death, or the threat of performing ineptly outside the family and being subjected to ridicule or rejection. In addition, a person fears that his lack of competence will prevent him from mastering problematic situations and reaching his goals. In the developmental period, many of the potential sources of fear are relatively quiescent because the child has the protection and support of his kin group. As he gets older, he is propelled into confronting some of these "dangerous" situations on his own and is expected to draw on his own repertoire of gradually developing skills to deal with them.

When the development of new skills has not yet caught up with new demands, the individual may be fearful of failure, public show of incompetence, and ridicule. In addition to the concerns about not being able to satisfy the expectations for mature behavior, he may continue to be vulnerable to any threats to his closeness to and dependency on key figures —and thus is subject to fears of abandonment and rejection. Besides his fears about establishing autonomy and mastering problems, the individual fears that his own sense of individuality and freedom may be taken away because of external domination and restriction.

Curiously, the fears of behaving incompetently may persist long after a person has developed a broad range of competence. The development of skills does not necessarily expunge the sense of incompetence or fear of failure. A late adolescent who has developed an ability to initiate conversations, make requests, and present his ideas publicly may still have strong residual fears of appearing foolish and awkward. Thus, a person at this stage of development has three related sets of problems: fear of being incompetent; fear of appearing incompetent; and fear of loss of support of key figures. These fears are central in the development of many cases of anxiety disorder and social phobia.

In addition to the fears related to competence in dealing with problems are fears of externally imposed mishaps, such as accidents or illness. These adverse events are not only uncontrollable but to varying degrees require outside assistance in order for their effects to be mitigated. Within the family or school situation, help is automatically available to staunch bleeding, make diagnoses, and summon medical care. The price of increasing autonomy, however, is the decreased access to this kind of help. People who develop fears of having some overwhelming physical, mental, or behavioral derangement, thus, maintain their "need" for access to a caregiver and are threatened by situations that limit this access. The coupling of fear of disaster with fear of distancing from a caregiver is dramatized in agoraphobia but is present to a lesser degree in many anxiety states.

It appears that a person is influenced by two opposing modes: self-confidence, based on a demonstrated degree of success in managing challenges; and vulnerability, derived from earlier periods of actual lack of competence. When a person's self-confidence—or "self-efficacy estimates" (Bandura 1982)—is firmly established, his self-doubts and uncertainties may be temporarily quiescent. When the vulnerability or insecurity mode is activated, however, he may strongly question the basis of his self-confidence. The insecurity imposes severe strictures on his attempt to confront threats, challenges, and demands. These strictures are expressed in the form of crippling inhibitions, painful anxiety, and generalized patterns of avoidance, all of which impair functioning and lead to further fear of incompetent performance and consequent failure and depreciation.

A generalized anxiety disorder may derive from a reactivation or extension of developmental fears regarding a person's capability of mastering problems and his acceptability to other people. Thus, we often see the precipitation of the disorder when a person's life has shifted in the direction of increased demands and expectations; when there is a decrease in the amount of support from significant others; or when he undergoes experiences that sharply undermine self-confidence and sense of acceptability.

In this sense, generalized anxiety disorder may be distinguished from social phobia. In the former, there is generally a reduction in self-confidence from a previous level. In the case of social phobia, the individual has not yet mastered the skills demanded by social interaction. For example, he may have a sense of incompetence in approaching strangers, in interacting socially with members of the opposite sex, or in negotiating with authorities. However, he is still comfortable in familiar situations and, with further psychological maturation, shows progressive improvement in social skills and self-confidence.

The crucial feature of the social performance of the individual with a generalized anxiety disorder is that he is impaired not simply by a relative deficiency of skills and low self-confidence but by an active *inhibition* of the skills he has already acquired, and thus he becomes more vulnerable to being insulted, ridiculed, and taken advantage of in the vicious cycle we have already described (pages 73–74).

SPECIFIC FEARS

The widely accepted concept of generalized anxiety disorder as a disturbance in which the source of the anxiety is unknown creates an unfortunate tautology. Since, by definition, the patient is unaware of the source of anxiety, the clinical investigator or therapist is unlikely to make a thorough exploration of the patient's phenomenal field. The patient's spontaneous explanations are likely to be discounted as rationalization rather than as pertinent data (Marks 1981). Although generalized anxiety disorder has conventionally been conceived of as diffuse and not related to specific situations, the investigator or therapist is able to pinpoint situations that appear to generate or exacerbate anxiety. Moreover, by factoring into the analysis one's anxiety *prior* to entering a problematic situation (anticipatory anxiety) and *after* leaving it (retrospective anxiety), an investigator is able to provide at least a partial explanation of one's anxiety episodes.

Using a "cognitive analysis," the therapist may establish even more precisely that the anxiety is not "diffuse" but is related to specific fears. Some of the fears are like discrete phobias in that they are attached to specific situations. Generalized anxiety states differ from phobias in that the former fears cut across a heterogeneous group of situations. Moreover, these fears may be active even when the person is not in a "threatening" situation. They can be understood in terms of ultimate "consequences," such as dying or being rejected or attacked. Some cross-situational fears are concerned with psychosocial traumas. Other fears are more pervasive and are related to the possibilities of losing control, not being able to cope, failing, or having a potentially fatal disease (such as heart disease). In some cases, especially following a brush with disaster or an actual trauma, there is a pressure of ideation related to the trauma; hence, the person may have frequent thoughts of being traumatized (dying, falling, getting mutilated, suffocating, drowning). These traumas are similar to those classified as "post-traumatic stress disorders," but the anxiety states do not qualify for that diagnosis since they are not stresses "outside the range of usual human experience."

"Social anxiety" or "interpersonal anxiety" appear to be the cornerstone of most cases of generalized anxiety disorder, as shown in systematic studies by A. T. Beck, R. Laude, and M. Bohnert (1974); by N. A. Fox and Beck (1983); and by G. A. Hibbert (1984). These individuals are apprehensive of any interaction where they would risk being dominated, devalued, rejected, or abandoned. Thus, whether at work, play, or home, they are continually experiencing fears and, consequently, anxiety. Before a job interview, for example, the GAD patient is anxious about how he *will* perform; during the interview, he feels anxious about how he *is* performing and about the outcome; and afterward, he feels anxious about how he *did* perform—specifically, about the possible negative consequences of inadequate performance.

Beck, Laude, and Bohnert (1974) found that their patients with GAD showed ideation (images and automatic thoughts) revolving around at least one of the following general fears: physical injury, illness, or death; mental illness; psychological impairment or loss of control; failure and inability to cope; and rejection, depreciation, domination. It is significant that the majority of the patients (70 percent) had fears in at least three of these areas. Patients without panic attacks focused on psychosocial rather than physical fears. Almost all patients with panic attacks had fears of physical or mental damage. Hibbert (1984) found that most of his GADs without panic had a central fear of not being able to cope with other people, whereas those with panic attacks had fears of a physical disaster.

The nature of the fears in GAD may be delineated by comparing them with the fears in phobias. The anxiety-producing situations in GAD are situations in which avoidance is not feasible. One of the major problems in GAD (especially in panic disorder) revolves around the persistence and escalation of distressing internal sensations which lead to a fear of loss of control or of some serious pathological process. These are "dangers" that *should be attended to* rather than avoided. If a person is bleeding or believes he is having a heart attack, it might save his life to feel helpless and to call for help.

Another source of danger lies in the domain of interpersonal relationships. If an individual is uncertain about his interpersonal skills in a threatening situation, it might be advantageous for him to experience anxiety as a spur to develop or polish these skills. An immature person who lacks social skills, and keeps getting rebuffed in social situations because of his ineptitude, eventually will be isolated from the social group and may become depressed. His anxiety, thus, deters him from actions that will elicit social reprisal and may increase the pressure to develop more adaptive behavior.

In essence, then, anxiety (along with several of the other negative affects, such as shame) is a powerful spur to socialization and maturity. It also helps to deter the individual from getting into dangerous situations that he should avoid (raging fires, shaky tree limbs, collapsible tunnels, deep water) and discourages rash behavior in social situations. A person's anxiety may be reduced to some extent in social situations by the development and application of social competences. (This factor may be the reason that training in social skills is often so effective in generalized anxiety.) As an alternative to self-development, the immature individual may take the option of leaning on a more skillful relative or companion for promoting his interests in social situations and, consequently, maintain juvenile dependency.

The fears of the GAD patient, thus, may be understood in terms of the excessive impact of the exposure to socialization. A major dread of these patients is that of being depreciated, ridiculed, or rejected. Generally, the trigger for such expectations is their perception of "inept behavior." Thus, a person who behaves immaturely is subject to epithets such as "You're a baby, grow up!" The fear of such a sanction stirs anxiety and stimulates him to monitor and control his behavior. If he feels like crying, for example, he inhibits its expression. Anxiety may lead further to overmonitoring and inhibition and thus can produce awkward behavior for which the patient may be criticized. Consequently, more anxiety is generated.

Another major fear, especially in panic attacks, is that of loss of control. This fear also tells us something about the rigidity of a person's standards: namely, that he considers the maintenance of control to be imperative and the prospect of loss of control to be a catastrophe. In a study of the fears of GAD patients at the Center for Cognitive Therapy, we found that about 75 percent reported fear of loss of control as a major fear.

Fear of failure and of being unable to cope with the demands and expectations imposed by oneself or others is a theme that runs—subtly— through the ideation of most cases of GAD. One factor activating this fear is the "paralysis" of function in acute confrontations: that is, inhibition of spontaneous movement and interference with speaking, thinking, and recall. A person fears confrontations because of the possibility that his apparatus for effective communication will shut down and leave him vulnerable and helpless. In addition, the generalized concept of himself as not being sufficiently skilled or competent to meet his goals haunts him whenever he undertakes an important task or attempts to solve a difficult problem.

Proximal Fears and Ultimate Fears.   To a large extent human beings are programmed to fear potentially harmful places and events. A specific fear can be formulated in terms of three different levels or points: fear of a specific place, situation, or object or event; fear of having an unpleasant affect or sensation (anxiety, panic, shame, physical pain, choking, and so on); and fear of the *outcome* or consequences of being in that particular place or of having that unpleasant sensation or feeling. The first two fears are labeled "proximal" in the sense that they represent the frightening place or object and the symptom (anxiety) activated as a person approaches it; thus, the patient has a fear of the situation and a fear of the anticipated anxiety and other symptoms.

These three "types" of fear are obviously components or aspects of the same process and have a logical relationship. For example, a young woman, notified that her boss wants to see her, initially feels anxious at the thought of entering his office (the "situation"). She shudders at this unpleasant experience (the "affect") and would like to terminate it. Then she fears that her anxiety will get worse and that she will be very uncomfortable. Finally, she is afraid of a specific outcome once she is in the situation: namely, that she will be fired (the "consequence"). In this case, the fear of the situation and of her anticipated symptoms may be labeled the "proximal fear"; and the fear of being fired, the "ultimate fear."

The three facets may be analyzed in terms of their function in the survival mechanism. The most pragmatic way to prevent dangerous encounters is to label as "dangerous" a concrete, identifiable object or place associated with a possible harmful encounter. For example, children are often afraid of the dark or of strange places. However, the actual danger, if any, is not the object or the place itself but what might occur *in* the situation (for example, one might be attacked by ghosts or strangers). The aversive place is tangible and thus easily identified. A person is programmed to perceive it as the danger and experiences anxiety as he approaches it. He may not "know" why it is dangerous. The global meaning of "dangerous" is sufficient to produce the anxiety and avoidance behavior.

The next level of fear is attached to the anticipation of anxiety. Just as one avoids exposing oneself to the risk of physical damage because of the fear of physical pain, so one avoids exposure to psychological trauma because of the fear of anxiety. The agoraphobic person may say, "I know that there is nothing unsafe about public places, but I also know I am afraid that I'll be very uncomfortable if I go there" (in this sense, the fear is "realistic": that person probably will feel discomfort if he goes there).

The final, ultimate level has to do with the anticipation of harmful consequences if one is in the dangerous situation. Thus, a person may decide against engaging in a hazardous activity because he determines the risk of being harmed is too great. He does not need anxiety to deter him;

the knowledge of the danger is sufficient. For the anxiety patient, the precise nature of the ultimate fear may not be apparent until he is actually in the situation. Thus, a person may feel tense on entering a classroom. Once there, he will recognize that his fear centers on the idea that he will look foolish when he is asked to perform.

The specific nature of the proximal fears may be understood in terms of the automatic protective (primal) functions of the organism. The early global fear is relatively primitive in that it is attached strictly to the physical, topographic classification of a dangerous situation. This focus on the physical features has the advantages of eliminating judgment from the fear reaction. The rule regarding the "dangerous" place is simple, unequivocal, and absolute; there is generally no need for delay or confusion in applying it. On the other hand, the breadth and rigidity of the classification make it overly inclusive; and consequently, the individual is likely to experience a number of false alarms. The warning system appears to be most effective if the concept of danger is shifted from a noxious event that *might* occur, were the individual in contact with the place or object, to the object itself. By attaching the label of danger to the concrete object, he is alerted to danger at the earliest point. Thus, the experience of anxiety and avoidance motivation impel him to *prevent* the danger from becoming actualized. Once he is in the situation, however, the automatic mechanisms are directed to escape, freezing, or seeking help.

The role of cognitive therapy, as we will point out, is to test whether a particular situation labeled dangerous is actually dangerous. Thus, through questioning the degree of danger, evaluating danger-laden automatic thoughts, and experimental exposure, the patient is enabled to detach and "extinguish" the fears that have been erroneously attached to a given situation or object.

Systematic Studies of Automatic Thoughts and Images.   A detailed analysis of the content of the ideation of thirty-two GAD patients (Beck, Laude, and Bohnert 1974) indicated that each patient anticipated being harmed physically or psychologically, or both. In acute-severe conditions, a patient's ideation revolved around the fear of a physical disaster or of some social, interpersonal catastrophe, or both. In more chronic and less severe conditions, this feared event or trauma was of a less "severe" nature—anticipation of being criticized or rejected or of failing.

The cognitions that occurred just before the onset or exacerbation of anxiety had the common theme of imminent danger. They were experienced as discrete thoughts, such as "I am having a heart attack," or "I will look foolish." In the more severe cases, the patient attached a high degree of probability to the occurrence of the feared event. Even in the less severe cases, the automatic thought of danger seemed plausible to the patient and the likelihood of being hurt seemed high. Despite a history of repeated disconfirmations, the expectation of danger recurred when a patient was exposed to the typical "dangerous" situation.

Of the thirty-two patients, thirty reported having experienced conscious images of an unpleasant or a disastrous experience. These visual experiences had the same content as the verbal cognitions. When asked to experience the fantasies during the interview, the patients were able to visualize the unpleasant event and felt anxious as the visualized scenario developed. Specific features of thoughts and images reported by a given patient often clearly related to unique aspects of his conceptual configurations and to his past experience. Therefore, these personal variations often shed the most light on the relation between the patient's mode of integrating his experiences and the arousal of anxiety.

For instance, eight of the thirty patients had recurrent, anxiety-associated ideation about dying. However, the nature of the feared event, the situations associated with anticipation of death, and the expected consequences of the anticipated catastrophe differed substantially. One woman patient, for instance, feared sudden death by heart attack or suffocation. This fear developed after two experiences, involving fainting associated with chest pain and dyspnea, that she had misinterpreted as heart attacks—an erroneous conclusion that was reinforced by the apparent concern of the doctors observing her in the hospital. However, no evidence of any disease was found.

Another woman was specifically fearful of dying from a slowly deteriorating illness, associated with chronic pain, wasting, and deformity. A close friend of hers had been afflicted with chronic, progressive neurological illness; and at the time our GAD patient experienced unexplained pains and paresthesia, which disappeared several years before her examination in the study. She interpreted almost every unusual sensation in any part of her body as indication of a progressive disease. These ideas ultimately culminated in her experiencing a severe anxiety attack.

A third patient, who had been raped by an armed man while alone at night, believed that the terrifying emotions aroused in her then were sufficient to permanently damage her mind. Being alone in her apartment or walking alone in the city activated fantasies of being attacked. It is important to recognize that the crucial object of her fear was not the danger of being raped again *per se*, but rather the disastrous consequences that she assumed would result from the terror she would feel. She believed it was likely that she would be at least momentarily paralyzed and might die from the terror.

A fourth patient was chiefly concerned with the consequences of dying suddenly and unexpectedly. From a strong orthodox Catholic background, she feared an afterlife of eternal punishment if she was not prepared for death. She had been warned several times during an impressionable period of early childhood that if she was lazy or sinful in her life, she might die in her sleep, unprepared and without warning, and wake up in hell. Subsequently, she believed that she was particularly vulnerable to some unpredictable event that could cause her death.

All of the other patients who were afraid of death traced their fears to actual life experiences that had frightened them. One woman, who was afraid of having a heart attack, had witnessed her mother doubled up with pain from attacks of angina, one of which culminated in her death. Another patient had a severe choking episode while receiving anesthesia during an operation and was continually haunted by the fear of choking to death. Still another patient had a severe allergic reaction to penicillin and was afraid of having a sudden fatal reaction at any time.

Fear of rejection was a prelude to anxiety in ten patients. The particular characteristics and consequences of the anticipated rejection, however, varied considerably among the individual cases. One patient had the specific fear that her behavior would be regarded as peculiar, foreign, and distasteful by her social peers, and that she would therefore be systematically and irreversibly excluded from her peer group. She anticipated that rejection would extend to total ostracism, and that she would lead a life of unbearable loneliness.

Another patient who anticipated catastrophic consequences of rejection leading to complete ostracism, however, feared that she would be found fundamentally lacking in wit and intellectual ability and would therefore not fit into her peer group. It is perhaps significant that these two patients also had fears of being physically attacked by other people.

The fear of rejection experienced by another patient was associated with imagery of collective exclusion by a social group, but the anticipated rejection was limited to certain specific situations—namely, large groups and interaction with men—and was not seen as complete ostracism extending to all social contexts. In six patients, the recurrent thematic content of anxiety-associated thoughts and imagery was disgrace and humiliation because of inept performance in specific situations. The patients anticipated rejection resulting from unfavorable comparison with other people in specific contexts, usually related to work, school, or social situations. However, they had no expectation of being completely ostracized by an entire class of people or of being excluded in all social interaction.

A more recent study by Fox and Beck (1983) of GAD patients demonstrated a similar relationship between the occurrence of automatic thought relevant to danger and the anxiety experienced. The theme of physical or psychological vulnerability was present in all cases. The themes relevant to psychosocial dangers centered in notions of deficient coping abilities; in fears of being observed, depreciated and isolated; and finally in fears of failure.

Similar themes were reported by Hibbert in his 1984 study of GAD patients. Those *with* panic attacks had fears centering on physical danger. Hibbert found that those patients *without* panic attacks primarily had fears of not coping with psychological problems.

These studies clearly demonstrate the presence of a cognitive component in anxiety neurosis. The specific cognitions that occurred both in verbal form and in visual images centered on the theme of personal danger. These specific cognitions were reported as consistently as the affective and physiological components of the anxiety syndrome.

The most regular sequence observed weekly in the self-reports of those patients who received psychotherapy was that the anticipation of danger generally preceded the onset or the exacerbation of anxiety. As the patient's belief in the probability of harm was reduced by information or clarification from the therapist, by increased attention to reality testing, and by improved discrimination between fantasy and fact, his subjective distress gradually dissipated.

SELF-CONCEPT IN GENERALIZED ANXIETY DISORDER

The general definition of the self-concept in the literature varies from a cluster of beliefs regarding the effectiveness of a highly specialized skill in a particular confrontation to a generalized global view of the self, such as a weakling or an inadequate personality—unable to cope with ordinary life demands, expectations, and problems—or a superman or genius.

For the severely anxious patient, most life situations pose a threat because "inadequate" performance makes him feel constantly vulnerable to negative evaluation and rejection. The notion of vulnerability may progress into the concept of hopeless ineffectuality, which leads to ideas of quitting, of abandoning normal goals and the prospect of getting normal rewards. At this point, the self-concept has moved from anxious to depressive.

The notion of the self-concept in GAD can be illustrated by an analysis of the reactions to situations of immediate interpersonal confrontation, such as (1) confrontation with an authority (for example, teacher, boss); (2) confrontation with the group (for example, public speaking); (3) subjection to immediate evaluation of ability (for example, test taking, athletic competition); (4) subjection to social evaluation (for example, asking for a date); or (4) confrontation with a stranger (for example, a sales clerk).

Each of the preceding confrontations involves important facets of an individual's life—namely, his perceived competence in dealing with problematic situations and his ability to obtain respect and acceptance of his individuality, his rights as a person. The individual is being judged (or at least believes that he is) in evaluative terms. Even if he is not being judged by others, he may judge his performance severely since he believes he has a great deal to lose. A lowered self-confidence results in susceptibility to anxiety or in an actual persistent low level of anxiety. With this background anxiety, further lowering of efficacy by factors such as fatigue negates the sense of control over thinking and performing. In addition, an acute confrontation may produce inhibitions of speech and action and thus further limit effectiveness and reduce self-confidence.

The GAD patient is different from the depressive in that he can see the positive aspects of his personality and also can separate the consequences of inadequate behavior from the durable concept of himself. He can regard himself as having a behavioral deficit without a characterological deficit. Thus, he can think and say, "I made a fool of myself"—a statement indicating that he did not consider himself a fool *before* the performance, and that he does not regard being a fool intrinsic to his personality or as a durable characteristic. The depressive, on the other hand, would view inept performance as a manifestation of an inadequate personality.

The self-image of the anxious person may fluctuate according to the degree of risk he perceives in a situation. Thus, he may view himself as competent and effective in an unthreatening situation but switch to an image of himself as childlike, small, and inept when confronted with threatening situations such as confrontation with authority.

This observation—which could be labeled the "shrinking phenomenon" —suggests that such a person has at least two images of the self: one, competent, mature, and confident; the other, incompetent, immature, and insecure. It is conceivable that these conflicting self-concepts have motivational properties and lead to behavior that is consistent with them. Further, it is possible that they serve some adaptive function, the negative concept serving as a check against excessive, prolonged ventures into precarious activities. In any event, the negative image of being weak, tongue-tied, immobile may appear at the time a person reacts to a threat with inhibitions.

SELF–CRITICISM IN ANXIETY AND DEPRESSION

Another aspect of the negative concept is self-criticism. It is apparent that, even in specific threat situations such as taking tests or preparing reports, anxious people are likely to criticize themselves for not having prepared better, for not concentrating well, and for not doing as well as other students or workers. As we have said, the anxious person is unlike the depressive, who criticizes himself in more global terms, in that he criticizes specific lacks in preparation performance and ability. In fact, the criticisms produce anxiety—as though the individual were simply warning himself about the dire consequences of his deficiencies.

The differences between the two groups may be summarized in terms of the target of criticism: The anxious person tends to reproach himself for specific flaws ("behavioral self-blame"), such as not preparing adequately, not spending time optimally, or misunderstanding a question. The depressive blames himself for global deficits ("characterological self-blame"), such as being stupid, lazy, or generally inadequate (Beck 1976; Peterson and Seligman 1984).

THE DIFFERENCES BETWEEN ANXIETY AND DEPRESSION

There is a significant overlap between anxiety and depression in that patients with GAD often are depressed and depressed patients often are anxious. Moreover, even "pure" cases of each disorder show roughly similar characteristics in terms of depreciated self-concept (as pointed out earlier), negative predictions, and negative bias in appraising current experiences. The differences between the two groups, however, are revealing and illuminate the specific nature of each disorder:

1. In depression, negative appraisals are pervasive, global, and exclusive; in anxiety, they are selective and specific, do not encompass all aspects of functioning, and do not exclude consideration of positive factors.

2. The anxious patient sees some prospects for the future; he has not voluntarily given up. The depressed patient sees the future as blank; he believes he has already lost an "essential" relationship or been defeated, and he has given up voluntarily.

3. The anxious person does not regard his defects or mistakes as irrevocable, as indicating rottenness in the central core of his personality, or as justifying self-loathing. The depressed patient sees his mistakes as meaning that he is defective "through and through" and is beyond redemption.

4. The anxious patient is tentative, uncertain in his negative evaluations; the depressed person is absolute. The differences between the two syndromes will be highlighted in the examination of their specific dimensions.

5. The anxious patient anticipates possible damage to his relations with others, to his goals and objectives, to his ability to cope with problems and perform adequately, and to his health or survival. The depressed patient *regrets* that he has lost sources of gratification, that he has been deprived of significant other people, that he has been defeated in his objectives, that he is already diseased, and that he is incapable of doing anything to change his adversities or improve his performance.

6. The depressed individual has a global view that nothing will turn out right for him; and for this, he feels regretful and sad. However, when faced with a specific confrontation—say, with a boss or an audience—he reacts the way a GAD patient might—with anxiety. The anxious patient predicts only that certain specific events may go badly—for example, confrontations.

The cognitive-motivational-behavioral difference between generalized anxiety disorder and the affective disorders may be discussed in terms of specific psychological functions or dimensions:

Avoidance. The depressive has given up on routine tasks—for example, making phone calls, answering letters, balancing his checkbook, getting out of bed, tending to chores, going out for a walk, preparing meals.

The anxiety patient, as we have said, avoids only those specific tasks that endanger his vital interests and present some probability of confrontation or failure or of not being able to cope (public appearances, calling a person for a social engagement, or asking for a raise). If in such a situation the possibility of the danger is lessened, the patient gains confidence in being able to cope with it and is less likely to avoid the situation; indeed, he might be motivated to enter it. In this case, the anxious patient is much more sensitive to fluctuations in a negative confrontation and adjusts his approach-avoidance behavior to them.

Motivation and Energy. Depressives "lack" the energy to carry out tasks. They experience a decathexis of the motivational-motor apparatus, which is manifested by a *loss of will power* and by *psychomotor retardation*.

The anxiety patient often has the energy to undertake a project (study for an examination, enter a contest) but may be inhibited (countercathexis). He has a subjective sense of some internal force that automatically opposes or offers *resistance to his wishes* and that also may be manifested in active inhibition of action and of effective mental activity. Some patients have described this as a kind of rigid motor paralysis (all the muscles of the body become taut) and mental paralysis. If the inhibition is lifted, then one has abundant energy to carry out the task. For example, a young man felt a rigid inhibition when he prepared himself to call a girl for a date (difficulty in talking, blank mind). When he was informed that she was very eager to hear from him and wanted to go out with him, the inhibition disappeared; he was able to carry on a long, animated conversation with her. He could not have done this had he been depressed.

The depressive has given up on whole categories of objectives and so sees no use in trying. The anxious patient would like to pursue these objectives but feels straitjacketed by a sense of vulnerability, by a fear of being hurt, and by automatic reflexive inhibitions.

Expectation of Failure.   The depressed patient expects failure. He feels regret—as though the failure has already occurred—even though he has not yet undertaken a task. When he contemplates his activities for the day, he thinks, "I won't be able to do it——I won't know what to say——I won't accomplish anything today." He feels sad and discouraged. In more severe cases, the patient has already decided that the burden of a task is too great, and that he will not even make an effort. Thus, even in the early morning, he has "written off" the day as a failure.

The anxiety patient is actively afraid of failure and the consequences of failure, but he views the event as still in the future. A student, for example, may think, "If I don't finish the paper, I will flunk out." He may even believe that he will probably flunk, but he has not taken the expected failure as a *fait accompli*. Nonetheless, since he does consider the consequences of flunking a source of future pain, he experiences anxiety (not sadness, because the failure has not yet occurred).

We should note that the anxiety patient is not concerned about failure unless a vital interest is concerned. For example, a generally anxious medical student decided to take the Law School Admissions Test just to see how well he would do and also to fulfill a bet. Although he had always been anxious about taking medical exams in the past, he had no anxiety about failing the law exam since he had nothing at stake in regard to his needs or expectations of himself. His motivation to do well, however, was high because a good score represented a source of satisfaction. In contrast, a depressed college student, interested in law, wanted to avoid taking the examination. He could see no point in subjecting himself to failure, as he believed that he was totally incapable of performing the task.

Self-Concept. The differences in self-concept have already been discussed in the section on that topic (pages 101–2). In brief, the anxious patient focuses on specific areas of vulnerability in his repertoire of skills, coping mechanisms, and strategies for solving problems; his uncertainties are related in that any of these areas of uncertainty *can* show weakness under conditions of stress or confrontation. The depressed patient is generally unrealistic in his sweeping negative generalizations about himself.

It should also be noted that the anxious patient sees the consequences (disgracing himself) of his failure as occurring *after* the possible failure and therefore as something to worry about and possibly fear. The depressed patient, on the other hand, sees the consequences as starting *right now,* since he has already "incorporated" the failure and is passing judgment on himself for "having failed." Whether he takes the exam is irrelevant to him: either way he is a failure.

Automatic Thoughts. Automatic thoughts that are followed by anxiety are different from those followed by sadness and reflect the differences in ideational content between depression and anxiety disorders. In a systematic study, outpatients were asked to check typical thoughts in specific situations and to indicate the associated feeling. The following automatic thoughts occurred frequently on entering a social situation and were associated with anxiety but not with sadness:

"I will make a fool of myself."

"I won't know what to say."

"People will laugh at me."

Automatic thoughts followed by sadness included:

"I'm a social failure."

"I'll never be as good as other people are."

Anxiety-producing thoughts when the patient works on a project were as follows:

"What if I fail?"

"Other things might get in the way."

"I won't have enough time to do a good job."

"I'm falling behind."

Typical thoughts associated with sadness were:

"I'll never be as capable as I should be."

"I'm not as capable as I used to be."

In the category of physical health, anxiety was found to be associated with the possibility of a specific injury or illness ("What if I get sick and become an invalid?"), and sadness, with a sweeping generalization ("I am a defective human being").

Panic Disorder

DESCRIPTION

Charles Darwin wrote the following vivid description of the somatic and behavioral characteristics of acute terror in animals:

> With all or almost all animals, even with birds, Terror causes the body to tremble. The skin becomes pale, sweat breaks out, and the hair bristles. The secretions of the alimentary canal and of the kidneys are increased, and they are involuntarily voided, owing to the relaxation of the sphincter muscles, as is known to be the case with man, and as I have seen with cattle, dogs, cats, and monkeys. The breathing is hurried. The heart beats quickly, wildly, and violently; but whether it pumps the blood more efficiently through the body may be doubted, for the surface seems bloodless and the strength of the muscles soon fails. . . . The mental faculties are much disturbed. Utter prostration soon follows, and even fainting. A terrified canary-bird has been seen not only to tremble and to turn white about the base of the bill, but to faint; and I once caught a robin in a room, which fainted so completely, that for a time I thought it dead. [1872, p. 77]

Darwin went on to develop the concept that fear, derived from innumerable injuries in the course of evolution, prepares the animal for possible injury and automatically mobilizes the body for defense.

Compare Darwin's description with the verbatim description of a panic attack experienced by a young woman, and note the similar symptoms—shallow breathing, rapid heart rate, profuse sweating, faintness, difficulty in thinking:

> My breathing starts getting very shallow. I feel I'm going to stop breathing. The air feels like it gets thinner. I feel the air is not coming up through my nose. I take short rapid breaths. *Then I see an image of myself gasping for air and remember what happened in the hospital.* I think that I will start gasping. I get very dizzy and disoriented. I cannot sit or stand still. I start pacing. Then I start shaking and sweating. I feel I'm losing my mind and I will flip out and hurt myself or someone else. My heart starts beating fast and I start getting pains in my chest. My chest tightens up. I become very frightened. I get afraid that these feelings will not go away. Then I get really upset. I feel no one will be able to help me. I get very frightened I will die. I want to run to some place safe but I don't know where.

The patient's description of her panic disorder illustrates the misery of this most dramatic of psychiatric disorders. D. V. Sheehan (1982) reports that panic disorder occurs in 2 percent to 5 percent of the general population and in 10 percent to 14 percent of patients in a cardiology practice. In its most severe form, the panic attack is manifested by a variety of intense, unpleasant, strange experiences, as follow:

1. Such reactions are generally qualitatively different from previous experience. Some patients compare the strangeness of the experience to adverse reactions to drugs or to having a nightmare. External familiar objects seem peculiar, distorted, or unreal. The patient's *internal* experiences seem strange and peculiar. He may experience loss of normal sensations in his extremities or in the interior of his body. He may experience peculiar sensations or numbness (paresthesia) in his limbs. His body may feel very heavy or weightless.

2. Perhaps the most frightening aspect of the panic attack is the *slippage of controls* that the individual has always taken for granted. He has to struggle to retain or regain voluntary control over focusing, concentration, attention, and action. At times, the difficulty in focusing extends into a sense that he is losing consciousness, but actual loss of consciousness is rare. He has difficulty framing his thoughts or pursuing a consistent logical line of thinking or reasoning. His awareness of his surroundings is altered, and he may feel remote or detached from events. Paradoxically, however, he may be exquisitely sensitive to certain stimuli, especially those of a frightening nature: another person's voice may seem to boom and resonate (Beck 1976, p. 78).

3. He often feels *confused and disoriented*. Even though he may correctly identify who he is and where he is, he feels unsure that "this is really me." The extreme form of this disturbance has been labeled a "catastrophic reaction." The uncanny experiences may be described in terms such as "I don't feel that I'm really here——I feel different——Things look different." The quality of the eerie experience is captured by expressions such as "I feel I am ready to pass out"; "I feel I'm losing my grip"; "I'm going out of my mind"; "I'm coming apart"; "I'm dying"; "I'm going crazy"; or, "I'm having a stroke." Although patients often interpret "weird feelings" as a sign of insanity, they are specific signs of acute neurotic reactions rather than of psychosis.

4. Of course, the striking characteristic of the panic attack is the feeling of being engulfed by uncontrollable anxiety. This feeling has been described as "unendurable pain" and "the worst experience I could imagine." Another essential feature of the panic attack is the automatic suppression of reasoning powers. The individual may be aware that the panic attack may be a "false alarm," and he may even be able to recall previous panic

attacks that turned out to be innocuous. However, he cannot bring this reasoning to bear against the onslaught of symptoms and frightening ideas. He cannot get out of his mind the overwhelming notion that "this time it is the real thing. *I really am dying (losing control, choking, going crazy).*"

5. In addition, the patient has a variety of symptoms associated with parasympathetic or cholinergic activation and motor "collapse": faintness and pervasive weakness. These symptoms are usually more frightening than the more familiar palpitations and generalized sweating associated with acute anxiety. Further, a number of symptoms, such as peculiar sensations in the extremities and a sense of losing consciousness, may be a consequence of rapid shallow breathing or gasping (hyperventilation syndrome).

Although panic attacks have been described as "spontaneous," we have found that patients who are trained to monitor their anxiety can identify "inexplicable" physiological sensations (such as faintness or "palpitations") followed by frightening automatic thoughts as a prelude to an attack. Also, patients have specific fears during an attack. From their standpoint, the danger is real and plausible. What do we learn if we ask a patient, "What are you afraid of during an attack?" At first, his attention may be so fixated on his anxiety, his peculiar feeling states, and his loss of control that he may find it difficult to focus on the question. With a minimum of introspection, however, it is possible for him to respond. Often—but not always—he is overwhelmed by thoughts that he is dying. The fear of dying may be activated by his unexpected physical sensation for which he has no benign explanation. He interprets the physical distress as a sign of a devastating physical disorder and becomes more anxious and symptomatic; and a chain reaction is set up.

MEANING OF PANIC ATTACKS

Panic attacks seem to signify helplessness in the face of serious danger. The sense of helplessness appears to be the result of an internal mechanism that leads a person to believe that he is trapped in a dangerous situation or is overwhelmed by an internal derangement. The fear of his own vulnerability interacts with psychological and affective responses to produce a vicious cycle. With the onset of the symptomatology, the person has a sequence of responses.

For example, a patient experienced abdominal distress after a dietary indiscretion. His various systems were activated in the following sequence:

1. *Cognitive:* "Something terrible could be happening."
2. *Physiological:* Activation of autonomic nervous system—rapid heart beat, faintness, more abdominal sensations ("butterflies"), sweating.
   Affective: Anxiety.
   "Mental": Blocking, distraction, confusion.
3. *Cognitive:* "Something terrible is happening. I can't control my thinking, feeling, behavior. This could be a sign that I am dying (going insane, losing control, and so on)."
4. The *cognitive* elaboration escalates: "This must be pretty bad if I can't stop the feelings. This means it can go all the way (say, death, insanity, homicide). If I don't get help, I'm a goner."

The cognitive-affective-physiological mechanism almost appears to be *designed* to produce (1) the belief that he is endangered by internal disturbance that he cannot control, (2) the fear that the derangement will progress to an ultimate disaster, and (3) the belief that he should turn to a caregiver for help.

The specific fear engendered by this mechanism varies from person to person but seems to be relevant to the particular sensations:

Symptoms of abdominal or chest pain plus faintness = heart attack.
Peculiar sensations in limbs, freezing, tremor, weakness of muscles = stroke.
Changes in mental functioning (difficulty in focusing, fogginess, depersonalization, and so on) = incipient insanity or cerebral accident.
Faintness = passing out in public and being disgraced or loss of consciousness leading to coma and death.
Difficulty catching breath = "I will stop breathing and will die."
Generalized sense of loss of control over internal sensations = uncontrollable or bizarre behavior; insanity; homicidal or other antisocial acts; suicide; flagrant sex "misbehavior."

The crucial devastating symptom is the inability to control one's mental, physical, and affective symptoms. When the anxiety becomes so intense that the person believes he cannot control it by himself and that it will not subside spontaneously, he starts to catastrophize: "This cannot be simply an emotional upset. I'm having a heart attack (stroke, ruptured intestine)"; "I'm going crazy (lapsing into a coma)"; or, "I will be driven to bizarre behavior (suicide, destructive acts, sexual acting out)."

In the case of the "simple phobias" (fear of animals, heights, closed spaces), escape from the phobic situation offers relief. However, if escape is not possible, then the individual may have a panic attack similar to the one just described. In agoraphobia, the individual is trapped and, consequently, "needs" help in order to be rescued. In order to avoid having panic, he either takes a guardian with him or makes certain that he has ready access to the guardian.

The importance of loss of control is supported by the following observations: First, it has been reported that panic attacks associated with performance anxiety can be controlled by drugs that block the peripheral action of the sympathetic nervous system (beta adrenergic blocker). These drugs reduce tachycardia and tremors (but not the other symptoms of panic). Thus, the individual recognizes that there is a limit to the escalation of the symptoms, that they are being controlled (by the drug), and he no longer fears the "disastrous" consequences of not being able to perform. The "beta blockers" do not have any effect on generalized anxiety (Sheehan 1982). When a patient's problem is primarily premonitory (anticipatory) anxiety, drugs to prevent escalation of symptoms are not called for since the problem at this stage does not center around such escalation. Valium has an effect on generalized anxiety but not on panic attacks: as it acts primarily on the subjective experiences of anxiety but not on the behavioral or physiological reactions, it does not put a "stopper" on the acute symptoms of the emergency reaction (tachycardia, faintness, freezing).

FUNCTIONAL ANALYSIS OF PANIC ATTACKS

The acute primal mechanisms take over in these conditions. These mechanisms are not under volitional control but are, in fact, contravolitional. Depending on the particular situation, a person's primal physical reaction will be freezing (to cope with ambiguous danger), tonic or atonic immobility (to prevent falling), gagging and coughing (to prevent obstruction of the airway), ducking or jumping (to avoid a moving object). These reflexes are programmed to *prevent* death or injury but actually may increase vulnerability because they are automatic and stereotyped, are triggered by psychological as well as physical danger, and actually undermine coping. These reflexes are not an expression of anxiety. Indeed by interfering with skillful performance, they may increase anxiety. These primal mechanisms may have some survival value in children—prior to their developing more mature coping skills. Their persistence into adulthood may be a behavioral manifestation of the phenomena of neoteny (or juvenilization).

Panic attacks differ qualitatively as well as quantitatively from the feeling of anxiety generally experienced in GAD. Not only are affective and cognitive symptoms more intense, but the person experiences additional symptoms, such as change in perceptions of the self and the outside world (depersonalization and derealization) and an inhibition of cognitive functions relevant to reasoning, recall, and perspective-taking. The loss of the ability to reason is often the most prominent symptom, exceeding in intensity the subjective anxiety and physiological symptoms. The parasympathetic response involving fainting or actual fainting and involuntary defecation and urination suggests a more profound reaction than that involving the more familiar experience of anxiety. These qualitative differences suggest that the emergency response involving panic may denote the activation of a *different program* from that involved in the usual anxiety reaction. This program may be designed to deal with emergency situations in which the usual defensive strategies are inadequate. Although the "panic program" may be different from the other programs, it should be regarded as one component of the broader system. However, the alarm (panic) response should be investigated in terms of its own peculiar cognitive, behavioral, and neurophysiological correlates. The fact that panic attacks seem to be ameliorated by the administration of "antidepressive" drugs such as imipramine but not by "antianxiety" drugs such as benzodiazepam (Klein, Rabkin, and Gorman, in press) supports the notion of a separate organization.

PRECIPITATION OF PANIC ATTACKS

Although the attacks are often described as "spontaneous," we have found that some experience seems to activate a person's "alarm system" involving cognitive-affective and physiological components. The antecedent experience often consists of some change in a person's physiological status. He may, for example, feel faint after getting up quickly from a chair, get a flushed feeling when going from an air-conditioned room into a hot street, or experience rapid heart beat or shortness of breath from running up a flight of stairs. He interprets these normal physiological changes as signs of serious internal disorders. Of great importance is the fact that his ability to "reason" with himself regarding the gravity of these symptoms is impaired by fatigue, cognitive strain, use of drugs, and so on; and the vicious cycle is set up.

Not all cases of panic disorder involve the threat of internal derangement. Some cases center on terror of an overwhelming external psychosocial threat. For example, a patient who was a social worker had completed a difficult session with a client earlier in the day. As she reflected over her interview, she began to experience the following (in her own words): "intense anxiety . . . mounting nausea, feel hot, sweating, sense of removal from immediate reality, which makes me reluctant to drive home and is connected to a sense of doom, of foreshortening, of the future being cut off. Afterward, feel cold."

Automatic thoughts: "I messed it up. Her husband will make off with their car and money and leave her [the client] destitute. I'll have brought about exactly what she fears. . . . Her life will be ruined. She'll sue me and ruin my career. I'll lose my house—will have to pay court costs and a settlement. Martin [her fiancé] will be stuck with me, a failure, and question his love. I'll be barred from the profession. I'll be found out as an incompetent. I'll never have the marriage and professional status I want." She also had the following image: "Myself in Martin's apartment, alone. I have no job, no respect, nothing to do. His child despises me."

The waves of panic became so strong that she ran to the nearby office of Jim, a colleague. After talking to him, she was able to reason with herself, and her panic promptly subsided. Her rational response was: "People don't, and generally can't, do things like make off with the money in the way I envision. If they do, there are legal remedies for the wife. I would not be responsible for his behavior, in any case. According to Jim, I handled the client correctly. He also says that I have a distorted notion of what it takes to be sued for malpractice, and that I have blown this affair way out of proportion. Finally, I didn't create the situation, the couple did, over a period of twenty years."

The social worker's reaction illustrates what may be the essential ingredient of panic attacks, namely, the loss of ability to reason regarding the problem, whether it is physical or interpersonal.

The 1974 study by Beck, Laude and Bohnert (pages 98–100) included two groups of patients with generalized anxiety. The first, a psychotherapy group, had twelve patients. The second, patients seen on admission to the outpatient clinic at the Hospital of the University of Pennsylvania, consisted of twenty patients. Panic attacks were described in all but two patients in each sample—that is, twenty-eight out of thirty-two patients. The acute anxiety attacks were *superimposed on the base level of anxiety.* The acute panic attacks came on rapidly, caused severe distress, and were often totally disabling. They lasted from several minutes to a few hours, and their frequency for a given patient varied considerably from daily to once a month.

There is considerable clinical evidence that psychological factors can precipitate panic attacks. M. Raskin, H. V. Peeke, W. Dickman, and H. Pinsker (1982) described ten patients who experienced panic attacks following separations. Typically, the first series of panic attacks occurred shortly after each patient had left home; a subsequent attack occurred after the loss or possible loss of a "loved one." A variation of this theme was reported by a patient whose original panic attacks followed the death of her fiancé. Subsequent attacks occurred whenever she became sufficiently involved with a man to make him emotionally important to her; her attacks abated when she gave up the attachment. A somewhat analogous conflict occurred in the case of three male patients who reported a specific sequence of events leading to their initial panic attacks. Each had been ridiculed or abused frequently by his father throughout childhood and adolescence. The first panic attack for each occurred in late adolescence immediately following an act of open rebellion against his father. Some subsequent panic attacks followed conflicts with authority figures.

The conflicts leading to the panic attacks seem to represent threats to an individual's dependency or autonomy. For example, a patient in our clinic who experienced attacks only when deeply involved in a relationship would feel that she was losing her independence. The patients who experience attacks after rebellion against an authority figure may feel upset by the threat to their support system or may fear retaliation. In any event, a variety of fears stirred up by specific life situations impinging on the patient's vulnerabilities may provide the ingredients necessary to precipitate an attack.

Reading 3
Cognitive Therapy of Personality Disorders

Cognitive Therapy
of Personality Disorders

Judith S. Beck

Cognitive therapy, as Aaron T. Beck, M.D., first conceived it, was primarily a short-term, problem-focused form of psychotherapy for the treatment of depression, although Beck also noted its application to anxiety (Beck, 1964, 1967). Since the 1960s, Beck and his colleagues worldwide have expanded cognitive therapy both conceptually and clinically. One notable expansion has been to the area of personality disorders (Beck, Freeman, & Associates, 1990). While many cognitive and cognitive-behavioral theorists have written about a cognitive approach to personality disorders (e.g., Linehan, 1993; Liotti, 1992; Safran & McMain, 1992), this chapter focuses on the theory and approach derived directly from Beck's work.

There has been little controlled research on the efficacy of cognitive therapy for personality disorders. Most of the research conducted to date has consisted of uncontrolled clinical reports, single-case design studies, and studies of the effects of personality disorders on treatment outcome. In general these studies indicate that cognitive therapy is a promising approach (Pretzer & Beck, 1996). Turkat and Maisto (1985) reviewed a number of single-case experimental design studies using individualized conceptualizations with specific treatment plans. In general, they found that the implementation of these individualized treatment plans was more effective than treatment that matched interventions to symptoms. Beck et al. (1990) conclude that "standard" cognitive therapy, utilized for straightforward cases of depression and anxiety, is often ineffective for personality disorder cases and that research is essential to test whether a more comprehensive approach, such as that outlined in the 1990 book by Beck and his colleagues, is efficacious for this difficult population.

Personality disorder patients, according to the fourth edition of the *Diagnostic and Statistical Manual of Mental Disorders* (DSM-IV; American Psychiatric Association, 1994), are characterized by "an enduring pattern

165

of inner experience and behavior that deviates markedly from the expectations of the individual's culture, is pervasive and inflexible, has an onset in adolescence or early adulthood, is stable over time, and leads to distress or impairment" (p. 630). The pervasiveness, early onset, rigidity, chronicity, and enduring dysfunctionality help separate Axis II personality disorders from the usually more acute, episodic Axis I disorders. The inflexibility, dysfunctionality, and compulsive use of certain behavioral strategies distinguish the personality disorder patient from patients who also display "enduring patterns of perceiving, relating to, and thinking about the environment and oneself that are exhibited in a wide range of social and personal contexts" (American Psychiatric Association, 1994, p. 630) but whose personality traits are relatively more flexible and who can vary their behavior more adaptively, according to the situation.

Beck became interested in Axis II disorders when he recognized that a significant number of patients who had recovered from a major depression still experienced reduced but enduring or intermittent distress and continued to demonstrate faulty thinking and maladaptive behavior patterns (Beck, in press). Simultaneously, he began to explore the connection between evolutionary theory and psychiatric disorders. Mankind, he noted, has developed behavioral strategies to promote the primary evolutionary goals of survival and reproduction. The inflexible, maladaptive, compulsive use of these strategies in the current environment is one of the most salient characteristics of personality disorder patients.

DYSFUNCTIONAL STRATEGIES

Evolutionarily derived patterns of functioning include such behaviors or strategies as competitiveness, dependence, avoidance, resistance, suspiciousness, dramatics, control, aggression, isolation, and self-aggrandizement. Beck (in press) notes that the strategies "represent each individual's unique solutions to the problems of reconciling internal pressures for survival and bonding and external obstacles, threats and demands."

The healthy individual in our technologically advanced society flexibly employs many, if not all, of these strategies in adaptive ways, in specific circumstances. It is functional, for example, for an individual to be suspicious, vigilant, and on guard in a crime-ridden part of town. An individual whose task it is to persuade a group to adopt a certain viewpoint may need to be somewhat dramatic or theatrical. In a championship match it is to the individual's advantage to be highly competitive.

The personality disorder patient may display these same behaviors but tends consistently to overutilize a small set of strategies in an inflexible, compulsive way, when doing so is often distinctively disadvantageous. Unlike the individual with a healthier personality, he or she lacks the ability to assess particular situations realistically and select from a wide spectrum of strategies. For example, a paranoid patient may react quite suspiciously in interactions with people even when objective data and his own experience indicate they are most likely trustworthy. A histrionic patient may act in a highly unsuitable, dramatic fashion in a serious situation such as a formal job interview. A narcissistic patient may act in a self-aggrandizing, competitive manner when assigned to an egalitarian team at work.

Beck notes that not all individuals with a significantly skewed distribution of genetically influenced traits or strategies experience significant distress. Some seek an environment that accommodates their characteristic strategies. A dependent, help-seeking individual may select friends and mates who are strong, decisive caretakers. A suspicious, overly guarded individual may choose to live alone, in a rather anonymous fashion, and seek a job that requires little interaction with others. A compulsive, perfection-driven individual may create an environment that is highly structured and ordered. Note, too, that some individuals with inflexible strategies may not experience much subjective distress themselves but may inflict distress on others. Individuals who consistently act in a superior, entitled, demanding way often have disturbed relationships, for example, as do those who are manipulative, exploitive, and aggressive.

SCHEMAS AND BELIEF SYSTEMS

Early in their developmental period, children seek to make sense of themselves and their world. They develop schemas, or cognitive structures, to organize the massive amount of data they are constantly receiving. Schemas are the means by which they understand what they are experiencing and decide how to proceed. Beck drew on the works of Bartlett, Piaget, and Kelly in his elaborated conception of schemas (Weishaar, 1993).

The content of some schemas is often idiosyncratic for a given person. A schema relevant to policemen will elicit a positive response in one child, for example, or an anxious, contemptuous, or neutral reaction in others. Schemas "provide the instructions to guide the focus, direction, and qualities of daily life and special contingencies" (Beck et al., 1990, p. 4).

Schemas have various characteristics. At any given time a schema might be highly activated or completely dormant or somewhere in between. A schema can be relatively narrow or broad, rigid or modifiable, prominent or relatively quiescent. When highly activated, a schema influences how the individual is processing information. The hypervalence of one schema may inhibit the activation of contrary schemas that are more adaptive to the specific situation (Beck, 1967).

An avoidant patient, for example, may have a prepotent schema of threat or danger activated even when she is with nonjudgmental coworkers who are actively making supportive comments to her. A passive–aggressive patient with a schema relevant to vulnerability may inaccurately perceive his supervisor as trying to control him when the supervisor is actually trying to help.

According to Beck et al. (1990), there are in addition to cognitive schemas, affective, motivational, action (or instrumental), and control schemas. The avoidant patient who is describing his project to his coworkers has an activation of his cognitive schema (threat), his affective schema (anxiety), his motivational schema (desire to avoid), and his action schema (mobilization to deal with threat by fleeing).

Young (1990) elaborates on the characteristics and functioning of "early maladaptive schemas," or "extremely stable and enduring themes that develop during childhood and are elaborated upon throughout an individual's lifetime . . . [which are] templates for the processing of later experience" (p. 9). He notes that these schemas are accepted as a priori truths, self-perpetuating, difficult to change, significantly dysfunctional, activated by environmental events, and associated with high levels of affect. He describes three processes of schemas: schema maintenance (the individual processes information in such a way as to reinforce the schema), schema avoidance (the individual avoids thinking about situations that might trigger a schema, avoids negative feelings associated with a schema, or behaviorally avoids situations that might trigger a schema), and schema compensation (the individual consistently acts in a way opposite to what might be expected from their schemas).

Beck (1967) terms the content of cognitive schemas as "beliefs," which represent individuals' understanding of themselves, their world, and others. The healthy personality has stable, adaptive, relativistic basic or core beliefs ("I am a reasonably competent person; my world has some danger but is predominantly a safe enough place for me; other people may be beneficent, neutral, or malevolent toward me"). Personality disorder patients, in contrast, have extreme, negative, global, rigid beliefs ("I am incompetent; my world is out of my control; other people are untrustworthy"). When their schemas are activated, they apply these beliefs to situations that do not warrant such a negative view. They act and react as if their perceptions are accurate, despite sometimes strong evidence to the contrary. They develop a perceptual bias that interferes with reasonable and adaptive information processing.

One individual, for example, when presented with an intellectually challenging assignment at which he usually excels suddenly feels terrified because his beliefs "I am inadequate" and "Others will judge and criticize me" have been activated. Another person with a strongly activated belief such as "Others always take advantage of me" feels quite angry in this same situation. Thus individuals' schemas influence how they process information and which beliefs will guide their reactions. The personality disorder patient often selectively attends to, distorts, stores, and retrieves information in a dysfunctional way.

The rigidity and inflexibility of the personality disorder patient's beliefs and strategies can be understood by a lack of accommodation to new environmental input in a meaningful and useful manner. A histrionic patient, for example, may fail to notice that she is often more appreciated when she interacts with others in a subtle, low-key way. An antisocial patient may believe others did not exploit him because they didn't have a clear opportunity to do so. A paranoid patient may recognize that another person did not treat her badly on a number of occasions but account for the lack of mistreatment to a hidden motive. People who have relatively healthier personalities are able to assimilate incoming information in a more appropriate way, adjust their schemas to match the reality of their worlds more accurately, and develop a wider range of behavior patterns that are relatively more adaptive and functional.

Beck (in press) proposes that core beliefs about the self are of central importance in conceptualizing personality disorder patients. He describes these negative beliefs as falling into two categories: those beliefs associated with helplessness (e.g., "I am helpless," "I am powerless," "I am inadequate," "I am not good enough [in achievement]," "I am weak," "I am vulnerable," "I am trapped") and those associated with unlovability (e.g., "I am unlovable," "I am unworthy," "I am defective," "I am undesirable," "I am not good enough [to be loved by others]"). These core beliefs are quite painful to patients and they develop strategies to help them cope with or prevent the activation of these distressing ideas.

These strategies are often expressed as rules (e.g., "I must not let others take advantage of me"), attitudes (e.g., "It would be terrible if others saw me as weak"), and conditional assumptions (e.g., "If others take advantage of me, then it means I'm a thoroughly weak person"). Patients may not articulate their core beliefs and assumptions until therapy when their therapist probes to uncover the underlying meaning of their current perceptions across situations. For the most part, dysfunctional beliefs are not difficult to identify and therapists build their conceptualizations based on patients' characteristic perceptions of, meanings attributed to, and reactions in a variety of problematic situations.

Each personality disorder has a specific set of beliefs and accompanying behavioral pattern (Beck et al., 1990). Dependent personality disorder patients, for example, believe that they are incompetent and unable to cope. Therefore, they tend to have overdeveloped strategies of relying on others and avoiding important decisions and challenges, but they are underdeveloped in autonomy and decisiveness. Avoidant personality disorder patients believe they are unlovable and vulnerable. They tend to avoid intimacy, criticism, and negative emotion and are thus underdeveloped in openness, assertion, and emotional tolerance. Obsessive–compulsive personality disorder patients believe that they are vulnerable to their world's falling apart and therefore overemphasize rules, responsibility, and control and are deficient in spontaneity, lightness, and flexibility. Borderline personality disorder patients share a number of extremely rigid, negative beliefs with other personality disorders (Layden, Newman, Freeman, & Morse, 1993) ("I am defective," "I am vulnerable," "I am out of control," "I can't cope," "I will be abandoned") leading to more extreme patterns of behavior.

Patients who suffer from an Axis I disorder without a comorbid Axis II disorder may also demonstrate extreme, negative beliefs. Depressed patients, for example, may view themselves as total failures or as completely unlovable. Patients with an anxiety disorder may believe "I am vulnerable." These beliefs, however, become activated only during the acute episode and become latent once the Axis I disorder remits, when their relatively more positive core beliefs once again predominate. Axis II patients, in contrast, describe themselves as "always feeling this way" about themselves, others, and their world, though the degree of belief may intensify during a concomitant Axis I episode. The development of such beliefs, according to Beck (in press), is partly genetically influenced but also significantly affected by childhood events.

DEVELOPMENT EXPERIENCE

Core beliefs originate as individuals develop and start to make sense of themselves, their personal world, and other people. Most healthy children are able to incorporate both positive and negative events and adopt a balanced, stable view of themselves and others. Personality disorder patients, on the other hand, usually had either subtly or dramatically traumatic childhoods, during which they began, accurately or inaccurately, to view themselves in a distinctively negative way. Some trauma is blatant: sexual, physical, verbal abuse. Other trauma is less acute but agonizingly chronic: highly critical parents, demeaning siblings or peers, overly harsh teachers or caretakers. Since not all children who experience early trauma develop personality disorders, however, Beck (in press) proposes that some individuals may be genetically predisposed to develop a more extreme personality disorder or may have lacked supportive figures who would have helped to buffer the childhood traumas.

As children begin to develop a negative core belief, based on their experiences, they begin to process information in a distorted way. They interpret negative events as broad, global confirmation for their negative core beliefs. Positive events are either unnoticed, and therefore unprocessed, or distorted so that the core belief is not undermined (J. S. Beck, 1995). For example, a child who believes he is inadequate may not recognize his increasing mastery of skills or challenges or may discount them ("Anyone can do this," "This [task] might not be hard for me, but most other things are"). The process of readily incorporating negatively perceived data and omitting or discounting positive data solidifies dysfunctional schemas in the individual's formative period. The specific beliefs and strategies that the child develops are, again, idiosyncratic to the individual.

One child with an alcoholic parent, for example, may view himself as unprotected, vulnerable, and helpless when the parent rages at the family during bouts of drinking, and these beliefs about himself may become more generalized and global. He may begin to believe "I am vulnerable" or "I am helpless" in a range of situations in which these judgments are wholly or at least partially invalid. Depending on certain biases in his genetic make-up, the child may develop strategies of overcontrol, and overresponsibility and may become overly rule-driven in order to cope in an environment he experiences as chaotic. Another child might become quite avoidant, blame himself for his parent's dysfunctional behavior, start to believe that he is defective, and distance himself from other people who he fears will also find him lacking. A third child with a relatively healthier sense of self may accurately perceive that she is not in acute danger and that it is her parent, rather than she herself, who has problems. This third child, who perhaps has better insight due to a better "genetic shuffle," develops a healthier personality without a skewed set of overdeveloped and underdeveloped strategies. Thus it is that children develop their own characteristic ways of perceiving and relating to their world.

REACTIONS TO CURRENT SITUATIONS

Personality disorder patients often have strong emotional reactions to current situations. Their underlying beliefs influence their perceptions and interpretations. These perceptions are often distorted, yet are accepted as true, and, in turn, influence patients' emotional, physiological, and behavioral reactions. Thus a narcissistic patient who believes "If people don't treat me in a special way, they are being unfair or unreasonable" may have automatic thoughts such as "How dare they treat me like this" and may become quite angry and belligerent when he is forced to wait for an appointment or denied a request. An obsessive–compulsive patient may become very upset if others create even minor disorder because of her belief, "Terrible things can happen if everything is not done in just the right way." Automatic thoughts such as "What if the work isn't good enough? What if it isn't finished in time? What if the project doesn't get approved?" in a work situation may lead to anxiety and to her spending an inordinate amount of time on relatively unimportant tasks.

In order to facilitate the modification of these dysfunctional reactions, it is important to conceptualize for patients the relationship between the activation of their core beliefs in specific current situations and their automatic thoughts, emotional response, and behavior. Figure 8.1 presents a Cognitive Conceptualization Diagram for Kim, a personality disorder patient described later in this chapter. Filling in this diagram with patients (based on data they present) helps them understand how their childhood experiences have led to the development of their dysfunctional beliefs and assumptions and maladaptive behavior patterns (J. S. Beck, 1995).

Therapist's name: Judith Beck, PhD

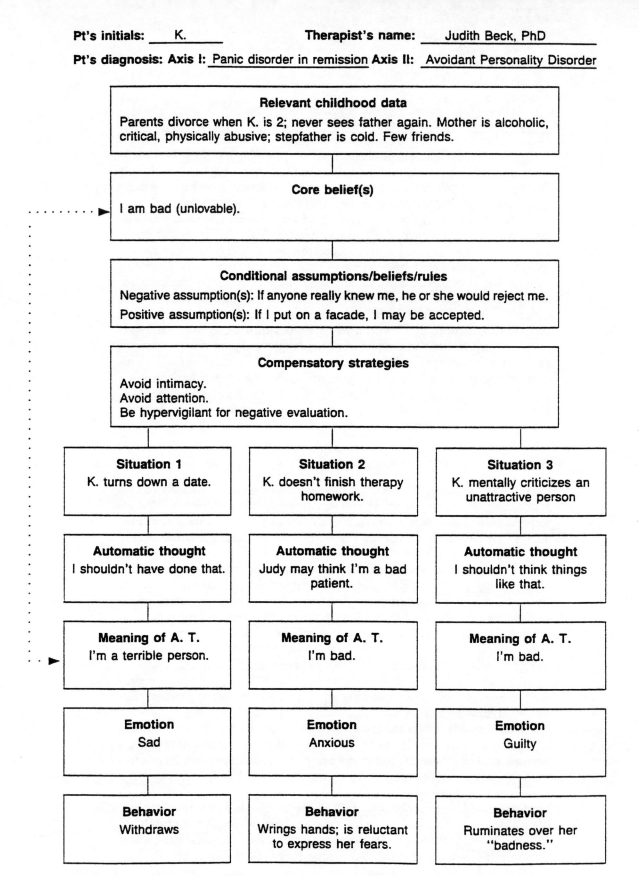

FIGURE 8.1. Cognitive Conceptualization Diagram. Copyright 1996 by Judith S. Beck, PhD. Reprinted by permission.

TREATMENT OF PERSONALITY DISORDER PATIENTS

The treatment of this difficult population shares some commonalties with cognitive therapy for Axis I depression and anxiety disorders. The therapist emphasizes collaboratively setting goals, solving problems, modifying dysfunctional thoughts and beliefs, changing dysfunctional behavior, and preventing relapse through teaching patients to be their own therapists. Treatment usually focuses first on the more acute Axis I diagnosis, if one is present. Collaborative empiricism and guided discovery are emphasized, though more persuasive techniques are often used in order to modify strongly held beliefs.

Several notable differences do exist, however, between Axis I and Axis II treatment. Perhaps of paramount importance is the establishment and maintenance of a sound therapeutic alliance (essential for all patients but often challenging for patients who characteristically exhibit disturbed relationships within and outside of therapy). Also, there is a much stronger focus on modifying core beliefs and assumptions, in addition to recognizing and responding to automatic thoughts. This additional emphasis requires a focus not only on the here and now (as therapists and patients analyze patients' distressed reactions to current situations both within and outside of therapy sessions) but also on the developmental origins of dysfunctional beliefs, through both "rational" and "emotional" or experiential methods. Modification of Axis II–related beliefs requires consistent work over a considerable period of time and treatment may continue for 9 months to 2 years or even longer for severely disordered patients. (See Beck et al., 1990, and Fleming & Pretzer, 1990, for additional guidelines in treating personality disorders.)

Case Example

Kim (see Figure 8.1) was an avoidant personality disorder patient in her mid-20s. She originally sought treatment for panic disorder and after 12 sessions this Axis I disorder fully remitted. However, she chose to remain in therapy to ameliorate some of her long-standing problems in relationships and work.

Kim had few friends and was not intimate with those she did have. She was hypersensitive to criticism from other people and consistently misread neutral or even slightly positive reactions from other people as negative. She was inhibited in social situations and tried to avoid drawing attention to herself. She avoided challenges at work even though she was competent and talented. Kim behaved in this dysfunctional manner in large part because of her strong core belief that she was bad and unlovable. She was certain that if people really got to know her, they would reject her because they would find out just how bad she really was. Although she appeared to others to be an attractive, well-groomed, articulate, intelligent, accomplished person, she believed almost completely that she was actually the opposite. She occasionally had images of "contaminating" innocent people with her badness by just being in their presence.

How did Kim develop such a distorted self-view? Kim's parents divorced when she was quite young and her mother continuously attributed the divorce to Kim's birth. Her mother was alcoholic, highly critical, and physically abusive. She may have had a borderline personality disorder herself. Her mother remarried when Kim was 10 and she and Kim's stepfather subsequently had two children whom they blatantly favored over Kim. Kim's stepfather was volatile and alcoholic and he, too, was quite verbally critical of Kim.

At a very early age Kim developed the idea that she must be bad and unlovable for her mother (and later her stepfather) to treat her so badly. She believed this negative idea so strongly that once she started school and was exposed to others, she began to withdraw from her classmates, neighborhood children, and most adults. She describes herself as having been a physically unattractive child who wore her hair in her face so that people couldn't really see her or get to know her. Her inhibition and withdrawal contributed to Kim's having few friends as she grew up. Her interpretation of lack of friends was that other children could see that she was bad and unlovable and therefore did not make overtures to her. Of course, a more likely explanation is that Kim did not present herself as a desirable or attractive person because her beliefs that she was bad and unlovable were so intense.

In addition to frequent physical abuse from her mother, Kim experienced many small traumas from her family on a daily basis. For example, whenever she received good grades her mother would say to her, "Don't think you're so smart. The teacher probably gave you good marks because you're well-behaved or you're quiet." When Kim won a statewide math competition, her mother characteristically remarked, "I hope you don't think too highly of yourself here. The judges probably gave you that award because they felt sorry for you." Kim's core belief, "I'm bad and unlovable," became stronger with each passing year. Although she did have occasional positive experiences (some teachers and a cousin treated her warmly), she did not interpret these events in a positive way. Instead, she discounted them, believing, "They only like me because they don't really know me well enough."

Kim's college years away from home were relatively better. With the diminishing influence of her family, she began to realize, to a limited degree at least, that other people did find her appealing. However, she once again interpreted this positive experience in a distorted way. "The reason they like me is because I put on a facade. If they really knew me, they would reject me."

Kim's personality disorder treatment had two major focuses. The first involved helping her solve problems, adaptively respond to her distorted thinking in current situations, learn new skills, and change her behavior. Second, toward the middle and end of therapy, her therapist strongly emphasized both testing Kim's assumption that if anyone really knew her she would be rejected and modifying her core belief of being bad and unlovable.

Kim will be used as an example to illustrate the following principles of treatment:

Establishing and Maintaining a Therapeutic Alliance

As mentioned above, the personality disorder patient brings the same negative assumptions about relationships outside of therapy to the therapy session itself. While this is an impediment in eliciting the full cooperation and trust of the patient, these problems within the session also provide an opportunity to conceptualize the patient's difficulties in relationships, to test the patient's assumptions about the therapist, and to learn new, more functional ways of relating to other people.

Kim, for example, was initially anxious in therapy because she assumed, "If my therapist really knew me, she would reject me." This assumption resulted in numerous automatic thoughts Kim had during the therapy session itself that interfered with her ability to relate important data to the therapist. She felt certain that if she revealed her problems (and especially her troubled history with her mother) the therapist would evaluate her negatively, verbally criticize her, and terminate the therapeutic relationship. Kim continually believed that she was on the brink of rejection.

Kim's anxiety within the therapy session allowed the therapist to conceptualize Kim's difficulties on the spot. First the therapist attempted to elicit Kim's automatic thoughts in the session. Fearful of the therapist's reaction, Kim replied that she couldn't relate what was going through her mind. The therapist did not push her to identify her cognitions but instead elicited her fears about revealing her thoughts. Kim was able to relate that she feared negative evaluation and rejection by the therapist. The therapist then helped her test that thought by examining supporting and disconfirmatory evidence, based on Kim's experience in prior therapy sessions. Through Socratic questioning, Kim realized that it was unlikely the therapist would judge her harshly and eject her from therapy.

After several sessions in which the therapist helped Kim realistically evaluate her fears of rejection, Kim's anxiety reduced and she was able to be more open. In small steps over several more sessions, Kim revealed her mother's abusiveness toward her when she was a child. The therapist anticipated that Kim might misread her reaction to these revelations and so encouraged Kim to question her directly. Kim's therapist then provided her honest reaction: She felt sad for Kim that she had undergone such trauma, she was sorry Kim had suffered, she was pleased that Kim had trusted her enough to confide in her, and she was also pleased because such information was vital for the therapist to be able to conceptualize Kim's present difficulties and plan her treatment. After several such interventions in which Kim discovered her fears about her therapist to be groundless, she was able to generalize what she had learned to other relationships. Over time Kim became less fearful of rejection by others, more willing to risk intimacy, and more successful in establishing and maintaining good, productive relationships.

Thus, establishing the therapeutic relationship poses both a challenge to therapists (when patients bring dysfunctional assumptions to therapy) and an opportunity for therapists to gain a "window" into the patients' reactions to other people. And monitoring their own emotional responses to patients' behavior also provides therapists with a window into how others may in turn be reacting to the patient.

Patients provide a variety of different challenges in therapy according to their dysfunctional beliefs and strategies. The narcissistic patient who has a belief "If others don't treat me in a special way, it means I'm nothing" may demand extra time with a therapist. The dependent patient who believes "If I rely on myself, I'll fail" may avoid tackling problems she can solve on her own. The passive–aggressive patient who believes "If I do what others want me to, it means they're controlling me" may fail to do homework assignments suggested by the therapist. The obsessive–compulsive personality disorder patient who believes "If my therapist doesn't understand me perfectly, I won't get helped" may insist on relating numerous unnecessary details. The histrionic patient who believes "If I'm not entertaining to my therapist, she won't like me or pay enough attention to me" may regale the therapist with amusing stories instead of focusing on her problems. Identifying and modifying these dysfunctional beliefs within the therapy relationship enables the patient to learn additional strategies to relate to others.

Modifying Underlying Assumptions and Beliefs

In general the therapist initially focuses on the patient's distressing automatic thoughts in specific current situations and teaches the patient how to identify thoughts and images and systematically evaluate them. Automatic thoughts are usually less rigid and global than beliefs and thus more easily modifiable. For example, Kim had little difficulty in evaluating and adaptively responding to her automatic thought, "It's terrible that I didn't pay my utilities bill." Modifying her global core belief "I'm a bad person," however, took months of sustained work with many types of interventions, as described below.

The use of a Cognitive Conceptualization Diagram (Figure 8.1) can aid the therapist in formulating a case and identifying the patient's core beliefs, underlying assumptions, compensatory strategies, and reactions to current situations (J. S. Beck, 1995). The therapist can fill in the diagram itself with a patient or verbally review its contents (without presenting the diagram) in several parts over several sessions. It is important for patients to understand their cognitive profile and how their core beliefs shape their interpretations of reality. By reviewing examples of their faulty information processing, the therapist shows patients how their negative core beliefs have become strengthened over time while positive, more realistic beliefs never developed or became attenuated. These explanations help patients comprehend why their beliefs can "feel" so true and yet be untrue or mostly untrue.

Having educated patients about their core beliefs, the therapist helps them identify advantages and disadvantages of modifying them. Through Socratic questioning the therapist fortifies each advantage and undermines each disadvantage. ("An advantage to seeing myself as an okay person is that I'll be more likely to initiate new relationships, improve the relationships I already have, speak my mind, be more interesting to people, have more fun, not feel like I'm always on the brink of rejection, not have to guard everything I say and do." "A disadvantage is that I'll feel anxious about questioning my sense of self but the anxiety will be time-limited, I'll most likely be able to tolerate it, and there may be a big payoff in seeing myself less negatively, more realistically.")

Initial interventions aimed at modifying core beliefs of personality disorder patients are present focused. A Core Belief Worksheet (Figure 8.2) allows the patient to recognize when she is processing information in a distorted way and thereby reinforcing a negative core belief. It aids the patient in reframing her negative interpretations and in attending to positive data that she might otherwise fail to recognize or discount. The worksheet also helps therapist and patient monitor over time the progress made toward attenuating the negative core belief and strengthening a new, more realistic belief (J. S. Beck, 1995).

Therapists must be creative to devise interventions that demonstrate the invalidity of patients' core beliefs. Extreme contrasts helped Kim carefully analyze how she differed from someone she considered to have even more of a negative quality than she herself had. Through Socratic questioning, for example, Kim compared herself to a public figure whom she viewed as a truly bad person and she recognized that she shared few attributes with him. A cognitive continuum, in which she ranked acts of "badness," helped her realize that she was not 100% bad for inadvertently misleading a coworker but rather only 1% bad. Her therapist helped her begin to judge her own and others' behavior by creating "yardsticks" of reasonable, borderline, and unreasonable behavior. Through guided questioning, Kim was able to provide examples of clearly unreasonable, mean-spirited responses to a man's request for a date and to judge that she herself had declined the date in a reasonable manner. This realization undermined her belief that she was bad for not accepting an invitation from a man she didn't like. Through evaluating others' behavior via a "yardstick," she began to recognize when they were acting unreasonably toward her. She stopped labeling herself as "bad," for example, when she resisted her housemate's unreasonable demands.

Behavioral experiments helped Kim test her assumptions. She believed that a friend would reject her if she proposed they see a movie different from

Name: Kim

Old core belief: I'm bad

How much do you believe the old core belief right now?   (0–100) 70%

*What's the most you've believed it this week?   (0–100) 95%

*What's the least you have believed it this week?   (0–100) 70%

New belief: I'm okay

How much do you believe the new belief right now?   (0–100) 50%

Evidence that contradicts old core belief and supports new belief	Evidence that supports old core belief with reframe
Jean asked me to have lunch with her.	I didn't want to go to the movies with my housemate *but* that doesn't mean I'm bad; it means I'm a normal person with reasonable preferences.
I took time to show (the new secretary) around the office.	I complained to Judy during therapy *but* she didn't consider it complaining and I'm supposed to bring up problems.
I called my sister and offered to help her move.	
(Boyfriend) invited me to a family wedding.	I told Norman that I was too busy to talk to him *but* he was really bugging me. I told him nicely, and okay people are appropriately assertive with others.

*Should situations related to an increase or decrease in the strength of the belief be topics for the agenda?

FIGURE 8.2. Core Belief Worksheet. Copyright 1996 by Judith S. Beck, PhD. Reprinted by permission.

his initial suggestion and that her boss would view her as critical and "uppity" if she made a constructive suggestion for improvement. After discussing and role-playing these situations, Kim approached her friend and her boss and discovered that they responded positively. "Acting as if" Kim believed a new, more functional belief (before she actually did) helped her modify her core belief and practice more functional behavior. Kim's therapist had her imagine in detail what she would do at a particular social gathering if she truly believed that she was an "okay" person whom others would like. Even though Kim did not yet hold this new belief strongly, she was nevertheless able to imagine herself acting more functionally and then actually did so at a party. Such behavioral change in many situations fortified the new, more adaptive belief. And as the new belief grew stronger, Kim found herself more and more easily able to "act as if."

The interventions described above are all present oriented. Personality disorder patients also benefit from a reexamination of the validity of their core belief from a developmental perspective. Kim and her therapist conducted a historical review (see Young, 1990) in which they examined her life in chunks of years (actually by school periods). Kim first recalled evidence that seemed to support her negative core belief for each time period. Then through Socratic questioning she identified evidence that contradicted the core belief and fortified the new, more functional belief. Next the therapist helped Kim to reframe each piece of negative data in a more adaptive way. Finally, Kim summarized this time period, more realistically assessing the validity of the core belief.

"Emotional" level interventions may be necessary for patients who develop an intellectual realization that their core beliefs are not valid but still "feel" them to be true. During rational/emotional role plays, Kim portrayed her "emotional" side that held a core belief strongly while her therapist played the "intellectual side" that recognized the core belief to be false or mostly false. Her therapist urged Kim to argue as strongly as she could so all of her "emotional" reasons could be voiced aloud. The therapist countered each emotional reason with a more realistic viewpoint, based on data Kim had provided in previous sessions. When Kim exhausted all her "emotional" reasons, they switched parts. Now the therapist expressed the same emotional reasons and Kim provided the more reasonable interpretations, having just heard these rational counters in the previous role play. Later in therapy Kim was encouraged to play both roles with the therapist intervening only when she was unable to produce an appropriate rational response.

A final intervention for patients who still "feel" their core beliefs to be true even though they intellectually understand them to be invalid involves restructuring the meaning of earlier memories (J. S. Beck, 1995; Edwards, 1989). Kim's therapist had her vividly reexperience in imagination early traumas that contributed to the origination or maintenance of her core belief. When Kim related an intense activation of her core belief and intense emotion her therapist interviewed Kim's "younger self." The therapist helped Kim reinterpret the experience, by suggesting that another person or her "older self" enter the image immediately following the trauma and help the younger Kim understand an alternative explanation for what had just transpired. During several therapy sessions Kim vividly recalled her mother's physical abuse for imagined or minor infractions. Through her therapist's suggestions, she was able to imagine her older self comforting her younger self, explaining that the 5-year-old Kim was not bad but rather that her mother had serious problems of her own and so treated Kim badly. By eliciting and then responding to the younger Kim's doubts about the validity of such an interpretation, the younger Kim (actually the "emotional" part of Kim's mind) was able to change the meaning of these experiences.

CONCLUSION

Thus the treatment of personality disorder patients shares many commonalities with the treatment of the Axis I patient, especially the initial emphasis on solving here-and-now problems, learning to identify and modify dysfunctional thoughts in current situations, and behavioral change. A solid formulation of the case is critical in identifying the core beliefs, assumptions, and compensatory strategies in order for patients and therapist to understand the patients' reactions to current situations. A strong emphasis on modifying patients' assumptions and beliefs is necessary for patients to see themselves and others in a more realistic way, leading to more functional behavior, decreased reliance on just one or a few compensatory strategies, and greater ability to reach their goals.

When Aaron T. Beck conceived of cognitive therapy as a treatment for depression, he had little notion of its wide applicability to the range of Axis I disorders, much less characterological disorders. His elaboration of schemas, his application of evolutionary theory to individuals' current functioning, his notions of information processing, and his development of specific cognitive profiles for each of the personality disorders led to the development and refinement of an effective treatment for Axis II patients. This major accomplishment is, of course, but one of the extraordinary contributions Beck has made to the fields of psychiatry and psychotherapy.

REFERENCES

American Psychiatric Association. (1994). *Diagnostic and statistical manual of mental disorders* (4th ed.). Washington, DC: Author.

Beck, A. T. (1964). Thinking and depression: 2. Theory and therapy. *Archives of General Psychiatry, 10,* 561–571.

Beck, A. T. (1967). *Depression: Clinical, experimental, and theoretical aspects.* New York: Harper & Row.

Beck, A. T. (in press). Cognitive aspects of personality disorders and their relation to syndromal disorders: A psychoevolutionary approach. In C. R. Cloninger (Ed.), *Personality and psychopathology.* Washington, DC: American Psychiatric Press.

Beck, A. T., Freeman, A., & Associates. (1990). *Cognitive therapy of personality disorders.* New York: Guilford Press.

Beck, J. S. (1995). *Cognitive therapy: Basics and beyond.* New York: Guilford Press.

Edwards, D. J. A. (1989). Cognitive restructuring through guided imagery: Lessons from Gestalt therapy. In A. Freeman, K. M. Simon, L. E. Beutler, & H. Arkowitz (Eds.), *Comprehensive handbook of cognitive therapy* (pp. 283–297). New York: Plenum.

Fleming, B., & Pretzer, J. (1990). Cognitive-behavioral approaches to personality disorders. In M. Hersen, R. Eisler, & P. Miller (Eds.), *Progress in behavior modification* (Vol. 25, pp. 119–151). Newbury Park, CA: Sage.

Layden, M., Newman, C., Freeman, A., & Morse, S. (1993). *Cognitive therapy of borderline personality disorder.* Boston: Allyn & Bacon.

Linehan, M. M. (1993). *Cognitive-behavioral treatment of borderline personality disorder.* New York: Guilford Press.

Liotti, G. (1992). Egocentrism and the cognitive psychotherapy of personality disorders. *Journal of Cognitive Psychotherapy: An International Quarterly, 6,* 43–58.

Pretzer, J. L., & Beck, A. T. (1996). A cognitive theory of personality disorders. In J. F. Clarkin & M. F. Lenzenweger (Eds.), *Major theories of personality disorder.* New York: Guilford Press.

Safran, J., & McMain, S. (1992). A cognitive-interpersonal approach to the treatment of personality disorders. *Journal of Cognitive Psychotherapy: An International Quarterly, 6,* 59–68.

Turkat, I. D., & Maisto, S. A. (1985). Personality disorders: Application of the experimental method to the formulation and modification of personality disorders. In D. H. Barlow (Ed.), *Clinical handbook of psychological disorders: A step-by-step treatment manual* (pp. 503–570). New York: Guilford Press.

Weishaar, M. E. (1993). *Aaron T. Beck: Key figures in counseling and psychotherapy.* Thousand Oaks, CA: Sage.

Young, J. (1990). *Cognitive therapy for personality disorders: A schema-focused approach.* Sarasota, FL: Professional Resource Exchange.

Reading 4
Cognitive-Behavioral Methods with Children

COGNITIVE-BEHAVIORAL METHODS WITH CHILDREN

LAUREN BRASWELL
PHILIP C. KENDALL

Cognitive-behavioral therapy with children, as with adults, includes a variety of strategies and procedures. These methods follow from a number of different theoretical tenets, but as stated by Kendall (1985), the cognitive-behavioral methods share an "emphasis on (a) both the learning process and the influence of the contingencies and models in the environment while (b) underscoring the centrality of mediating/information-processing factors in both the development and remediation of childhood disorders" (p. 359). Cognitive-behavioral approaches emphasize the complex interaction among cognitive events, processes, products, and structures, affect, overt behavior, and environmental context and experiences as contributing to various facets of dysfunctional behavior. Similarly, the diverse approaches agree that learning has a pivotal role in the acquisition and maintenance of deviant and adaptive behavior, and like operant theories (but to a lesser degree) recognize the importance of environmental consequences—particularly those provided by the social environment—in these processes. Unlike operant theories, however, cognitive/social-learning theories postulate that most learning is a function of how the individual cognitively processes stimulus and consequence information (Foster, Kendall, & Guevremont, in press).

A fundamental premise underlying the cognitive-behavioral theories as applied to adults is that much of maladaptive behavior and negative emotion arises from *distorted* cognitively mediated representations of external events. Distorted processing and world views are causally linked to problems of depression, anger, anxiety, and other disturbances of thought and behavior (e.g., Beck, 1976; Beck, Rush, Shaw, & Emery, 1979; Ellis, 1970). In contrast with certain childhood disorders, such as attentional difficulties, impulsivity, hyperactivity, and some types of acting out, the child is considered to manifest a deficiency, that is, an absence of effective mediating strategies for controlling behavior. In such cases, the task of the cognitive-behavioral therapy is to train the child in the use of verbal mediation strategies for developing more reflective problem-solving behavior and self-

167

control. With other more internalizing types of disorders, such as school phobia, childhood depression, and social withdrawal, the child's symptoms are believed to result, at least in part, from cognitive distortions (errors or misperceptions) in thinking similar to those described for anxious and depressed adults. With these children, intervention addresses the client's need to recognize and test the mistaken misperceptions, expectations, and/ or attributional preferences.

THEORETICAL PRÉCIS

The theoretical lines of influence that gave rise to cognitive-behavioral techniques used with adults, such as the development of behaviorists' interest in the phenomenon of self-control and the emergence of cognitive learning theories of psychotherapy, also contributed to the rise of cognitive-behavioral interventions with children (Kendall & Hollon, 1979). In addition, cognitive-behavioral interventions with children have benefited from the theoretical and empirical contributions of various areas in developmental psychology, such as studies of the development of self-control, social cognition, memory, metacognitive skills, and attributional processes.

The study of both the development of self-control and the factors interferring with self-control has contributed to the development of cognitive-behavioral intervention with children. The work of Luria (1961) and Vygotsky (1962), for instance, provided an initial theoretical formulation for understanding the emergence of verbal control or mediation of behavior. Failures or deviations from this developmental process are speculated to result in poor self-regulation in the child. This formulation ultimately became the basis for the development of self-instructional training procedures (Meichenbaum & Goodman, 1971).

The term social cognition (Shantz, 1975) refers to internal events or processes that are thought to mediate actions related to other people and their affairs. While Piaget (1926) began to address the child's development of social perspective taking over 60 years ago, developmentalists did not display intensive research interest in this area until the 1970s (Chandler, 1973; Hudson, 1978; Shantz, 1975). New theories have developed, such as the four level view of Selman (Selman, 1980; Selman & Byrne, 1974). According to this view, in the first stage the child lacks social perspective-taking abilities, and thus fails to consider the point of view of others. At the next level, the child can consider another's ideas and can recognize that these ideas may be different from his or her own, but has only a beginning awareness of the views of others. At the third level, the child continues to have difficulty considering different views at the same time but can, in sequence, consider his or her own view and then consider the perspective of the other. At the fourth and final level, the child is capable of simultaneously considering his or her own perspective as well as those of others. Accomplishing this requires some ability to step back from the social interaction and adopt what Selman (1984) calls "third-person" perspective. This theory provides one view of how the perspective-taking process emerges. Recognition of the developmental nature of this ability has resulted in theorizing about the extent to which anomalies in the development of perspective-taking account for certain types of behavioral disturbance.

Research on children's memory and metacognitive skills has influenced the development of cognitive-behavioral strategies (see discussions by Cohen & Schleser, 1984, and Reeve & Brown, 1985). An understanding of children's memory capacities and of the age at which children can begin to recognize their own need to employ specific strategies has provided treatment researchers with informational tools necessary for shaping age-appropriate interventions.

Children's expectations and attributional processes have also been an increasing focus of research (Braswell, Koehler, & Kendall, 1985). The findings of this body of literature suggest that children's attributions for specific events and their preferences for particular kinds of explanations (i.e., their attributional styles) have important therapeutic implications, both in their impact on the therapy process and outcome and in their potential to be the specific targets of intervention (Dweck, 1975; Andrews & Debus, 1978).

Some of these areas of theory and research will be discussed in greater detail as they relate to specific intervention methods, but the current brief account of these views highlights the extent to which advances in developmental theory and research have influenced the emergence of cognitive-behavioral methods with child populations.

The impact of developmental psychology upon the creation of cognitive-behavioral interventions with children belies the necessity of recognizing factors that distinguish intervention with children from intervention with adults. While there are many obvious differences between children and adults as targets for intervention, the factors having perhaps the greatest bearing on differences within cognitive-behavioral treatments include issues of the level of cognitive and affective development, referral status, and the role of the family and social context of children.

While attention to the cognitive and affective development of the client is important, even if one works only with adult clients, attention to these matters is crucial if children are the subjects of intervention. As alluded to above, an understanding of the subject's memory capacity is important to successful intervention, as well as an understanding of factors such as attentional capacity, verbal fluency and comprehension, and the capacity for conceptual reasoning. Many of the cognitive strategies that would be appropriate for use with adult clients may not be fully understood or managed by children. As children progress through adolescence they typically become cognitively and emotionally prepared for more adult-like interventions, but the problem of adequate cognitive and emotional preparation is a genuine issue for elementary school age and preschool children. For example, the successful application of Albert Ellis's rational–emotive therapy (Ellis, 1970) or Aaron Beck's cognitive therapy for depression (Beck, Rush, Shaw, & Emery, 1979) assumes that the client has the cognitive capacity to distinguish between rational and irrational, logical and illogical thinking, once this distinction has been discovered and identified by the therapist and client. While later in the chapter we shall discuss variations of cognitive therapy for working with depressed children, it would not be safe to assume that a randomly selected elementary-school-age child understands such distinctions. A child may be likely to perceive the confrontation of irrational thinking as a scolding, as well as finding it difficult to comprehend the intended outcome of philosophical change. Effective RET with children could involve preventive efforts, when children are taught rational expectations as a method of reducing subsequent psychological dysfunction.

Work with child versus adult clients also differs in terms of the typical method of referral for treatment. While a small number of adult clients are ordered into treatment by authorities such as the court system, the majority of adults receiving psychotherapy services make a personal choice to seek out this type of care. Children, however, do not typically call to initiate their own appointments for treatment, even if they are in great psychological pain. Rather, they receive treatment as a result of the concern of the adults around them, in most cases their parents or teachers. This difference in how one comes to therapy yields some interesting differences regarding what types of adults versus children are most typically seen for outpatient care. Adults tend to seek care for conditions that are causing pain to themselves, such as depression or anxiety problems. Children are most likely to be brought in for care when they display behaviors that are causing pain or irritation to the adults in their lives. Thus, children displaying difficulties with impulsivity, poor self-control, and/or various types of antisocial behavior are the ones most likely to be brought in for treatment. In recent years, the problems of depression and anxiety in children have received greater attention, and the general public is becoming more able to recognize symptoms of these difficulties. It is hoped that this change in public awareness will result in depressed and anxious children receiving the treatment that they need. At the current time, however, children presenting with externalizing problems continue to be more likely to be brought to the attention of mental health professionals. As a result, cognitive-behavioral interventions with children have tended to focus on meeting the treatment needs of externalizing rather than internalizing children. In a subsequent section discussing the applications of various cognitive-behavioral strategies, some examples of work with internalizing children will be presented, but these efforts are relatively few compared to the numerous studies focusing on the problems of poorly self-controlled, hyperactive, and/or aggressive children—those referred by others for treatment.

The child client is also much more embedded in the social context of his or her peers (Hartup, 1983), family, and school than is typically the case for adult clients (Craighead, Meyers, & Craighead, 1985). This state of affairs has implications both for the identification of the ongoing causes of the child's difficulties and for the preferred treatment. The recognition of the role of the parents and other powerful people in the child's life and the inclusion of these individuals in some aspect of the intervention process, whether it is in the actual context of the therapy or in a more educational role, becomes a crucial component to the successful treatment of the child client. Peers are potentially useful aids in child (Howard & Kendall, 1987) and adolescent (Kendall & Williams, 1986) treatments.

Recognition of these differences in the nature and context of the child client can lead to some interesting speculations regarding why some interventions are less successful or why their results fail to generalize maximally to the child's real-world environments. It is our belief that successful intervention requires careful attention to the cognitive and affective level of the development of the child client and recognition that he or she does not typically make a conscious choice to enter treatment. The child is there because some of his or her behavior is disturbing to adults, making the inclusion of parents, teachers, and others who play a significant role in the child's world for the achievement of a successful therapeutic outcome.

In the discussion that follows, we offer suggestions about evaluating a child's appropriateness for cognitive-behavioral intervention and then describe the procedures and components most common to cognitive-behavioral interventions with children. These descriptions will include attention to the theoretical and historical underpinnings of these key components. The methods of presenting or training these components will also be described, along with selected examples of clinical research applications. Special emphasis will be given to problem solving and self-instructional training interventions, since these are the most commonly evaluated types of cognitive-behavioral therapy with children. Finally, concerns relevant across the various treatment procedures, such as the lack of treatment generalization and the impact of subject variables, will be considered.

ASSESSMENT CONCERNS

As with adult clients, careful evaluation of the child client is crucial for discerning the child's true intervention needs. For example, children who are homogeneous with regard to their attentional deficits may vary tremendously in terms of their level of self-esteem and the quality of their peer relations. These factors may affect the type and content of the intervention enacted and the adjunctive treatments to be considered. The child is embedded in his or her familial context and expected to follow certain rules, and this fact further complicates the assessment process. The clinician must carefully weigh the extent to which the child's reported behavior represents a condition meriting treatment or reflects the parent's difficulty in coping with unpleasant but perhaps developmentally appropriate behavior on the part of the child. Given clarity on such questions, the clinician will be able to make a reasonable decision regarding whether treatment should focus on the child, the parents, or the entire family. The following comments are offered as brief guides to assessment, but the reader is referred to Kendall and Braswell (1982; 1985), Kendall, Pellegrini, and Urbain (1981), Harris (1985), and Roberts and Nelson (1984) for further details.

The intake interview is usually the primary source for gathering relevant information in implementing cognitive-behavioral interventions with children. When interviewing the parents, the clinician encourages them to translate terms such as "out of control" or "hyper" into specific behavioral examples. In accordance with a behavioral tradition, the interviewer works to clarify the current antecedents and consequences for these specific behaviors and the modes of intervention the parents have tried on their own. The cognitive-behaviorally oriented clinician views this data as providing information about the child *and* about the parents' problem-solving ability. Questions about what the parent thinks is responsible for creating the child's current symptoms can yield a preliminary picture of the parent's attributional processes and belief systems regarding the child. Obtaining a developmental history from the parents can be useful for detecting factors suggestive of gaps or lags in certain key areas of development and/or indications of the parent's role in the development of the current difficulties (e.g., unusually high expectations or difficulty allowing the child independent functioning).

The interview with the child can address his or her awareness and level of understanding of his or her current difficulties, and can solicit the child's explanation for the symptoms in order to begin to understand his or her attributional processes and world view. Asking the child what he or she thinks will be necessary to change the current circumstances, whether he or she feels capable of enacting these changes, and whether he or she thinks change will be noticed and appreciated by parents or teachers can provide important clues about the child's level of self-efficacy regarding behavior change, motivation for change, and level of interpersonal sophistication. Structured questionnaires, developed for specific programs, are recommended.

Behavior rating scales can be useful for presenting a global view of the child's behavior from the perspective of his or her parents and teachers. Broad spectrum rating scales such as the Child Behavior Checklist (CBCL: Achenbach, 1978; Achenbach & Edelbrock, 1978) or the Conners' Teacher and Parent Questionnaires (Conners, 1969) provide information about the extent to which the child displays a number of different types of behavior problems, while other scales, such as the Self-Control Rating Scales (SCRS: Kendall and Wilcox, 1979; Kendall, Zupan, & Braswell, 1981; Robin, Fischel, & Brown, 1984) can be more relevant for assessing specific targets for cognitive-behavioral intervention. The SCRS was developed to assess self-control in elementary school children as rated by their classroom teacher and/or parents (as in Kendall & Braswell, 1982). This 33-item measure is based on a cognitive-behavioral conceptualization of self-control, wherein self-controlled children are said to possess the cognitive skills necessary to generate and evaluate alternatives and the behavioral skills needed to inhibit unwanted behavior and engage in desired action.

Various task performance measures have been developed to assess children's level of impulsivity, attentional difficulties, perspective-taking, and problem-solving abilities. Measures such as the Porteus Maze Test (Porteus, 1955) and the Matching Familiar Figures Test (Kagan, 1966) allow the clinician to observe the child's potential to be impulsive on cognitive tasks. Cognitive impulsivity represents a potential problem in its own right and is associated with deficient cognitive processing in attentional difficulties and hyperactivity (Fuhrman & Kendall, 1986; Homatidis & Konstantareas, 1981). Selman's measure of interpersonal awareness (Selman, 1980) permits the assessment of the child's ability to recognize the thoughts and feelings of others and take the perspective of another. The Purdue Elementary Problem-Solving Inventory (PEPSI: Feldhusen, Houtz, & Ringenbach, 1972); and the Means–Ends Problem-Solving task (MEPS: Shure & Spivack, 1972) permit the assessment of the child's cognitive skills for solving interpersonal dilemmas. Dodge, McClaskey, and Feldman (1985) have developed a formalized role-play assessment to evaluate social competence. With this method, the experimenter initiates the role play and the child provides a verbal and behavioral response that is audiotaped for later coding. The role play situations were identified by teachers and clinicians as being problematic for children manifesting peer difficulties, and they include issues such as peer group entry, response to peer provocation, and response to failure. All of these measures have some problematic features, yet we prefer those that provide the clinician with an "in the office" opportunity to observe how the child negotiates a problem-solving situation. Beyond yielding a certain score, the evaluator can observe what if any problem-solving strategies the child possesses.

Self-report assessment of the child's expectancies, attributions, and self-talk can be quite valuable in preparation for a cognitive-behavioral intervention. Unfortunately, the assessment of these constructs in children is only beginning to receive the intense level of research attention associated with the adult literature. For example, while findings of research with adults are converging to suggest the existence of a depressotypic set of cognitive contents (self-talk) specific to depression (Dobson & Shaw, 1986; Hollon, Kendall, & Lumry, 1986; Ingram, Kendall, Smith, Donnelly, & Ronan, 1986), such a consensus has not yet developed in the child-related literature. Nonetheless, there is growing curiosity on the part of researchers and clinicians regarding the extent to which these variables have impacts on the child. For example, therapists and researchers have addressed the impact of expectancies upon behavior, particularly as defined by Bandura's concept of self-efficacy expectations (Bandura, 1977). According to this view, an individual's self-efficacy is the extent to which he or she feels capable of successfully executing the behaviors leading to desired outcomes. Changes in self-efficacy have been posited as the common underlying cognitive process that accounts for changes in behavior. Keyser and Barling (1981) have developed and replicated (Barling & Snipelisky, 1983) a 20-item self-report scale assessing children's academic self-efficacy beliefs. Brief assessments of self-efficacy expectations could be incorporated into traditional testing sessions by simply asking children how confident they are that they will be able to complete the task at hand, and then evaluating the fit between the child's expectations and the actual outcome of the task.

The concept of attributions is closely related to that of expectations, but attributions concern how we explain an event *after* it has occurred. The attributions children offer to explain their own task behavior can be quite interesting. For example, Asarnow and Callahan (1985) have developed a two-part interview assessment of social cognitive processes that includes attributional data. The first segment of the evaluation is referred to as the Knowledge of Interpersonal Problem-Solving Strategies Assessment, and involves presenting the child with four vignettes and asking what he or she thinks the child in the story should do. After the free response phase, the child is then asked to rate a series of prepared response alternatives. In the second part, labeled the Attributional Style Assessment, the child is again presented with four situations, but is now asked how he or she would feel and think in each situation. After the child has had an opportunity to respond freely, he or she is presented with possible self-statements and is asked to rate how likely it is that he or she may feel and think this way. This method has been demonstrated to distinguish elementary-school-aged boys of positive and negative peer status. The assessment of attributional biases in depressed children is not as advanced as the adult literature in this area; however, Haley, Fine, Varriage, Moretti, and Freeman (1985) have developed the Cognitive Bias Questionnaire for Children (CBQC). This method involves the presentation of 10 brief vignettes describing school, home, and social situations. Each vignette is followed by four response alternatives that reflect depressed-distorted, depressed-nondistorted, nondepressed-distorted or nondistorted-nondepressed interpretations/reactions to the situations. This measure has been able to discriminate successfully affective from nonaffective disordered children. A child's attributional style may also mediate treatment outcome. For example, children who attribute task success to their personal effort may be more likely to show improvement following cognitive-behavioral intervention than those who attribute their success to luck, fate, or other factors external to themselves (Braswell, Koehler, & Kendall, 1985).

A self-report assessment of test-anxious children's self-talk has been developed by Zatz and Chassin (1983, 1985). This scale consists of 40 yes–no items that begin with the stem "I thought _____" The items include both positive and negative self-statements and on- and off-task thoughts. The child endorses each item on a 4-point scale reflecting the frequency with which he or she experiences that thought during a test.

These various types of self-report measures can help the clinician understand what the child expects of him- or herself, how he or she explains personal success or failure, and the extent to which the child's cognitions are affecting his or her mood and performance. In the absence of well-established norms for many of these measures, clinicians should exercise caution in their interpretation of results, but these measures can be viewed as rich sources of idiographic data.

Behavioral observations at home and/or school, sociometric data, and archival data (grades, number of trips to the principal's office, number of skipped classes, etc.) provide information on the specific problems the child is experiencing and possibly on the conditions maintaining these problems. These forms of "objective" data can also be useful in detecting any positive and/or negative distortions on the part of the parent or child. For example, if there is concern that the parent tends to distort the intensity and frequency of the child's inappropriate school behavior, it would be valuable to know that the child has never been suspended or sent to the principal's office. Sociometric data could prove useful in helping the clinician confirm or disconfirm a child's belief that no one in the class likes him or her. Admittedly, behavioral observations, archival data, or sociometrics are often seen as difficult to obtain during the course of traditional clinical practice, but the effort can yield information that is quite valuable for both assessment and treatment.

The choice of assessment methods is ultimately guided by the nature of the clinician's questions. In evaluations prior to possible cognitive-behavioral intervention, the child clinician shares the questions of adult clinicians regarding the nature of the presenting problem and, as indicated previously, seeks to determine the child's developmental level across a range of cognitive and social-emotional variables. In addition, the child clinician must determine the extent to which cognitive deficiencies versus cognitive distortions contribute to the problem and the extent to which the child's family or school environment has contributed to the development of the problem. The clinician then considers how family and school personnel can be most effectively included in the treatment plan.

COMMON TREATMENT APPROACHES

PROBLEM-SOLVING TRAINING

The problem-solving component of treatment merits discussion before all others for two reasons. First it represents a specific type of training commonly seen in cognitive-behavioral interventions. For example, most applications of self-instructional training incorporate methods for systematically approaching and evaluating problem situations (see Kendall & Braswell, 1985; Kazdin, Esveldt-Dawson, French, & Unis, 1987). In addition, the adoption of a problem-solving approach to behavioral or interpersonal dilemmas is a general orientation or attitude that is common to interventions within this category. It is characteristic for the cognitive-behavioral therapist to approach the child's or family's difficulties as problems to be solved rather than the inevitable outcome of a specific disease process or family circumstance. This does not mean that the therapist ignores relevant biological, historical, or family systems data, but rather that he or she incorporates this data while collaborating with the child and parents/teachers to create a problem formulation. Various types of cognitive-behavioral interventions recommend that the therapist use this problem-solving orientation not only when addressing the specific issues of the client but also when confronting dilemmas that may occur during the course of the therapy. For example, the therapist would not only assist a family in problem solving that deals with how to cope with an attentionally disordered child's difficulty in complying with bedtime rules, he or she would also employ problem-solving with the family to handle issues such as their attendance at therapy sessions, their difficulties locating suggested training materials, or issues of emotional reactance that the family experiences as a result of being in therapy.

The study of human cognitive problem solving has a very long history (Davis, 1966; Duncan, 1959; Jahoda, 1953). The 1970s witnessed a number of attempts to formulate problem solving as a set of skills relevant for clinical endeavors (D'Zurilla & Goldfried, 1971; Mahoney, 1977). Spivack, Shure, Platt, and their associates hypothesized that effective interpersonal cognitive problem solving (ICPS) demands a number of subskills such as sensitivity to human problems, the ability to generate alternative solutions, the capacity to conceptualize the appropriate means to achieve a given solution, and a sensitivity to consequences and cause–effect relationships in human behavior (Shure & Spivack, 1978; Spivack, Platt, & Shure, 1976).

Spivack, Shure, and others have examined the nature of the relationship between these skills and overt social adjustment (Spivack & Shure, 1974; Larcen, Spivack & Shure, 1972; Platt, Spivack, Altman, Altman, & Peizer, 1974; Platt & Spivack, 1972). Their work has been valuable in focusing research atttention on a problem solving view of adjustment, although other research groups have not confirmed the original conceptualizations of the relationship between interpersonal cognitive problem-solving skills and social behavior (see Krasnor & Rubin, 1983; Rickel & Burgio 1982; Rickel, Eishelman, & Loigman, 1983). In addition, Kendall and Fischler (1984) found only a negligible relationship between adjustment and the ICPS skills in a sample of 6- to 12-year-old children when IQ was carefully controlled (see also Kendall, 1986).

While the exact relationship between adjustment and the specific ICPS skills deficits proposed by Spivack, Shure, and their colleagues is unclear, other investigators have found support for the notion that children with adjustment problems differ from normal children in some of their social problem-solving processes. In a series of studies, Dodge and his colleagues (Dodge & Frame, 1982; Richard & Dodge, 1982) have observed that aggressive boys do display social cognitive biases and deficits that distinguish them from normal children. In comparing delinquents and nondelinquents at ages 10 to 11 and 14 to 15, Hains and Ryan (1983) found that while these two groups were similar on certain dimensions of social problem solving, the delinquents were less exhaustive or thorough in their consideration of different aspects of social problem solving. These findings led the authors to conclude that the acting-out behavior of these boys may be based, at least in part, on deficient or distorted inferences made from social situations. Their conclusions regarding delinquents are highly similar to those Dodge and his colleagues with school-aged acting-out children who have not yet been identified as delinquent.

Further research is needed to pinpoint clearly the problem-solving deficits associated with various types of childhood disorders, but the existing theoretical and empirical literature has provided a foundation for the development of problem-solving interventions. Most interventions of this type provide children with formal training in the application of problem-solving sequences, such as those proposed by D'Zurilla and Goldfried (1971), D'Zurilla (1986), Mahoney (1977), or Spivack and Shure (1974) with interpersonal problem situations. Problem-solving interventions, like other types of cognitive-behavioral therapies, vary in the extent to which the intervention focuses solely on the child or includes other members of the child's family. Programs also vary in the extent to which they include explicit behavioral contingencies as an aid to problem-solving training.

Problem-Solving Training with the Child

The turtle technique (Robin & Schneider, 1974; Robin, Schneider, & Dolnick, 1976; Schneider & Robin, 1976) is one of the earliest problem-solving approaches developed to help emotionally disturbed elementary-school-aged children inhibit aggressive or impulsive responding in social situations and generate alternate responses. This training is presented in four phases. First the children are taught the "turtle response" of pulling in one's limbs and lowering one's head to withdraw from a provoking situation. Next, the children are instructed in relaxation skills that they can utilize while "doing the turtle." Social problem-solving skills of generating alternative solutions and examining their consequences are then introduced. Finally, to encourage maintenance of the response, the problem children and their classmates are given social rewards for cueing and supporting a child who is "doing the turtle." The program was designed to require 15 minutes of instruction per day for 3 weeks. At the end of the 3-week period, sessions can be reduced to twice a week and then gradually faded. Following a successful but uncontrolled demonstration of treatment effectiveness by Robin and Schneider (1974), Robin *et al.* (1976) evaluated this procedure via a multiple baseline design and obtained significant decreases in aggressive behavior.

Problem-solving training was conducted by Sarason (1968) and Sarason and Ganzer (1973) with institutionalized delinquents. In his pilot work, Sarason (1968) found that a program emphasizing a problem-solving approach to problematic situations via modeling and role playing was effective in producing improved staff ratings of behavior. Sarason and Ganzer (1973) examined the effectiveness of this same program in a more extensive investigation. The modeling condition, as the authors labeled it, emphasized a practical approach to social problems. The subjects met in groups of four, with two models or tutors per group. The models demonstrated positive and negative approaches to certain problem situations and then asked the subjects to role play the same situations. These role plays were taped and played back for discussion. The discussion treatment condition covered the same content as the modeling group but no role play was involved. Those receiving the modeling treatment attained more favorable case outcomes, were more likely to evaluate their institutional experience as positive, displayed greater memory for the goals of the treatment, and demonstrated less recidivism than controls.

Building on this successful intervention with delinquents, Sarason and Sarason (1981) developed a problem-solving training package that was administered in a class format to high school students who were at risk for dropping out of school and becoming delinquents. Following treatment, an unobtrusive behavioral measure (behavior in a job interview) indicated the experimental subjects were able to present themselves in a more appropriate and effective manner than the controls. At 1-year follow-up, the experimental group tended to display fewer absences, lower rates of tardiness, and few referrals for disciplinary action.

Lochman and colleagues (Lochman, Burch, Curry, & Lampron, 1984; Lochman & Curry, 1986; Lochman, Nelson, & Sims, 1981) have conducted a series of studies evaluating the effects of an anger-coping training program with aggressive 9- to 11-year-old boys. This program involves 12 sessions of group training in interpersonal cognitive problem-solving skills. The effectiveness of the program in reducing aggressive behavior was initially established in the Lochman et al. (1981) study. Lochman et al. (1984) compared the effectiveness of the anger-coping program with and without a goal-setting component versus goal setting only. The goal-setting intervention involved having the boys establish weekly behavioral goals, which were then monitored daily by their classroom teacher. If the goals were met, the boys received contingent reinforcement. The results indicated both anger-coping groups achieved significant reductions in disruptive and aggressive off-task behaviors at the 4- to 6-week follow-up. Parent ratings suggested that there was some generalization of treatment effects to the home environment for both anger-coping groups and that the boys in these groups manifested an increase in home-related self-esteem. The addition of the goal setting tended to accentuate the treatment effects obtained in the classroom. Despite the evidence of change in behavioral observations of aggression, teacher and peer perceptions showed no significant change.

Lochman and Curry (1986) compared the effectiveness of an 18-session version of the anger coping program with a program including training in the anger-coping skills plus self-instructional training. Both conditions included the goal-setting component previously described. Both treatments were found to be effective in reducing passive off-task behaviors and reducing parent ratings of aggression. Both groups also yielded increases in self-esteem. In addition, the anger-coping groups displayed significant reductions in disruptive and aggressive off-task behavior. As in the previous study, there was a lack of change in teachers' ratings of aggression.

Problem-Solving Training with Families

Blechman and colleagues (Blechman, Olson, & Hellman, 1976; Blechman, Olson, Schornagel, Halsdorf, & Turner, 1976) examined the impact of a procedure called the Family Contract Game. This technique used a board game format to develop problem-solving and contingency-contracting skills in families experiencing significant parent–child conflict. Component problem-solving skills, such as identifying problems in behavioral terms, gathering relevant information, generating behavioral alternatives, choosing a specific alternative, and evaluating the outcome of the selected alternative, were taught within the game context. After a successful case study

(Blechman, Olson, Schornagel, *et al.*, 1976), Blechman, Olson, and Hellman (1976) implemented the Family Contract Game with six mother–child dyads. As in the case study, the use of the game procedure resulted in a significant increase in on-task behavior and decreased off-task behavior during problem discussion. This change was apparent in the first intervention session and remained fairly constant throughout treatment. Unlike the findings of the case study, these changes did not persist in the post-treatment problem discussions. Similar results were obtained by Robin, Kent, O'Leary, Foster, & Prinz (1977). Their problem-solving training produced highly significant increases in the use of problem-solving behaviors in the audiotaped discussions of both real and hypothetical conflicts, but ratings completed by the parents and adolescents failed to indicate improvement in home problem-solving and communication behaviors. These interventions appear capable of altering behavior but the altered patterns do not seem to generalize to real-world settings.

On the whole, the results of these studies indicate that problem-solving training can have an impact on the behavior of the child and his or her family, although generalization of in-treatment results remains a concern. Some research has raised a question regarding the most effective way to include the parents. For example, Kirmil-Gray, Duckham-Shoor, & Thoresen (1980) achieved positive results in the attempt to maintain appropriate behavior in severely hyperactive children undergoing complete withdrawal or significant reduction of their stimulant medication. There was, however, no indication that problem-solving training with the children added significantly to the effects achieved by providing the parents with behavior management training. Going a step further, Coyne, Meyers, and Clark (1985) examined the effects of conducting a behavioral weight-loss program for obese children in which one group of parents and children received training in behavioral weight-loss techniques, while children in another group received training in behavioral management and the parents received problem-solving training that would facilitate maintenance of the behavioral program. Children in the behavior management plus problem-solving condition lost significantly more weight during the 8-week treatment and maintained these changes at 3- and 6-month follow-up. Thus, the inclusion of parents, whether in treatment with the children or as recipients of training through separate parent groups, appears to result in improved outcome for the child.

The case of Sean provides a clinical example of problem-solving training involving both the child and parents. Sean, age 11, was referred for treatment by his parents due to concentration difficulties, restlesss behavior, and disobedience. He had previously been diagnosed as manifesting an attention deficit disorder with hyperactivity and was maintained on psychostimulant medication during the school year. In school he was able to achieve at an average to above average level and was considered to be only a moderate behavior problem, but his parents were very distressed over his persistent noncompliance in the home. After the initial assessment, the family was presented with treatment options and chose to enter a program that focused on the needs of attentionally disordered children and their families. This program emphasized training both the child and his or her parents in cognitive problem-solving methods via self-instructional training, role-play exercises, and reinforced practice.

Sean soon entered the first phase of the program, in which he received two individual sessions that introduced him to cognitive problem solving and to an explanation of how such an approach could be applied to academic and social problems. He quickly grasped the concept of using a series of problem-solving steps to cope with difficult situations.

The family then entered the second phase of the program, with Sean participating in a group of children with similar behavioral backgrounds while his parents met in a separate group with the parents of the other children. In the children's group, Sean received training in self-monitoring and problem recognition. In addition, he engaged in repeated practice in applying a problem-solving process with dilemmas that would arise in the group. The format of the group included ongoing behavioral contingencies that rewarded the members for identifying and coping with problems in their own behavior or the behavior of other group members. The children were also rewarded for relating examples of how they had attempted to use a problem-solving strategy with situations occurring outside of group. Sean was able to master the self-monitoring and problem recognition exercises with ease. He could demonstrate effective use of problem-solving strategies in the group context, but through the first six of the eight group sessions he could not identify examples of home use of the training strategies. In the parent group sessions, the adults were introduced to cognitive problem-solving strategies and were encouraged to cue and reward their child for using these strategies in the home. Sean's parents reported that he was, in fact, refusing to apply the problem-solving methods to his home behavior. The parents were extremely frustrated by his defiance and felt they were facing yet another power struggle with Sean.

Fortunately, between group sessions six and seven, all families met with the group leaders for individual family sessions. The goal of these sessions was to address any difficulties the families were experiencing in applying the methods and tailor the procedures to better meet their needs. During the session with Sean's family, the therapist encouraged the parents to use the problem-solving methods to deal with issues that affected the husband and wife but did not necessarily involve Sean. The parents then role played strategy use to deal with some of their work-related and household management concerns while Sean observed them. This seemed to spark his interest, for he then asked if the parents were the only ones who could identify family problems or if the children could too. The parents stated that they were receptive to Sean identifying formal problems but that then he would need to be willing to participate in the problem-solving process. The events of this session seemed to be quite significant for Sean, for in the remaining two groups he was able to bring in several examples of home applications and his parents reported that he had become much interested and cooperative regarding problem solving in the home. Obviously, Sean's resistance and subsequent change of heart appears to be related to some complexities of family interaction patterns. The therapist was able to work with these issues in the context of a problem-solving intervention and ultimately achieved a positive outcome, as self-reported by the child and parents.

These highlights from research and clinical applications of problem-solving training demonstrate that behavior change can be achieved through this method and the generalization to extra-therapy settings, while not universal, can be achieved. In addition to the further exploration of the impact of parent involvement, we would also encourage evaluation of added gains produced by peer involvement (Howard & Kendall, 1987; Kendall & Williams, 1986).

VERBAL SELF-INSTRUCTIONAL TRAINING

Self-instructions as an element of child cognitive-behavioral theory are the self-directed statements of an internal dialogue that an individual uses to guide him- or herself through a problem-solving process. Self-instructing occurs in an automatic manner and it may be most observable when an individual is attempting a new task. Self-instructional training programs with children are usually directed toward providing the child with a thinking strategy—not what to think, but how to think. The self-statements serve as guides for the child to follow through the process of problem solving.

As noted by Meichenbaum (1979) and Craighead (1982), two bodies of theoretical and empirical work have provided the background of current self-instructional training programs. The work of Soviet psychologists Luria (1959, 1961) and Vygotsky (1962) details the process through which verbal mediation of behavior is achieved. Vygotsky hypothesized that internalization of verbal commands is the key step in the child's establishment of verbal control over his or her behavior. Luria, a student of Vygotsky, elaborated a development theory of verbal control. Although this theory is not without its critics (Jarvis, 1968; Miller, Shelton & Falvell, 1970), it has proven quite valuable as a model for teaching children who display an apparent lack of verbal mediation of their behavior. It has also encouraged others to continue to explore the developmental significance of children's self-directed speech (Copeland, 1983; Zivin, 1979). The second body of research is represented by the work of Mischel and colleagues on the phenomenon of the delay of gratification. In his 1974 review, Mischel summarized data suggesting that self-generated strategies, such as self-instructions and self-praising statements helped children reduce the frustration they experienced during delay-of-gratification tasks. Patterson and Mischel also examined verbal self-control in a series of studies on verbal mediation strategies for use in resisting distraction (Mischel & Patterson, 1976; Patterson & Mischel, 1976). Their results indicated that preschoolers did not spontaneously produce instructions to help themselves cope with distracting stimuli, but that when these children were provided with a specific cognitive strategy they were able to work longer in the distracting environment. Similar strategies have been employed in studies of rule-following behavior (Monohan & O'Leary, 1971; O'Leary, 1968), with the data suggesting verbalization of simple self-statements can reduce rule breaking in some children.

In examining the myriad of experimental applications of self-instructional training, one can observe examples that conform more closely to the model of the Mischel and Patterson work in that the training provided is very brief and typically involves the experimenter simply instructing the child to say a particular sentence or think a particular thought in response to a well-defined problematic situation. The current authors have referred to this type of training as noninteractive, for the training involves the experimenter/clinician simply telling the child what to do or say. Studies that reflect more of the influence of Luria's stage theory are labeled interactive, for training involves a much greater degree of therapist–child exchange. Other investigators have labeled this interactive training based on the Luria model as the faded rehearsal method of self-instructional training, for the experimenter/clinician typically guides the child through a series of steps in using the self-instructions. The experimenter first models appropriate use of the self-instructions him- or herself and then has the child carry out a task while the clinician states the appropriate self-instructions. The child is then given practice in solving problems while verbalizing the self-instructions, and finally the child practices solving problems while making covert use of the self-instructing statements. Within recent years another mode of training has emerged. The directed discovery method, as developed by Schleser, Meyers, and Cohen (1981), involves the clinician leading the child to "discover" a specific set of self-guiding strategies through a Socratic dialogue. As indicated in our selective review of self-instructional training studies, this area of research is becoming increasingly well elaborated as experimenters attempt to create maximally effective treatment packages.

Self-Instructional Training with Behaviorally Disordered Children

Self-instructional training has frequently been applied with samples identified by teachers as being disruptive and/or impulsive in their classroom behavior. Meichenbaum and Goodman (1971) initiated the application of self-instructional training with children displaying a lack of self-control. Second graders who had been teacher-identified as hyperactive or lacking in self-control were randomly assigned to cognitive training, attention control, or assessment control conditions. The experimental and control groups received four 30-minute training sessions. Both groups used the same training tasks but only the experimental group received training in self-instructions. The results indicated that the self-instructional group improved significantly more than the two control groups on task performance measures of impulsivity. This pattern of relatively positive results was maintained at 4-week follow-up. However, the classroom measures revealed no significant group differences on behavioral observations or teacher ratings of classroom behavior. The design of this study has served as the model for many subsequent outcome studies.

Following this introduction of the self-instructional procedures, numerous studies have sought to attain the elusive goal of behavioral generalization. Kendall and colleagues have examined the efficacy of Meichenbaum and Goodman's self-instructional procedures when used in conjunction with various additional strategies such as explicit behavioral contingencies. After obtaining positive results on both task performance measures and behavior ratings in a preliminary case study (Kendall & Finch, 1976) and group outcome study (Kendall & Finch, 1978), Kendall and Wilcox (1980) examined the contribution of different types of self-instructional training with behavioral contingencies to the attainment of generalized change. Self-instructional training that focused on the specific training task (concrete labeling) was compared with training that was relevant to the task but was also general and could be applied to other situations (conceptual labeling). Training tasks included cognitive and interpersonal problems. Using 8- to 12-year-old teacher-referred subjects, they obtained results indicating that both concrete and conceptual self-instructional training produced increased self-control and decreased hyperactivity at posttest and 1-month follow-up, with the treatment effects stronger for the conceptual labeling group. Thus, generalization of treatment effects to the classroom was found. In addition, Kendall and Wilcox provided data on the self-control ratings of nonreferred children to give some guidelines or norms for assessing treatment impact. At both posttreatment and follow-up, the mean ratings of the conceptual treatment group fell just within one standard deviation of the mean for the nonreferred children. At 1-year follow-up (Kendall, 1981), teacher ratings showed differences favoring the conceptually trained children, but with the small number of children available, the differences did not reach statistical significance. It was observed that conceptually trained children showed significantly better recall of the material they had learned when compared with the concrete and control groups.

Kendall and Zupan (1981) examined the relative effectiveness of individual versus group training using subjects and procedures similar to those of Kendall and Wilcox (1980), but increasing the number of 1-hour treatment sessions to twelve. At posttreatment the group and individual treatment conditions demonstrated significant improvements on the self-control ratings. The changes in teacher's ratings of hyperactivity paralleled the self-control ratings, though the changes were significant for all three conditions. Both individual and group treatments produced changes in interpersonal perspective taking at follow-up; a nonspecific control condition did not. In terms of normative comparisons, the mean self-control and hyperactivity ratings of cognitive-behavioral treatment conditions at posttreatment were within one standard deviation of the normative mean. These improvements, resulting from lengthier treatments, were greater than those reported in Kendall and Wilcox (1980). At 1-year follow-up (Kendall, 1982) improvements were found for subjects across treatment conditions. Structured interviews indicated that individually treated children showed significantly better recall of the ideas they had learned and produced significantly more illustrations of use of the ideas than either group treatment or the nonspecific treatment conditions.

A component analysis of the Kendall treatment package was conducted by Kendall and Braswell (1982). A cognitive-behavioral treatment condition received self-instruction training via coping modeling and behavior contingencies, while the behavioral treatment condition involved only task modeling and contingencies. Following 12 individual treatment sessions, the cognitive-behavioral group showed significant improvement and maintenance of improvement on the ratings of self-control, while the behavioral and control groups did not. On the teacher ratings of hyperactivity, both the cognitive-behavioral and behavioral groups showed significant change at posttest and maintenance of change at follow-up. The two treatment groups also produced significant improvement and maintenance on the latency aspect of the impulsivity measure, while all three groups displayed significant improvement and maintenance on the error score. The cognitive-behavioral group produced more significant change on an achievement measure than did the behavioral group, and only the subjects in the cognitive-behavioral groups showed improvement on a self-concept measure. Classroom observations yielded a high degree of variability, but the cognitive-behavioral group displayed improvement in the categories of off-task verbal and physical behaviors. In terms of normative comparisons, subjects within the cognitive-behavioral group achieved self-control ratings within one standard deviation above the means of a nonreferred group when assessed at posttest. Parent ratings of behavior in the home environment did not reveal significant treatment effects. Thus treatment generalization to the classroom did occur, as indicated by the teacher ratings and classroom observations, but generalization to the home did not. At 1-year follow-up, significant group differences did not persist on any of the treatment outcome measures.

These studies suggest that when self-instructional training with disruptive/impulsive children is conducted with social as well as cognitive problem-solving tasks *and* when the training is accompanied by behavioral contingencies, it is possible to achieve some change on both cognitive and social/behavioral measures.

The experience of 9-year-old Jason is similar to many of the children participating in the studies of Kendall and his colleagues. Jason was referred to the intervention project by his 4th-grade teacher because he displayed an impulsive work style that resulted in numerous errors on homework and tests. He also displayed outbursts of aggression on the play ground that typically followed disputes with peers over appropriate game rules and procedures. Testing indicated Jason scored on the low average of general intellectual functioning, and that he was rated as functioning particularly poorly on subtests assessing verbal IQ. Jason's therapist initially began to train him in simple self-instructional statements while working on matching games and other psychoeducational tasks, but sensed that although Jason could "say the words," he was not grasping the concepts behind the self-instructional statements. Further information was obtained from Jason and his teacher to determine what types of games or activities were particular areas of competence for Jason. On the basis of this information, the therapist then began to teach Jason self-instructions for use in addressing dilemmas that arise in ice hockey games. Using a content area more familiar to him, Jason began to display a greater understanding of the meaning and purpose of the self-instructional steps. The therapist was then able to move on to the application of the self-instructional methods with academic materials and interpersonal problem situations. At the end of the intervention, ratings completed by Jason's teacher indicated improvement in self-control and a decrease in hyperactive behavior. She commented that she had observed Jason quietly talking himself through math problems during testing situations. Jason also displayed improvement on a measure of cognitive impulsivity.

While Kendall and others have been successful in achieving some behavior change with disruptive/impulsive teacher-referred children from regular schools, the results of self-instructional training with children meeting the full DSM-III criteria for attention deficit disorder with hyperactivity have been much more equivocal.

Elaborating on related cognitive-behavioral strategies Hinshaw, Henker, and Whalen (1984a) conducted a fascinating study assessing the effects of cognitive-behavioral training and methylphenidate hydrochloride (Ritalin) on the behavior of hyperactive boys in an anger-inducing situation. Hinshaw *et al.* recruited 24 hyperactives (8 to 13 years old) to participate in daily cognitive-behavioral training sessions during the course of a 5-week summer program. The children met in groups of four, with half of each group on medication and the other half receiving a placebo. All children were exposed to general cognitive-behavioral concepts such as self-instructions during the first 2 weeks. Then during the 3rd week the trainers introduced a behavioral provocation situation modeled on Goodwin and Mahoney's (1975) circle game, with each child serving a turn as the target of name calling by the others. The children were presented an array of different coping strategies and were encouraged to practice the strategies of their choice. Children in the control condition were instructed in the concept of perspective taking and received exposure to the general concepts of social problem solving but did not learn about their own anger cues or practice specific methods of coping. The behavioral provocation situation was then reintroduced. The results of pre–post comparisons of the children's behavior indicated that the treatment group scored significantly higher on a global rating of self-control and displayed significantly more purposeful coping strategies. Relative to the pretest, all children displayed less fidgeting, laughter, and verbal aggression and more neutral statements in response to provocation. The one significant effect for medication was observed in global ratings of the intensity of the children's behavior, with medicated children displaying less intensive behavior. These findings support the efficacy of the self-instructional, coping skills procedures as a means of changing the actual content of the child's behavior in a stressful situation.

Brown and colleagues (Brown, Borden, Wynne, Schleser, & Clingerman, 1986; Brown, Wynne, & Medenis, 1985) have also examined the individual and combined effects of stimulant drug therapy and cognitive training with 6- to 11-year-old hyperactive boys. The cognitive training involved individual twice-weekly 1-hour sessions for a total of 24 meetings. The therapists also worked with both the parents and teachers to help them apply the training strategies in extra-therapy environments. The training followed an elaborated version of Meichenbaum and Goodman's (1971) self-instructional training. Children received training in breaking tasks into component parts and using general problem-solving strategies with academic and social problem situations. No explicit behavioral contingencies accompanied the treatment. Treatment effects were assessed via tests of attention deployment and cognitive style, academic achievement, and behavioral ratings completed by parents and teachers. The results of Brown *et al.* (1985) indicated that those children receiving medication, whether with or without cognitive training, attained improvement on the measures of attention deployment and the behavior ratings. Those in the cognitive therapy only condition displayed improvement on measures of attention deployment. These findings of cognitive change in the absence of behavioral changes are similar to those obtained by Douglas, Parry, Marton, and Garson (1976).

Brown *et al.* (1986) also examined the efficacy of medication and cognitive methods similar to those used in Brown *et al.* (1985); however, in contrast to the earlier study, those in the medication conditions did not continue to receive medications during the posttest assessments. With this methodological change, it appeared that the effects of the medication treatment dissipated rapidly (within 1 week) and no main effects for medication, or cognitive training or the combined condition were obtained. Other investigators have also failed to obtain significant increments in behavioral change with cognitive therapy (Abikoff & Gittelman, 1985). It should be noted, however, that there are meaningful concerns regarding the Abikoff and Gittleman study such as the absence of contingent rewards and specific training for generalization (Kendall & Reber, 1987).

It appears that self-instructional training, when combined with related cognitive and behavioral procedures, is capable of producing some generalizable behavior change in children displaying subclinical levels of disturbance. Changes in subjects' response to provocation and performance on attentional measures have also been achieved with clinical samples of attentionally disordered, hyperactive children. Consistent, across-setting changes in overall behavior have not been observed with clinical samples.

Self-Instructional Training with Learning-Disabled Children

Self-instructional strategies have been used as means of treating educational difficulties. This application of cognitive-behavioral procedures has become increasingly popular in the past 5 years, as perspectives on learning-disabled children have changed. Current theories of learning disability in children emphasize difficulties in the self-regulation of planful behaviors as opposed to some type of inability to learn or execute certain strategies or some type of specific deficit. This view is supported by research suggesting the performance of disabled children who fail to produce spontaneously appropriate task strategies, can be improved by mild prompts or direct instruction in strategy usage (Hallahan & Reeve, 1980; Torgeson & Kail, 1980). Harris (1986) examined differences in the private speech of learning-disabled and normally achieving children. She found that while these groups had the same rate of private speech, the learning-disabled children had more task-irrelevant speech. Further research is needed to understand more about the nature of these self-regulation difficulties, but other investigators have used currently existing data to devise interventions. The earliest academically oriented self-instructional interventions successfully treated cognitive impulsivity using methods like those employed in the Meichenbaum and Goodman (1971) and Kendall and colleagues studies (see Nelson & Birkimer, 1978; Palkes, Stuart, & Kahana, 1968). Some treatments have focused on developing general learning strategies that can be applied with a variety of subject areas, while others have focused on interventions for specific academic contents, such as reading, math, and writing.

The work of Deshler, Alley, Warner, and Schumaker (1981) provides an example of an intervention that was designed to promote the acquisition and generalization of learning strategies that could be employed with a variety of academic content areas. Severely learning-disabled adolescents were trained individually via a series of steps that included an initial examination of the student's current learning habits, the instructor's description of the strategy to be learned, the instructor's modeling of the strategy, the student's verbalization of the strategy until mastery, the student's practice of implementing the strategy with specially selected materials, and finally practice of the strategy with classroom materials. In addition to the sequential approach for training strategy usage, these investigators included features designed to promote generalization, such as training with a variety of examples of usage and a variety of training formats, helping the students learn to cue others to provide reinforcement for the strategy use, providing the student with intermittent reinforcement once the student has mastered the strategy, and providing the student with explicit instructions to generalize their strategy usage (see also Hall, 1979; Zakraski, 1982).

Other investigators have examined the efficacy of self-instructional methods as a means of remediating deficits in specific academic content areas. Leon and Pepe (1983) compared the effectiveness of verbal self-instructional methods with traditional direct instruction for training math skills in learning-disabled and educable mentally handicapped children. The self-instructional methods produced superior results and induced greater generalization of the skills. Johnson (1983) obtained similar results with a sample of normally achieving first graders. In addition to comparing the efficacy of self-instruction and direct instruction methods, Johnson examined the impact of the specificity of the self-instructions. General problem-solving self-instructions plus specific task-oriented self-instructions proved to be the most effective, particularly for the less competent students in this sample.

Self-instruction interventions have been developed for addressing different types of written language skills. Both Robin, Armel, and O'Leary (1975) and Graham (1983) obtained results suggesting cognitive-behavioral techniques may not be appropriate for intervention with handwriting problems; however, Wong (1985) indicated that these studies may have failed because they did not address the issue of adequate preskills. She holds that if a child is still struggling to master basic letter knowledge, he or she may not have the linguistic skills necessary to implement a procedure such as self-instructional training. In support of this point, Kosiewicz, Hallahan, Lloyd, and Graves (1982) successfully improved the handwriting of a 9-year-old boy via self-instruction and self-correction procedures. Wong hypothesizes that the subject in this intervention did possess adequate letter knowledge and linguistic ability.

Written composition skills have also been the targets of cognitive-behavioral instructions. Scardamalia, Bareiter, and Steinbach (1984) trained novice writers in a thinking aloud process that involved self-questioning during the composition planning phase and the statement of strategy questions that helped the subject resolve conflicting ideas. The results indicated that this method yielded improvement in the writer's ability to reflect on ideas and improvement in the structure of the compositions. Using self-control strategies like those employed by Deshler *et al.* (1981) Harris and Graham (1985) were able to achieve improvement in the written composition skills of two learning-disabled 6th graders. Generalization from the skill-training setting to the children's work in their resource room was also accomplished, and was maintained through a 6-week follow-up period. An assessment at 14 weeks after the intervention did not yield continued evidence for skill maintenance. Interestingly, when the children were questioned, they could repeat the specific steps for writing good stories that they had learned during the training phase, despite the fact that they had ceased to apply the steps.

Echoing the concerns of Kendall and Wilcox (1980), other research teams have examined the merits of task-specific versus general self-instructional statements with academic problems. Schleser, Meyer, and Cohen (1981) compared the efficacy of task-specific versus general self-statements for training math skills with same-age children who varied in terms of level of cognitive development (Piaget's pre-operational versus concrete operational stages). The specific self-statement group showed the greatest posttest improvement on the task of training, while the general self-statements group manifested greater improvement on a generalization task. Cognitive level also affected performance; concrete operational children out-performed the preoperational group on both tasks. Thackwray, Meyers, Schleser, and Cohen (1985) obtained similar results, with those receiving specific self-instructions showing improvement on a test assessing training task materials, while those receiving general self-instructions did significantly better on tests in other academic content areas. The authors suggest that subjects in the general self-instructions condition were able to practice tailoring general problem-solving strategies to fit the demands of a specific task, in this case math problems, and such practice may have made it possible for them to successfully tailor these strategies for use with other subject areas. Unfortunately, despite test indications of change, teacher ratings of academic skills did not evidence improvement. Swanson (1985) did obtain successful generalization across settings and tasks using global strategies plus specific skill training for remediating academic deficits in conduct-disordered children. Swanson's intervention also included a token program that provided rewards for accuracy and appropriate conduct.

Self-instructional techniques have been employed to reduce anxiety that might interfere with adequate performance in mathematics. Working with 7th grade girls whose math achievements were below grade level and reading achievements were above grade level, Genshaft and Hirt (1980) compared the relative effectiveness of tutoring, tutoring plus self-instructions, and a no-treatment control condition. In this intervention the self-instructions focused on helping the student monitor her attention, make positive self-statements, and reduce arousal, rather than focusing on the details of the task. Results indicated that all three groups made improvements on a standardized math test, but the tutoring plus self-instructions group displayed the greatest improvement on the computational subtest and greater improvement in attitudes toward math.

Thus, self-instructional interventions appear to have demonstrated some potential for improving skills in reading, math, and written language, with treatments that include both task-specific self-instructions and general, problem-solving self-instructions being particularly likely to produce successful results. Self-instructional methods, often of a more concrete variety, are also beginning to be effectively used in the training of mentally retarded children (Whitman, Burgio, & Johnston, 1984) and of children experiencing fears and anxieties (Graziano & Mooney, 1980; Peterson & Shigetomi, 1981).

ATTRIBUTION RETRAINING

As indicated earlier in this chapter, a growing body of research in clinical, social, and developmental psychology suggests that children's attribution for specific events and their preferences for particular kinds of explanations (attributional styles) may have important therapeutic implications (Braswell, Koehler, & Kendall, 1985). Attributions have been of interest for their potential both to have an impact on therapy outcome and to be the actual targets of intervention.

Attributional retraining studies have a basis in the cognitive theories of motivation put forth by Bandura (1977) and Weiner (1979). These viewpoints emphasize how the child's causal explanations for why he or she is doing well or poorly have implications for his or her behavioral persistence, expectancies for future performance, and affective reactions to success and failure. Exploratory research has indicated that poor readers, learning-disabled students, and mentally retarded children all tend to make attributions that interfere with their optimal performance in achievement situations (Butkowsky & Willows, 1980; Pearl, 1985; Weisz, 1979). Even students of high ability have been found to make maladaptive attributions in some cases (Dweck & Reppucci, 1973).

Most efforts at attribution retraining attempt to create a training environment in which the child learns to take more individual credit for his or her achievements, thus encouraging the child's experience in positive control and/or self-efficacy. It is the goal of these interventions not only to increase the amount of behavioral persistence that these children display but also to foster the long-term maintenance of the beliefs and expectations that lead to these behavioral changes.

The seminal treatment research in the area of attribution retraining was conducted by Dweck (1975). Subjects for this original study were elementary-school-age children who were prone to expect failure and be debilitated by it. These children received 25 daily sessions, with each session consisting of 15 trials of solving math problems. In the attribution retraining condition, the children experienced some failure as they solved problems, and when this occurred they were told by the experimenter, "Failure means you should try harder." The attribution retraining condition was contrasted with a success-only condition, in which children solved math problems that were well within their ability and that would insure success. The results indicated that the attribution retraining condition was more successful in changing children's response to failure. Those in the treatment condition persisted longer in their attempts to solve problems. In addition, children receiving attribution retraining showed a change in their beliefs, with an increased tendency to attribute failure to a lack of effort rather than a lack of ability. Thus cognitive and behavioral changes were attained.

Further research has suggested that attribution retraining is most likely to be successful with students who are not applying the knowledge or skills they already possess or in conjunction with teaching new problem-solving strategies (Schunk, 1983). Pearl (1985) has emphasized that it is important to target for training those children who are truly making maladaptive attributions rather than assuming that poor academic performance is by definition the result of maladaptive thinking. Pearl notes that research also suggests the importance of linking attributional statements with specific behavioral efforts. When this is not done, one is less likely to achieve a positive outcome. For example, Short and Ryan (1984) had children make effort-oriented statements prior to reading a story passage rather than after having had difficulty with a specific passage. Their results indicated the attribution manipulation was largely ineffective.

Within this area of training, there currently seems to be a shift towards promoting the attribution of failure as the result of the use of ineffective strategies rather than as inevitably the result of a lack of effort (Clifford, 1984). Obviously, attribution focused interventions would be highly inappropriate when there is reason to believe the presenting problem or symptom is the result of an actual skills deficit (Fincham, 1983). In such cases the skills deficit must be remediated and then the child's attributional status can be reassessed. Another caution concerns the nature of internal versus external attributions. As Braswell, Koehler, and Kendall (1985) have stated, while the aim of encouraging a child's "internality" may be appropriate in some cases, an inappropriately internal attributional style can also be associated with maladaptive functioning (Dweck & Reppucci, 1973; Seligman et al., 1982). To give a clinical example, one would not want a child to attribute his parents' divorce to some behavior or lack of effort on the child's part. For the purposes of subsequent adjustment, attributions of causality must be reality-based and accurate. Different attributions are useful and appropriate for different situations at different points in time.

Attribution-retraining interventions have received much less research attention than problem-solving or self-instructional interventions. The demonstrated effects of attribution retraining have been rather specific and focused, but they suggest that interventions can have an impact on the child's emerging beliefs about the reasons for experiencing failure. By apparently changing these beliefs, behavioral persistence may be improved.

TREATMENT APPROACHES WITH INTERNALIZING DISORDER

The development and evaluation of cognitive-behavioral treatments for children experiencing anxiety, depression, and other types of internalizing symptomatology lags far behind the existing work with adults experiencing these disorders. Fortunately, research attention to this area is increasing in conjunction with our knowledge base regarding the manifestation of these disorders in childhood. The interventions that have been proposed thus far are developmentally tailored extensions of techniques used with adults and/ or combinations of the methods previously described in this chapter.

Emery, Bedrosian, and Garber (1983) argue that cognitive therapy techniques that have proved useful with depressed adults such as self-monitoring, activity scheduling, graded task assignments, and hypothesis testing of distorted beliefs can be effective with children. They also believe that children can be taught to generate alternate attributions regarding negative events or beliefs and can learn to "decatastrophize" about negative outcomes. These authors note the importance of including parents in the therapy process, particularly as aides when the child is attempting activity scheduling or hypothesis testing. Their contentions are buttressed by developmental research suggesting that latency-age children do have the capacity for such cognitive operations (Flavell, 1977). The authors presented case study data supporting the effectiveness of these procedures, but did not provide formal outcome data.

Stark, Kaslow, and Reynolds (1985) conducted one of the few group outcome studies that addresses the efficacy of cognitive-behavioral interventions with depressed children. Using 9- to 12-year-old subjects, these authors compared the efficacy of a self-control therapy and a behavior therapy based on Lewinsohn's (1974) model of depression. The self-control therapy was modeled after work by Fuchs and Rehm (1977) and involved teaching the children skills such as setting more realistic standards for performance, setting realistic subgoals, applying self-reinforcement, learning to self-punish less, and learning to examine one's attributions. Training in self-monitoring, with special attention to monitoring pleasant activities was also included. The behavioral therapy included training in self-monitoring, pleasant event scheduling, problem solving about social situations, and gaining an understanding about the relationship between feelings and social behavior. After 12 group sessions, both treatments produced statistically and clinically significant reductions in depressive symptomatology relative to a waiting-list control group. The positive results were most pronounced for the self-control therapy group, suggesting that the cognitive change strategies employed in this treatment were within the capacity of the target children.

The current authors have applied these concepts with individual cases of depressed children and adolescents. The case of 15-year-old Sharon provides an interesting example. When initially seen, she was extremely dysphoric, experienced recurrent suicidal ideation, and displayed a number of vegetative signs of depression. A psychiatric consultation was obtained and she was placed on antidepressant medication. In individual therapy she was introduced to a cognitive-behavioral approach to depression, and she completed self-monitoring and mood ratings on a regular basis. She was able to understand how her mood was affected by her thoughts and behavior and was able to engage in behavioral planning to increase the occurrence of pleasure and mastery-oriented events. Sharon manifested extremely high standards for evaluating her performance in a number of areas, and it became clear that her parents also ascribed to these standards, so that family therapy sessions were held to encourage Sharon and her parents to re-evaluate their standards.

Sharon had difficulty with the notion of changing her standards and noted that when she was not depressed she actually valued her perfectionism. At that point she resisted the therapy because she perceived it as trying to change something she valued in herself. With this in mind, we began to explore and identify those situations or domains in which her perfectionism worked for her and when and how it might work against her. She became increasingly comfortable with this perspective and decided she wanted to continue to set high standards regarding her performance in mathematical coursework (which was a clear area of strength), but she did not need to be so demanding of herself regarding art or physical education. Her parents were very willing to adjust their expectations for Sharon because of their great concern for her, but over time it became clear that the parents were quite demanding of themselves. Eventually Sharon was able to identify this familial pattern and became comfortable with the notion that she could choose different expectations for herself than her parents had adopted for themselves.

A cognitive-behavioral program for treating school phobia has been described in Kendall, Howard and Epps (in press). This program incorporates components of previous treatments that have demonstrated effectiveness, including *in vivo* exposure, modeling, social reinforcement, coping-skills training and parental involvement. In addition, the program addresses the cognitions of the child and parent and includes problem-solving training to cope with the new situations that arise from the child's return to school (e.g., peer relations difficulties, needing to elicit help from teachers, conflicts over homework). This treatment package offers a promising approach to returning the school-phobic child to school and improving the quality of his or her functioning at school. However, it awaits empirical confirmation of its efficacy.

These cognitive-behavioral approaches to the treatment of internalizing disorders represent the field's beginning attempts to address these serious problems in children. It is our hope that the pursuits in this area will build on knowledge gained by the earlier efforts with more externalizing types of children.

KEY METHODS OF TRAINING DELIVERY

While the cognitive-behavioral interventions we have described differ from each other in emphasis, they do share the goal of altering the child's thoughts and thinking processes in ways that lead to behavioral and emotional changes. These therapies also share some of the methods through which the content of the treatment is delivered or trained. The training methods of modeling, role play, and use of behavioral contingencies deserve special attention because they are so widely used in interventions with children.

MODELING

Virtually all effective cognitive-behavioral interventions with children involve some form of active modeling as a means of conveying the coping methods the therapist wishes to train. The therapeutic use of modeling involves the exposure of the client to an individual who actually demonstrates the behaviors to be learned by the client. Modeling as an intervention in its own right has been demonstrated as effective in achieving the elimination of behavioral deficits, the reduction of excessive fears, and the facilitation of social behavior (see Bandura, 1969, 1971; Rosenthal & Bandura, 1978). As a component in cognitive-behavioral interventions, modeling has been presented in a number of different forms, including filmed modeling, graduated modeling, symbolic modeling, and participant modeling.

The phenomenon of modeling has received significant research attention. Several factors or dimensions that influence the effectiveness of modeling have been delineated and some of these have particular implications for the therapeutic use of modeling. Having the model talk out loud, verbalizing his or her own thoughts, has been demonstrated to produce superior results relative to a model who does not verbalize (Meichenbaum, 1971). It appears that as the model speaks, he or she provides the observer with a demonstration of how to think him- or herself through a particular problem or situation. Talking out loud while performing an action also provides the learner with auditory as well a visual cues for acquiring the new behavior.

Another factor with therapeutic implications is the distinction between mastery and coping models. A *mastery model* demonstrates successful task performance without indications of anxiety or difficulty. In contrast, the *coping model* may demonstrate task performance that includes some mistakes. A coping model may also demonstrate some anxiety or feelings of discomfort while approaching and accomplishing the task and yet be able to fulfill the task requirements with persistent effort. Data from a number of different researchers suggest that the coping model produces superior behavioral results relative to the mastery model (Kazdin, 1974; Meichenbaum, 1971; Sarason, 1975). It is hypothesized that the superior effects of the coping model arise from the fact that this model appears to be more similar to the client, who is also likely to face difficulties when attempting to execute a new behavior. The coping model not only shows the client how to execute this behavior but also demonstrates how this can be accomplished despite cognitive, emotional, and/or behavioral difficulties.

In addition to the formal modeling that takes place during the process of teaching the child various problem-solving or self-instructional strategies, many intervention programs also emphasize the role of informal modeling. Through informal modeling the therapist is able to demonstrate how one copes with various dilemmas that may arise during the course of conducting the therapy. For example, in the cognitive-behavioral program developed by the current authors (Kendall & Braswell, 1985) therapists are encouraged to model problem solving when facing dilemmas such as locating the right room for conducting the therapy, obtaining the necessary materials, handling situations involving the loss or absence of materials, and handling details such as scheduling, which may require coordination with the child, parents, and school. Such examples provide natural demonstrations of the problem-solving process.

ROLE PLAYING

Role-playing methods are used in almost all cognitive–behavioral intervention programs that focus on social or classroom behaviors. Through role-playing exercises, the cognitive-behavioral therapist provides the client with performance-based learning experiences. In addition to serving as a vehicle for training, role-playing exercises also provide a method of ongoing assessment of the extent to which the client is able to produce the newly learned skills, at least in the context of the therapy setting. In this way, the therapist can continually monitor the type of feedback the client requires and detect any gaps or incomplete behavioral information that has been provided to the client. Role plays typically involve the therapist and child; however, there is an increasing tendency to design interventions so that children can participate in role-playing situations with age-appropriate peers (Bloomquist & Braswell, 1987; Hinshaw, Henker, & Whalen, 1984a; Sarason & Sarason, 1981).

Another variation of role-playing techniques includes the use of videotaped role playing, so that the participants can receive auditory and visual feedback about their performance (Chandler, 1973; Sarason & Ganzer, 1973). Sarason and Ganzer found that the effectiveness of the type of feedback may be mediated by certain subject variables. Hypothesizing that high test-anxious delinquents would be upset by televised feedback of their role-playing performance, these investigators compared the behavioral outcomes of high anxiety subjects who received audiotape feedback versus those receiving televised feedback. In support of their hypothesis, only 1 of 15 high anxious subjects in the televised modeling group received positive behavior ratings, while 14 of 19 test-anxious subjects in the nontelevised group received positive ratings.

Some investigators have made special attempts to make the role-playing situations particularly realistic in their potential for emotional arousal. Goodwin and Mahoney (1975) used a technique called the circle game to train hyperactive boys to control their responses to the verbal taunts of others. This procedure involved having the child play a game in which each one in turn was verbally assaulted by the other subjects. The children were then exposed to a model who appeared to remain calm and demonstrated the use of a series of self-statements to cope with the verbal taunts. Repeated exposure to this model was alternated with practice at "playing" the circle game. Posttreatment observations of the game indicated improvement in the children's ability to remain calm while exposed to the taunts of others and observations of the boys in the classroom indicated a decrease in disruptive behavior. As was stated previously, this method was also found to be an effective vehicle for training by Hinshaw, Whalen, and Henker (1984a) in their work with attention-deficit disordered children. Indeed, the nonsupportive data reported recently by Abikoff and Gittelman (1985) in which cognitive training did not enhance medication effects with hyperactive children has been criticized by Kendall and Reber (1986) for failing to bring the children's actual problem situations into role-play sessions.

BEHAVIORAL CONTINGENCIES

Interventions for children that are viewed as cognitive-behavioral vary to a surprising degree in the extent to which actual behavioral contingencies are used to reinforce the learning of new cognitive and behavioral skills (see reviews by Kendall & Braswell, 1985, and Urbain & Kendall, 1980).

The cognitive-behavioral package developed and evaluated by the authors (Kendall & Braswell, 1982; Kendall & Wilcox, 1980; Kendall & Zupan, 1981) provides an example of how multiple behavioral contingencies can be applied with cognitive techniques such as self-instructional and problem-solving training. The specific contingencies included in this treatment package were general social rewards and self-rewarding self-statements, response cost for errors, rewarded performance on homework assignments, and rewarded accurate self-evaluation.

Therapists are encouraged to use socially rewarding phrases liberally throughout each therapy session. These phrases are recommended not only to provide the child with immediate feedback about his or her behavior but also as a means of setting a positive tone in the therapy session. Such social rewards could take the form of phrases such as "Good," or "Nice job" or any number of phrases that represent appropriate social rewards with children. Braswell, Kendall, Braith, Carey, and Vye (1985) analyzed the verbal behavior of therapists in the context of this type of intervention and found that statements of encouragement such as "Keep up the good work," or "I see you're really working hard at this," were associated with more positive child outcomes than were simply confirming statements such as "That's correct," or "Right." The child is also encouraged to use positively self-rewarding statements. In this particular intervention package, the final step of the self-instructional sequence requires the child to make a self-rewarding statement in recognition of positive task performance. If the child makes an error he or she is encouraged to make a coping statement such as "The next time I'll go more slowly. That will help me do a better job." The coping statement is included because children are expected to encounter challenges and they need to be prepared with cognitive controls to avoid acting out when frustrated.

Mild punishment in the form of a response-cost contingency that operated throughout all sessions is also used in this treatment package. With this type of contingency the child receives a given number of reward tokens at the beginning of each session and is instructed regarding how tokens can be lost for the commission of certain specific behaviors. In the treatment packages that have been formally evaluated, there were three reasons a child could lose a token, including failure to use the self-instructions, going too fast on the assigned task, or getting the wrong answer on a task. Thus, the response-cost contingency serves not as a serious negative consequence but as a cue to inhibit action, to help the child slow him- or herself down and to use the self-instructions appropriately. When the therapist enacts a response cost, the reason for the loss is clearly and calmly stated so that the child knows exactly what he or she must do to improve performance on the next task. At the end of each session, the child is given an opportunity to cash in some or all of his or her remaining tokens for a prize. The child has the choice of buying a small prize and saving some tokens toward the purchase of a larger prize or of spending all the tokens at the end of each session. While this contingency operates effectively with the majority of children we have treated, we have encountered a small number of kids who have significant emotional reactions to the response-cost contingencies. The reader is referred to Kendall and Braswell (1985) for a discussion of how to manage these cases.

The Kendall program does include other opportunities for children to earn bonus tokens by completing "homework assignments." In this particular treatment package, homework assignments involve having the child think of a situation in which he or she might have been able to use the self instructions in an extra-therapy situation and then be able to describe this situation to the therapist.

Opportunities to earn bonus rewards through accurate self-evaluation are included. At the end of each session, the therapist shows the child a simple 5-point rating scale that reflects how the child performed during that session. The therapist tells the child that the therapist will pick a number that he or she thinks best described the child during that session. The child is then asked to pick a number. If his or her number equals or is within 1 point of the therapist's rating, the child earns a bonus token or chip. Hinshaw, Whalen, and Henker (1984b) trained self-evaluation skills in the context of a comprehensive behavioral training program with attention-deficit disordered children and found that children engaging in reinforced self-evaluation of their social behavior were able to display more appropriate behavior in a free play setting relative to children receiving more traditional external reinforcement for appropriate social behavior. Stimulant medication was also found to increase the accuracy of children's self-evaluations. Self-evaluation coupled with self-monitoring has yielded improvement with cognitive and academic performance of attention deficit disordered children (see Abikoff, 1985 for a review).

Other investigators have combined cognitive techniques with explicit behavioral contingencies. Lochman et al. (1984) included behavioral contingencies by adding a goal-setting component to their anger-coping training program. This procedure involved having the child establish weekly behavioral goals with the help of the group. These goals were then monitored by the child's classroom teacher and contingent reinforcement followed appropriate goal attainment. The authors believe that the addition of the goal setting tended to augment the treatment effects in the classroom. Positive results, including generalization across tasks and settings, were obtained by Swanson (1985) who combined self-instructional training for academic deficit with a token program that rewarded accuracy and appropriate behavior.

It seems unfortunate that many otherwise well-designed and intensive intervention programs have failed to incorporate explicit behavioral procedures (e.g., Abikoff & Gittleman, 1985) as a means of motivating the child to learn new cognitive strategies, rewarding rehearsal of these strategies and reducing off-task behavior that can significantly interfere with learning and rehearsal.

CONTINUING CONCERNS

SUBJECT VARIABLES

Given the demonstration of some positive treatment effects across these various forms of cognitive-behavioral intervention, it becomes relevant to examine individual difference factors that may moderate treatment gains. The variables of age, type of the disorder, sex, cognitive level, socioeconomic status (SES), ethnicity, and attributional style have all been suggested as possible influences on outcome (Copeland, 1982). In a similar vein, Abikoff (1985) has emphasized the need for a comprehensive skills analysis of the child in order to understand if he or she possesses the necessary preskills for the particular intervention to be applied. Unfortunately, even though the client uniformity myth (Kiesler, 1966) is well recognized, journal articles still omit potentially interesting information regarding the effects of subject variables. Thus our conclusions must be based on relatively small bodies of information and be related to findings from other areas of inquiry. Our discussion will focus on two subject variables that we believe have important implications for treatment outcome: developmental level and attributional/expectational style.

Developmental Level

Children are not a homogeneous group. Indeed, the "developmental uniformity myth" (Kendall, 1984) is an unfortunate belief, since children differ in meaningful ways in terms of cognitive and physical development, peer and family status, and the nature of the behaviors that define competence and skill across the ages.

Cognitive-behavioral interventions have been applied with children ranging in age from preschool to adolescence, although the majority of the reported studies are with elementary-school-aged children. Consideration of the child's level of development facilitates proper assessment and intervention.

With regard to evaluating the normality or abnormality of behavior, one must consider the symptoms against a background of developmental norms. As indicated in earlier discussions, problem-solving abilities and capacities for verbal mediation of behavior are all considered developmental phenomena. Egocentrism and/or impulsivity in a 3- or 4-year-old child are considered normal and would not merit intervention in the vast majority of cases. For example, considering the Lurian developmental model from which self-instructional training was derived, one might not expect language-based self-control to fully appear in "normal" children before the age of 6. The inconsistent results of cognitive-behavioral interventions with preschoolers may be the product of attempting to intervene before the child is developmentally ready for or in need of the skills to be trained. It may be the case, however, that when parents identify the child's normal developmental status as problematic, then the parents may be in need of an educational intervention that would inform them about the child's cognitive and emotional development and help them formulate more age-appropriate expectations. Cognitive-behavioral parent training, an idea whose time has come, would incorporate such material into behavioral programs.

The implications of developmental level for how one might best intervene are somewhat predictable. Copeland (1982) concluded that a broad age range of children do appear to benefit from self-instructional training, but specified that younger children may require more structured and specific training than do older children. Pressley (1979) also discussed the need for more concrete training with younger children. Bender (1976) found specific strategy training more effective than a general type of training with a sample of impulsive 1st graders, and Kendall and Wilcox (1980) found conceptual training more effective than concrete training among non-self-controlled 8- to 12-year-olds. But Schleser *et al.* (1981) and Thackwray *et al.* (1985) found specific plus general self-statements to be the most effective treatment for improving task performance and obtaining cross-task generalization in an elementary-school-aged sample. If development is conceptualized in terms of Piagetian stages, Schleser *et al.* (1981) found that concrete operational children outperformed preoperational children on both training task and generalization assessments.

Attributional/Expectational Styles

While we have addressed attributions as the target for intervention, the child's attributional style may also be an important mediator of treatment effects. Kopel and Arkowitz (1975) suggested that a child's feelings of personal control might influence his or her responsiveness to any type of self-control intervention. Studies examining a child's attributional style or generalized expectations, such as locus of control, speak to this issue. Beliefs and expectancies regarding personal control have been found to differ for a number of populations. For example, blacks tend to be more external in their locus of control relative to whites (Battle & Rotter, 1963; Ramey & Campbell, 1976) and hyperactive, attentionally disordered children have been observed to be more external than peers when matched for sex, age, mental age, and SES (Linn & Hodge, 1982).

In a study of the role of expectations and the differential effectiveness of external versus internal monitoring, Bugental, Whalen, and Henker (1977) provided treatment for hyperactive and impulsive boys, half of whom were receiving methylphenidate. Treatment was conducted twice a week for 8 weeks, with the experimenter tutors utilizing either self-instructional training or contingent social reinforcement. Both interventions were aimed at increasing the child's attention and correct performance on academic tasks. The results indicated that children whose attributional styles were congruent with their treatment (high personal control/self-control training or high external control/social contingency management) achieved better Porteus scores than those in noncongruent combinations. Also, self-instructional training was more effective with nonmedicated children, while external control was superior with the medicated subjects. As Bugental *et al.* state, "change strategies (behavioral management, educational programs, psychotherapy, medical intervention) have implicit attributional textures which interact with the attributional network of the individual to influence treatment impact" (p. 881). Unfortunately, neither intervention produced changes on a teacher rating scale.

The Bugental *et al.* (1977) results are consistent with the findings from the learning research of Baron and Ganz (1972). These researchers administered the Intellectual Achievement Responsibility (IAR) scale (Crandall, Katkovsky, & Crandall, 1965) to 5th-grade lower-class black males. Subjects scoring in an internal or external direction then executed a simple discrimination task under one of three feedback conditions. In the external condition the experimenter provided correctness feedback, in the internal condition the child checked his own choices, and in the combined condition the child received both types of feedback. The combined feedback proved to be equally effective for both internally and externally oriented children, while internals made more correct choices than externals in the internal feedback condition. Children scoring as externals showed greater performance improvement in the external feedback condition than did the internals. Baron, Cowan, Ganz, and McDonald (1974) replicated these findings with lower-class white children. Thus, a subject's pretreatment level of internality versus externality may facilitate his or her responsiveness to interventions that have matching assumptions regarding the individual's control over his or her behavior. Braswell (1984) obtained results consistent with this contention in an evaluation of the effects of self-instructional training in a racially and economically diverse sample of children. Those children who obtained improvement on the teacher ratings of classroom behavior tended to be more internal in locus of control at pretest and were more likely to provide effort-oriented attributions for their own change at posttest.

In addition to predicting treatment response, research also suggests that one's attributional style or generalized expectancies may change as a result of treatment. In a 6-month follow-up of the Bugental *et al.* (1977) intervention, Bugental, Collins, Collins, and Chaney (1978) found that the self-instructional training group as a whole had increased their perceptions of personal control (become more internal) relative to the social reinforcement group. Teacher ratings, however, indicated that the social reinforcement group showed more improved classroom behavior. In this case, increasing internality did not seem to be associated with greater behavioral change, at least from the perspective of the classroom teacher. Dweck's (1975) study on reattribution training also suggests that a child's perception of personal control can be altered via intervention. Both Bugental et al. (1978) and Dweck (1975) provide examples of children becoming more internal in their perceptions of control, but, as previously stated, an exclusive focus on making children more internal may be a less desirable goal than helping children develop an appropriately flexible attributional system in which one's perceived sense of personal control matches the reality of one's current situation.

GENERALIZATION AND ITS ABSENCE

One cannot review this literature without becoming keenly aware that while short-term or specific gains are achieved in many studies, there is an overall lack of generalization of treatment effects across behavioral domains and settings and a lack of maintenance of effects across time. These limitations may seem particularly disappointing in light of the original expectations that cognitive-behavioral methods would improve upon traditional interventions and produce lasting and far-reaching effects.

With over 10 years of research activity, researchers and readers have to accept the fact that boundless generalization of treatment effects seems to be and perhaps will continue to be something of a pipedream. As Foster et al. (in press) have noted, while cognitive strategies may be more efficient to teach due to their broad applicability, they may not generalize more readily than behavioral skills. As ever, generalization of both cognitive strategies and behavioral skills is not a magical process, but it is a trainable goal. But how is generalization best trained? A number of authors (Bransford, 1979; Cohen & Schleser, 1984; Kendall, 1977) have offered consistent suggestions. One common thought is to have training sessions resemble potential generalization targets as much as possible. This similarity could occur on a variety of dimensions. Considering the training tasks, it is no longer common wisdom to assume that one can train a child on psychoeducational tasks and obtain changes in performance on classroom academic tasks and class behavior. Overlap between training tasks and generalization targets is necessary for obtaining optimal gains. Training in applying the new skills to a variety of tasks provides the child with opportunities to learn how the strategies can be adapted to an as yet unexperienced situation. As Cohen and Schleser (1984) suggest, such training would involve analyzing task similarities and differences and considering how the differences may affect strategy application.

Overlap or similarity in the social context of the intervention may also enhance generalization. Thus, if the goal of the intervention is to obtain improved peer behavior, it would seem wisest to conduct at least a portion of the intervention in a peer group context (see also Howard & Kendall, 1987). If generalization to home or school is desired, then the intervention could be planned to include parents and teachers. The outcome studies we have reviewed indicated that the inclusion of peers, teachers, and/or parents in the treatment process certainly does not guarantee success, but it may heighten one's probability of making the intervention have an impact.

The provision of treatments of longer duration, allowing the child to reach an adequate level of skill mastery, would enhance treatment generalization. Implicit in this suggestion is the recognition that children acquire skills at varying rates and, therefore, treatment length should be flexible enough to allow for such variation. Clinical application, as opposed to research programs, have followed flexible timetables and there is presently a need for the evaluation of this approach.

Discussions about lengthening treatments may not be popular in light of the changing nature of health care delivery and funding, for the emphasis in many sectors is on providing brief treatment. It must be acknowledged, however, that the process of acquiring a more reflective thinking style or changing one's mode of attributing causality is a developmental process, not an event (Mahoney & Nezworski, 1985). In fact, some investigators emphasize that the goal is to change underlying cognitive structures rather than discrete cognitive events, and while these structures are viewed as malleable, they are not as readily changed as discrete thoughts or behaviors (see Foster et al., in press; Ingram & Hollon, 1986; Kendall & Ingram, 1987).

As stated previously and elsewhere (e.g., Kendall, 1985), we can not overemphasize our concern that cognitive-behavioral therapists undermine their own potential for impact when they fail to include ongoing behavioral contingencies in their training. We risk letting newly trained skills suffer an early extinction when we fail to establish rewards for skill use in the child's natural settings. The assumption that the child's new reflective thinking will immediately result in natural rewards is another example of magical thinking on the part of the experimenter/therapist. We have engaged in this type of thinking and the design of some of our treatment studies attests to this fact. Some researchers are attempting to rectify this difficulty. For example, Deshler et al. (1981) included a component in which the subjects—learning-disabled adolescents—were trained in how to cue others to provide them with reinforcement for their strategy use. Bloomquist and Braswell (1987) have developed an experimental training program for attention deficit disordered children and their parents that includes training the parents to observe and reinforce their children's fledgling attempts to engage in reflective problem solving in the home setting. Reports of more cognitive-behavioral training programs in which the child returns to an environment that shapes the use of the cognitive skills would be welcome additions to the literature.

REFERENCES

Abikoff, H. (1985). Efficacy of cognitive training interventions in hyperactive children: A critical review. *Clinical Psychology Review, 5,* 479–512.

Abikoff, H., & Gittelman, R. (1985). Hyperactive children treated with stimulants: Is cognitive training a useful adjunct? *Archives of General Psychiatry, 42,* 953–961.

Achenbach, T. M. (1978). The Child Behavior Profile: I. Boys aged 6–11. *Journal of Consulting and Clinical Psychology, 46,* 478–488.

Achenbach, T. M., & Edelbrock, C. S. (1978). The classification of childhood psychopathology: A review and analysis of empirical efforts. *Psychological Bulletin, 85,* 1275–1301.

Andrews, G. R., & Debus, R. L. (1978). Persistence and the causal perception of failure: Modifying cognitive attributions. *Journal of Educational Psychology, 70,* 154–166.

Asarnow, J. R., & Callahan, J. W. (1985). Boys with poor adjustment problems: Social cognitive processes. *Journal of Consulting and Clinical Psychology, 53,* 80–87.

Bandura, A. (1969). *Principles of behavior modification.* New York: Holt, Rinehart & Winston.

Bandura, A. (1971). Psychotherapy based upon modeling procedures. In A. Bergin & S. Garfield (Eds.), *Handbook of psychotherapy and behavior change.* New York: Wiley.

Bandura, A. (1977). Self-efficacy: Toward a unifying theory of behavior change. *Psychological Review, 84,* 191–215.

Barling, J., & Snipelisky, B. (1983). Assessing the determinants of childrens' academic self-efficacy beliefs: A replication. *Cognitive Therapy and Research, 7,* 371–376.

Baron, R. M., Cowan, G., Ganz, R. L., & McDonald, M. (1974). Interaction of locus of control and type of performance feedback: Considerations of external validity. *Journal of Personality and Social Psychology, 30,* 285–292.

Baron, R. M., & Ganz, R. L. (1972). Effects of locus of control and type of performance of lower-class black children. *Journal of Personality and Social Psychology, 21,* 124–130.

Battle, E. S., & Rotter, J. (1963). Children's feelings of personal control as related to social class and ethnic groups. *Journal of Personality, 31,* 482–490.

Beck, A. T. (1976). Cognitive therapy and the emotional disorders. New York: International Universities Press.

Beck, A. T., Rush, A. J., Shaw, B. F., & Emery, G. (1979). *Cognitive therapy of depression.* New York: Guilford.

Bender, N. (1976). Self-verbalization versus tutor verbalization in modifying impulsivity. *Journal of Educational Psychology, 68,* 347–354.

Blechman, E., Olson, D., & Hellman, I. (1976). Stimulus control over family problem-solving behavior: The family contract game. *Behavior Therapy, 7,* 686–692.

Blechman, E., Olson, D., Schornagel, C., Halsdorf, M., & Turner, A. (1976). The family contract game: Technique and case study. *Journal of Consulting and Clinical Psychology, 44,* 449–455.

Bloomquist, M. L., & Braswell, L. (1987). *A comprehensive child and family intervention program for attention deficit disorder.* Unpublished manuscript, North Memorial Medical Center, Minneapolis.

Bransford, J. D. (1979). *Human cognition: Learning, understanding and remembering.* Belmont, CA: Wadsworth Publishing.

Braswell, L. (1984). Cognitive-behavioral therapy with an inner-city sample of non-self-controlled children. Unpublished doctoral dissertation, University of Minnesota, Minneapolis.

Braswell, L., Kendall, P. C., Braith, J., Carey, M. P., & Vye, C. S. (1985). "Involvement" in cognitive-behavioral therapy with children: Process and its relationship to outcome. *Cognitive Therapy and Research, 9*, 611–630.

Braswell, L., Koehler, C., & Kendall, P. C. (1985). Attributions and outcomes in child psychotherapy. *Journal of Social and Clinical Psychology, 3*, 458–465.

Brown, R. T., Borden, K. A., Wynne, M. E., Schleser, R., & Clingerman, S. R. (1986). Methylphenidate and cognitive therapy with ADD children: A methodological reconsideration. *Journal of Abnormal Child Psychology, 14*, 481–497.

Brown, R. T., Wynne, M. E., & Medenis, R. (1985). Methylphenidate and cognitive therapy: A comparison of treatment approaches with hyperactive boys. *Journal of Abnormal Child Psychology, 13*, 69–87.

Bugental, D. B., Collins, S., Collins, L., & Chaney, L. A. (1978). Attributional and behavioral changes following two behavior management interventions with hyperactive boys: A follow-up study. *Child Development, 49*, 247–250.

Bugental, D. B., Whalen, C. K., & Henker, B. (1977). Causal attribution of hyperactive children and motivational assumptions of two behavior-change approaches: Evidence for an interactionist position. *Child Development, 48*, 874–884.

Butkowsky, I. S., & Willows, D. M. (1980). Cognitive-motivational characteristics of children varying in reading ability: Evidence for learned helplessness in poor readers. *Journal of Educational Psychology, 72*, 408–422.

Chandler, M. (1973). Egocentrism and anti-social behavior: The assessment and training of social perspective-taking skills. *Developmental Psychology, 9*, 326–332.

Clifford, M. M. (1984). Thoughts on a theory of constructive failure. *Educational Psychology, 19*, 108–120.

Cohen, R., & Schleser, R. (1984). Cognitive development and clinical interventions. In A. W. Meyers & W. E. Craighead (Eds.), *Cognitive behavior therapy with children.* New York: Plenum.

Conners, C. K. (1969). A teacher rating scale for use in drug studies with children. *American Journal of Psychiatry, 126*, 884–888.

Copeland, A. P. (1982). Individual differences factors in children's self-management: Toward individualized treatments. In P. Karoly & F. H. Kanfer (Eds.), *Self-management and behavior change: From theory to practice.* New York: Pergamon.

Copeland, A. P. (1983). Children's talking to themselves: Its developmental significance, function and therapeutic promise. In P. C. Kendall (Ed.), *Advances in cognitive-behavioral research and therapy* (Vol. 2). New York: Academic Press.

Coyne, T., Meyers, A., & Clark, L. (1985, November). *Behavioral treatment for obese children: Does parental problem solving solve the problem?* Paper presented at the meeting of the Association for Advancement of Behavior Therapy, Houston.

Craighead, W. E. (1982). A brief clinical history of cognitive-behavioral therapy with children. *School Psychology Review, 11*, 5–13.

Craighead, W. E., Meyers, A. W., & Craighead, L. W. (1985). A conceptual model for cognitive-behavior therapy with children. *Journal of Abnormal Child Psychology, 13*, 331–342.

Crandall, V. C., Katkovsky, W., & Crandall, V. G. (1965). Children's beliefs in their own control of reinforcement in intellectual academic achievement situations. *Child Development, 36*, 91–109.

Davis, G. (1966). Current status of research and theory in human problem-solving. *Psychological Bulletin, 66*, 36–54.

Deshler, D. D., Alley, G. R., Warner, M. M., & Schumaker, J. B. (1981). Instructional practices for promoting skill acquisition and generalization in severely learning disabled adolescents. *Learning Disability Quarterly, 6*, 231–234.

Dobson, K. S., & Shaw, B. F. (1986). Cognitive assessment with major depressive disorders. *Cognitive Therapy and Research, 10*, 13–29.

Dodge, K. A., & Frame, C. L. (1982). Social cognitive biases and deficits in aggressive boys. *Child Development, 53*, 620–635.

Dodge, K. A., McClaskey, C. L., & Feldman, E. (1985). Situational approach to the assessment of social competence in children. *Journal of Consulting and Clinical Psychology, 53*, 344–353.

Douglas, V. I., Parry, P., Marton, P., & Garson, C. (1976). Assessment of a cognitive training program for hyperactive children. *Journal of Abnormal Child Psychology, 4*, 389–410.

Duncan, C. P. (1959). Recent research on human problem-solving. *Psychology Bulletin, 56*, 397–429.

Dweck, D. S. (1975). The role of expectations and attributions in the alteration of learned helplessness. *Journal of Personality and Social Psychology, 31*, 674–685.

Dweck, C. S., & Reppucci, D. (1973). Learned helplessness and reinforcement responsibility in children. *Journal of Personality and Social Psychology, 25*, 109–116.

D'Zurilla, T. (1986). *Problem-solving therapy*. New York: Springer.

D'Zurilla, T. J., & Goldfried, M. R. (1971). Problem-solving and behavior modification. *Journal of Abnormal Psychology, 78*, 107–126.

Ellis, A. (1970). *The essence of rational psychotherapy: A comprehensive approach to treatment*. New York: Institute for Rational Living.

Emery, G., Bedrosian, R., & Garber, J. (1983). Cognitive therapy with depressed children and adolescents. In D. P. Cantwell & G. A. Carlson (Eds.). *Affective disorders in childhood and adolescence: An update*. New York: Spectrum Publications.

Feldhusen, J., Houtz, J., & Ringenbach, S. (1972). The Purdue Elementary Problem-Solving Inventory. *Psychological Reports, 31*, 891–901.

Fincham, F. D. (1983). Clinical applications of attribution theory: Problems and prospects. In M. Hewstone (Ed.), *Attribution theory: Social and functional extensions*. Oxford: Blackwells.

Flavell, J. (1977). *Cognitive development*. New Jersey: Prentice Hall.

Foster, S. L., Kendall, P. C., & Guevremont, D. (in press). Cognitive and social learning theory and therapy. In J. Matson (Ed.), *Handbook of treatment approaches in childhood psychopathology*. New York: Plenum.

Fuchs, C. Z., & Rehm, L. P. (1977). A self-control behavior therapy program for depression. *Journal of Consulting and Clinical Psychology, 45*, 206–215.

Fuhrman, M. J., & Kendall, P. C. (1986). Cognitive tempo and behavioral adjustment in children. *Cognitive Therapy and Research, 10*, 45–50.

Genshaft, J. L., & Hirt, M. (1980). The effectiveness of self-instructional training to enhance math achievement in women. *Cognitive Therapy and Research, 4*, 91–97.

Goodwin, S., & Mahoney, M. J. (1975). Modification of aggression through modeling: An experimental probe. *Journal of Behavior Therapy and Experimental Psychiatry, 6*, 200–202.

Graham, S. (1983). The effect of self-instructional procedures on LD students' handwriting performance. *Learning Disability Quarterly, 6*, 231–234.

Graziano, A. M., & Mooney, K. C. (1980). Family self-control instructions for children's nighttime fear reduction. *Journal of Consulting and Clinical Psychology, 48*, 206–213.

Hains, A. A., & Ryan, E. B. (1983). The development of social cognitive processes among juvenile delinquents and nondelinquents peers. *Child Development, 54*, 1536–1544.

Haley, G. M. T., Fine, S., Marriage, K., Moretti, M. M., & Freeman, R. J. (1985). Cognitive bias and depression in psychiatrically disturbed children and adolescents. *Journal of Consulting and Clinical Psychology, 53*, 535–537.

Hall, R. J. (1979). *An information processing approach to the study of learning disabilities*. Unpublished doctoral dissertation, University of California, Los Angeles.

Hallahan, D. P., & Reeve, R. E. (1980). Selective attention and distractibility. In B. K. Keogh (Ed.), *Advances in special education: Basic constructs and theoretical orientations* (Vol. 1). Greenwich, CT: JAI Press.

Harris, K. R. (1985). Conceptual, methodological, and clinical issues in cognitive-behavioral assessment. *Journal of Abnormal Child Psychology, 13,* 373–390.

Harris, K. R. (1986). The effects of cognitive-behavior modification on private speech and task performance during problem solving among learning disabled and normally achieving children. *Journal of Abnormal Child Psychology, 14,* 63–67.

Harris, K. R., & Graham, S. (1985). Improving learning disabled students' composition skills: Self-control strategy training. *Learning Disabilities Quarterly, 8,* 27–36.

Hartup, W. W. (1983). Peer relations. In E. M. Hetherington (Ed.), Mussen's *Handbook of Child Psychology* (Vol. 4). New York: Wiley.

Hinshaw, S. P., Henker, B., & Whalen, C. K. (1984a). Self-control in hyperactive boys in anger-inducing situations: Effects of cognitive-behavioral training and of methylphenidate. *Journal of Abnormal Child Psychology, 12,* 55–77.

Hinshaw, S. P., Henker, B., & Whalen, C. K. (1984b). Cognitive-behavioral and pharmacologic interventions for hyperactive boys: Comparative and combined effects. *Journal of Consulting and Clinical Psychology, 52,* 739–749.

Hollon, S. D., Kendall, P. C., & Lumry, A. (1986). Specificity of depressotypic cognition in clinical depression. *Journal of Abnormal Psychology, 95,* 52–59.

Homatidis, S., & Konstantareas, M. M. (1981). Assessment of hyperactivity: Isolating measures of high discriminant validity. *Journal of Consulting and Clinical Psychology, 49,* 533–541.

Howard, B., & Kendall, P. C. (1987). *Child interventions: Having no peers?* Manuscript submitted for publication: Temple University, Philadelphia.

Hudson, L. M. (1978). On the coherence of role-taking abilities: An alternative to correlational analysis. *Child Development, 49,* 223–227.

Ingram, R. E., & Hollon, S. D. (1986). Information processing and the treatment of depression. In R. E. Ingram (Ed.), *Information processing approaches to clinical psychology.* New York: Academic Press.

Ingram, R., Kendall, P. C., Smith, J., Donnelly, C., & Ronan, K. (in press). Cognitive specificity in emotional distress. *Journal of Personality and Social Psychology.*

Jahoda, M. (1953). The meaning of psychological health. *Social Casework, 34,* 349–354.

Jarvis, P. E. (1968). Verbal control of sensory-motor performance: A test of Luria's hypothesis. *Human Development, 11,* 172–183.

Johnson, M. B. (1983). *Self-instruction and children's math problem-solving: A study of training, maintenance, and generalization.* Unpublished doctoral dissertation, University of Notre Dame, South Bend.

Kagan, J. (1966). Reflection-impulsivity: The generality and dynamics of conceptual tempo. *Journal of Abnormal Psychology, 71,* 17–24.

Kazdin, A. E. (1974). Covert modeling, model similarity, and reduction of avoidance behavior. *Behavior Therapy, 5,* 325–340.

Kazdin, A. E., Esveldt-Dawson, K., French, N. H., & Unis, A. S. (1987). Problem-solving skills training and relationship therapy in the treatment of antisocial child behavior. *Journal of Consulting and Clinical Psychology, 55,* 76–85.

Kendall, P. C. (1977). On the efficacious use of verbal self-instructional procedures with children. *Cognitive Therapy and Research, 1,* 331–341.

Kendall, P. C. (1981). One year follow-up of concrete versus conceptual cognitive-behavioral self-control training. *Journal of Consulting and Clinical Psychology, 49,* 748–749.

Kendall, P. C. (1982). Individual versus group cognitive-behavioral self-control training: One year follow-up. *Behavior Therapy, 13,* 241–247.

Kendall, P. C. (1984). Social cognition and problem solving: A developmental and child-clinical interface. In B. Gholson & T. L. Rosenthal (Eds.), *Application of cognitive-developmental theory*. New York: Academic Press.

Kendall, P. C. (1985). Toward a cognitive-behavioral model of child psychopathology and a critique of related interventions. *Journal of Abnormal Child Psychology, 13*, 357–372.

Kendall, P. C. (1986). Comments on Rubin and Krasnor: Solutions and problems in research on problem solving. In M. Perlmutter (Ed.), *Cognitive perspectives on children's social and behavioral development: The Minnesota symposium on child psychology* (Vol. 18). Hillsdale, NJ: Erlbaum.

Kendall, P. C., & Braswell, L. (1982). Cognitive-behavioral self-control therapy for children: A components analysis. *Journal of Consulting and Clinical Psychology, 50*, 672–689.

Kendall, P. C., & Braswell, L. (1985). *Cognitive-behavioral therapy for impulsive children*. New York: Guilford.

Kendall, P. C., & Finch, A. J., Jr. (1976). A cognitive-behavioral treatment for impulsivity: A case study. *Journal of Consulting and Clinical Psychology, 44*, 852–857.

Kendall, P. C., & Finch, A. J., Jr. (1978). A cognitive-behavioral treatment for impulsivity: A group comparison study. *Journal of Consulting and Clinical Psychology, 46*, 110–118.

Kendall, P. C., & Fischler, G. L. (1984). Behavioral and adjustment correlates of problem-solving: Validational analyses of interpersonal cognitive problem-solving measures. *Child Development, 55*, 879–892.

Kendall, P. C., & Hollon, S. D. (Eds.). (1979). *Cognitive-behavioral interventions: Theory, research and procedures*. New York: Academic Press.

Kendall, P. C., Howard, B., & Epps, J. (in press). The anxious child: Cognitive–behavioral strategies. *Behavior Modification*.

Kendall, P. C., & Ingram, R. (1987). The future of cognitive assessment of anxiety: Let's get specific. In L. Michelson & M. Ascher (Eds.), *Anxiety and Stress Disorders: Cognitive-Behavioral Assessment and Treatment*. New York: Guilford Press.

Kendall, P. C., Pellegrini, D., & Urbain, E. S. (1981). Approaches to assessment for cognitive-behavioral interventions with children. In P. C. Kendall & S. D. Hollon (Eds.), *Assessment strategies for cognitive-behavioral interventions*. New York: Academic Press.

Kendall, P. C., & Reber, M. (1987). Cognitive training in treatment of hyperactive children. *Archives of General Psychiatry, 44*, 296.

Kendall, P. C., & Wilcox, L. E. (1979). Self-control in children: Development of a rating scale. *Journal of Consulting and Clinical Psychology, 47*, 1020–1029.

Kendall, P. C., & Wilcox, L. E. (1980). A cognitive-behavioral treatment for impulsivity: Concrete versus conceptual training in non-self-controlled problem children. *Journal of Consulting and Clinical Psychology, 48*, 80–91.

Kendall, P. C., & Williams, C. L. (1986). Adolescent therapy: Treating the "marginal man." *Behavior Therapy, 17*, 522–537.

Kendall, P. C., & Zupan, B. A. (1981). Individual versus group application of cognitive behavioral strategies for developing self-control in children. *Behavior Therapy, 12*, 344–359.

Kendall, P. C., Zupan, B. A., & Braswell, L. (1981). Self-control in children: Further analyses of the Self Control Rating Scale. *Behavior Therapy, 12*, 667–681.

Keyser, V., & Barling, J. (1981). Determinants of children's self-efficacy beliefs in an academic environment. *Cognitive Therapy and Research, 5*, 29–40.

Kiesler, D. J. (1966). Some myths of psychotherapy research and the search for a paradigm. *Psychological Bulletin, 65*, 110–136.

Kirmil-Gray, K., Dockham-Shoor, L., & Thoresen, C. R. (1980, November). *The effects of self-control instruction and behavior management training on the academic and social behavior of hyperactive children*. Paper presented at the meeting of the Association for Advancement of Behavior Therapy, New York.

Kopel, S., & Arkowitz, H. (1975). The role of attribution and self-perception in behavior change: Implications for behavior therapy. *Genetic Psychology Monographs, 92,* 175-212.

Kosiewicz, M. M., Hallahan, D. P., Lloyd, J. W., & Graves, A. W. (1982). Effects of self-instruction and self-correction procedures on handwriting performance. *Learning Disability Quarterly, 5,* 71-78.

Krasnor, L. R., & Rubin, K. H. (1983). Preschool social problem-solving: Attempts and outcomes in naturalistic interaction. *Child Development, 54,* 1545-1558.

Larcen, S., Spivack, G., & Shure, M. B. (1972, August). Problem-solving thinking and adjustment among dependent-neglected preadolescents. Paper presented at the meeting of the American Psychological Association, San Francisco.

Leon, J. A., & Pepe, H. J. (1983). Self-instructional training: Cognitive behavior modification for remediating arithmetic deficits. *Exceptional Children, 50,* 54-60.

Lewinsohn, P. M. (1974). A behavioral approach to depression. In R. M. Friedman & M. M. Katz (Eds.), *The psychology of depression: Contemporary theory and research.* New York: Wiley.

Linn, R. T., & Hodge, G. K. (1982). Locus of control in childhood hyperactivity. *Journal o Consulting and Clinical Psychology, 50,* 592-593.

Lochman, J. E., Burch, P. R., Curry, J. F., & Lampron, L. B. (1984). Treatment and generaliza tion effects of cognitive-behavioral and goal-setting interventions with aggressive boys *Journal of Consulting and Clinical Psychology, 52,* 915-916.

Lochman, J. E., & Curry, J. F. (1986). Effects of social problem-solving training and self instruction training with aggressive boys. *Journal of Clinical Child Psychology, 15,* 159 164.

Lochman, J. E., Nelson, W. M. III, & Sims, J. P. (1981). A cognitive behavioral program for us with aggressive children. *Journal of Clinical Child Psychology, 10,* 146-148.

Luria, A. R. (1959). The directive function of speech in development and dissolution. *Word, 15* 341-352.

Luria, A. R. (1961). *The role of speech in the regulation of normal and abnormal behavior.* New York: Liveright.

Mahoney, M. J. (1977). Reflections in the cognitive-learning trend in psychotherapy. *America Psychologist, 32,* 5-18.

Mahoney, M. J., & Nezworski, M. T. (1985). Cognitive-behavioral approaches to children problems. *Journal of Abnormal Child Psychology, 13,* 467-476.

Meichenbaum, D. (1971). Examination of model characteristics in reducing avoidance behav ior. *Journal of Personality and Social Psychology, 17,* 298-307.

Meichenbaum, D. (1979). Teaching children self-control. In B. B. Lahay & A. E. Kazdin (Eds Advances in Clinical Child Psychology, (Vol. 2, pp. 1-33). New York: Plenum.

Meichenbaum, D., & Goodman, J. (1971). Training impulsive children to talk to themselves: means of developing self-control. *Journal of Abnormal Psychology, 77,* 115-126.

Miller, S. A., Shelton, J., & Flavell, J. H. (1970). A test of Luria's hypothesis concerning t development of verbal self-regulation. *Child Development, 41,* 651-665.

Mischel, W. (1974). Processes in delay of gratification. In L. Berkowitz (Ed.), *Advances Experimental Social Psychology* (Vol. 7). New York: Academic Press.

Mischel, W., & Patterson, C. J. (1976). Substantive and structural elements of effective plans : self-control. *Journal of Personality and Social Psychology, 34,* 942-950.

Monohan, J., & O'Leary, K. D. (1971). Effects of self-instruction in rule-breaking behavi *Psychological Reports, 29,* 1051-1066.

Nelson, W., & Birkimer, J. C. (1978). Role of self-instruction and self-reinforcement in modification of impulsivity. *Journal of Consulting and Clinical Psychology, 46,* 18?

O'Leary, K. D. (1968). The effects of self-instruction on immoral behavior. *Journal of Expe mental Child Psychology, 6,* 297-301.

Palkes, H., Stewart, M., & Kahana, B. (1968). Porteus maze performance of hyperactive boys after training in self-directed verbal commands. *Child Development, 39*, 817–826.

Patterson, B. C., & Mischel, W. (1976). Effects of temptation-inhibiting and task-facilitating plans on self-control. *Journal of Personality and Social Psychology, 33*, 207–217.

Pearl, R. (1985). Cognitive-behavioral interventions for increasing motivation. *Journal of Abnormal Child Psychology, 13*, 443–454.

Peterson, L., & Shigetomi, C. (1981). The use of coping techniques to minimize anxiety in hospitalized children. *Behavior Therapy, 12*, 1–14.

Piaget, J. S. (1926). *The language and thought of the child.* New York: Harcourt-Brace.

Platt, J. J., & Spivack, G. (1972). Problem-solving thinking of psychiatric patients. *Journal of Consulting and Clinical Psychology, 39*, 148–151.

Platt, J. J., Spivack, G., Altman, N., Altman, D., & Peizer, S. B. (1974). Adolescent problem-solving thinking. *Journal of Consulting and Clinical Psychology, 42*, 787–793.

Porteus, S. D. (1955). *The maze test: Recent advances.* Palo Alto, CA: Pacific Books.

Pressley, M. (1979). Increasing children's self-control through cognitive interventions. *Review of Educational Research, 49*, 319–370.

Ramey, C. T., & Campbell, F. (1976). Parental attitudes and poverty. *Journal of Genetic Psychology, 120*, 3–6.

Reeve, R. A., & Brown, A. L. (1985). Meta-cognition reconsidered: Implications for intervention research. *Journal of Abnormal Child Psychology, 13*, 343–356.

Richard, B. A., & Dodge, K. A. (1982). School maladjustment and problem-solving in school-aged children. *Journal of Consulting and Clinical Psychology, 50*, 226–233.

Rickel, A. V., & Burgio, J. C. (1982). Assessing social competencies in lower-income preschool children. *American Journal of Community Psychology, 10*, 635–645.

Rickel, A. V., Eshelman, A. K., & Loigman, G. A. (1983). Social problem-solving training: A follow-up study of cognitive and behavioral effects. *Journal of Abnormal Child Psychology, 11*, 15–28.

Roberts, R. N., & Nelson, R. O. (1984). Assessment issues and strategies in cognitive-behavior therapy with children. In A. W. Meyers & W. E. Craighead (Eds.), *Cognitive behavior therapy with children* (pp. 99–128). New York: Plenum.

Robin, A. L., Armel, S., & O'Leary, K. D. (1975). The effects of self-instruction on writing deficiencies. *Behavior Therapy, 6*, 178–187.

Robin, A. L., Fischel, J. E., & Brown, K. E. (1984). *Validation of a measure of children's self-control.* Paper presented at the meeting of the Association for Advancement of Behavior Therapy, Toronto.

Robin, A. L., Kent, R., O'Leary, K. D., Foster, S., & Prinz, R. (1977). An approach to teaching parents and adolescents problem-solving communication skills: A preliminary report. *Behavior Therapy, 8*, 639–643.

Robin, A. L., & Schneider, M. (1974). *The turtle-technique: An approach to self-control in the classroom.* Unpublished manuscript, State University of New York, Stony Brook.

Robin, A. L., Schneider, M., & Dolnick, M. (1976). The turtle technique: An extended case study of self-control in the classroom. *Psychology in the Schools, 13*, 449–453.

Rosenthal, T., & Bandura, A. (1978). Psychological model: Theory and practice. In S. L. Garfield & A. E. Bergin (Eds.), *Handbook of psychotherapy and behavior change* (2nd ed.). New York: Wiley.

Sarason, I. G. (1968). Verbal learning modeling and juvenile delinquency. *American Psychologist, 23*, 254–266.

Sarason, I. G. (1975). Test anxiety and the self-disclosing model. *Journal of Consulting and Clinical Psychology, 43*, 148–153.

Sarason, I. G., & Ganzer, V. J. (1973). Modeling and group discussion in the rehabilitation of juvenile delinquents. *Journal of Counseling Psychology, 20*, 442–449.

Sarason, I. G., & Sarason, B. R. (1981). Teaching cognitive and social skills to high school students. *Journal of Consulting and Clinical Psychology, 49*, 908–918.

Scardamalia, M., Bereiter, C., & Steinbach, R. (1984). Teachability of reflective processes in written composition. *Cognitive Science, 8*, 173–190.

Schleser, R., Meyers, A., & Cohen, R. (1981). Generalization of self-instructions: Effects of general versus specific content, active rehearsal, and cognitive level. *Child Development, 52*, 335–340.

Schneider, M., & Robin, A. L. (1976). The turtle technique: A method for the self-control of impulsive behavior. In J. D. Krumboltz & C. E. Thoresen (Eds.), *Counseling Methods.* New York: Holt, Rinehart & Winston.

Schunk, P. H. (1983). Ability versus effort attributional feedback: Differential effects on self-efficacy and achievement. *Journal of Educational Psychology, 75*, 848–856.

Seligman, M. E. P., Peterson, C., Alloy, L., Abramson, L. Y., Kaslow, N. J., Tanenbaum, R. L., Kaysf, S., Semmel, A., Tolman, M., & von Baeyer, C. (1982). *Depressive symptoms, attributional style, and helplessness deficits in children.* Unpublished manuscript, University of Pennsylvania, Philadelphia.

Selman, R. L. (1980). *The growth of interpersonal understanding: Developmental and clinical analyses.* New York: Academic Press.

Selman, R. L., & Byrne, D. A. (1974). A structural developmental analysis of levels of role-taking in middle childhood. *Child Development, 45*, 803–806.

Shantz, C. V. (1975). The development of social cognition. In E. M. Hetherington (Ed.), *Review of child development and research* (Vol. 5). Chicago: University of Chicago Press.

Short, E. J., & Ryan, E. B. (1984). Metacognitive differences between skilled and less skilled readers: Remediating deficits through story grammar and attribution training. *Journal of Educational Psychology, 76*, 225–235.

Shure, M. B., & Spivack, G. (1972). Means–end thinking, adjustment and social class among elementary school-aged children. *Journal of Consulting and Clinical Psychology, 38*, 348–353.

Shure, M. B., & Spivack, G. (1978). *Problem-solving techniques in childrearing.* San Francisco: Jossey-Bass.

Spivack, G., Platt, J. J., & Shure, M. B. (1976). *The problem-solving approach to adjustment.* San Francisco: Jossey-Bass.

Spivack, G., & Shure, M. B. (1974). *Social adjustment of young children: A cognitive approach to solving real-life problems.* San Francisco: Jossey-Bass.

Stark, K. D., Kaslow, N. J., & Reynolds, W. M. (1985). *A comparison of the relative efficacy of self-control and behavior therapy for the reduction of depression in children.* Paper presented at the Fourth National Conference on the Clinical Application of Cognitive Behavior Therapy, Honolulu.

Swanson, H. L. (1985). Effects of cognitive-behavioral training on emotionally disturbed children's academic performance. *Cognitive Therapy and Research, 9*, 201–216.

Thackwray, D., Meyers, A., Schleser, R., & Cohen, R. (1985). Achieving generalization with general versus specific self-instructions: Effects on academically deficient children. *Cognitive Therapy and Research, 9*, 297–308.

Torgeson, J. K., & Kail, R. V. (1980). Memory process in exceptional children. In B. K. Keogh (Ed.) *Advances in special education: Basic constructs and theoretical orientations* (Vol. 1). Greenwich, CT: JAI Press.

Urbain, E. S., & Kendall, P. C. (1980). Review of social-cognitive problem-solving interventions with children. *Psychological Bulletin, 88*, 109–143.

Vygotsky, L. (1962). *Thought and language.* New York: Wiley.

Weiner, B. (1979). A theory of motivation of some classroom experiences. *Journal of Educational Psychology, 71*, 3–25.

Weisz, J. R. (1979). Perceived control and learned helplessness among mentally retarded and nonretarded children: A developmental analysis. *Developmental Psychology, 15*, 311–319.

Whitman, T., Burgio, L., & Johnston, M. B. (1984). Cognitive-behavioral intervention with mentally retarded children. In A. W. Meyers & W. E. Craighead (Eds.), *Cognitive behavior therapy with children* (pp. 193–227). New York: Plenum.

Wong, B. Y. L. (1985). Issues in cognitive-behavioral interventions in academic skill areas. *Journal of Abnormal Child Psychology, 13*, 425–442.

Zakraski, R. S. (1982). *Effects of context and training in the generalization of a cognitive strategy by normally achieving and learning disabled boys.* (Unpublished doctoral dissertation, University of Virginia, Richmond)

Zatz, S., & Chassin, L. (1983). Cognitions of test anxious children. *Journal of Consulting and Clinical Psychology, 51*, 526–534.

Zatz, S., & Chassin, L. (1985). Cognitions of test anxious children under naturalistic test-taking conditions. *Journal of Consulting and Clinical Psychology, 53*, 393–401.

Zivin, G. (1979). *The development of self-regulation through private speech.* New York: Wiley.

Reading 5
Cognitive-Behavioral Treatment of Personality Disorders in Childhood and Adolescents

Safran, J. D., & McMain, S. (1992). A cognitive-interpersonal approach to the treatment of personality disorders. *Journal of Cognitive Psychotherapy: An International Quarterly*, 6, 59–68.

Simon, K. M. (1983, August). *Cognitive therapy with compulsive patients: Replacing rigidity with structure.* Paper presented at the annual meeting of the American Psychological Assoiation, Anaheim, CA.

Stravynski, A., Marks, I., & Yule, W. (1982). Social skills problems in neurotic outpatients: Social skills training with and without cognitive modification. *Archives of General Psychiatry*, 39, 1378–1385.

Stephens, J. H., & Parks, S. L. (1981). Behavior therapy of personality disorders. In J. R. Lion (Ed.), *Personality disorders: Diagnosis and management* (2nd ed.). Baltimore: Williams & Wilkins.

Turkat, I. D., & Maisto, S. A. (1985). Personality disorders: Application of the experimental method to the formulation and modification of personality disorders. In D. H. Barlow (Ed.), *Clinical handbook of psychological disorders: A step by step treatment manual.* New York: Guilford Press.

Vallis, T. M., Howes, J. L., & Standage, K. (2000). Is cognitive therapy suitable for treating individuals with personality dysfunction? *Cognitive Therapy and Research*, 24, 595–606.

Veen, G., & Arntz, A. (2000). Multidimensional dichotomous thinking characterizes borderline personality disorder. *Cognitive Therapy and Research*, 24, 23–45.

Woody, G. E., McLellan, A. T., Luborsky, L., & O'Brien, C. P. (1985) Sociopathy and psychotherapy outcome. *Archives of General Psychiatry*, 42, 1081–1086.

Young, J. (1990). *Cognitive therapy for personality disorders: A schema-focused approach.* Sarasota, FL: Professional Resource Exchange.

Young, J., Klosko, J., & Weishaar, M. (2003). *Schema therapy: A practitioner's guide.* New York: Guilford Press.

Young, J., & Lindemann, M. D. (1992). An integrative schema-focused model for personality disorders. *Journal of Cognitive Psychotherapy: An International Quarterly*, 6, 11–24.

Young, J. E. (1983, August). *Borderline personality: Cognitive theory and treatment.* Paper presented at the annual meeting of the American Psychological Association, Anaheim, CA.

Chapter 15

Cognitive-Behavioral Treatment of Personality Disorders in Childhood and Adolescence

ARTHUR FREEMAN

The very title of this chapter raises discomfort and disagreement among clinicians. Can a child or adolescent have a personality disorder? What qualifies a child for a diagnosis of a personality disorder? Clinicians are often left in a confusing position. Child psychologists, child psychiatrists, classroom teachers, pediatricians, child care workers, and clinicians working in acute treatment and residential settings regularly see children and adolescents who meet criteria for personality disorders (Beren, 1998; Bleiberg, 2001; Kernberg, Weiner, & Bardenstein, 2001; Shapiro, 1997; Vela, Gottlieb, & Gottlieb, 1997; Freeman & Rigby, 2003). But can clinicians apply these "adult" diagnoses to this small, but visible group of children? What are the advantages and disadvantages of using these diagnoses for children and adolescents? What are the ramifications (in terms of placement, treatment, and politics) of using personality disorder diagnoses for children and adolescents? And, finally, does using these "adult" diagnoses have the effect of creating a "trash can" category that will be used for the most troubling and troubled of children or adolescents?

Bearing these questions in mind, I contend in this chapter that personality disorders can be manifested and identified among youth prior to age 18. These disorders can be diagnosed with the same criteria used for adults. Rather than trying to find euphemistic terms, titles, or diagnoses, or seeing the identified patterns as clinical precursors to the adult disorders, I believe that the clinical reality of personality disorders in childhood must be appropriately assessed, diagnosed, and treated. Although many would agree that some youngsters have certain traits that may be precursors to later personality disorders, most contemporary clinicians are loath to diagnose a child as having a personality disorder (Paris, 2003). Some reasons for this hesitance are theoretical, some conceptual, and some "legal."

The goal of this chapter is to extend Aaron T. Beck's pioneering work in applying cognitive therapy to the treatment of personality disorders (Beck, Freeman, & Associates, 1990; Beck, Freeman, Davis, & Associates, 2004) and to examine the premise and the diagnosis of personality disorders in children and adolescents. I hope to do this by raising and discussing the conceptual, theoretical, and "legal" issues. These are followed by a discussion of the cognitive-behavioral conceptualization and directions for future study.

Several questions emerge. At what point are the behaviors of children or adolescents seen and diagnosed as personality-disordered? At what point do they move from "precursor" or antecedent behaviors (Paris, 2003) to being diagnosable as fully meeting the criteria for personality disorders? When do traits and styles of responding become diagnosed as pathology? At what point should the mental health community step in and attempt to challenge or to modify the noted behaviors? Are there issues present that require the inclusion of the criminal justice system or the child protective systems into the treatment plan? At what point do troubled or troubling children get diagnosed as having personality disorders?

The most frequent answer to these questions is that children cannot be "legally" diagnosed as having a personality disorder, according to the fourth edition (text revision) of the *Diagnostic and Statistical Manual of Mental Disorders* (DSM-IV-TR; American Psychiatric Association, 2000). The rationale for this position comes from an interpretation of the prototypical DSM-IV TR (APA, 2000) introduction in to all of the criteria sets for the personality disorders. The introduction states that each personality disorder involves "a pervasive pattern of [descriptive statements], beginning by early adulthood and present in a variety of contexts," as indicated by [a number] or more of the following [criteria listing]." Without any further reading, this repeated statement gives the impression that personality disorders are manifestations of behavior, affect, and cognition that arise and can only be diagnosed beginning in the early adult years (which generally mean 18 years and up).

Clearly, however, the introduction states that the disorders are in place "by early adulthood" rather than "in early adulthood." The reader might

be inclined to see this as a piece of Talmudic *pilpul*.[1] Nevertheless, the term "personality disorder" implies an enduring pattern whose beginnings can, at the very least, be traced back to adolescence, and often to childhood. The one exception noted in DSM-IV-TR is the diagnosis of antisocial personality disorder, where a history of conduct disorder in childhood and adolescence is required (APA, 2000, p. 706). DSM-IV-TR states, "The features of a personality disorder usually become recognizable during *adolescence* or early adult life" (APA, 2000, p. 688; emphasis added).

DSM-IV TR (APA, 2000) also offers six broad criteria for defining a personality disorder. These six essential features of a personality disorder are as follows:

An enduring pattern of inner experience and behavior that deviates markedly from the expectations of the individual's culture and is manifested in at least two of the following areas: cognition, affectivity, interpersonal functioning, or impulse control (Criterion A). This enduring pattern is inflexible and pervasive across a broad range of personal and social situations (Criterion B) and leads to clinically significant distress or impairment in social, occupational, or other important areas of functioning (Criterion C). The pattern is stable and of long duration, and its onset can be traced back at least to adolescence or early adulthood (Criterion D). The pattern is not better accounted for as a manifestation or consequence of another mental disorder (Criterion E) and is not due to the direct physiological effects of a substance (e.g., a drug of abuse, a medication, exposure to a toxin) or a general medical condition (e.g., head trauma) (Criterion F). (p. 686)

According to these criteria, children can easily be diagnosed as having personality disorders. The patterns of behavioral disorders described in children are exhibited in a wide range of social, school, and interpersonal contexts. They are not better accounted for by another disorder on Axis I, III, or IV, or by some developmental stage. An arguable point is that a personality pattern must be stable and of long duration. If the pattern has been in place for 2 or 3 years, does that qualify as accounting for a "significant duration"? If we think of a 10-year-old child, then 2 years is 20% of his or her life, and therefore can be quite significant in terms of its chronic impact on the child's life. Finally, the patterns are not the result of some chemical or toxic reaction. Furthermore, DSM-IV-TR states:

Personality Disorder categories may be applied to children or adolescents in those relatively unusual instances in which the individual's particular

[1]*Pilpul* describes a method of reasoning and text understanding that involves the careful reading and interpretation of content, context, placement, order, and choice of language.

maladaptive personality traits appear to be pervasive, persistent, and unlikely to be limited to a particular developmental stage or an episode of an Axis I disorder. It should be recognized that the traits of a Personality Disorder that appear in childhood will often not persist unchanged into adult life. To diagnose a Personality Disorder in an individual under age 18 years, the features must have been present for at least 1 year. The one exception to this is Antisocial Personality Disorder, which cannot be diagnosed in individuals under age 18 years. (APA, 2000, p. 687).

Probably the easiest markers for understanding and identifying personality disorders are that the behaviors are inflexible (i.e., the individual seems to have little choice in his or her response style), compulsive (i.e., the individual will almost always respond in the same idiosyncratic way, even when he or she sees and understands that the behavioral choice may have negative consequences), and maladaptive (i.e., the behaviors may serve to get the individual into trouble), and that they cause significant functional impairment (i.e., the individual's adaptive function is limited or impaired) and subjective distress (i.e., the individual experiences marked and frequent discomfort).

Ideally, be mounted for maximizing the value of therapy by addressing behaviors before they have become more powerfully and frequently reinforced and habituated. For instance, I think that would be far better to address a clearly identified case of early borderline personality disorder in a 12-year-old child than when the same individual seeks therapy as a 25-year-old adult. The 13 years in which the problem is not treated, treated tangentially, or treated as some euphemistic precursor to borderline personality disorder will not serve the child. The behavioral, cognitive, and affective style will, in the 13-year period, become more firmly entrenched and habituated. It would make much better sense to treat the disorder as the disorder. Essentially, if it looks like a duck, walks like a duck, and quacks like a duck, it would make sense to call the animal a duck.

The behavioral characteristics that are used to define personality disorders in adults must also be distinguished from characteristics that are part of normal and predictable developmental patterns for children. Or behavioral patterns may emerge in response to specific situational or developmental factors. For example, the clinging and dependent behavior seen in a 3- or 4-year-old may be developmentally appropriate and should not then be used as diagnostic signs of a dependent personality. I am not suggesting that every behavioral pattern seen in childhood is fully, or even in part, a personality disorder. Nor am I positing that every pattern in childhood will persist into the adult years and eventually become a personality disorder.

MALADAPTIVE VISIBILITY

Behaviors may be seen by an objective observer to be strange or unusual when those behaviors are judged by the standards of the larger community or group. Of course, the characteristics that may meet criteria for a personality disorder may not be considered problematic by the identified child or the child's family, despite these behaviors' appearing to an objective observer to be self-defeating, self-injurious, or self- or other-punitive. The observed individual, or the members of that individual's family group or cultural subgroup, may be unperturbed by, sanguine about, or nonobservant of those same behaviors. For the family or cultural subgroup, the identified behaviors may be seen as acceptable and even laudable. Obviously, judgments about personality functioning must take into account the individual's cultural and psychosocial background. When clinicians are evaluating children from a background different from their own, it would be essential to obtain additional information from informants who are familiar with the children's sociocultural history, background, and experience.

Making the diagnostic process even more complex is the fact that under some circumstances, the behaviors that are diagnosed as a personality disorder in an adult individual may have been quite functional and strongly reinforced during that individual's childhood or adolescence. The patterns that are later used to establish a diagnosis of personality disorder may, during the childhood years, have had value and purpose that began to wear away as the child moved into the adult years. A personality style may move to disorder or be exacerbated following the loss of significant supporting persons (e.g., the death of a parent) or previously stabilizing social situations (e.g., changing schools, moving homes). It is not always the case that children with unusual behaviors go through school unnoticed. Olin et al. (1997) found that teacher ratings of adolescents subsequently diagnosed as having schizotypal personality disorder indicated observable analogues of the adult disorder in late childhood or early adolescence. Wolff, Townshend, McGuire, and Weeks (1991) found that of 32 children described as having schizoid personality in childhood, three-quarters later met DSM criteria for schizotypal personality disorder. In fact, some of these patterns may be apparent by the end of preschool, between ages 4 and 6 (National Advisory Mental Health Council, 1995).

For example, the child who is diagnosed by teachers as having a conduct disorder, and who resists authorities and terrorizes his peers, may be seen by his parents or others in their culture as a "real boy" or a "kid who doesn't take shit from anyone." The question is whether the aggression is isolated, occasional, and episodic, or whether it meets DSM-IV-TR criteria and is part of a pervasive pattern. If it is not pervasive, the DSM code V71.02 ("child or adolescent antisocial behavior") might be used.

ARGUMENTS AGAINST DIAGNOSING PERSONALITY DISORDERS IN CHILDHOOD

The argument can be made that children below the age of 18 years cannot, by definition, have a personality disorder. This argument posits that in childhood the personality is still forming, and that to label it as "disordered" gives the impression that the personality of the child is fully formed, fixed, and encased in stone. I would respond to this argument by pointing out that the age of 18 as the entry point to adulthood is not typical of all cultures. In certain cultures, the age at which children reach their majority may be as low as 13. It is at that point that the child may be married, begin bearing children, and have adult responsibilities

A second argument against diagnosing personality disorders in childhood is that personality is in a constant and rapid state of an individual's development throughout the developmental years. To take a "snapshot" of behavior at any point in those years and use that picture to draw conclusions gives an inaccurate view of the individual. These patterns may (and probably will) change. My response to this criticism is that *all* diagnoses are conditional, and can and should be revised as clinicians obtain additional data.

A third argument against using personality disorder diagnoses for children and adolescents has to do with the diagnosis or label "personality disorder."

Simply stated, the diagnosis of a personality disorder for a child may have the effect of therapists' and teachers' quickly giving up on the child without trying to help. An extension of this point is that the diagnosis will follow that child throughout his or her school years and may be used as an excuse for limiting or even withholding treatment. I would in fact agree with this argument, inasmuch as diagnoses in a child's record will be viewed, for good or ill, throughout the child's school career and possibly beyond. Indeed, I am very concerned that the acceptance of the present thesis of childhood personality disorders will result in malpractice among therapists, teachers, and institutions.

A fourth concern, and an extension of the point noted above, is that the personality disorder diagnosis will be applied inappropriately to socially or culturally different groups. It would then become an easy way for individual therapists or entire systems and institutions not to treat minority group children. Here again, I am very concerned that the diagnosis will be too quickly and inappropriately applied. If adults choose to "give up" on a child because the child has been diagnosed with a personality disorder, we will all have a very serious problem. In point of fact, however, the children who do qualify for such diagnoses are the ones who need to be identified, so that they can receive the best and most appropriate care. If doing this be-

comes a "copout" for therapists, then it is more a problem of the mental health system than it is of the need for, or the validity of, the diagnosis. The system is truly broken if it avoids treating those who clearly most need treatment.

ARGUMENTS FOR DIAGNOSING PERSONALITY DISORDERS IN CHILDHOOD AND ADOLESCENCE

It is generally agreed that personality pathology originates in childhood and adolescence. I believe that it makes sense to diagnose the problems at the earliest possible opportunity, not only for the sake of the affected individuals, but also for their families. Early detection and intervention may limit pervasiveness and chronicity. Identification and prevention become essential ingredients in the treatment (Harrington, 2001).

Since most adults with personality disorders can identify childhood and adolescent manifestations of their disorders, the therapy for children can include extensive parental involvement. This might serve to limit some of the damage that is consequent to impaired parenting. For example, youngsters abused in early childhood are four times more likely than nonabused children to be diagnosed with a personality disorder by early adulthood (Johnson, Cohen, Brown, Smailes, & Bernstein, 1999; Johnson et al., 2001; Johnson, Smailes, Cohen, Brown, & Bernstein, 2000). If the patterns of behavior and the abuse could be identified earlier, possibly intervention could be implemented. If necessary, child protective services could be brought into the case management along with intensive home-based services, as needed. The school could be involved as an agency that identifies children and could then participate in the treatment. There may be the need for agency intervention, and opportunities for postvention, over several years.

BIOLOGICAL, PHYSIOLOGICAL, AND NEUROCHEMICAL PERSPECTIVES

Various theorists have pointed to neurological disturbances that may be implicated in the onset of personality disorders. The occurrence of childhood abuse (verbal, physical, and/or sexual) experienced by many patients with personality disorders may precipitate neurological changes. Teicher, Ito, Glod, Schiffer, and Gelbard (1994) have suggested that childhood abuse agitates the limbic system in a way that produces impulsivity, aggression, affective instability, and dissociative states. Goleman (1995) posits that continual emotional distress can create deficits in a child's intellectual abilities and damage the ability to learn in such a way that as the child develops, and subsequent rational decision-making abilities are impaired.

DEVELOPMENTAL PERSPECTIVES

One explanation for the emergence of personality disorders in childhood centers on the mother–child relationship as described by object relations theorists (Kernberg, Weiner, & Bardenstein, 2000). According to this view, the child's intrapsychic structure develops through differentiation of self from object, with interrelated maturation of ego defenses (Masterson, 2000). Mahler (as discussed in Kramer & Akhtar, 1994) described four stages of development: autistic, symbiotic, separation–individuation, and object constancy. Problems encountered by the child in the separation–individuation phase in particular are implicated in the etiology of borderline personality disorder, for example. Kohut (as discussed in Kramer & Akhtar, 1994) examined the distortions of "self-object" that he believed to arise from narcissistic injury to the child at a particularly vulnerable moment or developmental stage. This injury was thought to lead to the formation of personality disorders.

Beck et al. (1990, 2004) have pointed out that certain behaviors observed in children, such as clinging, shyness, or rebelliousness, tend to persist throughout various developmental periods into adulthood—at which point they are given personality disorder labels, such as dependent, avoidant, and antisocial. There is evidence that certain relatively stable temperaments and behavioral patterns are present at birth. These innate tendencies may be reinforced by significant others during infancy, or modeled as appropriate and sought-after behaviors during early childhood. For example, the infant or toddler who clings and cries is much more likely to be singled out for attention by caregivers, which in turn reinforces the care-eliciting behavior. The difficulty arises when these patterns persist long after the developmental period in which they may be adaptive.

Kernberg et al. (2000) comment that enduring patterns of personality are increasingly being described in preschoolers. These include patterns of aggressive behavior, inflexible coping strategies, and insecure attachment. Adult manifestations of these patterns may include depression, drug use, and criminal behavior. The progression of childhood conduct disorder to antisocial personality disorder suggests that personality disorders have their origins in earlier developmental stages (Kasen et al., 1999). Impulsivity and empathy are both apparent in children as young as age 2, and deviations in both impulsivity and empathy are components of certain personality disorders. The presence of concrete operational thinking in

middle childhood makes it possible to discern thought disorders and impaired reality testing in school-age children.

FAMILY SYSTEM PERSPECTIVES

Problems in the family environment are important contributing factors in the development of personality disorders in childhood. The disruption of a child's attachment to primary caregivers through death, divorce, severe parental pathology, or otherwise chaotic family environments may elicit maladaptive personality patterns in the child.

Family and systemic factors contribute to the development of personality disorders in children by providing learning experiences that lead to the formation of maladaptive schemas, which persist throughout the developmental phases. These factors include the following:

1. *Parents' failure to teach frustration tolerance.* Even well-intentioned parents may fail to provide optimal training for dealing with frustrating experiences early in a child's life. This training would include the setting and maintaining of clear and consistent boundaries.

2. *Inappropriate child rearing and ignorance regarding child management skills.* Overly punitive or overly permissive parenting may initiate disturbances in the child's sense of boundaries and self-regulation.

3. *Skewed parental value systems.* For example, a highly achieving, perfectionistic child may be pushed by parents to excel, and reinforced by the parents' own need to succeed. Parents' beliefs are reflected in their choice of socialization strategies for their children, which in turn determine whether a child exhibits socially appropriate or socially deviant behavior (Rubin, Hymel, Mills, & Rose-Krasner, 1989). Cultural factors will also come into play (Harkness & Super, 2000).

4. *Parental psychopathology.* The relationship between parental psychopathology and childhood oppositional defiant disorder is quite strong. Hanish and Tolan (2001) and Hanish, Tolan, and Guerra (1996) have suggested that a parent with antisocial personality disorder, through the use of modeling and reinforcement, may transmit the idea to the child that it is acceptable to defy authority. As the child internalizes this belief, he or she begins to oppose the parent, and eventually other authority figures.

5. *Severe and persistent psychosocial stressors in the child's life.* Such stressors may include financial problems, displacement of the home, discord between the parents/parental figures, or stressors with the community. Hanish et al. (1996) found that marital/couple discord is a predictor of

childhood behavior problems—specifically noncompliant, disruptive behavior.

6. *Parental neglect and rejection.* Parental neglect and rejection may lead to the development of schemas suggesting to the child that he or she is disconnected from primary attachment figures, and thus may lead to a more pervasive sense of isolation.

7. *Difficult child temperament.* Children who are difficult infants may elicit responses from caregivers that contribute to the formation of maladaptive schemas. A crying, whining child may experience harsh punishment and more rejection, as well as excess attention from frequent attempts on the part of the parents to soothe the child themselves rather than fostering the infant's ability to self-soothe.

8. *Frequent and severe boundary violations.* These violations can occur on the part of both the child and the parent. For example, if the child is forced into a dependent role at the expense of normal development of autonomy because of a parent's own need for dependence, then the child will have difficulty with individuation. A child who is inclined to introversion may delay or inhibit natural steps toward autonomy, and an overly punitive parenting style may thwart the child's first steps toward a clearly defined self. Instances of physical and sexual abuse are clear and severe boundary violations that have been linked with the development of several personality disorders.

ASSESSMENT AND DIAGNOSTIC PERSPECTIVES

The clinician who suspects that the behavior of a child or adolescent may warrant an Axis II personality disorder diagnosis must thoroughly assess the child's behaviors, affect, and cognition across a variety of situations, as well as obtaining a thorough family and developmental history. The assessment should include contact or reports from the child's pediatrician and teachers in earlier grades. This is required to assess the chronicity and pervasiveness of the problem. Data can be collected through structured clinical interviews with the child and the child's parent(s); reports from teachers and other school personnel (administrators or counselors); psychological testing; behavioral observations at home and at school; repeated self-report measures when possible; symptom behavioral checklists; and school behavior report forms, family history, and the clinician's interview impressions.

Essential to making the diagnosis is a thorough grounding in developmental norms and an understanding of what is normative for that child, in that setting, at that time. For example, when one sees an adolescent who is contrary, argumentative, impulsive, antiauthority, and risk-taking, one can

easily label this youth as normal. The assessment questions include the following:

Does a reported and/or observed behavior have a normal developmental explanation?

Does the behavior change over time or setting? Is it cyclical, variable, and unpredictable, or is the behavior constant, consistent, and predictable?

Could the observed/reported behavior be the result of discrepancies between the child's chronological age and the child's cognitive, emotional, social, and/or behavioral ages?

Does the child function similarly in different environments (e.g., does the behavior relate to the child's placement at home or in school)?

Is the observed/reported behavior culturally related?

Who has made the referral, and why was it made at this point?

Is there agreement between parents, or between parent(s) and teacher(s), on the cause, need, or purpose of the referral?

What are the expectations that are being made of the clinician in responding to the referral?

How does the child's behavior compare or contrast with the behavior of other children in that family, that socioeconomic or sociocultural setting, or that age group?

What is the history of the child's behavior in terms of length of existence; duration when stimulated; and the child's ability to control, contain, or withdraw from the behavior?

Does the child have insight into the behavioral cues that trigger the behavior, or into the consequences of the behavior?

Does the child see the behavior as something he or she would be interested in modifying?

What are the differing views of the child's behavior? Are the clinician's sources of data reliable?

The parent report is important in terms of the child's behavior at home. How does the child relate to siblings, neighborhood friends, clubs, sports, organizations, church activities, adult relatives, pets, and self-care (activities of daily living)?

Has there been recurrent physical, emotional, sexual, or verbal abuse? The parental view of what constitutes discipline versus child abuse is a key element to be considered.

Within societal norms, is the parental behavior inappropriately sexual or seductive? Is incest suspected?

What is the parental view of privacy for the child? Are the parents inappropriately, unreasonably, or unjustifiably interfering with the child's relationships with other children?

Within societal norms, are the parents inappropriately involved with the child's personal hygiene beyond the child's necessity?

Kernberg et al. (2000) suggest a number of specific factors to be considered in the assessment. These include an evaluation of the child's temperament. This is probably based on biogenetic factors constituting a "disposition" that will influence the child's interactions with his or her world. This temperamental filter will influence the nature, style, frequency, "volume," and content of the child's approach to the world. Other factors to be considered include the following:

The child's internal, persistent, and developing internal mental construction of selfhood (identity) will need to be assessed.

Gender plays a role, inasmuch as gender carries with it both self- and other-expectations that are based in the culture. While certainly a component of identity, gender also carries with it significant societal norms and demands.

It is critical to be able to identify any neuropsychological deficits related to cognitive functioning. It is especially important to identify any problems in the manner in which the child organizes, processes, and recalls information.

The child's level, content, range, and repertoire of affect need to be assessed.

What is the child's characteristic mode of coping with internal and external stressors in his or her life? How does the child respond initially, and how do the attempts at coping increase or decrease as the stressors persist?

The clinician must assess the child's environment, which includes the child's family system, school experience, religious environment, and the stability of all of these. It will be important to assess the reactivity and reciprocal behavior of others within the systems.

The child's motivation and attempts to meet intrinsic and extrinsic needs are important. This will reflect the "why" of the child's actions. What is the goal of the child's drives and actions?

The child's social facility and repertoire of social interaction skills will assist the child in relating to, and coping with, significant others within his or her environment.

It is in light of the child's level of cognitive development and integration that his or her actions can be best understood. A child at preoperational levels cannot be expected to process information in the same manner as a child at the level of concrete or formal operations.

What are the most active and compelling schemas that the child uses to understand and organize his or her world?

Frequently, the euphemisms used to describe the child are suggestive of a particular personality disorder and can be added to the diagnostic mix. To give a few examples, a child described as "isolated and withdrawn" may have schizoid personality disorder; a child termed "chronically suspicious" may have paranoid personality disorder; a child called "excessively self-focused" may have narcissistic personality disorder; a child termed "very needy" may have dependent personality disorder; or a child described as "always conscientious and careful" may have obsessive–compulsive personality disorder.

Finally, there are a number of factors that can (and often do) complicate the differential diagnosis of personality disorder in adolescents:

First and foremost is the typical adolescent "neurosis." Adolescents are exploring new roles, shedding old roles, and confronting new challenges, all while trying to maintain a semblance of safety and stability. This describes much of adolescent behavior. Their actions are often responded to by parents' or other authorities' stating, "You should know better."

There are significant hormonal surges that will serve to influence the adolescent's behavior, cognitive processing, and affect. The significant mood shifts typical of adolescents are rooted in their physiology. These mood shifts may be similar to those seen in individuals with bipolar illness, or other disorders involving rapid alternation and shifting of mood.

Adolescence presents everyone with a Kafkaesque experience of metamorphosis. There are rapid (and often significant) changes in size, weight, and height, as well as in the development of secondary sex characteristics and therefore in body shape. These changes are usually expected and often taken in stride, with far greater equanimity than would be the case if an adult experienced these same physical changes in the same brief period of time. However, this is not always the case.

There are rapid alterations of identity, in which an adolescent moves from child to adult. The late Hank Ketcham, the cartoonist responsible for *Dennis the Menace*, once had Dennis state, "How come when I have to go to the doctor I am supposed to be a big boy, but when it's time for bed, I am still a little boy?" The adolescent tries out many identities in terms of dress, attitude, social circle, or relationship with family members. This shifting of identity could be mistaken as meeting criteria for a personality disorder.

Adolescents end up in conflicts with parents, school authority, or the justice system. Adolescence is filled with rebellion alternating with dependence. The push-pull of the relationship with parents is capsuled by an adolescent's wanting greater freedom while asking for financial or social support. This dichotomizing is also indicative of certain personality disorders.

The adolescent may rebel by joining an apparently neurotic or antisocial group. Parents may be concerned that the adolescent is hanging out with the "wrong group." In fact, the adolescent may make a very normal and appropriate adjustment to the group by how he or she acts, dresses, talks, responds to authorities, and responds to parents. The problem will be that the child or adolescent is not so much troubled as troubling to others.

The emergence of sexual behavior serves as another confounding variable. The onset of this new behavior has implications for adolescents' interpersonal action, responsibility for their safety, and adherence to parental demands and expectations. The dividing line between societally approved and disapproved sexuality as demonstrated by dress and action seems increasingly to be blurred. The adolescent icons seen on MTV or in advertisements for clothing, music, foods, or recreation are overtly sexual.

Finally, there is a normal body dysmorphia during adolescence that relates how one's body appears to oneself or may be viewed by others. A skin eruption at the time of a date or important school function may be viewed as more than a pimple. It may be perceived as a cause for cloistering oneself and not appearing in public.

COGNITIVE-BEHAVIORAL TREATMENT CONCEPTUALIZATION

The clinician must work to identify the schemas that are driving the child's cognitions, affect, and behavior (Freeman, 1983; Freeman & Leaf, 1989; Freeman, Pretzer, Fleming, & Simon, 2004; Beck et al., 1990, 2004). Since these schemas evolve through assimilation and accommodation, the clinician must assess the schemas that are being used to address life problems.. The range of schemas can encompass personal, family, gender, cultural, age group, and religious schemas, with varying degrees of power and credibility for the child. For example, religious schemas may have more credibility and power for the child in a devoutly religious family than for the child whose family has no religious affiliation. The more powerful the reinforcers are for schemas, and the more frequently they are reinforced, the more likely strong bonds will exist for those schemas. It is important to determine how early in life schemas are acquired, for the earliest-acquired schemas are the

most powerful. The clinician needs to be aware that schemas can be acquired through multifaceted, multisensory learning—through cognitive, behavioral, motor/kinesthetic, visual, olfactory, and gustatory modes, for example. This means that even infants have the capacity to acquire schemas; hence the ensuing difficulty in attempting to modify early-entrenched but maladaptive schemas.

Behaviors and beliefs can also be the result of modeling. The child observes significant others and learns that certain patterns of behavior are reinforced. The nature of a behavior may be adaptive or maladaptive, depending on the level of pathology present in parents. The child also gains reinforcement for a particular pattern of behaviors. Family environment and genetic predisposition may interact in a unique ways, resulting in the development of a child who manifests a pattern of behaviors.

TREATMENT COSTS

Is there a possibility or even a probability that the identified behavior pattern will spontaneously remit if treatment recommendations are refused, and treatment is not initiated? If there is a minimal environmental shift, will the behaviors then remit? Basically, the clinician must assess the "treatment costs" (financial and otherwise) to the child and family. For example, if the child and family are referred to therapy, is it possible that things may get worse for the child, the family, or both? Who in the family can be called upon and trusted to participate in the therapy? What supports can be offered or provided for the child and for the family? Who will fund the supports? For what period of time? In what context?

SELECTING THE OPTIMAL FOCUS FOR TREATMENT

The decision to engage the child in some form of psychological treatment is one that is ideally made in conjunction with, and with input from, a number of sources. At this point, it may be tempting to consider the child as the sole focus for treatment. However, such a singular emphasis on the child negates the reality that other forces have an impact on the child and are influencing the noted referral problem. If the referral problem is a result of a parent's lack of knowledge regarding normal development and norms of behavior in children and adolescents, then one aspect of treatment must include parenting information and education. The child's behavior may relate to parental behavior and expectations or to the parent's skills at parenting.

Given that a child spends half of his or her waking hours in school, it will be essential to engage not only the parents or other caretakers in the treatment plan, but also the school. The child likewise must be included in the treatment planning. The "problem" will need to be explained to the child, along with the reasons for intervention and the goals of treatment. Trying to treat a child who may have no idea why treatment is indicated may be a lost cause. The child may have little or no motivation to change, and may be frightened of and violently opposed to any changes in his or her behavior or world.

Depending on the child's age and level of cognitive development, treatment may have to be modified. For example, the child's developmental stage may not be adequate for verbal/abstract therapy, or an older child may have limited verbal skills and ability to generalize (an important factor in therapy). Most children will have great difficulty in being able to sit still, listen, concentrate, focus, and integrate the diverse pieces that arise in typical psychotherapy. Even spending an extended amount of time alone with an adult may be viewed as somewhere between strange and frightening by the child. Session length may have to be limited, based on the child's ability to attend for a prescribed length of time.

THE THERAPY PROCESS

Once therapy has been agreed to, the actual therapy session is a small part of what must be viewed as an integrated whole. On a regular basis, the clinician needs to review the occurrence of target behaviors since the last session (based on parent and/or teacher report). Goals of therapy include expanding the child's "emotional vocabulary" to describe positive and negative feelings, helping the child to identify and dispute dysfunctional ideas, teaching self-instructional techniques, teaching problem-solving skills (including consequential thinking and finding alternatives), and role-playing specific skills. When possible, significant others can act as therapy assistants by reinforcing learned skills in the child's home and/or school environment. Continued monitoring by parents and school personnel is encouraged for the purposes of collecting data, as well as fostering a sense of involvement and efficacy in those closest to the child.

It is assumed that the clinician has made a decision concerning the use of therapy to treat the child, one or both parents, the family, or the family system. The judicious use of time is essential. The clinician will want to set the agenda to allow the child and his or her parents to be alert to the goals of the session. When possible, both the child and the parents can suggest agenda items for discussion. Parents and teachers may be involved in assisting the child with homework assignments given in session, or providing additional reinforcement of skills learned in session. The amount of time that is allocated to child work, parent work, or family work will depend on the clinician's assessment of where the focus must be at any particular point in the treatment.

The clinician will ascertain the child's capacity to "uncover" or "process" experience, based on the child's cognitive level and response to therapy. For example, a child who is at the concrete operational level of thinking may respond best to therapeutic interventions that provide a limited range of choices for behavior. The focus of therapy should be on the change process itself. The therapist must develop the working alliance with the child by assessing the child's ability and willingness to connect both cognitively and emotionally. The therapist will be aided by an understanding of the basics of neuropsychology, the effects of anxiety on performance, and the impact on adaptive functioning of learning problems, as well as of developmental psychology.

DISCUSSION AND CONCLUSIONS

"Cognitive therapy with children, as is work with adults, is founded upon the assumption that behavior is adaptive, and that there is an interaction between the individual's thoughts, feelings, and behaviors" (Reinecke, Dattilio, & Freeman, 2003, p. 2). Cognitive-behavioral treatments are of benefit to children because they can be modified and tailored to meet their specific needs. Therapeutic interventions focus on such concrete concepts as misinterpretation of information, reality testing, adaptive responses along a continuum, and basic problem-solving skills, rather than emphasizing insight. Everyday problems at school or home are addressed with the goal of developing a wider and better repertoire of coping skills. Within this basic framework, various cognitive-behavioral interventions can be utilized: time management skills training, assertiveness training, problem-solving training, relaxation training, social skills training, self-management training, behavior analysis skill training, activity scheduling, self-monitoring, and developing adaptive self-talk.

Cognitive-behavioral therapy with children emphasizes the effects of maladaptive or dysfunctional beliefs and attitudes on current behavior. The presumption is made that a child's reaction to an event is influenced by the meanings he or she attaches to the event (Reinecke et al., 2003). When a child's behavioral and emotional responses to an event are maladaptive, it may be because the child lacks more appropriate behavioral skills, or because his or her beliefs or problem-solving capacities are in some way disturbed (the cognitive elements). With this framework in mind, cognitive-behavioral therapists attempt to enable children to acquire new behavioral skills and provide children with experiences that foster cognitive change.

There is a great need for protocols and research on each of the personality disorders in children and adolescents. We must develop new and more effective diagnostic tools, and sharpen our experience with existing tools. We also have to evaluate "best practices" for treatment. What works best, with whom, in what time frame, and under what circumstances? We will need to evaluate what are the idealistic goals for treatment, and what are the more realistic goals. Finally, we will have to be ready to pay the price in clinician effort, and economic cost to treat these children.

Choosing to ignore the reality of personality disorders among children and adolescents, to downplay the problem, or to search for euphemistic terms is to disregard the severity and impact of these disorders. The sooner that we can accept their reality, the sooner we will focus our efforts on treatment, and the sooner we can relieve the suffering of these children.

REFERENCES

American Psychiatric Association (APA). (2000). *Diagnostic and statistical manual of mental disorders* (4th ed., text rev.). Washington, DC: Author.

Beck, A. T., Freeman, A., & Associates (1990). *Cognitive therapy of personality disorders*. New York: Guilford Press.

Beck, A. T., Freeman, A., Davis, D. D., & Associates. (2004). *Cognitive therapy of personality disorders* (2nd ed.). New York: Guilford Press.

Beren, P. (1998). *Narcissistic disorders in children and adolescents*. Northvale, NJ: Aronson.

Bleiberg, E. (2001). *Treating personality disorders in children and adolescents: A relational approach*. New York: Guilford Press.

Freeman, A. (1983). Cognitive therapy: An overview. In A. Freeman (Ed.), *Cognitive therapy with couples and groups* (pp. 1–10). New York: Plenum Press.

Freeman, A., & Leaf, R. (1989). Cognitive therapy of personality disorders. In A. Freeman, K. M. Simon, L. Beutler, & H. Arkowitz (Eds.), *Comprehensive handbook of cognitive therapy* (pp. 403–434). New York: Plenum Press.

Freeman, A., Pretzel, J., Fleming, B., & Simon, K. M. (2004). *Clinical applications of cognitive therapy* (2nd ed.). New York: Kluwer Academic.

Freeman, A., & Rigby, A. (2003). Personality disorders among children and adolescents: Is it an unlikely diagnosis? In M. A. Reinecke, F. M. Dattilio, & A. Freeman (Eds.), *Cognitive therapy with children and adolescents* (2nd ed.). New York: Guilford Press.

Goleman, D. (1995). *Emotional intelligence*. New York: Bantam Books.

Hanish, L. D., Tolan, P. H., & Guerra, N. G. (1996). Treatment of oppositional defiant disorder. In M. A. Reinecke, F. M. Dattilio, & A. Freeman (Eds.), *Cognitive therapy with children and adolescents* (pp. 62–78). New York: Guilford Press.

Hanish, L. D., & Tolan, P. H. (2001). Antisocial behaviors in children and adolescents: Expanding the cognitive model. In W. J. Lyddon & J. V. Jones, Jr. (Eds.), *Empirically supported cognitive therapies: Current and future applications* (pp. 182–199). New York: Springer.

Harkness, S., & Super, C. M. (2000). Culture and psychopathology. In A. J. Sameroff, M. Lewis, & S. M. Miller (Eds.), *Handbook of developmental psychopathology* (pp. 197–214). New York: Kluwer Academic/Plenum.

Harrington, R. C. (2001). Childhood depression and conduct disorder: Different routes to the same outcome? *Archives of General Psychiatry, 58*(3), 237–238.

Johnson, J. G., Cohen, P., Brown, J., Smailes, E. M., & Bernstein, D. P. (1999). Childhood maltreatment increases risk for personality disorders during early adulthood. *Archives of General Psychiatry, 56*(7), 600–606.

Johnson, J. G., Cohen, P., Smailes, E. M., Skodol, A. E., Brown, J., & Oldham, J. M. (2001). Childhood verbal abuse and risk for personality disorders during adolescence and early adulthood. *Comprehensive Psychiatry, 42*(1), 16–23.

Johnson, J. G., Smailes, E. M., Cohen, P., Brown, J., & Bernstein, D. P. (2000). Associations between four types of childhood neglect and personality disorder symptoms during adolescence and early adulthood. Findings of a community-based study. *Journal of Personality Disorders, 14*(2), 171–187.

Kasen, S., Cohen, P., Skodol, A. E., Johnson, J. G., Smailes, E. M., & Brook, J. S. (2001). Childhood depression and adult personality disorder: Alternate pathways of continuity. *Archives of General Psychiatry, 58*(3), 231–236.

Kernberg, P. F., Weiner, A. S., & Bardenstein, K. K. (2000). *Personality disorders in children and adolescents*. New York: Basic Books.

Kramer, S., & Akhtar, S. (Eds.). (1994). *Mahler and Kohut: Perspectives on development, psychopathology, and technique*. Northvale, NJ: Aronson.

Masterson, J. (2000). *The personality disorders: A new look at the developmental self and object relations approach*. Phoenix, AZ: Zeig, Tucker.

National Advisory Mental Health Council. (1995). Basic behavioral science research for mental health, a national investment: Emotion and motivation. *American Psychologist, 50*(10), 838–845.

Olin, S. S., Raine, A., Cannon, T. D., Parnas, J., Schulsinger, F., & Mednick, S. A. (1997). Childhood precursors of schizotypal personality disorder. *Schizophrenia Bulletin, 23*(1), 93–103.

Paris, J. (2003). *Personality disorders over time: Precursors, course, and outcome*. Washington, DC: American Psychiatric Press.

Reinecke, M. A., Dattilio, F. M., & Freeman, A. (Eds.). (2003). *Cognitive therapy with children and adolescents* (2nd ed.). New York: Guilford Press.

Rubin, K. H., Hymel, S., Mills, R. S., & Rose-Krasner, L. (1989). Sociability and social withdrawal in childhood: Stability and outcomes. *Journal of Personality, 57*, 238–255.

Shapiro, T. (1997). The borderline syndrome in children. In K. S. Robson (Ed.). *The borderline child*. Northvale, NJ: Aronson.

Teicher, M. H., Ito, Y., Glod, C. A., Schiffer, F., & Gelbard, H. (1994). Early abuse, limbic system dysfunction, and borderline personality disorder. In K. R. Silk (Ed.), *Progress in psychiatry: No. 45. Biological and neurobehavioral studies of borderline personality disorder* (pp. 177–207). Washington, DC: American Psychiatric Association.

Vela, R., Gottlieb, H., & Gottlieb, E. (1997). Borderline syndromes in children: A critical review. In K. S. Robson (Ed.), *The borderline child*. Northvale, NJ: Aronson.

Wolff, S., Townshend, R., McGuire, R. J., & Weeks, D. J. (1991). Schizoid personality in childhood and adult life. II. Adult adjustment and the continuity with schizotypal personality disorder. *British Journal of Psychiatry, 159*, 620–629.

Reading 6
The Treatment of Depression

The Treatment of Depression

A discussion of the treatment of depression has a special place in any book on Cognitive Therapy. Depression was, after all, the first problem area to which Beck (1967, 1976) applied Cognitive Therapy. It is also the clinical problem that has been most extensively studied in terms of the efficacy of Cognitive Therapy (Simon & Fleming, 1985). Finally, depression, by itself and in combination with other disorders, is arguably the most common problem seen in clinical practice (Seligman, 1975).

The term *depression* refers to a broad range of affective disorders. Rather than being a unitary phenomenon, it is a highly complex, multidimensional clinical syndrome. In its clinical presentation, depression may be mild or severe, obvious or masked, episodic or chronic. Depression has emotional and behavioral manifestations, as well as distinctive cognitive patterns and neurochemical changes. There can be chronic, low-level depression with very subtle symptoms, or severe depression with definite and extremely problematic symptoms. The clinical symptomatology of depression is observed in every age, racial, and ethnic group, both sexes, and across the socioeconomic spectrum. Depression manifests itself both interpersonally and intrapersonally and can have major impact on the individual, the couple, and the family (Freeman, Epstein, & Simon, 1986).

The goal of this chapter is twofold. For readers who are familiar with Cognitive Therapy of depression, it will refresh their knowledge, while also discussing aspects of Cognitive Therapy of depression that have not been emphasized in previous discussions of this subject. For readers who are not familiar with Beck's approach to depression (Beck, Rush, Shaw, & Emery, 1979), it will provide an overview of Cognitive Therapy of depression and will introduce many of the concepts, strategies, and interventions that will be adapted in subsequent chapters for use with other disorders.

ASSESSMENT

Because depression is not a unitary phenomenon, the clinician is faced with the task of discriminating between a number of related disorders

81

ranging from Adjustment Disorder with Depressed Mood through Dysthymic Disorder and Cyclothymic Disorder to Bipolar Disorder, Depressed, and Major Depression. The assessment process is further complicated by the fact that complaints of depression can be secondary to other disorders and that depressed individuals may present symptoms of other disorders rather than complaining of depression. The distinctions between these various disorders are not academic; they can have important implications for intervention. Fortunately, the detailed information provided by the type of initial evaluation described in Chapter 2 provides the information needed to draw these distinctions.

Consider the following case example:

"Frank" was a 45-year-old, married man with three children who had been employed as a machine tool salesman. At the time when he sought treatment, Frank had been unemployed for several months and was feeling quite depressed and hopeless over his career difficulties and the prospect of not being able to provide well for his family. He had become increasingly withdrawn and inactive, was unable to job hunt effectively, and spent most of his time sitting around the house brooding about his problems and feeling miserable.

The mildest of the various forms of depression is Adjustment Disorder with Depressed Mood (see Table 4). In this form of depression, an individual whose premorbid functioning has been unremarkable experiences an identifiable stressor and becomes depressed, but his or her depression does not satisfy the diagnostic criteria for other disorders. It is sometimes assumed that no intervention is needed with adjustment disorders because they tend to be time limited without intervention. However, if effective intervention can decrease the client's distress, speed recovery, improve the outcome, and decrease the risk of the client's problems progressing to the point where they qualify for a more serious diagnosis, then it could be

TABLE 4. DSM-III-R Diagnostic Criteria for Adjustment Disorder
with Depressed Mood

A. A reaction to an identifiable psychosocial stressor (or multiple stressors) that occurs within 3 months of onset of the stressor(s).
B. The maladaptive nature of the reaction is indicated by either of the following:
   1. Impairment in occupational (including school) functioning or in usual social activities or relationships with others
   2. Symptoms that are in excess of a normal and expectable reaction to the stressor(s).
C. The disturbance is not merely one instance of a pattern of overreaction to stress or an exacerbation of one of the mental disorders previously described.
D. The maladaptive reaction has persisted for no longer than 6 months.
E. The disturbance does not meet the criteria for any specific mental disorder and does not represent Uncomplicated Bereavement.

TABLE 5. DSM-III-R Diagnostic Criteria for Dysthymic Disorder

A. Depressed mood for most of the day, more days than not, as indicated either by subjective account or observation by others, for at least 2 years.
B. Presence, while depressed, of at least two of the following:
    1. Poor appetite or overeating
    2. Insomnia or hypersomnia
    3. Low energy or fatigue
    4. Low self-esteem
    5. Poor concentration or difficulty making decisions
    6. Feelings of hopelessness
C. During a 2-year period of the disturbance, never without the symptoms in A for more then 2 months at a time.
D. No evidence of an unequivocal Major Depressive Episode during the first 2 years of the disturbance.
E. Has never had a Manic Episode or an unequivocal Hypomanic Episode.
F. Not superimposed on a chronic psychotic disorder, such as Schizophrenia or Delusional Disorder.
G. It cannot be established that an organic factor initiated and maintained the disturbance.

quite valuable. In Frank's case, his initial reaction to being fired would have satisfied the diagnostic criteria for this disorder, but his depression soon progressed further.

Dysthymic Disorder (Table 5) and Cyclothymic Disorder (Table 6) are characterized by more chronic and persistent problems than result from an adjustment disorder but milder symptomatology than either Major Depression or Bipolar Disorder. It would be natural to assume that Dysthymic Disorder and Cyclothymic Disorder would respond to treatment more quickly than Major Depression and Bipolar Disorder because the symptoms are milder and result in less impairment. However, the high instance of substance abuse among clients with Cyclothymic Disorder and the high incidence of personality disorders among clients with Dysthymic Disorder greatly complicate and slow treatment.

TABLE 6. DSM-III-R Diagnostic Criteria for Cyclothymic Disorder

A. For at least 2 years, presence of numberous Hypomanic Episodes and numerous periods with depressed mood or loss of interest or pleasure that did not meet Criterion A of Major Depressive Episode.
B. During a 2-year period of the disturbance, never without hypomanic or depressive symptoms for more than 2 months at a time.
C. No clear evidence of a Major Depressive Episode or Manic Episode during the first 2 years of the disturbance.
D. Not superimposed on a chronic psychotic disorder, such as Schizophrenia or Delusional Disorder.
E. It cannot be established that an organic factor initiated and maintained the disturbance.

In fact, the individual with Dysthymic Disorder is probably the most difficult depressed patient to treat. This client gains little pleasure from life without being severely debilitated and often without having obvious precipitants for his or her depressed moods. Severely depressed clients are powerfully motivated to change by the intensity of their distress, though the severity of their depression may initially mask this motivation to change. However, the dysthymic experiences a much more tolerable level of distress and thus is less motivated to change. Furthermore, initial interventions with seriously depressed clients often produce noticeable changes early in therapy, and when client's level of depression changes from a BDI score of 32 to a score of 21, there is great clinical change. The client feels better, does more, and thinks differently and is encouraged to persist in therapy because it obviously is helping. With dysthymic clients, initial changes usually are slower and less obvious. When the dysthymic goes from a BDI score of 13 to an 11, the change is barely noticeable, and the client sees little indication that therapy is accomplishing anything. Given the small changes, whatever motivation for treatment the client had initially tends to disappear altogether.

The DSM-III R (APA, 1987) criteria for Major Depressive Disorder are given in Table 7. As can be seen, this is the diagnosis given for severe, episodic depressions that are extremely incapacitating for the individual. It is sometimes assumed that clients who are this severely depressed need antidepressant medication or hospitalization or some more "powerful"

TABLE 7. DSM-III-R Diagnostic Criteria for Major Depressive Disorder

At least five of the following symptoms have been present during the same 2 week period and represent a change from previous functioning; at least one of the symptoms is either (1) depressed mood, or (2) loss of interest or pleasure. (Do not include symptoms that are clearly due to a physical condition, mood-incongruent delusions or hallucinations, incoherence, or marked loosening of associations.)

1. Depressed mood most of the day, nearly every day, as indicated either by subjective account or observation of others
2. Markedly diminished interest or pleasure in all, or almost all, activities most of the day, nearly every day
3. Significant weight loss or weight gain when not dieting (e.g., more than 5% of body weight in a month), or decrease or increase in appetite nearly every day
4. Insomnia or hypersomnia nearly every day
5. Psychomotor agitation or retardation nearly every day (observable by others, not merely subjective feelings of restlessness or being slowed down)
6. Fatigue or loss of energy nearly every day
7. Feelings of worthlessness or excessive or inappropriate guilt (which may be delusional) nearly every day (not merely self-reproach or guilt about being sick)
8. Diminished ability to think or concentrate or indecisiveness, nearly every day
9. Recurrent thoughts of death (not just fear of dying), recurrent suicidal ideation without a specific plan, or a suicide attempt or a specific plan for committing suicide

TABLE 8. DSM-III-R Diagnostic Criteria for Bipolar Disorder

A. Current (or most recent) episode involves the full symptomatic picture of both Manic and Major Depressive Episodes (except for the duration requirements of 2 weeks for depressive symptoms), intermixed or rapidly alternating every few days.
B. Prominent depressive symptoms lasting at least a full day.

---

intervention rather than "talking therapy." In fact, Cognitive Therapy works well even with clients who are quite severely depressed, and it has been found to be at least as "powerful" as the other treatment options (see Simon & Fleming, 1985, for a recent review of research on the effectiveness of Cognitive Therapy). At the time of his initial evaluation, Frank clearly met the diagnostic criteria for Major Depression. He reported a constant depressed mood and appeared quite depressed; he reported that he no longer felt any interest in or enjoyment from his usual activities; he had a constant problem with waking in the early morning hours and being unable to get back to sleep; he reported chronic fatigue; and he felt totally worthless.

Bipolar Disorder is perhaps more widely known by the older term, Manic-Depressive Disorder. Many persons assume that this disorder is characterized by a regular alternation between manic and depressive episodes but in actuality the essential feature of Bipolar Disorder is a history of one or more manic episodes accompanied by one or more depressive episodes. From the diagnostic criteria shown in Table 8, it is clear that the pattern of manic and depressive episodes can vary considerably from client to client. The presence of manic episodes complicates treatment of depressed clients who have a Bipolar Disorder. First, clients usually fail to come in for therapy during manic episodes despite the degree of impairment that can result from a manic episode. Second, no cognitive interventions have been demonstrated to be effective in treating manic episodes. Therefore, there is a consensus that Cognitive Therapy is an appropriate treatment for depressive episodes in clients with Bipolar Disorder as long as appropriate medication is used to control the manic episodes.

It is important to note that both Cyclothymic Disorder and Dysthymic Disorder can co-occur with Bipolar Disorder or Major Depression. When a sufficiently detailed history of the client's symptoms is available, it is possible to diagnose both disorders by examining the pattern of symptomatology over time. However, often a detailed history is not available, and the Cyclothymic or Dysthymic Disorder is not apparent until the client's Major Depressive Episode has been at least partly treated.

Although the term *masked depression* is not a diagnostic label, it still is a concept that the clinician needs to consider. When a client complains of being "blue," "down," or "sad," his or her depression is easy to recognize.

However, individuals differ widely in the extent to which they are able to recognize and express their emotions and in the extent to which they are willing to acknowledge having psychological problems. Depressed individuals may seek help either without recognizing their depressed mood or without being willing to admit that they are depressed. When this is the case, they are likely to present "nonpsychological" symptoms such as sleeping difficulty, eating problems, loss of appetite, loss of libido, or a lack of motivation without mentioning feelings of sadness or depression. Often if these individuals are asked directly about depressed mood, periods of tearfulness, and so forth, it is possible to determine if they are indeed depressed. In addition, the Beck Depression Inventory (see Chapter 2) can be useful in determining the extent to which a client's complaints correspond to symptoms of depression. Obviously, when a client's "medical" complaints are symptoms of depression, effective treatment of the depression should alleviate the symptoms.

Conversely, a client's depressed mood may reflect a "secondary depression," where the depressed mood is a response to some other medical or psychiatric problem (Shaw, Vallis, & McCabe, 1985). Problems ranging from cardiac surgery to agoraphobia can elicit a depressed mood or a full depressive disorder as a reaction to either the actual impact the problem has on the client's life or the client's expectations about the effects it will have. Whether the depression is primary or secondary, cognitive therapy techniques can be used for treatment of the depression. However, when depression is a response to another psychiatric disorder, it may be more appropriate for therapist and client to focus most of their efforts on treating the primary disorder because the depression is likely to lift if the primary disorder can be resolved.

Cognitive Therapy can also be applied to helping clients deal with objectively tragic or saddening life problems. Many life situations cause realistic sadness, frustration, or grief. For example, Holmes and Rahe (1976) found the death of a loved one to typically be the most powerful stressor that persons experience. DSM-III-R (p. 361) states that individuals experiencing "uncomplicated bereavement" frequently suffer a full depressive episode and may enter therapy for associated symptoms. Assessment of the client who is responding to a life crisis does not differ from that of any other client. The therapist must assess the degree to which the client's response is realistic as well as any distortions in the client's thinking that aggravate the situation. When dysfunctional beliefs and cognitive distortions do not disrupt the normal grieving process, support and reassurance from the therapist may be sufficient. However, when cognitions about the loss intensify the grief or block the normal grieving process, Cognitive Therapy can be quite useful.

Even when a client presents with classic symptoms of depression, it is important for the therapist to be certain that depression is, in fact, the problem. A wide range of medical problems can contribute to depression or produce symptoms that mimic depression. Therefore, if the client has not had a complete physical exam in the past year, he or she should be directed to get one early in treatment to rule out the possibility that a medical disorder is involved. Obviously, treating a low thyroid level or congestive heart failure with Cognitive Therapy or with any other psychotherapy will be ineffective and may even constitute malpractice.

As outlined in the Beck Depression Inventory, a wide variety of symptoms are associated with depression, including feelings of sadness and depression, pessimism, and hopelessness, feelings of failure, dissatisfaction with activities, guilt, dissatisfaction with self, self-criticism, suicidality, tearfulness, irritation, loss of interest in others, difficulty making decisions, dissatisfaction with appearance, lack of motivation, early-morning waking, fatigue, loss of appetite, weight loss, overconcern with health, and decreased sexual desire. In addition to the distinction between the various diagnostic categories, the therapist must also assess the pattern of depressive symptomatology for a particular client.

Two individuals coming for treatment may have identical levels of depression, but the particular constellation of symptoms on the BDI may be very different. If both individuals have a score of 25 (out of 63), it would indicate a moderate to severe clinical depression. However, for one individual, the major manifestation of his or her depression might be interpersonal, whereas for the other the manifestations might be intrapersonal. The individual whose symptom picture is primarily interpersonal might have difficulty because of a loss of libido, loss of interest in other people, and a general dissatisfaction and boredom with everything. The patient whose symptom picture is primarily intrapersonal might have problems with self-blame, guilt, self-criticism, disappointment, and self-hate. Both of these patients might have other symptoms in common such as feelings of hopelessness, with a corresponding risk of suicidality for both. Any number of combinations of symptoms may occur and account for much variability between one depressed client and the next. When the therapist understands the client's symptom pattern, interventions can be selected that focus on the specific problem areas that are posing difficulties for the client.

In addition to correct diagnosis and assessment of the pattern of depressive symptomatology, the therapist must also determine whether the client can be effectively treated with outpatient psychotherapy or whether he or she should be hospitalized. This, of course, would depend upon the client's level of functioning, support system, and suicidality, among other factors. Hospitalization is most commonly needed when the client is suicidal and interventions within the session have not been sufficiently effective to alleviate the risk of a suicide attempt. This is discussed more fully in Chapter 5.

CONCEPTUALIZATION

The cognitive view is that depression is characterized by a "cognitive triad" of a negative view of the self, a negative view of the world,* and a negative view of the future (Beck, 1976; Beck *et al.*, 1979). This cognitive triad is manifested in the content of the individual's "automatic thoughts," his or her immediate, involuntary, nonreflective cognitive response to a situation. In Frank's case, he made many negative statements that reflected these automatic thoughts, such as "I'm not good enough," "I've never really been successful," "I'll never get anywhere," and "I'll fail," and he believed these statements implicitly. These views contributed to Frank's depressed mood, his low motivation for job hunting ("I'm not good enough. I'll fail. Why bother?"), and to his pervasive sense of hopelessness and dissatisfaction.

If Frank's negative views had been accurate, his mood and his actions would have been easy to understand. However, when the situation was examined in detail, it turned out that Frank lost his job as part of a major work force reduction resulting from a recession. Not only had the layoff been based on seniority rather than on any lack on Frank's part, but he actually had received very positive evaluations on the job and had been promoted regularly before the firm's economic difficulties. Frank's former supervisor had a high opinion of his abilities and expressed confidence that Frank would be able to get a good job and do well in it. By all accounts (except Frank's), his view of himself as a failure, his pessimistic outlook, and his subsequent lack of motivation were completely unrealistic. How could an intelligent, well-educated man develop such an unrealistically negative view of himself?

The cognitive view argues that an individual's schemas, beliefs, and assumptions constantly and automatically shape his or her perceptions and interpretations of events. In the course of growing up, Frank had been taught, both explicitly and implicitly, that success was essential for one to be worthwhile, to be liked, and to enjoy life. In addition, he had been taught that the way to succeed was to set very high standards and to push very hard in trying to meet those standards. Consequently, he viewed most situations in terms of success and failure, had a lifelong pattern of setting unrealistically high standards for himself, and tried to do things perfectly. These beliefs and assumptions predisposed him to be unreasonably self-critical and to react strongly to perceived failures.

Frank's cognitive distortions intensified the impact of his dysfunctional beliefs. He was particularly prone to the distortions of "dichotomous

---

*It is important to note that Beck uses the phrase *negative view of the world* to refer to the depressed individual's negative view of his or her personal experience, not a negative view of the world in general.

thinking" and "labeling". For example he viewed success and failure in absolute terms. As he saw it, anything that was not a complete success was clearly a total failure, and if he failed at a task, then he was a failure. Because being laid off, whatever the reason, was not success, then by definition he was a failure. This view of himself had a broad impact. After all, what prospective employer would choose to hire a failure? Frank's view was that even if he was able to fool someone into hiring him, it would lead inevitably to disaster because he was a failure. Thus it was not surprising that Frank was unable to motivate himself to actively apply for another job. From his point of view, job hunting seemed futile at best and potentially disastrous.

The combination of his unrealistically high standards for himself and his dichotomous thinking about success and failure was particularly devastating for Frank. Because his standards for judging his performance as success were excessively severe, he was doomed to frequently fall short of his standards. When the "failure" was relatively minor, Frank simply became quite upset with himself and redoubled his efforts, but each time a significant "failure" occurred Frank would begin to consider himself a complete failure. He would then expect to fail at anything he tried and would lapse into a depression. This pattern of cognitions had been responsible for his history of recurrent episodes of depression in response to perceived failures.

The third factor that completed the picture of Frank's depression was the impact his mood had on his cognition. As discussed in Chapter 1, perception and evaluation of personally relevant events is negatively biased during depression. Thus Frank showed a tendency to selectively recall previous failures and shortcomings and to be biased toward interpreting ambiguous situations negatively. Because both recall of sad events and biased perception of events would tend to elicit a depressed mood, the tendency of moods to bias cognition in a mood-congruent way perpetuated and amplified Frank's depressed mood.

These three factors set the stage for the "downward spiral of depression" (Figure 7). In Frank's case, his schemas and basic assumptions about failure and self-worth predisposed him to depressive reactions when confronted by "failure." When he was laid off, these beliefs about the significance of failure were activated, and a stream of negative automatic thoughts about himself, his situation, and his future prospects resulted. Given his proclivity for dichotomous thinking, these negative thoughts were quite extreme and seemed completely plausible to him. These negative thoughts then elicited a depressed mood that further biased Frank's perception and recall in a depression-congruent way. This resulted in his selectively remembering past failures while overlooking experiences that were inconsistent with his negative views. Thus his thoughts became increasingly negative, his mood increasingly depressed, and so on. As a

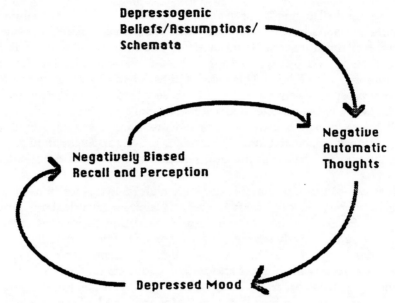

FIGURE 7. The downward spiral of depression.

result, it was possible for Frank's reaction to being laid off to spiral from shock and disappointment to significant depression over a short period of time.

A number of additional factors commonly tend to perpetuate depressions once they occur. The depressed individual's lack of motivation often results in a decrease in activity that has several effects: The unoccupied time provides additional opportunity for depressing ruminations, the depressed individual may become concerned or self-critical over his or her decreased productivity, and the individual has fewer experiences that he or she might possibly enjoy or find worthwhile. Also, the changes in the depressed individual's behavior as well as his or her expressions of depressed mood may affect interpersonal interactions in a way that is likely to perpetuate the depression.

STRATEGIES FOR INTERVENTION

The cognitive conceptualization of depression in terms of the "downward spiral of depression" suggests that it is important to break the depression-perpetuating cycle of *negative automatic thoughts* → *depressed mood* → *biased recall and perception* in order to alleviate the depression. This cycle can be broken at any point. Thus Frank's therapist hypothesized that if Frank could be induced to take a more balanced view of himself, his experiences, and his future prospects, or if his mood could be improved, or if the biasing impact of his depressed mood on perception and recall could be counteracted, the cycle that perpetuated his depression could be broken, and his depression should subside. However it can be seen from Figure 7 that if Frank and his therapist accomplished only this without modifying his dysfunctional beliefs, Frank would still be at risk for a relapse whenever he experienced a setback or failure that could restart the downward spiral. In order to achieve lasting results, it would be necessary to modify the beliefs and assumptions that predisposed Frank to depression and to help him plan effective ways to handle situations that might precipitate a relapse.

The general strategy of first attempting to disrupt the cycles that perpetuate the client's depression and then attempting to modify the beliefs and assumptions that predispose the individual to depression can be implemented in many ways within the framework of "collaborative empiricism" outlined in Chapter 1. A wide variety of techniques for modifying automatic thoughts, dysfunctional beliefs and assumptions, dysphoric moods, and maladaptive behavior are available to the therapist. If it is possible to develop a clear understanding of each client and use this as a foundation for an individualized treatment plan, the therapist can intervene more effectively than if he or she uses a "standard" approach to all depressed clients.

COGNITIVE AND BEHAVIORAL TECHNIQUES

After working to establish a collaborative therapeutic relationship, Cognitive Therapy for depression often begins either with behavioral interventions designed to improve the client's mood or with cognitive interventions focused on identifying and challenging dysfunctional automatic thoughts. In Frank's case, his depression was so intense that he was largely inactive at home and was fairly unresponsive during the session. Frank's answers to the therapist's questions were slow and terse and he was not able to participate actively in a collaborative approach to dealing with his problems. This led the therapist to conclude that it would be quite useful to focus initially on improving Frank's mood in the hope that this would increase his responsiveness to verbal interventions and his motivation to take an active part in therapy. Despite Frank's lethargy, it was possible to use a guided discovery approach to analyzing the differences between times when Frank's depression was particularly intense and times when it was less intense and to demonstrate that his level of activity had an important impact on his mood. This made it possible to introduce Frank to activity scheduling (Chapter 3) in a way that resulted in his being willing to try it as a "homework assignment."

When Frank tried to intentionally be more active despite his depression, he quickly discovered that by simply increasing the number of things that he did each day, he was able to improve his mood substantially. Although this intervention did not eliminate Frank's depression or his procrastination, it resulted in Frank's being much more responsive and motivated during sessions and provided him with clear evidence that he was not helpless in the face of his depression. At this point, it was possible to engage Frank more actively in collaboration and clarify his goals for therapy.

The productive targets for initial cognitive interventions can be selected by paying special attention to the cognitive triad, the client's negative views of self, world, and future. Just as symptoms differ, the relative importance of issues relating to self, world, and future differ for each client. By assessing the importance of each of the three factors, the therapist can determine which of the three to emphasize in initial interventions. In addition, another aspect of the early phase of therapy is to orient the client to the cognitive view of depression and to establish a collaborative relationship. This assessment of the roles of each aspect of the cognitive triad in the client's depression can be visualized in a way that can be used to help the client have a better understanding of the focus of the therapy.

The cognitive triad can be pictured as an equilateral triangle. One can draw a perpendicular line from each of the three sides (Figure 8), with the degree of importance of a particular factor represented by the length of the line such that the shorter the line, the greater the degree of importance of that factor for the individual and the longer the line, the less important that particular factor is. Thus, the intersection of the three lines will be closest to the factor or factors that are most strongly represented in the client's cognitions. For example, a client who voices many statements reflecting low self-esteem and a negative view of his or her experiences but who does not emphasize a negative view of the future would be seen as having problems primarily with negative views of self and world and would be represented graphically by Pattern "A" in Figure 8. The client's concerns would be voiced by statements reflecting low self-esteem and negative views of world and experience. When questioned about current hopelessness and suicidality, this client might say, "Kill myself? Oh, No! I'll just continue to live my poor, miserable life because I deserve to." It must be remembered, of course, that the representation of negative thoughts of the self, world, and future can change at any time. Thus, the therapist should not be lulled into complacency regarding the future suicidal potential of a client who is not currently hopeless.

If the client's concerns focus primarily on self and future, the verbalizations might include those reflecting low self-esteem and suicidal thoughts, for example, "What good am I? I deserve to die. The world seems to get along pretty well; it's me that is at variance with the rest of the

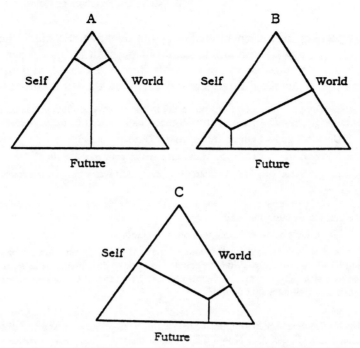

FIGURE 8. Graphic representation of the relative importance of components of the cognitive triad.

world." In Frank's case, by far the most important aspect of the cognitive triad was his negative view of himself. He was preoccupied with the belief that he was a complete failure, and to a lesser extent with the belief that he was doomed to remain a failure. His view of the world was the least distorted of the three aspects of the cognitive triad but was also the aspect on which he focused the least. This is shown in Pattern "B" in Figure 8.

Finally, if the client's concerns involve a negative view of the world and the future (Pattern "C"), a view that is common among clients who have Axis II diagnoses as well, the client's verbalizations might include a diatribe against the ills and evils of the world and a multitude of reasons as to why the client is powerless to improve things. When asked about self-esteem or personal contributions to their difficulty, this type of individual will often go on in great detail about how he or she has tried and not succeeded because of the world's problems and present him or herself as an innocent victim.

Interventions directed toward challenging negative automatic thoughts typically play a major part in Cognitive Therapy with depressed clients. In working with Frank, the therapist's next goal was to demonstrate the connection between automatic thoughts and mood to Frank and to work to help him learn to challenge his negative automatic thoughts. This was done by asking Frank to identify a point in the past when he had experienced a noticeable increase in his depressed mood and then pinpointing the automatic thoughts that occurred in that situation as follows:

Therapist: Can you think of a particular point in the past week when you became noticeably more depressed? A time when your mood took a turn for the worse?

Client: Um . . . I guess I got pretty depressed Thursday morning.

Therapist: What was the situation at the time when your mood shifted?

Client: Let me think. . . . The mail had just come, and I was sitting on the couch flipping through it.

Therapist: Do you remember what thoughts were running through your mind as you sat there flipping through the mail?

Client: No, I don't think anything was on my mind.

Therapist: Let's try something that should make it easier to remember whatever you might have been thinking. What I'm going to ask you to do is imagine that situation over again as realistically as you can. People often find that that makes it easier to remember the details. How does that sound?

Client: Ok.

Therapist: So settle back in a comfortable position, close your eyes to shut out distractions, and let yourself relax. . . . Now I'd like you to imagine being back in that situation as realistically as you can. It's Thursday morning, the mail has just come, and you're flipping through it. Imagine the room just the way it was on Thursday, the mail in your hands, the whole situation. . . . How do you feel as you imagine that?

Client: I'm starting to feel depressed like I did then.

Therapist: What thoughts are running through your head?

Client: I'm thinking about the bills.

Therapist: What I'd like you to do is try to quote the thoughts as much as possible in the same words as when they ran through your head because sometimes the wording can make a big difference.

Client: "Look at all these bills! I'll never be able to pay them off. How's Jack ever going to go to college?"

Therapist: Ok. Stop imagining and open your eyes. Do you think those thoughts might have something to do with your getting more depressed right then?

The therapist was then able to explain the cognitive view of the impact of automatic thoughts on mood using Frank's reactions to illustrate his points. He was then able to introduce the idea of challenging negative automatic thoughts as follows:

Therapist: When you went ahead and opened the mail, how did it turn out?

Client: Well, they weren't all bills, and it wasn't as bad as I expected.

Therapist: Are you going to be able to pay them off?

Client: Yeah. I'm getting unemployment, and my wife works part time so we haven't had to dip into our savings yet.

Therapist: How do you think you would have felt if instead of thinking "I'll never be able to pay them off," you'd been thinking "These damn bills are a pain It's a good thing I've got unemployment and some money in the bank"?

Client: I'd probably have felt better.

Therapist: Which would have been closer to the truth?

Client: That they're a pain.

After discussing the merits of looking critically at automatic thoughts and "talking back" to the ones that are exaggerated or distorted, the therapist was able to demonstrate the use of the Dysfunctional Thought Record (Chapter 2) by showing Frank how the therapist had recorded Frank's thoughts on a DTR sheet. Frank's next homework assignment was to use the DTR to record his automatic thoughts at times when his mood worsened and to begin reading *Feeling Good* (Burns, 1980) in addition to maintaining his increased activity level.

One of the most frequently used strategies in Cognitive Therapy is that of developing adaptive responses to dysfunctional thoughts (see Chapter 3). In Frank's case, negative thoughts relating to his self-worth, judgments of his performance, and the futility of trying to find another job frequently occurred at the times when he became more depressed. Most of Frank's negative thoughts were not actually true (as is the case with most depressives), and therefore could be challenged with specific disconfirming evidence from his life. By correcting exaggerations and distortions in his automatic thoughts, Frank was able to improve his mood considerably. However, as Frank examined his automatic thoughts, he discovered some of them to be "true, but not useful." For example, Frank experienced periods during which he ruminated over the possibility that his savings might eventually be exhausted. Although such an eventuality was possible and would have posed a serious problem were it to occur, Frank's periods of ruminating about this were very depressing to him and did nothing to forestall the problem. Dysfunctional thoughts of this type can be handled adaptively by the client's learning to control the occurrence of these thoughts through techniques such as "thought stopping" and "scheduling worries," through replacing them with more adaptive thoughts, or through developing effective plans for preventing or handling the anticipated problem. In Frank's case, he found that when he took active steps to find a new job, these worries subsided.

Often the automatic thoughts or themes among automatic thoughts that come up most frequently are the most important to address. Frank's conviction that he was "a complete failure" was a recurrent theme among the thoughts that he recorded on the DTR and thus was selected as the next target for intervention. This view of himself probably could have been addressed in the abstract through a philosophical analysis; however, it was simpler and more powerful for the therapist to guide Frank to examine the evidence bearing on the question of whether Frank was indeed a complete failure. The therapist discovered that Frank had been laid off, purely on the basis of seniority, in a work force reduction after years of being one of the better salesmen at his firm and of providing well for his family. Once this evidence had been made explicit, Frank no longer accepted the view that he was "a complete failure" and instead endorsed the view that he had failed at some things and succeeded at others.

The discussion of success and failure highlighted Frank's long-standing tendency to set unrealistically high standards for himself and the negative consequences this had for him. The therapist chose to intervene here by examining the pros and cons of holding very high standards for oneself. Frank initially expressed a strong conviction that it was necessary to do his work perfectly in order to be successful, but as he and his therapist considered the available evidence, he quickly realized that this approach resulted in considerable stress and pressure, resulted in his often becoming preoccupied with trivial imperfections in his work, and resulted in his interpreting performance with which his superiors were quite pleased as being inadequate. In addition to continuing to use DTRs, he agreed to try a behavioral experiment (Chapter 3) of doing a "good but not perfect" job on several household tasks in order to test whether setting more moderate standards for himself was actually a good idea.

Noncompliance with homework assignments can be very useful in identifying important issues that have not yet been addressed. It was at this point in therapy that Frank suddenly found himself unable to get around to doing the homework despite having been quite reliable about doing it previously. At the same time, he began experiencing upsetting visual images and disturbing dreams of himself ending up as a vagrant. When he and his therapist examined the thoughts that occurred when he tried to do his homework and when the images occurred, they uncovered an intense fear that if Frank relaxed his perfectionism at all, the consequences would be disastrous. Once the fear was identified, Frank and his therapist were able to challenge it successfully, and Frank's work on reducing his perfectionism then proceeded without a hitch.

At this point in therapy, Frank's depression had subsided to nonclinical levels and he had begun active job hunting. When the client's goals for therapy have been attained and he or she is free of depression, it may seem that the time for termination has arrived. However, if therapy is stopped before identifying and challenging the client's dysfunctional assumptions and preparing him or her to handle future setbacks, he or she will continue to have a predisposition toward depression. The middle stage of Frank's therapy began with identifying the basic assumptions that predisposed him to depression by looking for patterns among the automatic thoughts collected thus far in therapy and use of the "downward arrow" technique (Chapter 2). Once the assumptions were identified, it was possible to help Frank to look at them critically, to work to develop more adaptive alternative beliefs, and to test them through behavioral experiment (Chapter 3). For example, one of Frank's basic assumptions that had been uncovered in examining his difficulty through the antiperfectionism home work assignments was the idea that in order to succeed he must constantly set very high standards for himself and work as hard as possible or, in his own words, "If I quit pushing I might end up there [as a vagrant on a streetcorner]." When asked whether he had any evidence that would support this view Frank pointed to his poor performance when depressed. However, the therapist was able to remind Frank that they knew from previous sessions that he did not lower his standards for himself or quit trying to force himself to work hard when he was depressed; the problem was that when he was depressed this approach to motivating himself was ineffective. In fact, the approach to self-motivation that had proven effective in overcoming his inactivity and procrastination included setting moderate, clearly manageable goals rather than high standards for himself and focusing on what he hoped to accomplish through the activity rather than pushing himself or dwelling on the bad consequences that would occur if he did not act. After reviewing his experiences in several other situations, it was clear to Frank that the available evidence was incompatible with his initial assumption.

Although this review of the evidence did not completely eliminate his belief in the assumption that a more positive, less pressured approach to work would lead to disaster, it prepared Frank to test the assumption through a "behavioral experiment" in which he tried his new approach to self-motivation with job hunting tasks and compared the results with the results he had achieved by setting high standards and putting a lot of pressure on himself. He was surprised to discover that the new approach not only was much more pleasant but also resulted in his completing more applications and being able to present himself more confidently in interviews. After this experience, he no longer accepted his former assumption that it was necessary to set high standards for himself and constantly push himself.

Work on relapse prevention generally focuses on clearly identifying situations that would be likely to present a risk of relapse and pinpointing early warning signs of relapse. The next step is to develop plans for coping with those situations should they arise. With Frank, it was already clear that work-related "failures" were the primary situation in which there would be a risk of another depression. From a review of Frank's response to earlier work-related setbacks, he and his therapist learned that a consistent early sign that he was starting down the path to depression was when he began to feel increasingly pressured and to focus solely on work. Knowing this, he and his therapist were able to formulate a plan for handling setbacks that included intentionally resisting his tendency to withdraw and become inactive, using adaptive self-statements (such as "Failing at one task doesn't make me a failure in general" and "The thing to do is to plan ahead rather than dwelling on this setback"), taking active steps to deal with the situation, rereading the portions of *Feeling Good* (Burns, 1980) that he had found particularly useful, and returning to therapy for a "booster session" if necessary.

Particular attention was paid to Frank's expectations regarding future problems. Initially he expected never to feel depressed again and was at risk for reacting to a future period of sadness or depression with thoughts like, "Oh my God, I'm depressed again! Cognitive Therapy didn't work, it really is hopeless." Obviously, these unrealistically optimistic expectations regarding the long-term effects of therapy might be encouraging initially but could predispose him to relapse when he encountered future problems. His adoption of the more realistic view that Cognitive Therapy had equipped him with the skills he needed to cope effectively with depression and to prevent depressed moods from becoming major problems decreased the risk of his overreacting to future setbacks and should decrease the risk of relapse.

The final stage of therapy is termination. It is usually a collaborative process during which therapy sessions are gradually scheduled less frequently so that therapist and client have an opportunity to see whether the gains achieved in therapy persist without frequent intervention by the therapist. In Frank's case, termination was more abrupt than usual because soon after he and his therapist began discussing termination he began a new job some distance away and was unable to come in for therapy at the times when the therapist could be available. Therefore it was necessary to handle the final steps of work on relapse prevention and termination by telephone. At the close of therapy, Frank had been completely free of depression for 3 weeks, had been able to actively pursue job hunting without procrastination, had resumed his normal family and social activities, had begun a new job about which he was enthusiastic, and was experiencing substantially less stress and pressure than he had previously experienced when starting other jobs. Because termination had been more abrupt than usual, there had not been an opportunity to observe how Frank coped with a significant setback or failure, but he had a clear plan for handling failures adaptively, was confident that he would be able to do so, and was comfortable with the idea of returning for a booster session if necessary.

CONCLUSION

Because Beck originally developed Cognitive Therapy specifically for the treatment of depression, it is not surprising that the majority of outcome studies of Cognitive Therapy have involved the treatment of depression. In controlled outcome studies, Cognitive Therapy has been found to be an effective treatment for depression, to be at least as effective as treatment with antidepressant medication and often to be superior, and possibly to have a lower dropout rate than treatment with antidepressant medication (Simon & Fleming, 1985). In almost all comparisons between Cognitive Therapy and alternative treatment approaches, Cognitive Therapy has been found to be at least as effective as the alternatives and often more effective.

The cognitive approach to the treatment of depression is not only a well-developed, well-validated approach to effectively treating an important problem, it is also the "standard" Cognitive Therapy approach that serves as a foundation for the cognitive approach to other, more complex disorders. Thus a solid understanding of Cognitive Therapy of depression is strongly recommended.

Reading 7
Anxiety Disorders

Anxiety Disorders

Interest in the anxiety disorders has increased greatly in the past few years with the recognition that anxiety disorders are among the most prevalent psychiatric conditions. The results of a recent epidemiological survey indicate that phobias are the most frequently occurring DSM-III disorders among women and the second most frequent among men (Myers, Weissman, Tischler, Holzer, Leaf, Orvaschel, Anthony, Boyd, Burke, Kramer, & Stoltzman, 1984). In addition, the problem of anxiety goes far beyond just the DSM-III anxiety disorder diagnoses. Complaints of anxiety are among the most common problems among clients seeking help from general medical practitioners, far outnumbering other emotional or behavioral problems. One study showed anxiety as the fifth most common reason for visits to a primary care physician, ahead of all other emotional concerns (Marsland, Wood, & Mayo, 1976). These statistics only include those people whom primary care physicians recognize as having anxiety and those people who are actively seeking help. Beyond this, individuals with severe anxiety and panic often present to health practitioners with any one of a number of related physical problems (e.g., headaches, irritable bowel syndrome, difficulty breathing) and the majority of people with anxiety problems simply never seek help.

Although anxiety is one of the most common of emotional responses, it need not be problematic at all. When experienced in moderate intensity, anxiety can serve to motivate, energize, and mobilize the individual to heights of performance and spectacular deeds. Many people claim to "work best under pressure," that is, when their anxiety level is high enough to motivate them to exert additional effort. It is only when the anxiety level is so high that it debilitates the individual or causes emotional or physical discomfort that anxiety becomes a problem.

ASSESSMENT

At first glance, it seems that differential diagnosis of anxiety disorders would be a simple, straightforward task. If people report a fear of flying,

119

they must be simple phobics; if they cannot leave home, they must be agoraphobics. In actuality, however, the distinctions are much more complex, and a simple checklist of symptoms is not sufficient to adequately diagnose anxiety disorders or to determine the most useful type of treatment. Upon careful assessment, for example, symptoms of fear of flying *may* turn out to be part of a broader agoraphobic syndrome; staying at home *could* turn out to be due to depression rather than agoraphobia; and fear of people *could* be part of a Borderline Personality Disorder rather than a Social Phobia.

The diagnoses of anxiety disorders have been changed significantly in DSM-III-R. One major change is that Agoraphobia and Panic Disorder are no longer two separate diagnostic categories (as in DSM-III, APA, 1980). The essential feature of Panic Disorder is still the presence of recurrent, unexpected panic attacks, but in DSM-III-R (see Table 9), Panic Disorder can exist with or without Agoraphobia (defined as the fear of being where escape might be difficult or help not available in the event of a panic attack). There is also a separate category of Agoraphobia without History of Panic Disorder. The presence of panic attacks alone is not sufficient evidence to conclude that a client has an anxiety disorder, much less Panic Disorder. A past study found that 34% of normal young adults had experienced at least one panic attack in the previous year (Norton, Harrison, Hauch, & Rhodes, 1985), and panic attacks have been found to be present in varying degrees in a wide range of disorders (Boyd, 1986). When the panic attacks are due to another disorder such as Schizophrenia or Somatization Disorder, the diagnosis of Panic Disorder is not made. Also, the presence or absence of panic attacks is insufficient to distinguish *among* the anxiety disorders. In Simple Phobia or Social Phobia, the person may have panic attacks, but these occur only in the presence of specific phobic stimuli. The diagnosis of Panic Disorder is made only when attacks are unexpected and do not occur immediately before or during exposure to a specific situation that almost always causes anxiety.

The distinction between Panic Disorder with and without Agoraphobia can be a difficult one if the agoraphobic avoidance is mild. When asked if they avoid many situations, clients with panic attacks may answer "No," leading one to conclude that they have Panic Disorder without Agoraphobia. However, patterns of avoidance may be subtle or may have continued for so long that the client does not recognize the avoidance. It may be necessary to specifically ask about the frequency of their involvement in a number of activities (e.g., driving on freeways, flying, traveling far away from home, attending concerts, plays, and sporting events), both alone and accompanied, and about any special conditions needed to enable them to face feared situations (e.g., having a glass of water available when speaking in public), in order to accurately ascertain the extent of the Agoraphobia.

TABLE 9. DSM-III-R Diagnostic Criteria for Panic Disorder

At some time during the disturbance, one or more panic attacks (discrete periods of intense fear or discomfort) have occurred that were (1) unexpected, i.e., did not occur immediately before or on exposure to a situation that almost always caused anxiety and (2) not triggered by situations in which the person was the focus of others' attention.

Either four attacks, as defined in Criterion A, have occurred within a 4-week period, or one or more attacks have been followed by a period of at least a month of persistent fear of having another attack.

At least four of the following symptoms developed during at least one of the attacks:
1. Shortness of breath (dyspnea) or smothering sensations
2. Dizziness, unsteady feelings, or faintness
3. Palpitations or accelerated heart rate (tachycardia)
4. Trembling or shaking
5. Sweating
6. Choking
7. Nausea or abdominal distress
8. Depersonalization or derealization
9. Numbness or tingling sensations (parathesias)
10. Flushes (hot flashes) or chills
11. Chest pain or discomfort
12. Fear of dying
13. Fear of going crazy or of doing something uncontrolled

Note: Attacks involving four or more symptoms are panic attacks; attacks involving fewer than four symptoms are limited symptom attacks (see Agoraphobia without History of Panic Disorder).

During at least some of the attacks, at least four of the C symptoms developed suddenly and increased in intensity within 10 minutes of the beginning of the first C symptom noticed in the attack.

It cannot be established that an organic factor initiated and maintained the disturbance, e.g., amphetamine or caffeine intoxication, hyperthyroidism.

Note: Mitral valve prolapse may be an associated condition, but does not preclude a diagnosis of Panic Disorder.

Agoraphobia: Fear of being in places or situations from which escape might be difficult (or embarrassing) or in which help might not be available in the event of a panic attack. (Include cases in which persistent avoidance behavior originated during an active phase of Panic Disorder, even if the person does not attribute the avoidance behavior to fear of having a panic attack.) As a result of this fear, the person either restricts travel or needs a companion when away from home or else endures agoraphobic situations despite intense anxiety. Common agoraphobic situations include being outside the home alone, being in a crowd or standing in line, being on a bridge, and traveling in a bus, train, or car.

Social Phobia is a fear of exposure to the scrutiny of others, particularly e fear of embarrassment or humiliation due to one's actions while others e watching (see Table 10). Although seemingly straightforward, the diag- sis of Social Phobia can be a complex one to make. The presence of social xiety in and of itself is not sufficient to warrant the diagnosis of Social obia. For example, social anxiety resulting from intense fear of intimacy

TABLE 10. DSM-III-R Diagnostic Criteria for Social Phobia

A. A persistent fear of one or more situations (the social phobic situations) in which the person is exposed to possible scrutiny by other and fears that he or she may do something or act in a way that will be humiliating or embarrassing. Examples include being unable to continue talking while speaking in public, choking on food when eating in front of others, being unable to urinate in a public lavatory, hand trembling when writing in the presence of others, and saying foolish things or not being able to answer questions in social situations.

B. If an Axis III or another Axis I disorder is present, the fear in A is unrelated to it, e.g., the fear is not of having a panic attack (Panic Disorder), stuttering (Stuttering), trembling (Parkinson's disease), or exhibiting abnormal eating behavior (Anorexia Nervosa or Bulimia Nervosa).

C. During some phase of the disturbance, exposure to the specific phobia stimulus (or stimuli) almost invariably provokes an immediate anxiety response.

D. The phobic situation(s) is avoided or is endured with intense anxiety.

E. The avoidant behavior interferes with occupational functioning or with usual social activities or relationships with others, or there is marked distress about having the fear.

F. The person recognizes that his or her fear is excessive or unreasonable.

G. If the person is under 18, the disturbance does not meet the criteria for Avoidant Disorder of Childhood or Adolescence.

Specify generalized type if the phobic situation includes most social situations and also consider the additional diagnosis of Avoidant Personality Disorder.

in a person with Borderline Personality Disorder or from hypersensitivity to potential rejection in a person with Avoidant Personality Disorder would not necessarily lead to a separate diagnosis of Social Phobia. There must be a persistent fear of one or more situations in which the person is exposed to possible scrutiny by others and fears that he or she may act in a way that will be humiliating or embarrassing. Social Phobias often include fear that one's anxiety will be noticed by others. Thus a social phobic may be unwilling to write in the view of others for fear that his or her hand will tremble or may avoid social situations for fear of being so nervous that he or she will perspire excessively.

One difficult but important differential diagnosis is that between Social Phobia and Paranoia. Social phobics are often concerned that people are watching them and talking about them and thus might be diagnosed as paranoid. However, it would be more appropriate to consider these individuals as acutely self-conscious rather than paranoid. These clients are often so worried about people noticing their anxiety that they feel as if they are the center of attention. However, unlike individuals with true Paranoia, they do not ascribe malicious intentions to other people and do not feel that they are in danger of anything worse than humiliation.

Both agoraphobics and social phobics often become anxious in public but in different ways and for different reasons. Social phobics are not concerned about having panic attacks, as are agoraphobics, and generally do not feel a need to be accompanied by a friend or family member. Although agoraphobics often do worry about embarrassing themselves in public by having a panic attack, they can be distinguished from social phobics by the fact that they worry not only about embarrassment but also about being unable to escape from the situation or unable to get help if they do panic.

A Simple Phobia is a persistent fear of a specific object or situation and is usually quite circumscribed (see Table 11). Fears of specific stimuli such as heights, insects, snakes, and so on are quite common but would be considered to be Simple Phobias only if the fear and/or avoidance resulted in significant impairment or distress. Simple phobias encountered in clinical practice range from the commonplace, such as fear of flying, to the idiosyncratic, such as fear of the wind. It is important to remember that if the consequence that the individual fears is embarrassment or humiliation, a diagnosis of Social Phobia is likely to be more appropriate than a diagnosis of Simple Phobia. For example, most clients who enter therapy complaining of a fear of breaking into a sweat in social situations would not be classified as Simple Phobia (fear of sweat) but, rather, as Social Phobia because they are actually less concerned about sweat *per se* than they are that others will notice their excessive perspiration and that they will then be humiliated and embarrassed.

When a client seeks therapy for what appears to be a fear or phobia, it is important to ascertain whether the symptoms involve compulsive rituals or not. For example, many clients who report a fear of germs or dirt have developed elaborate hand washing or cleaning rituals as a result of their fears. It is often necessary to explore this area carefully because clients may be so used to their extensive strategies for preventing harm that they no longer view them as rituals and may not think to mention them. Even if

---

TABLE 11. DSM-III-R Diagnostic Criteria for Simple Phobia

A. A persistent fear of a circumscribed stimulus (object or situation) other than fear of having a panic attack (as in Panic Disorder) or of humiliation or embarrassment in certain social situations (as in Social Phobia).

Note: Do not include fears that are part of Panic Disorder with Agoraphobia or Agoraphobia without History of Panic Disorder.

B. During some phase of the disturbance, exposure to the specifc phobic stimulus (or stimuli) almost invariably provokes an immediate anxiety response.
C. The object or situation is avoided or endured with intense anxiety.
D. The fear or the avoidant behavior significantly interferes with the person's normal routine or with usual social activities or relationships with others, or there is marked distress about having the fear.
E. The person recognizes that his or her fear is excessive or unreasonable.
F. The phobic stimulus is unrelated to the content of the obsessions of Obsessive Compulsive Disorder or the trauma of Post-Traumatic Stress Disorder.

TABLE 12. DSM-III-R Diagnostic Criteria for Obsessive-Compulsive Disorder

A. Either obsessions or compulsions:

Obsessions—1, 2, 3, and 4:

1. Recurrent and persistent ideas, thoughts, impulses, or images that are experienced, at least initially, as intrusive and senseless, e.g., a parent's having repeated impulses to kill a loved child, a religious person's having recurrent blasphemous thoughts
2. The person attempts to ignore or suppress such thoughts or impulses or to neutralize them with some other thought or action
3. The person recognizes that the obsessions are the product of his or her own mind, not imposed from without (as in thought insertion)
4. If another Axis I disorder is present, the content of the obsession is unrelated to it, e.g., the ideas, thoughts, impulses, or images are not about food in the presence of an Eating Disorder, about drugs in the presence of a Psychoactive Substance Use Disorder, or guilty thoughts in the presence of a Major Depression

Compulsions: 1, 2, and 3:

1. Repetitive, purposeful, and intentional behaviors that are performed in response to an obsession, or according to certain rules or in a stereotyped fashion
2. The behavior is designed to neutralize or to prevent discomfort or some dreaded event or situation; however, either the activity is not connected in a realistic way with what it is designed to neutralize or prevent, or it is clearly excessive
3. The person recognizes that his or her behavior is excessive or unreasonable (this may not be true for young children; it may no longer be true for people whose obsessions have evolved into overvalued ideas)

B. The obsessions or compulsions cause marked distress, are time consuming (take more than an hour a day), or significantly interfere with a person's normal routine, occupational functioning, or usual social activities or relationships with others.

---

fears and phobias do exist, if a person also has significant obsessions or compulsions, she or he would be diagnosed as having an Obsessive-Compulsive Disorder (see Table 12) rather than a phobia. Treatment for the rituals would generally need to precede any treatment addressed at the fears or phobias.

The criteria for Generalized Anxiety Disorder are much more specific in DSM-III-R than they were in previous diagnostic systems (see Table 13); however, the use of the term *generalized* still leads many to mistakenly assume that the anxiety is continuous, pervasive, and "free floating." Careful cognitive and behavioral assessment of individuals with Generalized Anxiety Disorder makes it clear that there are definite variations in the presence and intensity of anxiety, depending on the situation and cognitions of the client at the time. Even though it is common for clients to initially experience their anxiety as occurring spontaneously for no apparent reason, the concept of free-floating anxiety (i.e., anxiety that occurs "out of the blue" for no reason) does not seem to be borne out when careful assessment takes place. With systematic monitoring of both behaviors and

TABLE 13. DSM-III-R Diagnostic Criteria for Generalized Anxiety Disorder

A. Unrealistic or excessive anxiety and worry (apprehensive expectation) about two or more life circumstances, e.g., worry about possible misfortune to one's child (who is in no danger) and worry about finances (for no good reason), for a period of six months or longer, during which the person has been bothered more days than not by these concerns. In children and adolescents, this may take the form of anxiety and worry about academic, athletic, and social performance.

B. If another Axis I disorder is present, the focus of the anxiety and worry in A is unrelated to it, e.g., the anxiety or worry is not about having a panic attack (as in Panic Disorder), being embarrassed in public (as in Social Phobia), being contaminated (as in Obsessive Compulsive Disorder) or gaining weight (as in Anorexia Nervosa).

C. The disturbance does not occur only during the course of a Mood Disorder or a psychotic disorder.

D. At least 6 of the following 18 symptoms are often present when anxious (do not include symptoms present only during panic attacks):

Motor tension
1. Trembling, twitching, or feeling shaky
2. Muscle tension, aches, or soreness
3. Restlessness
4. Easy fatigability

Autonomic hyperactivity
5. Shortness of breath or smothering sensations
6. Palpitations or accelerated heart rate (tachycardia)
7. Sweating or cold clammy hands
8. Dry mouth
9. Dizziness or lightheadedness
10. Nausea, diarrhea, or other abdominal distress
11. Flushes (hot flashes) or chills
12. Frequent urination
13. Trouble swallowing or "lump in throat"

Vigilance and scanning
14. Feeling keyed up or on edge
15. Exaggerated startle response
16. Difficulty concentrating or "mind going blank" because of anxiety
17. Trouble falling or staying asleep
18. Irritability

E. It cannot be established that an organic factor initiated and maintained the disturbance, e.g., hyperthyroidism, Caffeine Intoxication.

cognitions, it becomes apparent that the anxiety was indeed triggered by particular stimuli, although often by thoughts or interoceptive cues that may not be obvious to the external observer.

Post-Traumatic Stress Disorder (PTSD) has received much attention in recent years due to the high incidence of PTSD among combat veterans. However, it should be noted that PTSD can occur following any extraordinary traumatic event such as a natural disaster, a major accident, or a

Table 14. DSM-III-R Diagnostic Criteria for Post-Traumatic Stress Disorder

A. The person has experienced an event that is outside the range of usual human experience and that would be markedly distressing to almost anyone, e.g., serious threat to one's life or physical integrity; serious threat or harm to one's children, spouse, or other close relatives and friends; sudden destruction of one's home or community; or seeing another person who has recently been, or is being, seriously injured or killed as the result of an accident or physical violence.

B. The traumatic event is persistently reexperienced in at least one of the following ways:
   1. Recurrent and intrusive distressing recollections of the event (in young children, repetitive play in which themes or aspects of the trauma are expressed)
   2. Recurrent distressing dreams of the event
   3. Sudden acting or feeling as if the traumatic event were recurring (includes a sense of reliving the experience, illusions, hallucinations, and dissociative [flashback] episodes, even those that occur upon awakening or when intoxicated)
   4. Intense psychological distress at exposure to events that symbolize or resemble an aspect of the traumatic event, including anniversaries of the trauma

C. Persistent avoidance of stimuli associated with the trauma or numbing of general responsiveness (not present before the trauma), as indicated by at least three of the following:
   1. Efforts to avoid thoughts or feelings associated with the trauma
   2. Efforts to avoid activities or situations that arouse recollections of the trauma
   3. Inability to recall an important aspect of the trauma (psychogenic amnesia)
   4. Markedly diminished interest in significant activities (in young children, loss of recently acquired developmental skills such as toilet training or language skills)
   5. Feeling of detachment or estrangement from others
   6. Restricted range of affect, e.g., unable to have loving feelings
   7. Sense of a foreshortened future, e.g., does not expect to have a career, marriage, or children, or a long life

D. Persistent symptoms of increased arousal (not present before the trauma), as indicated by a least two of the following:
   1. Difficulty falling or staying asleep
   2. Irritability or outbursts of anger
   3. Difficulty concentrating
   4. Hypervigilance
   5. Exaggerated startle response
   6. Physiologic reactivity upon exposure to events that symbolize or resemble an aspect of the traumatic event (e.g., a woman who was raped in an elevator breaks out in a sweat when entering any elevator)

E. Duration of the disturbance (symptoms in B, C, and D) of at least 1 month.

Specify delayed onset if the onset of symptoms was at least 6 months after the trauma.

victimization (see Table 14). Clinically, it is valuable to distinguish between PTSD resulting from a single traumatic event and PTSD resulting from recurrent trauma. Persons with PTSD stemming from recurrent trauma appear to be much more difficult to treat effectively.

In making a DSM-III-R diagnosis, as well as in the treatment of anxiety disorders, cognitive assessment is especially important because the same outward behavior patterns and reported fears may reflect very different disorders depending on the personal meaning of the situations to the client. Any given phobic stimulus may be part of a Simple Phobia, Social Phobia, or Panic Disorder, depending on the cognitions behind the fear. Two clients seeking treatment for driving phobia, for example, may have different disorders depending on their cognitions. One client may report only such thoughts as "I could have an accident and die," "People drive like maniacs," and "This is too dangerous," indicating a Simple Phobia. The second client may report all these cognitions plus thoughts like "What if I have a panic attack and can't get home?" "I'll be stuck on the highway all alone" and "No one will be there to help me," indicating the possibility that the client may be agoraphobic and be likely to have other areas of avoidance as well.

Cognitive assessment with anxiety clients can be challenging because they are frequently unaware of their thoughts related to their anxiety and avoidance. When asked exactly what they are afraid of or nervous about, the most typical response is, "I don't know, I just feel afraid" or, "I don't have any particular thoughts, I just feel bad." One client who complained of a fear of bridges insisted that she had no thoughts whatsoever about bridges, knew there was nothing to be afraid of, and just got an intense physical feeling of fear any time she approached a bridge. Given the frequent lack of awareness of cognitions, it may be necessary to be creative in eliciting automatic thoughts from anxiety clients. In this case, the therapist started off using the fairly traditional approach of simply asking what thoughts ran through the client's mind as she approached a bridge. When that was ineffective, the therapist decided to try using imagery by asking the client to close her eyes and imagine herself driving toward a particular bridge while the therapist described the scene in detail. When the client was able to vividly imagine herself approaching the bridge, she was able to report all the physical feelings of fear that she was experiencing and in the midst of her descriptions of her feelings she reported the thought, "What if I fall off the edge?"

If imagery is not vivid enough to elicit automatic thoughts, it may be useful to use *in-vivo* exposure (actually going into the feared situation with the client) for the purpose of collecting automatic thoughts. With the therapist along to help focus the client's attention on thoughts and with the level of anxiety rising as the object or situation becomes closer, most clients are able to report some of their cognitions. In some cases, role playing can be useful in eliciting automatic thoughts, especially those occurring in interpersonal situations.

Because many clients have been told by family and friends that their fears are silly, they may be inhibited from disclosing their automatic thoughts. They know the thoughts are irrational and are often concerned about being rejected by the therapist. The therapist can reassure the client that although thoughts may sound silly on the surface, those fears can be very intense and just as strong as if a gun were put to their head.

Cognitive assessment is generally discussed in terms of assessing verbal thought. In a study of anxiety, however, 90% of clients reported visual images of being in danger prior to and concomitant with their anxiety (Beck, Laude, & Bohnert, 1974). Many clients who have difficulty pinpointing specific verbal automatic thoughts will be able to graphically describe images of disaster when asked whether they get any pictures, images, or scenes that flash through their mind when they are anxious. Therefore, assessment of imagery should always be a part of cognitive assessment of anxiety. Just as imagining a scene in systematic desensitization evokes similar emotional reactions to those that would be experienced if exposed to the actual stimulus, so too does imagining a catastrophe evoke emotional responses similar to those that would occur in reaction to an actual catastrophe. Therefore, in Cognitive Therapy it is just as important to be able to pinpoint and modify mental imagery as it is to pinpoint and modify verbal automatic thoughts.

Given the wide variety of physical symptoms experienced by clients with anxiety disorders, it is crucial to have the client receive a complete physical examination to rule out physiological disorders that require medical treatment. DSM-III-R has introduced the diagnosis of Organic Anxiety Syndrome that is marked by prominent, recurrent panic attacks or generalized anxiety caused by a specific organic factor. Certain endocrine disorders can cause symptoms similar to anxiety disorders, as can withdrawal from substances such as sedatives or alcohol and intoxication from caffeine or amphetamines. These conditions would be given the diagnosis of Organic Anxiety Syndrome and not be considered anxiety disorders. The practice of requiring a physical examination before giving a diagnosis of anxiety disorder is important in ruling out Organic Anxiety Syndrome, but it has other important advantages in the treatment of anxiety disorders as well. Many anxiety clients have catastrophic thoughts about their symptoms, thinking they are dying or having a stroke or heart attack. It is crucial for both the client and the therapist to know whether there is a rational basis for the fears or not. Thus having a thorough physical examination can be the first step in challenging the catastrophic thoughts.

It is also important to pay careful attention to symptoms of depression when dealing with clients with anxiety disorders. Depressive symptoms are quite common in anxiety clients, especially in clients with Panic Disorder or Obsessive-Compulsive Disorder, and frequently the symptoms are severe enough to fit the DSM-III-R criteria for Major Depression. In fact, when attempting to conduct a study that required subjects with agoraphobia but without symptoms of depression, one of the authors found it almost impossible to find such subjects even among a sample of hundreds of agoraphobics.

The crucial distinction to make when a person shows symptoms of both an anxiety disorder and depression is whether the depression is primary or secondary. If the client has no history of Major Depression prior to the onset of the anxiety disorder, if the depression clearly began after the agoraphobia, or if he or she reports that the depression is due to the limitations resulting from agoraphobia, then the person would be given both the diagnoses of Panic Disorder with Agoraphobia and Major Depression and the depression would be considered secondary to the agoraphobia. In such cases, treatment primarily focusing on agoraphobia would be appropriate, although it may be necessary to address some aspects of the depression early in the treatment. If, however, the depression predated the agoraphobia or is clearly independent of it, the depression would not be considered secondary to the agoraphobia and successful treatment of the agoraphobia would not be expected to alleviate the depression. Obviously, if the client is avoiding situations because he or she is too depressed and cannot deal with the outside world, then the individual would not be given a diagnosis of Panic Disorder, and treatment for depression would be more appropriate.

Many clients use alcohol or other substances to reduce their anxiety, often to the point of abuse or dependence. Because these clients often underreport their use of these substances, it is crucial to get a careful and detailed history of the client's use of alcohol and other substances and to ask specific questions about his or her current practices. Research has consistently provided evidence of state-dependent learning (e.g., Eich, 1977), and this indicates that any type of desensitization procedures administered under the influence of alcohol may not generalize to a dry state. Thus, any alcohol or substance abuse would need to be treated before an anxiety treatment program is likely to be beneficial. Even clients who do not actually abuse alcohol may count on its availability as a coping strategy and, if so, they will need to stop using alcohol in this way and learn alternative coping strategies in order for treatment to be effective.

CONCEPTUALIZATION

Anxiety is a part of everyday life and in many situations can be functional. Anxiety is generally considered a normal reaction if it is aroused by a present danger and if it dissipates when the danger is no longer present. If the degree of anxiety is greatly disproportionate to the danger or if no objective danger is present, then the reaction is considered to be abnormal. The precise boundaries between what is considered to be normal and abnormal anxiety are defined to a large degree by social norms.

According to Beck's cognitive theory of psychopathology (Beck, 1976), the thinking of the anxious client is dominated by themes of danger. The client anticipates threats to self and family, and those threats can be either physical, psychological, or social in nature. In phobias, the anticipation of physical or psychological harm is confined to specific situations. The fears are based on the client's exaggerated conception of specific harmful attributes of these situations. The phobic is not afraid of the situation or object in and of itself but rather is afraid of the consequences of being in the situation or in contact with the object. In Generalized Anxiety Disorder and Panic Disorder, the client anticipates danger in situations that are less specific and therefore more difficult to avoid. Thus, the thinking of the anxious client is characterized by repetitive thoughts about danger that take the form of continuous verbal or pictorial cognitions about the occurrence of harmful events.

A number of cognitive distortions are particularly common in anxious clients and tend to amplify their anxiety:

1. *Catastrophizing.* Anxious clients tend to dwell on the most extreme negative consequences conceivable, assuming that a situation in which there is any possibility of harm constitutes a highly probable danger. Simple phobics tend to expect disaster in the form of physical harm when faced with a specific situation or object, social phobics expect more personal disaster in the form of humiliation and embarrassment, and agoraphobics expect disaster as the consequence of their own internal experience of anxiety or panic attacks.

2. *Personalization.* Anxious individuals often react as though external events are personally relevant and are indications of a potential danger to him or her. Thus, if an anxious client hears about a car accident, she or he may decide that he or she is likely to have a car accident as well.

3. *Magnification and minimization.* When anxious, individuals tend to focus on signs of danger or potential threat to the exclusion of other aspects of the situation. Thus the anxious client tends to emphasize any aspects of a situation that might be seen as dangerous and minimize or ignore the nonthreatening or rescue factors in a situation.

4. *Selective abstraction.* The anxious person often focuses on the threatening elements of a situation and ignores the context.

5. *Arbitrary inference.* The anxious client frequently jumps to dire conclusions on the basis of little or no data. For example, a client may assume that any unusual feeling in the body must be a heart attack or that any turbulence means the airplane will crash.

6. *Overgeneralization.* The client may view a time-limited situation as lasting forever (i.e., "this panic attack will never end"), may assume that because a particular problem has occurred previously it is bound to reoccur frequently or may assume that if he or she had any difficulty in a particular situation that shows that the situation is dangerous.

Research has demonstrated that certain beliefs are characteristic of anxious individuals (Deffenbacher, Zwemer, Whisman, Hill, & Sloan, 1986; Zwemer & Deffenbacher, 1984). In a nonclinical population, these authors found that anxious individuals tended to believe that if something is or may be dangerous or fearsome, one should be terribly upset about it and continually think and worry about it (anxious overconcern), that one has to be thoroughly competent, adequate, and achieving in order to be worthwhile (personal perfection), that it is horrible when things are not the way they would like them to be (catastrophizing), and that it is easier to avoid than to face life's difficulties (problem avoidance). In a clinical study of the beliefs of phobics, Mizes, Landolf-Fritsche, and Grossman-McKee (1987) found that in addition to anxious overconcern and problem avoidance already discussed, phobics also endorsed the belief that it is essential to be loved and approved by all significant others (demand for approval). Significant, but weaker, correlations were found between level of phobic avoidance and both the idea that the past determines present feelings and behaviors that cannot be changed (helplessness) and the idea that one must do well at everything to be worthwhile (high self-expectations). Although research is not yet available on clinical populations of different types of phobics, it seems clear from clinical observation that social phobics are ruled by the belief that it is a dire necessity to be loved by everyone for everything they do. They also seem to hold the underlying assumption that it is essential to appear strong and in control at all times, and that any demonstration of weakness or anxiety is disastrous. Agoraphobics seem to be especially concerned with the issue of control and to hold the underlying assumption that one must have certain and perfect control over things. They also tend to hold a generalized belief that the world is threatening if confronted independently and that security from danger must be ensured either through the availability of a loved one or by being extremely cautious.

A cognitive model of anxiety (Figure 9) demonstrates how a number of cognitive factors work together in the development and maintenance of anxiety. An individual's perception of each situation he or she encounters is shaped by his or her beliefs and assumptions and can be biased by any cognitive distortions that occur. If a situation is perceived as presenting some degree of risk of threat, the individual automatically evaluates the degree of threat present as well as his or her capacity for handling the situation satisfactorily. Although the perception of threat elicits anxiety, belief in one's own self-efficacy (or ability to cope in that particular situation) moderates the perception of threat and hence the anxiety. Thus if one perceives a stimulus as dangerous but is convinced that he or she will be able to safely deal with the danger, the stimulus is seen as less of a threat and causes less anxiety. However, if one has low self-efficacy and feels incapable of dealing with the potential danger, anxiety is increased. Take

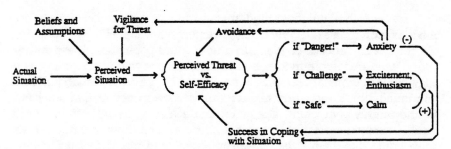

FIGURE 9. A cognitive model of anxiety.

the example of two people looking down from a steep cliff. One person is an experienced mountain climber. She can see that there is the risk of falling and that it would be dangerous to fall. However, she knows from her experience that she has the skills she needs to cope with the situation, so she experiences a sense of challenge, excitement, and enthusiasm. The other person has never done any mountain climbing before. He sees the threat of falling but, in addition, perceives that he does not have the ability to cope with the situation. Instead of a sense of challenge, he is overwhelmed with the sense of danger and experiences intense anxiety. A person's sense of self-efficacy is shaped by one's experience. If one perceives a situation as dangerous and is able to cope successfully with the situation, one's sense of self-efficacy is increased. The next time a similar situation is approached, that person is likely to feel less anxious and more able to cope. If, however, one experiences intense anxiety and is not able to cope effectively, one's sense of self-efficacy is decreased, and similar situations are likely to be viewed as even more dangerous in the future.

Intense anxiety tends to produce involuntary vigilance for signs of danger and, if any indications of danger are perceived, an involuntary fixation of attention on these danger signs. When one is objectively in danger, it seems only natural to focus one's attention on the danger until a solution has been found. However, the client with an anxiety disorder is unrealistically anxious and thus often is vigilant for signs of danger or is preoccupied with perceived dangers when this is not at all adaptive. As a result, the amount of attention remaining for focusing on specific tasks, recall, or self-reflection can be greatly restricted, and the client may well complain of inability to concentrate or of forgetfulness.

When faced with the experience of intense anxiety, an individual may choose to avoid or escape from the stimulus seen as dangerous. This can be a very effective short-term strategy and can successfully reduce anxiety for the moment. However, it has its cost. Because avoidance does nothing to change the perception of the stimulus as dangerous, the appraisal of threat is unmodified, and the stimuli continues to be seen as dangerous. In addition, avoidance does not help to increase self-efficacy. The client learns that the anxiety-provoking stimulus can be avoided but has no evidence that he or she is capable of handling it in any other, more direct way. Thus when again faced with the stimulus, the person may believe that he or she has no alternative but to again avoid or escape the situation. Thus avoidance reinforces future avoidance of the same and similar situations. Over time, consistent avoidance of problem situations can lower self-efficacy and increase the individual's anxiety. These patterns of avoidance can lead to any of the phobic disorders, the type of phobia differing primarily in the situations that elicit the anxiety and in the consequences that are feared.

If, instead of avoiding, the individual attempts to cope with the perceived danger through vigilance and worry and no catastrophe follows, he or she may conclude that the vigilance and worry proved effective. This pattern of response to perceived or anticipated threats can easily become habitual and result in frequent periods of stress and anxiety due to rumination about such threats. If such a pattern becomes sufficiently ingrained and the resulting anxiety becomes sufficiently intense, Generalized Anxiety Disorder could develop.

Obsessions go far beyond the distressing worries and rumination characteristic of individuals with Generalized Anxiety Disorder and are produced by a somewhat different pattern of cognitions. Most individuals occasionally experience thoughts, images, or impulses that they find repugnant. If the individual can accept that this experience is just a part of being human, no problem arises. However, if an individual believes that certain thoughts, feelings, or impulses are totally unacceptable, perhaps because they are a sign of insanity or moral depravity, then when such a thought, feeling, or impulse occurs, it is likely to be followed by catastrophic cognitions such as "God! How could I think such a thing? Only a freak would think that!" These cognitions elicit strong emotional reactions, including anxiety, and because anxiety produces an involuntary fixation of attention on signs of danger and vigilance for signs of danger (i.e., unacceptable thoughts), the individual can quickly become preoccupied with his or her unacceptable thoughts. This preoccupation tends to generate additional thoughts, images, or impulses on the same theme, and the flow of unacceptable cognitions can quickly become quite intense.

Compulsions arise when the individual tries a behavior or cognitive response that reduces his or her anxiety in the short run without dealing with the situation effectively. In this case, the anxiety soon returns, and the individual can easily become involved in a pattern of repeating the behavior or thought in order to obtain short-term anxiety relief without ever dealing effectively with the situation. One situation in which this is particularly likely to develop is when the individual is incorrectly attributing his or her anxiety to the situation at hand. For example, if an individual's belief that he or she is "dirty" is due to guilt over some transgression rather than being due to soiled hands, hand washing obviously will not eliminate the feeling of dirtiness, but it may provide enough temporary relief to become addicting. It has often been noted that clients with compulsions are often quite unwilling to acknowledge particular actions or feelings that they believe to be totally unacceptable. Obviously, an individual who is unwilling to acknowledge the problematic actions or feelings will be unable to deal with these directly and effectively and can easily become dependent on any strategy that provides temporary relief. Unfortunately, for many of these individuals, the relief is only momentary, and the "solution" becomes much worse than facing their "unacceptable" behavior or feelings would have been. Cognitive compulsions such as compulsive counting or compulsively repeating a particular prayer can develop as a way of blocking unacceptable thoughts, images, or impulses from awareness and then become "addictive" in the same way as compulsive acts.

PTSD can be conceptualized in terms of the individual's partially effective, partially dysfunctional attempts to avoid recalling his or her traumatic experiences. Individuals with PTSD attempt to avoid stimuli that might arouse recollections of the traumatic event(s) and attempt to avoid thoughts and feelings associated with the trauma, yet they are plagued by very distressing intrusive memories of the event(s). It is quite understandable that an individual who has undergone traumatic experiences would fear memories of the event and attempt to avoid them because these recollections are intensely distressing. However, he or she encounters the same problem as the person who is plagued by obsessions. The fear of memories, images, thoughts, and feelings associated with the traumatic event(s) results in a focus of attention on these cognitions and vigilance for stimuli that might elicit them. At the same time, the individual's determined avoidance of the cognitions blocks him or her from realizing that they are not dangerous, simply quite distressing.

Cognitive-behavioral theorists have devoted considerable effort to the task of developing and validating a theoretical model of Panic Disorder with Agoraphobia. Figure 10 presents a cognitive view of agoraphobia created by combining elements from the theories of agoraphobia presented by Goldstein and Chambless (1978) and by Mathews, Gelder, and Johnston (1981). This model is intended as a flow chart of the development of an anxiety disorder and is not meant to imply causality. The middle level of the chart illustrates the process of the development of the anxiety disorder, with the top and bottom levels showing predisposing and contributing factors.

People, particularly those with high levels of trait anxiety, may at some point in their lives experience a traumatic experience or an increase in stress that raises their anxiety to the point where new or more severe physical symptoms occur. This is particularly likely if the person already has a medical condition that is aggravated by stress and that has vague,

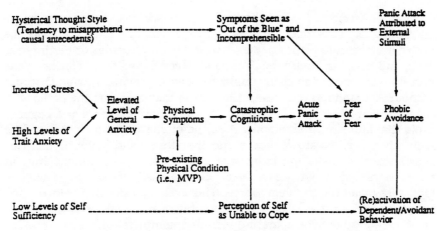

FIGURE 10. Cognitive model of Panic Disorder with Agoraphobia.

confusing symptoms.* Regardless of whether the symptoms experienced by the client are due to the interaction between increased anxiety and a vague physical condition or simply result from intensified anxiety, when the person notices these new and strange physical symptoms, he or she may begin to suspect that something is seriously wrong. These suspicions increase the client's anxiety and because the symptoms of concern are aggravated by anxiety, the symptoms increase in intensity. As the symptoms get worse, the suspicions seem to be confirmed, and they are replaced by catastrophic thoughts about the symptoms such as "I'm having a heart attack! I must be dying!" or "Oh no, I'm going to go crazy!" These thoughts serve to further increase the anxiety, intensifying the severity of the symptoms and stimulating further catastrophic thoughts. At the same time, the individual's increased attention to his or her physical sensations also aggravates the symptoms and makes them appear more severe and frightening. The anxiety symptoms and the fearful thoughts about the symptoms form a cycle that can spiral to peak levels of anxiety very quickly and produce an acute panic attack during which the individual is *certain* that he or she is dying, going crazy, or going "out of control."

*One physical condition that has been the source of much controversy recently in relation to anxiety disorders has been mitral valve prolapse. This is a generally benign heart condition that is often asymptomatic but that produces vague symptoms in some individuals. Empirical research into the relationship between mitral valve prolapse and agoraphobia have been conflicting with some studies showing a relationship and other studies failing to find such a relationship (summarized in Gorman, Shear, Devereux, King, and Klein, 1986). Whether a statistical connection between agoraphobia and mitral valve prolapse is substantiated or not, this syndrome is illustrative of how any physical syndrome with vague symptoms not clearly understood by the client can be part of the development of agoraphobia.

Once a panic attack has occurred, the person may become so frightened of having subsequent attacks that he or she begins to anticipate the possibility of future panic attacks, excessively monitors his or her internal state, and hence increases the likelihood of continued panic attacks. If the process stops here, the client might be seen as having a Panic Disorder without Agoraphobia. However, the person may associate the panic with the particular situation in which panic attacks have occurred and begin to avoid that and similar situations. Also, he or she may anticipate needing help when a panic attack occurs and therefore avoid being alone. This avoidance may make the individual more comfortable initially but, as noted previously, avoidance can easily decrease self-efficacy and is likely to gradually make the problem worse. This cycle can develop into the full syndrome of Panic Disorder with Agoraphobia and might eventually progress to the point where the individual is completely housebound. For example:

Jenny was a 28-year-old married female who was a housewife with a 3½-year-old son. Her husband was the pastor of a church in a small southern town. Jenny sought treatment because she had been having severe panic attacks for the past 2 years, and her life had become increasingly restricted. She was afraid of any situation out in public where she felt she might be trapped and unable to get home. She avoided stores, church, restaurants, waiting in line, theaters, and traveling alone. This had severely limited her life, and she felt depressed about it and had gained 20 lb in the past 2 years.

Jenny described herself as always having been "high-strung," but this had never been a problem for her in the past. As she saw it, her problems had begun about 2 years before during a church service when she got very light-headed, dizzy, her heart pounded, her hands got cold and clammy, she felt terrified and felt she had to leave. She left in the middle of her husband's sermon and was very embarrassed. This was the first in a series of panic attacks that always occurred when Jenny was out in public.

The first panic attack occurred at a time when Jenny had just moved from a large city to a small town, her son had just become a toddler, and her husband had a new parish and was spending much less time with her. However, Jenny did not attribute her physical symptoms to the stress she was under. Instead, she saw them as coming totally out of the blue and thought that it must be a physical problem. She sought medical attention, was diagnosed as having mitral valve prolapse, and her physician prescribed 150 mg of Imiprimine per day. She felt somewhat better on the medication but still had panic attacks and avoided a range of situations.

Two additional variables (shown in Figure 10) have been hypothesized by Goldstein and Chambless (1978) as predisposing an individual to continue through this entire process and develop Panic Disorder with Agoraphobia. The tendency to misapprehend causal antecedents (labeled *hysterical thought style* by Goldstein and Chambless) may increase the possibility that the anxiety symptoms will seem to come "out of the blue" and be totally incomprehensible. If Jenny had been able to think about her symptoms systematically and to draw accurate connections between cause and effect, she might have noticed her initial physical symptoms and thought, "Boy, I must really be under a lot of stress. Maybe I should take it easy for a while." This reaction would not have raised her anxiety level and thus would not have contributed to a panic attack. However, Jenny had a very impressionistic thought style and did not even realize that she had been under stress when the symptoms began until possible stressors were explored in detail in therapy 2 years later. Because she had drawn no connection between her increased stress and the physical symptoms, the symptoms seemed mysterious and frightening to her and thus were more likely to lead to catastrophic cognitions. A person who has difficulty thinking analytically is likely to look haphazardly for reasons for the symptoms, tending to attribute responsibility to the situation rather than to stress and anxiety. This makes it more likely that avoidance will ensue.

Low levels of self-sufficiency and self-efficacy can also predispose an individual to developing the full agoraphobic syndrome. A person who tends to be self-sufficient certainly could experience a panic attack if the situation were right, but he or she would then be likely to try dealing actively with the problem rather than avoiding situations associated with the panic attack and/or relying on others for security. The person who generally feels incapable of handling problems on his or her own is more likely to assume that there is nothing that he or she can possibly do to deal with the situation

STRATEGIES FOR INTERVENTION

The primary goal in treating clients with anxiety disorders is to eliminate both the client's disproportionate fears and any maladaptive patterns of avoiding or preventing anxiety that the individual may have developed. However, this is not easily done because the fears and the dysfunctional behaviors tend to perpetuate each other. The task is further complicated by the fact that rational responses do not have the same impact on anxiety as on other problematic emotions. It is quite common for a client to understand intellectually that he or she is in no danger but to continue to feel quite anxious and to avoid the feared situation.

The conceptualization of anxiety disorders presented in Figures 9 and 10 suggests a variety of points where useful intervention can occur. The client's overall level of anxiety can be reduced by training him or her in anxiety-reduction skills. The client's catastrophic cognitions regarding the feared situation, the anxiety symptoms, memories, thoughts, images, and the like and any hysterical thought style can all be challenged through cognitive restructuring. Avoidance, whether behavioral or cognitive, can be modified through intentionally exposing the client to the stimuli he or she fears (in collaboration with the client, of course). Finally, the client's sense of self-efficacy and self-sufficiency can be increased through cognitively challenging any unrealistically harsh appraisals of his or her capacities and through training in coping skills such as assertion. Each of these points of possible intervention can have an impact on the entire process of the anxiety disorder, but a more powerful impact is achieved when several aspects of the anxiety process are modified at the same time.

In general, individuals with anxiety disorders have allowed anxiety to take over their lives, investing a great deal of time and energy trying to fight, control, and/or avoid the anxiety. One widely used treatment tactic is to ask clients to give up their "control" of anxiety and instead to accept the experience of anxiety and expose themselves to situations in which their anxiety would be heightened. As they do so and discover that the consequences are not as catastrophic as they initially expected, the anxiety gradually fades away. However, in order to enable clients to face the situations they fear, it is necessary to first challenge their appraisal of threat cognitively. As long as clients truly believe that exposing themselves to the feared situation will cause them to risk dying, "going crazy," being humiliated, and so forth, they will not expose themselves to the situation, no matter how hard the therapist tries to encourage them. Only when the belief that disaster is inevitable has been effectively challenged, at least to some extent, will clients be willing to initiate approach behavior.

Exposure to the phobic stimulus, whether it is exposure to a single situation, a wide range of situations, or a range of internal cues, is a central part of the treatment of anxiety disorders. This exposure can be done in imagery or in the actual situations the client fears; it can be done in gradual steps or all at once, and it can be done as part of homework assignments or with the therapist's assistance. The coping skills used to reduce the client's general level of stress can be used to help reduce his or her anxiety during exposure to feared situations, but it is the experience of encountering the feared situations in such a way that disaster does not follow that is crucial.

Training in coping skills and exposure to phobic situations are not only useful in reversing avoidance and weakening the connection between the situation and the experience of anxiety. These interventions also serve to increase the client's sense of self-efficacy, leaving clients with a new sense that they can indeed cope with situations. These interventions are especially powerful because they provide the client with concrete accomplishments that provide particularly convincing evidence of self-efficacy (Bandura, 1977). An increase in self-efficacy should not only lower the client's anxiety level and contribute to improved coping but also should help reduce the client's likelihood of developing further anxiety reactions.

The process of monitoring and challenging dysfunctional thoughts is useful as a coping strategy in the situation where the client becomes anxious and also has the added effect of altering the client's "hysterical thought style." Cognitive restructuring can help him or her learn to take the time to look critically at the thoughts and feelings generated in various situations, thus reducing the tendency to automatically jump to conclusions and misunderstand the relationships between cause and effect. This facilitates more effective problem solving and reduces the likelihood of similar problems occurring in the future. (See Chapter 9 for additional suggestions for modifying a global, impressionistic thought style.)

Another type of intervention that has received much attention in recent years is the use of medication, especially for reducing or eliminating panic attacks. These medications are not necessarily incompatible with Cognitive Therapy; in fact, there is some research that indicates that medications may facilitate the process of exposure by helping the client be more willing to approach anxiety-provoking situations (summarized in Barlow & Waddell, 1985). However, because the relapse rates for medication treatment alone are alarmingly high and because many antianxiety medications are potentially addicting, the use of medication alone is not a sufficient treatment for any of the anxiety disorders. When medications are used in conjunction with Cognitive Therapy, it is important that the client be faded off the medication while Cognitive Therapy is still in progress to prevent relapse. At that time, any fears about discontinuing the medication can be addressed, and behavioral experiments can be performed to demonstrate convincingly to the client that progress can be maintained even without the medication.

COGNITIVE AND BEHAVIORAL TECHNIQUES

Many clients with anxiety disorders are frightened in part because their problems seem incomprehensible. Therefore, it can be quite valuable to begin treatment by educating the client about anxiety. After the initial evaluation, the therapist can explain the symptoms of anxiety to the client in detail, basing the explanation on the client's personal experience as much as possible. This brief didactic presentation helps the client to feel understood and to have confidence in the therapist as well as establishing a rationale for the interventions that will follow. Most clients with anxiety symptoms have been to many different medical and mental health professionals without receiving clear explanations and without feeling that aynone understands their problems. They often feel that their problems are unique and are quite reassured to discover that other people have had similar problems and have been successfully treated. A clear explanation can also be the first step in decatastrophizing the presence of the symptoms and helping clients become less excessively concerned with them.

One way to give anxious clients some relief while also beginning to challenge the belief that they are helpless and cannot handle situations is to increase their self-efficacy by teaching them specific skills to help them reduce their own anxiety. Rather than just challenging their feelings of helplessness verbally, learning coping skills provides convincing evidence that the client can, in fact, cope with anxiety. Once the client feels armed with tools that make him or her more adequate to deal with anxiety, he or she may be more likely to be willing to attempt some exposure to anxiety-provoking situations. Thus training in coping skills can serve two distinct purposes: (1) to actually help the person reduce anxiety and thus make exposure more comfortable and (2) to build the person's self-efficacy and make him or her more willing to try confronting his or her fears. Coping skills that are especially useful in reducing anxiety include relaxation methods and outward focus techniques.

A wide variety of relaxation training methods are useful clinically, ranging from simple deep breathing methods to elaborate, highly technical biofeedback procedures. (See Bernstein and Borkovec, 1976, for a good introduction to relaxation techniques.) The most important variable seems not to be which technique is used but, rather, that whatever technique is chosen is practiced consistently and that the client has faith in it. Any relaxation method that is practiced regularly with confidence will help the client achieve deeper levels of relaxation. The choice of relaxation method is important, however, because of the importance of teaching a method that will engage the client and is likely to maintain interest and cooperation. Taking a careful history of previous attempts at learning relaxation and eliciting current cognitions about relaxation are crucial steps needed before deciding which relaxation method is most likely to be effective with a particular client. Factors to consider include whether the individual finds a simple deep breathing method too boring or has difficulty keeping his or her mind from wandering (indicating a need for a somewhat more complex method, possibly with a tape recording to use to focus attention), whether he or she experiences physical pain that would make methods involving muscle tensing too uncomfortable, or whether his or her tension tends to build in one area of the body that is particularly difficult to relax (indicating possible benefits of tensing and then relaxing that area or using biofeedback regarding tension in that particular muscle group).

Relaxation can be helpful for clients with the full range of anxiety disorders and serves to reduce generalized anxiety, increase self-efficacy, and provide a coping tool for use when facing particularly stressful or anxiety-provoking situations. It also tends to increase clients' awareness of early stages of anxiety, so that they may be able to begin to deal with their anxiety while it is still reasonably low and prevent their symptoms from intensifying. It is important for the client to have realistic expectations about the likely effects of relaxation training. Clients with Generalized Anxiety Disorder may find that relaxation methods alone may help bring about a significant change in their symptoms; but for phobic clients, relaxation is only a first step in the treatment and cannot be expected to have a major impact on the symptoms in and of itself. In particular, although relaxation can be useful in preventing panic attacks by lowering the client's overall level of anxiety, once a panic attack has started, most clients do not find relaxation helpful in coping with the panic itself.

One of the major coping techniques used for the reduction of anxiety has often been referred to as "diversion" or "distraction." This terminology has led some therapists to criticize the technique as providing a way for the person to "escape" from the realities of the current situation and to see it as another mode of avoidance. Using the term *outward focus* makes the true purpose and usefulness of this technique more obvious. An excessive focus on the client's internal state serves to make the anxiety symptoms more severe and to decrease the more appropriate focus on the world outside of the client's body. Changing one's focus to specific items and events in the external world, however, is a very appropriate return to reality, rather than an avoidance of it. Although it can be very difficult for clients to simply ignore their symptoms, they can be taught the skill of focusing their attention on something specific outside of their body as an alternative to excessively focusing on their internal state. This technique is useful for most anxiety clients whenever they find their anxiety increasing and want to disrupt the cycle that amplifies it. Although it is very difficult for an individual to simply "stop worrying," it is not difficult to block catastrophic thoughts about one's internal symptoms by focusing on something else and occupying one's mind with that for a few minutes. This technique is particularly useful for clients who experience panic attacks because it is one coping skill that can be used effectively in the midst of even the strongest panic attack, often diffusing the panic in a matter of seconds.

When teaching outward focus as a coping technique, the therapist has the client rate his or her anxiety at a time when he or she is quite anxious, then instructs him or her to focus on some item in the office such as a lamp or pencil sharpener. The client is asked to describe the item in detail as if describing it to a Martian who has never seen a lamp before. What is its size, shape, color, texture? How would it look from different angles? What writing does it have on it? After this has continued for a few minutes, the client is again asked to rate his or her level of anxiety, which hopefully is lower than before the exercise, and the rationale for focusing on nonthreatening stimuli in order to block the cognitions that amplify his or her anxiety is explained. Other forms of outward focus that are useful in public situations can also be explained such as "eavesdropping" on the conversations of strangers, counting the number of people wearing red, singing along with songs on the car radio, watching for out-of-state license plates, and so forth. The client is then encouraged to practice this technique between sessions, whenever he or she has a panic attack, in order to both demonstrate its effectiveness and to become more skilled at using the technique. With social phobics, it is especially useful to help them learn to use focusing on the details of the face of the person they are taking to as a form of outward focus. With practice, this technique can be used to reduce anxiety during a conversation without anyone else noticing.

Intervention with Jenny occurred at many different points. Initially, she was taught relaxation and outward focus to lower her general level of anxiety. For Jenny, any focus on breathing in the relaxation was not helpful, because if she focused her attention on her breathing, she started to worry about whether she was breathing "right" or not. Instead, she learned an autogenic method where she focused on relaxing various muscle groups. She found that learning to change her focus of attention through the use of outward focus was particularly helpful to her because it changed her natural pattern of focusing on her symptoms. Together, graded exposure and training in coping skills led to early success and feelings of self-efficacy, so that each session started out with her proudly announcing all the accomplishments of the week.

Even while the therapist is educating the client about anxiety and teaching coping skills, he or she should be collecting data about the client's automatic thoughts and images. Learning to identify automatic thoughts is a crucial early step in Cognitive Therapy with anxiety. Once the client has learned to identify these automatic thoughts and images, possibly using the dysfunctional thought records discussed in Chapter 3, the full range of techniques can be used to challenge these thoughts. The therapist can also help the client challenge his or her thoughts by providing factual information that the client does not have (for example, facts about the physical consequences of physical symptoms or statistics about the odds of being killed in an airplane crash) and by helping the client explore possible rescue factors in the situation.

Jenny's treatment quickly moved to cognitive work to address her fear of the fear and catastrophic cognitions. Her main fears were of having a panic attack and either passing out or embarrassing herself in public. She began to write Dysfunctional Thought Records during the week whenever she attempted to do hierarchy items and at any other times that she felt particularly anxious. An example of an early DTR is shown in Figure 11. What she reported as being the most helpful in challenging her automatic thoughts was learning to distinguish specific symptoms of anxiety and other, normal feelings of discomfort from a full panic attack. In the past, if she noticed that she was feeling dizzy, for example, she would automatically conclude that she was going to have a full panic attack, pass out, and humiliate herself. As she got skilled at identifying and challenging her automatic thoughts, however, she was able to notice one symptom, check to see if there was any way she could understand why she might be having that symptom (stress from rushing around too fast, son cranky, fight with husband, expecting her period, etc.) and practice some coping skills to reduce the symptom.

Daily Record of Automatic Thoughts

Date	Situation Briefly describe the situation	Emotion(s) Rate 0–100%	Automatic Thought(s) Try to quote thoughts then rate your belief in each thought 0–100%	Rational Response Rate degree of belief 0–100%	Outcome Re-rate emotions
	Before shopping at Jacobson's	Anxious 65	I haven't been here since I had a panic attack here. What if I panic again?	There's no reason to believe I'll panic again. Besides, if I get anxious, I can do relaxation and concentrate on my shopping and I'll survive.	Anxious 20
	While shopping at Jacobson's	Anxious 25	I feel a bit disoriented and wobbly. Am I starting to panic?	The floor is made of plank and uneven. This may be just a natural response.	Anxious 0
	At church, sitting in the middle in a crowded service	Anxious 50	My heart is pounding	I'll be all right even if my heart pounds a great deal. (It didn't)	
			Without Joey here with me, I have no excuse to leave.	If I want to leave, I can even if Joey isn't here.	Anxious 0

FIGURE 11. A thought sheet from Jenny, an agoraphobic client.

One useful experience that occurred coincidentally after her sixth therapy session was that she was driving alone with her son, and her car broke down far away from home. Despite all her fears of what would happen if she were trapped away from home, she handled the situation appropriately. Later, as she looked back on that experience, she could see that she had been realistically anxious but had not panicked; and she was able to refer back to that experience throughout treatment whenever she began to confuse feelings of anxiety with panic.

Because catastrohizing is one of the major cognitive distortions in anxiety disorders, decatastrophizing is one of the major cognitive interventions. Through Socratic questioning, the therapist helps the client explore what could actually happen in the situation. In the treatment of anxiety disorders, the most commonly asked question is, "What is the worst that could happen?" The therapist has the client spell out in detail what he or she sees as the ultimate consequences so that the therapist and client can consider whether it would be possible to cope with the situation if the worst were to happen.

Amy came into treatment for her fears of eating and drinking in public that were severely limiting her life. As she was planning to go out for coffee with some friends (including Sarah, a woman she did not know well), she had been able to identify the thought, "What if I get upset and really start shaking?" She and the therapist explored the likelihood of that happening and concluded that it was possible (because that had happened before) but not very likely (because she had been quite anxious in a number of situations but had not had a severe shaking episode in a long time). The therapist then moved on to explore the worst possible scenario by asking, "Well, let's just say that you did get so upset that you shook harder than you ever have before. What's the worst what could happen?" Amy replied, "Sarah might notice and ask what's the matter with me." The therapist then asked, "And if she did notice and ask you, what's the worst that could happen?" Amy said, "I could be so nervous that I couldn't even answer her!" Again, the therapist asked, "And if that did happen, what is the worst that would happen next?" This time Amy thought for a second and answered, "Well, I'd be terribly embarrassed, and Sarah would probably think I was weird." Once more, the therapist asked, "And what's the worst that could happen then?" After thinking some more, Amy replied, "Well, Sarah might not want to have any more to do with me, but the other people there are my friends and probably would understand." Finally, the therapist asked, "And if that did happen?" Amy concluded, "I'd feel embarrassed, but I do have plenty of good friends, so I'd live without Sarah as a friend. Besides, if she's that narrow minded, who needs her anyway?"

In addition to challenging and modifying the verbal automatic thoughts, clients may need to learn how to modify images because images often have a strong effect on their anxiety.

As Amy's thoughts in this situation were discussed further, she was able to describe in detail an image she had of herself looking like one of the schizophrenic clients she had seen in a psychiatric hospital. The therapist was then able to use several techniques to begin to challenge that image. Amy was asked to practice acting very anxious in front of a mirror, and she was able to see the difference between looking anxious and looking "crazy." She was also asked to reimagine that picture of herself, but this time give the image a different ending. This time, she imagined herself using her coping skills and ending up looking and feeling much more relaxed. She and her therapist also worked on decatastrophizing her image, exploring what would happen in the unlikely event that she did end up looking that "crazy," and she came to a similar conclusion as when her verbal thoughts were challenged: Sarah might not want anything to do with her, she might even make some disparaging remarks, but that would have little lasting effect on Amy's life. Challenging that image also helped to identify another one of Amy's fears: that if she became extremely anxious, she would, in fact, go crazy. This fear was then challenged as well.

Other techniques that can be helpful in modifying imagery include using thought stopping to turn off the image, time projection (imagining the situation 6 months, a year, or several years from the present), developing a positive image to be substituted for the dysfunctional one and used for coping, and using imagery to practice coping skills.

Exposure techniques are an essential component of Cognitive Therapy with anxiety disorders. Purely verbal interventions have only a limited effect on problems involving significant anxiety. In order for treatment to be effective, the client must repeatedly confront the situation he or she fears, tolerate the anxiety, and cope effectively with both the situation and the anxiety. This exposure can be gradual, as in systematic desensitization, or massed, as in flooding, but it is quite important. After all, the most effective way to challenge thoughts is through behavioral experiments and the testing of specific hypotheses. Most exposure assignments serve as ways of testing the client's cognitive assumptions and expectations.

Although graded exposure hierarchies may be used both via imagery in the office or *in vivo*, the rationale for the use of these assignments is quite different from that presented by the strict behaviorists using similar techniques. These homework assignments are not used to "decondition" the connection between the stimulus and anxiety, but, rather, as a powerful way of challenging the client's thoughts and beliefs. Exposure homework assignments constitute behavioral experiments for the client to use to ascertain experientially the difference between his or her catastrophic expectations and the events as they actually occur.

One early part of Jenny's treatment involved reversing avoidance using graded exposure. She developed a hierarchy of increasingly anxiety-provoking situations, ranging from driving one block away from home alone (anxiety rating of 5) to driving alone and being caught in rush-hour traffic (100). She began practicing doing at least one of the lower level hierarchy items each day. She was very eager to get better and worked hard at her hierarchy items, so that she was able to drive alone to her therapy sessions by the third session and was very proud of herself. This experience was then used to challenge her belief that "if I drive alone, I'll panic and crash."

This distinction between using behavioral experiments to test cognitions and using desensitization to decondition anxiety is more than a semantic one and has definite implications for treatment. In classic systematic desensitization, because the goal is to break any possible connection between the stimulus and anxiety, it is crucial to proceed through the hierarchy slowly and systematically, making sure that the client does not at any point experience high levels of anxiety. In the cognitive approach to graded exposure, however, it is not considered crucial to protect the client from any anxiety. In fact, with agoraphobics, the belief that they cannot tolerate anxiety must be challenged, so it is important that during the course of treatment the client does experience anxiety and even panic attacks, learning that he or she can indeed tolerate and cope with them.

Teaching clients to tolerate anxiety lends itself nicely to the use of paradoxical techniques. Beck and his colleagues (Beck *et al.*, 1979) initially expressed disapproval with these techniques, primarily because of the belief that use of paradoxical techniques would risk disrupting the collaboration that is such an important part of treatment. As paradoxical techniques were originally used, the therapist would instruct the client to intensify a symptom, whereas the therapist, unbeknown to the client, assumed that this would actually decrease the symptom. Obviously, interventions based on this sort of hidden agenda could easily leave the client feeling manipulated and disrupt collaboration. With anxiety clients, however, this type of secrecy is unnecessary, and full collaboration can be maintained simply by sharing the rationale for the assignment with the client. For example, the type of paradoxical intervention that is most useful with clients who have panic attacks is that of prescribing the symptom, or in this case, asking the client to deliberately have a panic attack. It can be explained to the client that fear of the panic attack helps to maintain and intensify the panic. Therefore, the client is informed that the strongest way to combat this "fear of the fear" is to intentionally induce a panic attack by deliberately making the symptoms worse and then tolerating the anxiety without attempting to avoid it. Also, because it is necessary to have panic attacks in order to practice ways to cope with them, deliberately having a panic attack provides a good opportunity to practice coping skills. Thus the situation is set up as a no-lose situation: If fear of the fear is one of the major components of the panic, intentionally trying to panic may reduce the likelihood or the intensity of the panic. Even if the client does panic, this will then provide a useful opportunity to prove that he or she can survive the panic attacks and that the panic attacks do not lead to disaster. The task is paradoxical in that the client is trying to intensify something that he or she ultimately wants to eliminate, but because the rationale is fully shared with the client, no deception or loss of collaboration is involved. Whenever paradox is used, it is essential that the therapist and client have a good working relationship, that the client trust the therapist, and that the rationale is fully understood by the client. The same paradoxical intervention (such as saying, "Go ahead, let's see if you can have a heart attack") could be seen as cruel, sarcastic, or demeaning in one therapy relationship but seen as humorous, supportive, and caring within the content of a different therapeutic relationship.

Paradox can be particularly effective when used in a group therapy context, whether with agoraphobics or social phobics. Often, when the concept of paradox is first introduced, no matter how carefully the rationale is explained, the client comments, "Well, you clearly haven't had panic attacks, or you'd know that they are so awful that no one would deliberately encourage one." Of course, that idea can be challenged verbally, but in a group context, the client has the opportunity to watch other clients using paradox and hear their success stories, so it is much easier to convince him or her that it is worth a try. Also, the group can go out to a public place and practice paradox together, deriving a great deal of social support and encouragement for their attempts.

To actually address Jenny's fear of fear, it was necessary to have her experience panic attacks and deal with them rather than always working to keep her anxiety down. She was initially resistant to the idea of deliberately inducing panic because she had been able to cope well and had not been having spontaneous panic attacks. Unfortunately, there was no agoraphobia group available for her to join so that she could see how useful paradox had been to other clients. She decided to go ahead and try paradox after she spontaneously did have another panic attack and realized that she could not count on never panicking again no matter how skilled she was at coping. Because her main fear was of getting dizzy and fainting, she chose to go into a situation that was high up on her hierarchy (going to a restaurant where she had had a particularly bad panic attack 2 years before) and deliberately try to get dizzy and faint. She did get quite anxious, but as she tried to make it worse, she found that the symptoms decreased, and she was able to enjoy her lunch. Encouraged by the success of her attempt at not fighting the panic, she tried paradox in a variety of situations, especially when she felt that a panic attack was coming on.

Before attempting any behavioral experiments (whether paradoxical or part of a gradual exposure program), it is useful to go through a process of cognitive review in the office. Using imagery or verbal discussion to plan out the behavioral experiment step by step, the therapist can begin to desensitize the client to the situation, but it can also be a big help in identifying the automatic thoughts that are the most likely to occur in the actual situation. Once these have been identified, the therapist and the client can work together to develop an active coping plan and practice ways that the client can challenge the thoughts as they occur. It is particularly useful to attempt to identify and address all of the client's major fears about the particular situation before attempting a behavioral experiment in order to improve the chances that the client will prove willing to follow through with it. If the client changes his or her mind at the last minute, it is likely that this indicates that an important fear has not been addressed sufficiently.

The most commonly discussed behavioral treatment for Obsessive-Compulsive Disorder is response prevention, which can be seen in cognitive terms as the behavioral experiment of refraining from the obsessive-compulsive behavior as a test of whether or not the feared consequences occur. This intervention is appropriate and useful for both cognitive and behavioral rituals that are anxiety-reducing in nature because the individual is using the ritual to avoid anxiety, and thus preventing this response serves to help the client confront his or her fears. For example, if a compulsive hand washer is prevented from washing his or her hands even though he or she feels contaminated, the anxiety increases substantially, peaks, and begins to subside with no catastrophe following. The client discovers that the hand washing is unnecessary and that his or her anxiety can be reduced more effectively by confronting the fears.

Response prevention, however, would not be appropriate for obsessions that are anxiety evoking. For the treatment of anxiety-evoking obsessions, flooding with feared cognitions is necessary. These thoughts are maintained by the individual's fears and horror at the thoughts, and attempts at preventing these thoughts through procedures such as thought stopping could serve to support the view that the thoughts are terrible and could actually make the disorder worse. If the client is induced to confront the feared thoughts, images, or impulses and sufficient time is allowed for his or her anxiety to come to a peak and then subside, he or she discovers that they are unpleasant but not dangerous, breaking the cycle that perpetuated them.

Studies by Foa and her colleagues (Foa, Steketee, Grayson, Turner, & Latimer, 1984; Foa, Steketee, & Milby, 1980; Steketee, Foa, & Grayson, 1982) have shown that a combination of response prevention and prolonged exposure to obsessional cues was clearly superior to either component used alone for the treatment of Obsessive-Compulsive Disorder. For a detailed discussion of how to implement these procedures, see Steketee and Foa (1985).

Once the client has learned to successfully challenge his or her automatic thoughts and is actively confronting feared situations, the focus of treatment shifts to the underlying assumptions that predispose that person to anxiety. After having collected several weeks of automatic thoughts in a variety of situations, basic themes can generally be identified. In addition, the "downward arrow" technique (discussed in Chapter 3) can be used to pinpoint the specific underlying assumptions that seem most prominent for that client. Even though many anxious clients may share similar underlying assumptions, it is important not to assume that a given client holds a given belief. It is the most useful to identify the central idiosyncratic assumptions of the individual client and to specify them in the client's own words, so that challenging the assumptions will have the maximal impact.

As treatment went on, it became clear that Jenny strongly held the belief that because she was the minister's wife and a pillar of the community, she should be able to be perfect at whatever she did, which included not having any strong negative emotions. The prohibition against strong emotions included not only anxiety but also anger and sadness as well. She had already begun to see how fighting anxiety only made it worse and accepting it worked much better, so that was used as evidence that accepting strong emotions in general might be a more useful strategy than prohibiting them. With anger, she realized that she tended to hold her feelings in and pout when she was mad at her husband, which was not very useful because he was so busy he generally did not notice. Instead, she decided to accept her anger and work on assertive ways of expressing it. While working on assertion, she was able to pinpoint another underlying assumption: She felt she needed approval from everyone and that other people's reactions were extremely important. Assertion training served as a continual, and powerful, challenge to that assumption.

Many of the behavioral experiments being used to test out automatic thoughts will also serve as tests of some of the client's underlying assumptions, but it cannot be assumed that the client will draw those connections on his or her own. It is necessary to repeatedly restate the underlying assumption and discuss explicitly how a given behavioral experiment could be used as a challenge to that assumption. For example, an agoraphobic client may be practicing hierarchy items that involve being alone but may not spontaneously draw the connection that each successfully completed hierarchy item is further evidence to challenge the belief that he or she is incapable of functioning independently in the world.

In addition to consistently pointing out the steps the client is already taking to challenge his or her underlying assumptions, specific new behavioral assignments can be set up to directly test out these beliefs. For example, if a client has the belief that he or she needs to always be competent in all respects, an experiment could be set up where he or she deliberately does a task less than perfectly and observes the consequences. If the individual believes that total control over emotions is necessary at all times, he or she could practice being out of control (either by having a panic attack, or allowing him- or herself to have other strong emotions). The person who believes that it is necessary to get approval from everyone could deliberately do something that will clearly be disapproved of by someone else to test out that assumption.

Other basic beliefs can be successfully challenged by examining the advantages and disadvantages of maintaining those beliefs. Anxious over-concern, catastrophizing, problem avoidance, and helplessness are beliefs for which it is particularly useful to examine the price the client pays for holding the belief. Once the client can see that there is a choice as to whether to continue to pay that price, it can be useful to write out a new, more adaptive underlying assumption. For example, a client who decided that he no longer wants to maintain the belief that it is essential to be loved and approved of by everyone at all times could write a new belief, such as "It feels good to be loved and approved of, but it's even more important that I approve of what I'm doing." Then, without assuming that the client can change his or her belief automatically, the therapist can help the client outline how he or she would behave differently *if* he or she did endorse the new belief. Once the changes are elaborated sufficiently, the client could practice acting for 1 week *as if* he or she believed the new belief and observe the consequences (fixed-role therapy, Chapter 3).

In the treatment of Social Phobia, "decentering" is the process of having the client challenge the basic belief that she or he is the focal point of all events. The client is asked to collect concrete evidence to determine how often he or she actually is the focus of attention and what behaviors are being attended to by others. Thus, for example, a client may be asked to go to a mall or restaurant and count how many people actually are watching him or her sitting there. This exercise in itself requires a shift in focus because the person is required to adopt the perspective of other people.

Because control is often a major issue for individuals with anxiety disorders, it can be useful to help the client understand the distinction between the two different types of control discussed by Weisz, Rothbaum, and Blackburn (1984). Most American writings on the psychology of control focus on the view that perceived control results when individuals shape existing physical, social, or behavioral realities to fit their perceptions, goals, or wishes. This is what Weisz and his colleagues define as "primary control." For example, if a person begins to get anxious and uncomfortable in a crowded room when the lecturer continues to speak past the allotted time, he or she could exert primary control by changing the situation (leaving the room, opening a window, asking the lecturer to conclude his talk, etc.). In addition to this primary control, however, Weisz *et al.* argue that control is often sought via alternative paths that they label as *secondary control*. In secondary control, individuals attempt to align themselves with existing realities, leaving the realities unchanged but exerting control over the situation's psychological impact. In the above mentioned situation, the individual could exert secondary control by trying to better adapt to the situation as it is (deciding the information being imparted is worth running overtime, doing deep breathing to feel more comfortable, accepting that he or she gets anxious at times but does not have to do anything about it, etc.). Weisz *et al.* conclude that both types of control can be useful and that an important goal is to find an optimally adaptive blend of primary and secondary control. Anxiety clients, however, often feel out of control because they focus only on the aspects of the situation over which they feel no control. A discussion of primary versus secondary control and teaching the client to enumerate which factors are under his or her control can be very useful.

A 32-year-old male accountant was afraid to fly. When on an airplane, his thoughts focused on all the ways he was out of control, such as "I can't get out and leave no matter how much I want to" and "I have no say over how the pilot flies this plane." When the issue of primary versus secondary control was discussed with him, he realized that there are always many aspects of life over which he really had little or no control (i.e., the weather) but that he simply did not focus his attention on them so they did not bother him. He made up a list of all the things he did have control of during a flight (i.e., whether to read or nap, have a drink or eat, go to the bathroom or stay seated, write and challenge his dysfunctional thoughts, or practice relaxation training), and he found it very helpful to him to review this list when he took his next plane flight.

The final stage in therapy is work on relapse prevention. In addition to the usual process of identifying high-risk situations and planning how to handle them if they arise, it is important for clients recovering from anxiety disorders to understand the risks inherent in avoidance. The tendency to avoid situations that evoke anxiety is a very natural one; however, if a previously avoidant client gradually begins to again avoid the situations he or she avoided previously, the anxiety may well begin to return. In return, the client can expect that for some time following treatment, if he or she goes for some time without confronting a previously feared situation, mild anxiety will return. This is not a sign of relapse. All the client needs to do is to go ahead and confront the situation and the anxiety will fade quickly.

Later in Jenny's treatment, she wanted to get off of the medication, so it was necessary to address her attributions about her medications and fade her off of them (with the full cooperation of her physician). She was concerned that perhaps all her improvement was due to the medications, so she and her therapist conducted a behavioral experiment, having her redo all her hierarchy items once she was off of the medications. She also did thought sheets whenever she felt concerned about being medication free, and except for some initial anxiety when she first went off the medication, she was able to go through her hierarchy very quickly and successfully.

As Jenny and her therapist reviewed her goals and realized that she had made significant headway toward them, they decided to increase the time between sessions so that she could build up her confidence that she could continue her progress on her own. In the final sessions, treatment focused on getting her some time away from her son, increasing her involvement in activities she found rewarding without her husband, and scheduling enjoyable activities alone with her husband to improve their marriage. The therapy was terminated by mutual agreement after a total of 20 sessions, and contact 2 years later showed that she had maintained her progress and continued to improve further. She had had to deal with a number of serious stressors including the birth of a second child and her husband's having a serious illness, and she had found it difficult to resume her normal activities after long periods stuck at home with a new baby and sick husband; but she had managed to get through it all without a recurrence of the agoraphobia.

CONCLUSIONS

Although Cognitive Therapy is effective for the full range of anxiety disorders, Cognitive Therapy of anxiety appears to be somewhat more time consuming than Cognitive Therapy of depression. Whereas for depression the treatment is often effective within 10 to 12 weeks, Cognitive Therapy for anxiety often can take between 6 months and 1 year to be completed. This may be because individuals with anxiety disorders seem to have less access to their dysfunctional cognitions and also because avoidance behaviors can become so comfortable that they are difficult to change.

Research evidence for the efficacy of cognitive-behavioral therapies for anxiety has been accumulating over recent years, and several meta-analytic reviews have shown promising results (Barrios & Shigatomi, 1980; Dushe, Hurt, & Schroeder, 1983; Miller & Berman, 1983). In studies of the treatment of agoraphobia in particular, however, the findings are less clear. Some studies show an advantage to cognitive-behavioral approaches over behavioral treatments, but other studies show no such advantage, and other studies demonstrate a superiority of straight behavioral treatments over the cognitive-behavioral approaches (summarized in Michelson, 1987). Although further research is clearly needed, Michelson concludes that "a multimodal treatment approach would represent a more state-of-the-art treatment of this complex anxiety disorder by simultaneously addressing the three dimensions of the disorder (behavior, cognition, and physiology). Treatment integration of this nature is likely to result in improved outcome, synchrony, and maintenance and generalization effects" (1987, p. 264). Cognitive Therapy can provide such a multimodal, integrated approach.

Reading 8
Behavior Therapy and a Culturally Diverse Society

BEHAVIOR THERAPY 28, 347-358, 1997

Behavior Therapy and a Culturally Diverse Society: Forging an Alliance

GAYLE Y. IWAMASA

Oklahoma State University

As society continues to become increasingly culturally diverse, behavior therapy will need to adapt and develop in order to meet society's changing needs. I discuss behavior therapy's historical lack of attention to issues of diversity, why cultural diversity is important to behavior therapy, and recent developments on diversity in behavior therapy. Some positive implications of behavior therapists' establishing a commitment to issues of diversity in behavioral research are reviewed and recommendations regarding future research directions are offered.

The focus of this series of articles, "30 Years of Behavior Therapy: Promises Kept, Promises Unfulfilled," prompted me to examine my perspective of the relation between behavior therapy and cultural diversity. The invitation to contribute to this issue motivated me to review several influential classic chapters and books on behavior therapy (e.g., Emmelkamp, 1994; Kazdin, 1989; O'Leary & Wilson, 1987; Wilson, 1995; Wilson, Franks, Brownell, & Kendall, 1984; Wolpe, 1990). Although these writings clearly delineate the history and effectiveness of behavior therapy's techniques and methods, I found little mention of the actual characteristics of the people who were provided with such treatment. Indeed, the importance of cultural characteristics of individuals who undergo behavioral treatments (outside of diagnostic category) have not been adequately addressed or considered.

Indeed, findings from a recent review of the behavioral psychology literature suggest that, over the past several decades, only 1.31% of the articles published in three leading behavioral journals, *Behavioral Assessment*, *Behavior Modification*, and *Behavior Therapy*, focused on ethnic minority groups in the United States (Iwamasa & Smith, 1996). Likewise, a review of conference programs of the Association for Advancement of Behavior Therapy (AABT) was equally disappointing: only 2% of the 7,210 presentations given between 1983 and 1993 ($N = 39$) specified the ethnicity of the

Correspondence regarding this article may be addressed to Gayle Y. Iwamasa, Ph.D., Department of Psychology, 215 North Murray, Oklahoma State University, Stillwater, OK 74078; e-mail: iwamasa@okway.okstate.edu.

347

sample examined (Iwamasa, Nangle, & Larrabee, 1995). Such findings highlight behavior therapy's lack of attention and commitment to issues of diversity and support Landrine and Klonoff's (1995) contention that behavior therapy has been silent when it comes to cultural diversity. I believe, therefore, that it is fairly accurate to say that behavior therapy has never made any promises or commitment to cultural diversity.

Why Is Cultural Diversity Important to Behavior Therapy?

It is somewhat saddening that diversity issues need to be addressed at all. We live in an age where the media exploits, exacerbates, and manipulates cultural issues of race, ethnicity, religion, gender, and sexual orientation in order to receive higher ratings or to sell more newspapers and magazines. We also live in an age where too many individuals rely on this same media to obtain information about how diverse people relate to one another. I have often observed local and national television news reporters saying such things as "blacks and whites still split along racial lines on the O. J. Simpson trial verdicts. Stay tuned for the details!" Even worse, several years ago I watched in horror as my home town of Los Angeles went up in flames as numerous outraged citizens responded destructively to the acquittal of four white police officers accused of criminal wrongdoing toward Rodney King.

Although many may argue that ethnic tensions in the United States have subsided, covert hostility periodically becomes overt. Indeed, I have been the target of verbal slurs, and most ethnic minority individuals will agree that, at times, their physical characteristics have very high stimulus value for others. Such examples of actual events are readily available in the media—a man in Oklahoma City who was killed because his murderer thought he was homosexual, or a North Carolina couple who was doused with gasoline and set afire because they were black and in the "wrong neighborhood." The point here is that issues of ethnicity and culture affect behavior, and sometimes with very terrible consequences.

Claims that issues of diversity are unimportant is, in my view, an egregious error. For behavior therapists to say that issues of diversity have not proven to be important in our work is equally disturbing. Several times I have heard the argument that, by virtue of its methods, behavior therapy is "color blind." I would say the emphasis should be on the word "blind." Would a behavior therapist be blind to the fact that her client is an older adult, a woman, or walks with a limp? I would hope not. Then why do we appear blind when it comes to the cultural characteristics of the client? It may be that, because behavior therapists or researchers consider diversity to be unimportant, we remain ignorant of how diversity issues are important to clients or research participants. A friend once eloquently said, "a functional analysis of behavior may be more a function of who is doing the analysis, rather than what is being analyzed."

Several behavior therapists have suggested how behavior therapy can be modified to be culturally appropriate (e.g., Hayes & Toarmino, 1995; Matthews, 1997). Tanaka-Matsumi, Seiden, and Lam (1996) have even provided behavior therapists with a functional analysis specific to cross-cultural therapy dyads. Although these writings are very recent, they are a beginning, and behavior therapists would be irresponsible in failing to consider their ideas.

A small survey of ethnic minority cognitive behavioral therapists suggests that their work is greatly affected by their ethnic status (Iwamasa, 1996b). Perhaps this survey may serve as groundwork for examining how ethnicity and other cultural variables affect clients and therapists, not to mention researchers. Some nonminority behavior therapists may argue that they have never observed any differences between their ethnic minority and nonminority clients. From the client's perspective, however, the issues may be altogether different. Indeed, as a general rule, clients seek psychological assistance from individuals who are more likely to display sensitivity to the issues for which they are seeking treatment. For example, an African American male client who is experiencing distress from what he perceives as discrimination based on his ethnicity, would be unlikely to seek therapy from a therapist whom he perceives as insensitive to such issues. We should be cautious in assuming that cultural variables are unimportant in therapy based on limited information suggesting that they have not been unimportant in the past. Such views and assumptions may be more indicative of a therapist's own cultural values, rather than real issues that are of importance to the client.

Whether one accepts it or not, the United States is becoming more ethnically diverse. Recent census statistics indicate that ethnic minorities comprise 25% of the United States population, with estimates that by the year 2000, ethnic minorities will be the majority in five states and Washington, D.C. (U.S. Bureau of the Census, 1992). Add to this number other groups such as gays, lesbians, bisexuals, members of various religious groups, the poor, those who live in rural settings, and the elderly, and the United States is indeed quite multicultural. Behavior therapy will miss the boat if we do not demonstrate the applicability and appropriateness of behavioral approaches and interventions for these various groups.

Recent Developments on Diversity in Behavior Therapy

Despite behavior therapy's historical lack of responsiveness to issues of diversity, developments over the past few years indicate a promising change. It has been my observation that ethnic minority behavior therapists, and those behavior therapists who are committed to issues of diversity, are beginning to get more "air time." For example, although not a comprehensive list, recent articles in the Behavior Therapist (tBT) have focused on homosexuality and HIV issues (Campos, Bernstein, Davison, Adams, & Arias, 1996; Morales, 1995), rural populations (Rodrigue, Banko, Sears, & Evans, 1996), men's issues (Brodbeck, 1996), older adults (Lemsky, 1995, 1996; Malec, 1995), religious issues (Rowan, 1996), women's issues (Bell-Dolan & Peterson, 1994; Dancu & Hearst-Ikeda, 1994), culture-specific disorders (Kleinknecht, Dinnel, Tanouye-Wilson, & Lonner, 1994), and related clinical issues (Tanaka-Matsumi & Higginbotham, 1994). There was even a special edition of *tBT* focusing on "Understanding Diversity" (Miranda, 1993).

Although multicultural issues appear to be receiving a great deal of exposure in this "softer" behavioral publication, how has the refereed published literature fared? Unfortunately, not as well. Yet, there is still hope that things are changing, and for the better. I am pleased to have had the opportunity to guest edit a recently published special issue of *Cognitive and Behavioral Practice* (Iwamasa, 1996) devoted to ethnic and cultural diversity issues in behavior therapy (Iwamasa, 1996a). This groundbreaking issue provides behavior therapists with important, useful, empirically based practical information that can help guide their work with culturally diverse clients. The series of articles contained in this issue may even serve to generate ideas for culturally focused research in behavior therapy.

Recent issues of *Behavior Therapy* have moved diversity issues to the forefront with articles on diverse populations, as well as nonminority behavior therapists discussing the importance of diversity (e.g., Beck, 1997; Chambless & Williams, 1995; Forehand & Kotchick, 1996, Neff; Bill-Harvey, Shade, Iezzi, & DeLorenzo, 1995). Likewise, *Behavior Modification* has also brought diversity issues to the fore with articles on African American boys (Middleton & Cartledge, 1995), physically disabled groups (Donohue, Acierno, Hersen, & Van Hasselt, 1995; Rasing, Coninx, Duker, & van der Hurk, 1994), and a special issue on community integration of individuals with severe disabilities (Sisson & Lyon, 1995). These articles are a start, but they are clearly not enough to address the needs of an increasingly diverse society.

Does the lack of culturally focused publications in behavioral journals unequivocally imply that behavior therapists are not doing such work? Of course not. It is likely that behavioral researchers are publishing culturally relevant work in nonbehavioral journals. If so, they need to look for their work. In one nonbehavioral journal, for instance, Hayes (1995) reviewed the need for greater attention to issues of multiculturalism from a cognitive behavioral perspective. Although this article is not a comprehensive review of the literature, she does provide readers with a sense of the strengths and weaknesses in applying cognitive behavioral principles to culturally diverse populations, as well as providing suggestions for integrating cultural concerns in cognitive and behavioral practice.

The only ethnic-specific book in the behavioral realm that I was able to locate is a book by Turner and Jones (1982) on behavior modification with African Americans. Behavior therapy is still in need of comprehensive books addressing the application of behavior therapy for various ethnic and cultural groups. In the interim, behavior therapists must rely on chapters that focus

on treatment issues: Tanaka-Matsumi and Higginbotham (1989) discuss the applicability of behavioral approaches across cultures; Lewis (1994) discusses the use of cognitive behavioral approaches for women of color; and Allen (1995) presents a review of feminist theory and cognitive behaviorism.

How do we begin to further increase attention to diversity issues? First, behavioral researchers and clinicians must recognize that their skills and knowledge can and should be applied to largely understudied minority populations. Second, it must be recognized that it is in the best interest of behavior therapy to give attention to diverse populations. Just as I reviewed influential and classic books and chapters on behavior therapy for inclusion of issues of diversity, I also examined influential and classic multicultural psychotherapy books (e.g., Atkinson, Morten, & Sue, 1989; Locke, 1992; Sue & Sue, 1990; White & Parham, 1990) for inclusion of behavioral approaches. As expected, behavior therapy was conspicuously absent. Given the recent attention to ethnic issues in *tBT* and behavioral journals, the foundation has been laid to combine forces with multicultural mental health researchers to empirically demonstrate the utility of behavioral approaches with culturally diverse populations.

Recommendations for Future Behavioral Research

What is the next step for behavior therapy? Behavior therapists cannot afford to simply talk the talk, but we must also walk the walk. If we choose to ignore multicultural issues in behavior therapy and research, then we will fail to understand and know in any sense how such issues influence the behavior of the therapist or the client. Further, we will not know the extent to which behavioral interventions are appropriate and effective with some diverse populations, and perhaps not others. The paucity of data on diverse populations in behavior therapy has resulted in a situation where research in *any* area of mental health would be of benefit. The following are suggestions for places to start.

Back to the Basics

We need researchers to provide meaningful data on diverse groups that address a variety of issues such as conceptualization of psychopathology, beliefs about psychotherapy, and help-seeking behaviors. Although the first two issues may appear to be nonbehavioral, they often can and do play an important role in behaviors related to help seeking, which clearly has implications for the development and implementation of appropriate and effective treatment interventions. For instance, do socioeconomic group differences exist in beliefs about anxiety symptomatology and perceptions about the effectiveness of behavior therapy in treating anxiety disorders? Does providing psychoeducation about depressive symptoms and the benefits of behavior therapy increase the likelihood that Latinos will seek behavioral mental health services? What within-group difference variables, such as sex, generational status, acculturation level, and fluency in English, influence the conceptualization of depression among Puerto Ricans? We know so little about the mental health of ethnic minority populations that we cannot even begin to ascertain the effectiveness of behavior therapy for them. I will use my own research program to further illustrate this point.

Part of my current research program focuses on the conceptualization of depression and anxiety among Japanese Americans. Currently, empirical data on the mental health of Japanese Americans is sparse, and the existing data typically combine Japanese Americans with other Asian Americans. This has resulted in the potential for mental health professionals to use the general findings from such studies and apply them to any Asian American they may treat, regardless of that individual's ethnicity. An example of such overgeneralization is the mistaken belief that *all* Asian Americans express their distress somatically as opposed to psychologically or emotionally; a belief with little empirical support. In fact, our data suggest otherwise. That is, Japanese Americans emphasize cognitive symptoms when experiencing depression and anxiety, not somatic symptoms (Iwamasa, Hilliard, & Osato, 1997). Understanding how Japanese Americans experience psychological distress is important so that we can understand why, when experiencing that distress, Japanese Americans are not likely to seek the services of a behavior therapist. Perhaps more importantly, we need to ascertain who, if anyone, they may seek assistance from. In my work thus far as a Japanese American behavior therapist, I can say with certainty that we will be waiting a long time if we expect Japanese Americans to initiate behavior therapy. A more effective response, therefore, would be for us to bring behavior therapy to them.

If we discover that Japanese Americans, by nature of their cultural values, are more likely to seek help from other members of their community (e.g., church pastors) when experiencing distress, then we can then develop training programs and behavioral interventions that can be employed by community members to alleviate their distress. Although it might take some time to get used to the idea that someone besides a behavior therapist in an office setting is providing treatment, the more that our techniques and approaches are accessible to the public, the more the public will have the opportunity to observe their effectiveness. Additionally, this community-based approach to behavioral research is more likely to yield benefits in the prevention of future psychological distress. Regarding such community-based interventions, Franks (1984) points out that

> behavioral technologies are enticingly inexpensive . . . but their incorporation into a viable behavioral community model requires ingenuity, vision and experience with a variety of related disciplines. (p. 22)

Now is the time for behavior therapists to put their ingenuity to use and apply their knowledge base in creative and useful ways. Researchers already rec-ognize the utility of behavioral interventions for the prevention for specific disorders and problems (e.g. Foa, Hearst-Ikeda, & Perry, 1995; Hiss, Foa, & Kozak, 1994; Koerner, Prince, & Jacobson, 1995; Peterson, 1994; Peterson & Calhoun, 1995). However, what is now needed is the development of behavioral prevention strategies beyond those that are disorder-specific. I was quite pleasantly surprised to discover one study where behavior modification training was conducted with Asian American mental health personnel at a local community mental health center (Stumphauzer & Davis, 1983), and the results indicated that the staff members viewed the training as relevant and useful. Unfortunately, no other studies of this kind have appeared in the published literature.

Assessment, Therapy Process, and Treatment Outcome Issues

Clinicians and researchers must begin to examine the role of culture in the assessment process (Dana, 1994; Westermeyer, 1987). We have general models of case conceptualization (e.g., Persons, 1989), as well as culturally focused models (e.g., Tanaka-Matsumi et al., 1996). Behavior therapists should begin testing such models and publishing the results. In particular, the application of case conceptualization and functional-analytic models with a variety of groups is sorely needed. Although Persons, Curtis, and Silberschatz (1991) presented a comparison of control-mastery and cognitive behavioral case formulations with an Asian American client, cultural issues that may have influenced how the client viewed himself, his parents, and the world were not addressed in either case conceptualization. With this particular client, both case formulations did not include culturally based social support resources or interventions that would have augmented the therapist's usual repertoire of interventions. Acknowledging the role of the client's cultural values on his behavior, as well as the consequences of deciding whether to change some of those values, may have provided this particular client with additional relief from distress. In the behavioral literature, we should expect data on the utility of such idiographic models for diverse clients.

Additionally, we need to examine therapist and client behaviors in multicultural dyads during the therapy process, so that we will begin to understand how issues of culture influence the therapy process. For example, do therapists and clients exhibit different verbal and nonverbal behaviors in multicultural therapy (e.g., European American client and Latino therapist) as compared to therapy with a culturally similar therapist-client dyad? Do therapist beliefs about issues such as homosexuality affect the type of treatment provided (e.g., reorientation therapy vs. focusing on developing coping skills)? How does a therapist integrate and use information regarding a client's recent immigration from Southeast Asia to the United States in designing and implementing behavioral interventions? These are but just a few ideas to drive future research on therapy process issues.

Finally, we need outcome data. Given the small numbers of ethnically diverse clients in behavioral treatment, we must be more accepting of single-subject designs. Barlow and Hersen (1984) and Kazdin (1982) provide wonderful reviews on single-subject research methodology. Although our ability to generalize the results of such work might have its limitations, such studies will contribute to our understanding of how culture affects treatment outcome and of what (if any) unique variables and processes are involved.

Training Issues

My discussion of the future of behavior therapy would not be complete without mention of training issues. The field of behavior therapy cannot expect to keep up with societal needs unless we train behavior therapists to recognize the importance of diversity. Although the mainstream psychotherapy community has recognized the need to incorporate diversity issues in research and clinical training (Mio & Morris, 1990; Yutrzenka, 1995), behavior therapy has, by and large, lagged behind the rest of the mental health field. As discussed by Anderson and Crowther (1995), behavior therapists involved in training future behavior therapists must develop more flexible and effective methods of training if behavior therapy is to remain state-of-the-art. Failing to provide sufficient training in cultural diversity, or showing insensitivity to such issues, can have negative effects on students in behavioral training (e.g., Robbins-Brinson & Neal-Barnett, 1997).

The Future of Behavior Therapy: Everyone Is Responsible

My final comment is that we should not fall prey to the assumption that issues of multiculturalism are reserved only for the few who are women, ethnic minority, gay, lesbian, bisexual, and so on. The future of behavior therapy lies in the hands of behavior therapists. Behavior therapists must work together, toward mutual goals, to ensure the continued success and recognition of behavior therapy. Behavior therapists need to recognize that issues of diversity are sometimes difficult to examine directly and often involve systemic solutions. Elsewhere I have provided recommendations for how behavior therapists might begin to address diversity issues at the individual, institutional, and professional level (e.g., Iwamasa, 1996b; Iwamasa & Smith, 1996). My hope is that behavior therapists actually consider these recommendations and do something about them.

Although Scarr (1988) discussed risks associated with culturally focused research—the possibility of being viewed as politically reactionary or racist—she also emphasized the need for studies on race, gender, and the underrepresented. As Scarr put it.

. . . cowardice about minority and gender differences in research will lead us nowhere. . . . Unlike the ostrich, we cannot afford to hide our heads for fear of socially uncomfortable discoveries. (p. 56)

In the 21st century, behavior therapy will be left behind in mental health research if only culturally diverse behavior therapists focus upon culturally diverse issues. If behavior therapy is to remain a leader in psychological science and mental health, then behavior therapists must actively seek out and examine the issues that will continue to challenge us in this increasingly diverse society, and develop creative and innovative methods to address those issues. Behavior therapists and researchers have the ability and opportunity to demonstrate the applicability of behavioral treatments for an increasingly diverse population. The challenge, therefore, is for each behavior therapist to assess his or her role in shaping the future of behavior therapy. What are you doing in your clinical work or research to make behavior therapy applicable to a variety of populations? If you are not part of the solution, then you are likely part of the problem. I am optimistic that behavior therapists will rise to the challenge and advance our understanding of diversity issues in behavior therapy. I look forward to the next 30 years!

References

Allen, F. (1995). Feminist theory and cognitive behaviorism. In W. O'Donohue & L. Krasner (Eds.), *Theories of behavior therapy: Exploring behavior change* (pp. 495-528). Washington, DC: American Psychological Association.

Anderson, N. B., & Crowther, M. R. (1995). Some thoughts on cultural diversity in research training. *the Behavior Therapist, 18,* 17-21.

Atkinson, D. R., Morten, G., & Sue, D. W. (1989). *Counseling American minorities: A cross-cultural perspective* (3rd ed.). Dubuque, IA: William C. Brown.

Barlow, D. H., & Hersen, M. (1984). *Single-case experimental designs: Strategies for studying behavior change* (2nd ed.). New York: Pergamon.

Beck, J. G. (1997). Mental health in the elderly: Challenges for behavior therapy: Introduction to the special series. *Behavior Therapy, 28,* 1-2.

Bell-Dolan, D., & Peterson, L. (1994). Women in academic careers: The road to survival and success. *the Behavior Therapist, 17,* 207-212.

Brodbeck, C. (1996). Assessing role conflict in men: A critical review of the Gender Role Conflict Scale. *the Behavior Therapist, 19,* 85-86.

Campos, P. E., Bernstein, G. S., Davison, G. C., Adams, H. E., & Arias, I. (1996). Behavior therapy and homosexuality in the 1990s. *the Behavior Therapist, 19,* 113-125.

Chambless, D. L., & Williams, K. E. (1995). A preliminary study of African Americans with agoraphobia: Symptom severity and outcome of treatment with in vivo exposure. *Behavior Therapy, 26,* 501-516.

Dana, R. H. (1994). Testing and assessment ethics for all persons: Beginning and agenda. *Professional Psychology: Research and Practice, 25,* 349-354.

Dancu, C. V., & Hearst-Ikeda, D. (1994). Women in AABT: Their journeys, accomplishments, and comments on the field of behavior therapy. *the Behavior Therapist, 17,* 245-247.

Donohue, B., Acierno, R., Hersen, M., & Van Hasselt, V. B. (1995). Social skills training for depressed, visually impaired older adults: A treatment manual. *Behavior Modification, 19,* 379-424.

Emmelkamp, P. M. G. (1994). Behavior therapy with adults. In A. E. Bergin & S. L. Garfield (Eds.), *Handbook of psychotherapy and behavior change* (4th ed., pp. 379-427). New York: John Wiley & Sons.

Foa, E. B., Hearst-Ikeda, D., & Perry, K. J. (1995). Evaluation of a brief cognitive-behavioral involvement on the aggressive behaviors of African American males. *Behavior Modification, 19,* 192–210.

Mio, J. S., & Morris, D. R. (1990). Cross-cultural issues in psychology training programs: An invitation for discussion. *Professional Psychology: Research and Practice, 21,* 434–441.

Miranda, J. (1993). Understanding diversity: Introduction to a special edition of *the Behavior Therapist, 16,* 225.

Morales, P. C. (1995). Ethical responsibilities and sero-positive HIV clients. *the Behavior Therapist, 18,* 36–37.

Neff, N. A., Bill-Harvey, D., Shade, D., Iezzi, M., & DeLorenzo, T. (1995). Exercise participation with videotaped modeling: Effects on balance and gait in elderly residents of care facilities. *Behavior Therapy, 26,* 135–152.

O'Leary, K. D., & Wilson, G. T. (1987). *Behavior therapy: Application and outcome.* Englewood Cliffs, NJ: Prentice-Hall.

Persons, J. B. (1989). *Cognitive therapy in practice: A case formulation approach.* New York: W. W. Norton.

Persons, J. B., Curtis, J. T., & Silberschatz, G. (1991). Psychodynamic and cognitive-behavioral formulations of a single case. *Psychotherapy, 28,* 608–617.

Peterson, L. (1994). Child injury and abuse-neglect: Common etiologies, challenges, and courses toward prevention. *Current Directions in Psychological Science, 3,* 116–120.

Peterson, L., & Calhoun, K. (1995). On advancing behavior analysis in the treatment and prevention of battering: Commentary on Myers. *Journal of Applied Behavior Analysis, 28,* 509–514.

Rasing, E. J., Coninx, F., Duker, P. C., & van der Hurk, A. J. (1994). Acquisition and generalization of social behaviors in language-disabled deaf adolescents. *Behavior Modification, 18,* 411–442.

Robbins-Brinson, L. M., & Neal-Barnett, A. M. (1997). Defending my research or defending my ethnicity. *the Behavior Therapist, 20,* 17–19.

Rodrigue, J. R., Banko, C. G., Sears, S. F., & Evans, G. (1996). Old territory revisited: Behavior therapists in rural America and innovative models of service delivery. *the Behavior Therapist, 19,* 97–100.

Rowan, A. B. (1996). The relevance of religious issues in behavioral assessment. *the Behavior Therapist, 19,* 55–56.

Scarr, S. (1988). Race and gender as psychological variables: Social and ethical issues. *American Psychologist, 43,* 56–59.

Sisson, L. A., & Lyon, S. R. (Eds.). (1995). Community integration for persons with the most severe disabilities: Innovations in school, employment, and independent living settings [Special issue]. *Behavior Modification, 19*(1).

Stunphauzer, J. S., & Davis, L. C. (1983). Training community-based Asian-American mental health personnel in behavior modification. *Journal of Community Psychology, 11,* 253–258.

Sue, S., & Morishima, J. K. (1982). *The mental health of Asian Americans.* San Francisco: Jossey-Bass.

Sue, D. W., & Sue, D. (1990). *Counseling the culturally different: Theory and practice* (2nd ed.). New York: John Wiley & Sons.

Tanaka-Matsumi, J., & Higginbotham, H. N. (1989). Behavioral approaches to counseling across cultures. In P. B. Pedersen, J. G. Draguns, W. J. Lonner, & J. E. Trimble (Eds.), *Counseling across cultures* (3rd ed., pp. 269–298). Honolulu, HI: University of Hawaii Press.

Tanaka-Matsumi, J., & Higginbotham, H. N. (1994). Clinical application of behavior therapy across ethnic and cultural boundaries. *the Behavior Therapist, 17,* 123–126.

Tanaka-Matsumi, J., Seiden, D. Y., & Lam, K. N. (1996). The Culturally Informed Functional Assessment (CIFA) Interview: A strategy for cross-cultural behavioral practice. *Cognitive and Behavioral Practice, 3,* 215–234.

program for the prevention of chronic PTSD in recent assault victims. *Journal of Consulting and Clinical Psychology, 63,* 948–955.

Forehand, R., & Kotchick, B. A. (1996). Cultural diversity: A wake-up call for parent training. *Behavior Therapy, 27,* 187–206.

Franks, C. M. (1984). Behavior therapy: An overview. In G. T. Wilson, C. M. Franks, K. D. Brownell, & P. C. Kendall (Eds.), *Annual review of behavior therapy: Theory and practice* (Vol. 9, pp. 1–38). New York: Guilford.

Hayes, P. A. (1995). Multicultural applications of cognitive-behavior therapy. *Professional Psychology: Research and Practice, 26,* 309–315.

Hayes, S. C., & Toarmino, D. (1995). If behavioral principles are generally applicable, why is it necessary to understand cultural diversity? *the Behavior Therapist, 18,* 21–23.

Hiss, H., Foa, E. B., & Kozak, M. J. (1994). Relapse prevention program for treatment of obsessive-compulsive disorder. *Journal of Consulting and Clinical Psychology, 62,* 801–808.

Iwamasa, G. Y. (Ed.). (1996). Ethnic and cultural diversity in cognitive and behavioral practice [Special issue]. *Cognitive and Behavioral Practice, 3*(2).

Iwamasa, G. Y. (1996a). Introduction to the Special Series. Ethnic and cultural diversity in cognitive and behavioral practice. *Cognitive and Behavioral Practice, 3,* 209–213.

Iwamasa, G. Y. (1996b). On being an ethnic minority cognitive behavioral therapist. *Cognitive and Behavioral Practice, 3,* 235–254.

Iwamasa, G. Y., Hilliard, K., & Osato, S. (1997). *Anxiety and depression: Japanese American older adults' conceptualization.* Manuscript under review.

Iwamasa, G. Y., Nangle, D. W., & Larrabee, A. (1995). AABT and ethnic diversity: A review of convention programs of the past decade. *the Behavior Therapist, 18,* 49–51.

Iwamasa, G. Y., & Smith, S. K. (1996). Ethnic diversity in behavioral psychology: A review of the literature. *Behavior Modification, 20,* 45–59.

Kazdin, A. E. (1982). *Single-case research designs: Methods for clinical and applied settings.* New York: Oxford University Press.

Kazdin, A. E. (1989). *Behavior modification in applied settings* (4th ed.). Pacific Grove, CA: Brooks/Cole.

Kleinknecht, R. A., Dinnel, D. L., Tanouye-Wilson, S., & Lonner, W. J. (1994). Cultural variation in social anxiety and social phobia: A study of Taijin Kyofusho. *the Behavior Therapist, 17,* 175–178.

Koerner, K., Prince, S., & Jacobson, N. S. (1994). Enhancing the treatment and prevention of depression in women: The role of integrative behavioral couple therapy. *Behavior Therapy, 25,* 373–390.

Landrine, H., & Klonoff, E. (1995). Cultural diversity and the silence of behavior therapy. *the Behavior Therapist, 18,* 187–198.

Lensky, C. (1995). Understanding aging clients: Working with neurologically impaired elders [Introduction to the series]. *the Behavior Therapist, 18,* 166.

Lensky, C. (1996). Adapting behavioral interventions for brain injured older adults. *the Behavior Therapist, 19,* 9–12.

Lewis, S. (1994). Cognitive-behavioral approaches. In L. Comas-Díaz & B. Greene (Eds.), *Women of color: Integrating ethnic and gender identities in psychotherapy* (pp. 223–238). New York: Guilford Press.

Locke, D. C. (1992). *Increasing multicultural understanding.* Newbury Park, CA: Sage.

Malec, J. F. (1995). Behavior therapy and cognitive decline in the elderly. *the Behavior Therapist, 18,* 166–169.

Matthews, A. K. (1997). A guide to case conceptualization and treatment planning with minority group clients. *the Behavior Therapist, 20,* 35–39.

Middleton, M. B., & Cartledge, G. (1995). The effects of social skills instruction and parental

Turner, S. M., & Jones, R. T. (1982). *Behavior modification in Black populations*. New York: Plenum.

U.S. Bureau of the Census. (1992). *Census of population and housing: Summary tape File 3A, 1990 (CD90-3A) (CD-ROM)*. Washington, DC: Author.

Westermeyer, J. (1987). Cultural factors in clinical assessment. *Journal of Consulting and Clinical Psychology, 55*, 471–478.

White, J. L., & Parham, T. A. (1990). *The psychology of Blacks: An African American perspective* (2nd ed.). Englewood Cliffs, NJ: Prentice-Hall.

Wilson, G. T. (1995). Behavior therapy. In R. J. Corsini & D. Wedding (Eds.), *Current psychotherapies* (5th ed., pp. 197–228). Itasca, IL: Peacock.

Wilson, G. T., Franks, C. M., Brownell, K. D., & Kendall, P. C. (1984). *Annual review of behavior therapy: Theory and practice* (Vol. 9). New York: Guilford Press.

Wolpe, J. (1990). *The practice of behavior therapy* (4th ed.). New York: Pergamon.

Yutrzenka, B. A. (1995). Making the case for training in ethnic and cultural diversity in increasing treatment efficacy. *Journal of Consulting and Clinical Psychology, 63*, 197–206.

RECEIVED: March 9, 1997
ACCEPTED: May 13, 1997

Reading 9
Cognitive Therapy and Social Work Treatment

COGNITIVE THEORY AND SOCIAL WORK TREATMENT

JIM LANTZ

OVERVIEW OF THEORY

A cognitive approach to social work practice is based upon the idea that a person's thinking is the principal determinant of emotions and behavior.[46] As a result, cognitive theorists and cognitive social work practitioners believe that good social work treatment will include considerable effort directed toward helping the client identify, challenge, and change thinking patterns that result in dysfunctional forms of emotion, behavior, and problem solving.[20,21,44,45,46] As Werner[44,45] has noted, cognitive theory is not a system of ideas created by one or two individuals. Cognitive theory is rather a consistent and coherent orientation to understanding human functioning and human change that includes the ideas and contributions of many different individuals.[18,21,22]

HISTORICAL ORIGINS

The first cognitive therapist and practitioner was Alfred Adler.[1,2] Adler worked with Sigmund Freud and was initially an important member of the psychoanalytic movement in Vienna. Adler separated from Freud for a number of reasons. Adler believed that the personality is a unified whole and that it does not make sense to split the personality into the id, ego, and super-ego, as did Freud. Adler[1] also did not agree with Freud's understanding of human motivation. Adler believed that people are primarily motivated by social drives rather than by sexual drives. Adler[1,2] also believed that human cognition is of much greater importance than was suggested by Freud. For Adler,[2] a person's behavior is shaped by what Adler called the "life-style." For Adler,[2] the life-style consists of a person's ideas and beliefs about the self, self-ideal expectations, as well as the person's "picture of the world."[1,2] For Adler,[1,2] the life-

94

style also includes cognitive ideas about how to "correctly" solve problems and to exist in the world. For Adler,[1,2] psychotherapy and human service should include rigorous examination of the client's life-style assumptions as a way to initiate change.[22] Alfred Adler[2] is considered by many to be the first cognitive theorist in the mental health professions.[22,23,39]

IMPORTANT PRACTITIONERS AND PROPONENTS

Alfred Adler[1,2] was the first major cognitive theorist and practitioner, but there have been many other cognitive theorists and mental health practitioners. In 1954, Joseph Furst[12] reported that neurosis is a distortion and/or limitation of consciousness and that treatment should be considered to be "rational psychotherapy" that helps a client change cognitive distortions and expand conscious awareness.

In the late 1950s and the early 1960s, Albert Ellis[10] reported that dysfunctional emotion is reactive to a strongly evaluative kind of thinking. For Ellis,[10] dysfunctional emotion results from irrational self-talk cognitions. Ellis[10] believes that effective psychotherapy and counseling include help from a service provider who focuses the client upon identifying, challenging, and changing dysfunctional thinking and distorted cognitions. In 1962, Ellis[10] published his classic work, *Reason and Emotion in Psychotherapy,* which has served as a bible for many cognitive counselors and/or psychotherapists since that time.

William Glasser's[16] approach to psychotherapy, which he calls "reality therapy," has also been a popular approach to cognitive psychotherapy and mental health intervention. For Glasser,[16] there are two basic human needs: to give and receive love and to behave in a way that enables one to feel worthwhile to self and others. For Glasser,[16] effective psychotherapy helps the client find the courage needed to change, to use to identify responsible goals and responsible actions, and to use cognitive evaluation processes to identify opportunities for responsibility and the responsible awareness of reality.

Maxie Maultsby[38] is another mental health professional who has made significant contributions to cognitive theory and cognitive mental health practice. Maultsby's[38] major book, *Help Yourself to Happiness,* outlines his approach to "rational behavior therapy." Some of Maultsby's contributions include his use of cognitive theory in group psychotherapy, his promotion of cognitive self-help groups, his descriptions of the use of rational behavior therapy with adolescents, and his integration of hypnosis as a cognitive treatment strategy.[39]

Arnold Lazarus[32] published the extremely influential *Practice of Multimodal Therapy,* which is often considered the most systematic, comprehensive, and useful description of the use of cognitive theory in facilitating human change. In the Lazarus model,[32] the helping professional is first encouraged to assess seven modes of the client's functioning: behavior, affect, sensation, imagery, cognition, interpersonal living, and drugs-biology. Lazarus[32] calls this the "basic id" of assessment and intervention. For Lazarus,[32] it is important for the helper to use the basic id to outline a comprehensive treatment plan that will help in all areas of social functioning. For Lazarus,[32] the basic id is a way to tailor treatment to meet the specific and concrete treatment needs of the client who comes for help.

Arnold Lazarus[32] is a bit different from other cognitive psychotherapists in his ideas about the "sequence" of thinking, feeling, and human behavior. For Ellis,[10] Beck,[3] Maultsby,[38] and many other cognitive theorists, thinking almost always triggers and/or creates feeling and behavior. For Lazarus,[32] thinking is often reactive to feeling and behavior. For Lazarus,[32] an important part of assessment is to determine the sequence of cognition, affect, and behavior for each individual client requesting service. For Lazarus,[32] every client has a unique sequence of thinking, feeling, and behavior that needs to be assessed.

Don Tosi[42] is a cognitive psychotherapist who has made major contributions in the integration of hypnosis and cognitive therapy. The approach developed by Tosi[42] is called "rational stage directed hypnotherapy" and uses the stages of awareness, exploration, commitment, skill development, skill refinement, and redirection to focus hypnotic imagery in a way that helps the client change cognitions and "picture" thinking in a healthy direction.

Victor Raimy[39] is a psychotherapist who has used cognitive theory to understand self-concept and self-concept change. In Raimy's[39] classic work, *Misunderstandings of the Self,* he shows how the relationship between client and therapist can be used to help the client challenge and change cognitive misunderstandings of the self.

Rollo May[36,37] has not been listed consistently as a cognitive theorist or cognitive psychotherapist in most articles, books, or chapters on cognitive theory, yet his existential work does include significant cognitive elements. May[36,37] defines the unconscious as "unactualized being." For May,[36] an important part of psychotherapy is to help the client use freedom and responsibility to review his or her life, identify unactualized being, and "think" about ways that freedom and responsibility can be used to actualize being.

Like Rollo May, Viktor Frankl[13,14,15] is an existential psychotherapist who has not been identified consistently as either a cognitive theorist or a cognitive psychotherapist. In spite of this omission, it is this author's opinion that Frankl[14,15] should be understood as both an existential and a cognitive practitioner. In Frankl's[13,15] view, an important aspect of the treatment process is to utilize Socratic questions in a way that facilitates the client's thinking about the meanings and meaning potentials in his or her life. For Frankl,[14,15] the core of the treatment process is to help the client identify these meanings and meaning potentials through cognitive reflection. Frankl[13,14,15] calls this cognitive reflection on meanings and meaning potentials "existential analysis" or *"existenzanalysis."*

A final non–social work practitioner who has made significant contributions in cognitive treatment is Aron Beck. Beck is a psychiatrist who has utilized cognitive theory in the treatment of depression,[3] anxiety disorders,[4] and personality problems[5] with excellent results. In this author's opinion, Beck's[3,4,5] major contributions include "refining" cognitive treatment processes in a systematic and concrete way with a variety of psychiatric and mental health problems, and demonstrating through his research efforts and evaluation research studies[3] that cognitive therapy is effective with a wide variety of human problems. In recent years, Beck's daughter, Judy Beck,[6] has continued to expand the theory and practice of cognitive psychotherapy by building upon and refining her father's work.

PATH INTO SOCIAL WORK

Over the past three decades, numerous social work practitioners have made significant contributions to the theory of cognitive practice and the use of cognitive theory in the social work profession. Significant social work contributions have been made by Berlin,[7] Chatterjee,[8] Combs,[9] Epstein,[11] Goldstein,[17,18] Krill,[19] Lantz,[21] Reid,[40] Snyder,[41] Weiner and Fox,[43] Werner,[44,45,46] Witkin,[47] and Zastrow.[50] In spite of the excellent contributions to cognitive theory made by many of these social workers, this author will pay specific attention to the contributions of Werner, Goldstein, and Lantz.

Harold Werner[44,45,46] must be given credit for being the pioneer social worker in the use of cognitive theory in social work practice. Werner has contributed two outstanding books on the use of cognitive therapy in social work practice. In 1965, Werner published the classic *A Rational Approach to Social Casework.*[44] In 1983, he published another outstanding book, *Cognitive Therapy: A Humanistic Approach.*[45]

Although Werner is now recognized as a pioneer social work theorist,[46] he has not always received great respect in the social work profession. At the time of his early contributions, Werner was severely attacked by psychoanalytically oriented social workers who made very little effort to understand his work and to discuss it with him in a professional manner. In spite of this experience, Werner continued to publish and present his ideas. It is a tribute to Werner's efforts and vision that cognitive theory is so widely accepted and utilized in the social work profession today.

A second important pioneer in the use of cognitive therapy in social work practice is Howard Goldstein, who also produced a body of significant writings. He is the author of *A Cognitive Approach to Human Services*[17] and *Creative Change: A Cognitive-Humanistic Approach to Social Work Practice.*[18] Both books should be considered classics in the field. In addition to these two excellent books, Goldstein is the author of many articles that outline the creative and humanistic use of cognitive theory in social work.

The author of this chapter is responsible for the development of a cognitive-existential approach to social work practice.[24,25,26,27,28,29,30] Starting out as a classically trained cognitive practitioner,[20,21,22,23,31] this author was significantly influenced by the existential concepts of the Viennese psychiatrist Viktor Frankl[13,14,15] and the French philosopher Gabriel Marcel,[33,34,35] and as a result developed a treatment system that integrates cognitive theory with existential philosophy. This author's approach to cognitive-existential treatment is presented in his book *Existential Family Therapy: Using the Concepts of Viktor Frankl,*[27] as well as in numerous book chapters and journal articles.[24,25,26,28,29,30]

PRINCIPAL CONCEPTS AND ASSUMPTIONS

In a cognitive approach to social work practice, the central concept is that most human emotion is the direct result of what people think, tell themselves, assume, or believe about themselves and their social situation.[6,10,21] Albert Ellis[10] formulated a cognitive "ABC" theory of emotion based upon this primary cognitive concept. In the Ellis[10] framework, A represents the activating event; B represents what people believe, think, and tell themselves about themselves or the activating event; and C represents the emotional consequence of such beliefs, cognitions, and self-talk. According to Ellis,[10] when people's beliefs, thoughts, and self-talk are rational, they feel emotions that are functional. When their beliefs, thoughts, and self-talk are disturbed or irrational, however, people develop dysfunctional emotions, affect, and behavior. In cognitive social work practice, it is the social worker's responsibility to help clients change the disturbed and/or irrational cognitions, beliefs, and self-talk that create dysfunctional emotions and behavior.[21,44]

Raimy[39] has stated this primary premise of cognitive theory in a somewhat different way. In Raimy's[39] view, most dysfunctional human emotions and behaviors are a direct result of "misconceptions" that people hold about themselves or about various environmental situations. Raimy[39] also believes that most dysfunctional emotions can be changed when the person feeling the emotion is able to correct the misconceptions creating it.

A second basic concept in cognitive social work practice is that many misconceptions, irrational thinking, erroneous beliefs, and distributed cognitions are outside of a person's conscious awareness.[20,21,22,31] As a result, in many instances, the social work client does not know just what thoughts, ideas, beliefs, and misconceptions are creating his or her unpleasant or dysfunctional emotion. Maultsby[38] uses the example of learning to drive a car to describe this phenomenon. When a person first learns to drive a car, he or she engages in a great deal of active thinking and self-talk (i.e., a message from the self to the self) about driving. The person will actively tell him- or herself to step on the brake or to turn the steering wheel in order to stop or turn. After a period of time, this self-talk or thinking becomes so well learned that it becomes automatic and generally outside the person's awareness. A similar process occurs in the development of most dysfunctional human emotion. The person practices and learns misconceptions and irrational self-talk so well that these cognitive beliefs become "automatic" and create dysfunctional emotion without the person's conscious awareness of the specific content of his or her misconceptions, irrational beliefs, and irrational self-talk.[6,10,21,42,46] As a result, to help a client learn to change dysfunctional emotions, it is important that the social work practitioner help him or her to bring into active awareness the thoughts, beliefs, and misconceptions that are creating and maintaining dysfunctional emotions.[21,46]

Although cognitive social work practitioners consider most dysfunctional emotional states to be a direct result of the individual's misconceptions and irrational beliefs, a third cognitive concept is that there are exceptions to this rule. Some dysfunctional emotions may be the result of organic, physiological, neurological, or chemical problems.[21] Examples of such problems include thyroid imbalance, blood sugar imbalance, brain tissue damage, malnutrition, intake of toxic substances, aging, prolonged exposure to the elements, some forms of depression and schizophrenia, and any physical problem that can create an imbalance in brain chemistry.[21]

A fourth concept central to cognitive social work practice is that not all unpleasant emotions are dysfunctional and not all pleasant emotions are functional.[21] Maultsby[38] illustrates this point with the example of a person who feels very happy about being close to a rattlesnake. An individual who sees a rattlesnake that is set to bite and tells him- or herself that the rattlesnake is not dangerous is engaging in irrational self-talk. This misconception will result in a pleasant emotional state that is dysfunctional because it does not provide the person with the experience of fear that would motivate him or her to move away from the dangerous snake. In this situation, the happy feeling is dysfunctional because it is based upon a cognitive misconception that the rattlesnake is not dangerous.[38]

Because most cognitive social work practitioners base their opinion of the functionality of any emotional state on the rationality of the cognitive self-talk that produces it, practitioner and client can benefit from a basic definition of a rational thought as opposed to a misconception.[20,21,31] Maultsby[38] provides a definition of a rational thought that has proved helpful to many clients and practitioners of cognitive treatment. Maultsby[39] defines a rational cognition as any thought, idea, belief, attitude, or statement to the self that is based upon objective reality, is life preserving and productive for achieving one's goals, and that will decrease significant internal conflict and conflict with others. Although this definition of a rational thought does not "perfectly" solve the definitional problem, it is helpful and useful for many clients.[20]

NATURE OF PERSONALITY

In cognitive social work practice, it is believed that the human personality is flexible and can be influenced by both physical and social factors. Although cognitive practitioners recognize the influence of physical and environmental factors upon the manifestation of personality, most accept that people can decide to shape and change their external and internal environments.[1,5,10] Adler,[2] Ellis,[10] and Werner[44] all note that although people are not complete masters of their lives or fates, they can choose the posture they adopt toward life and fate. Adler's [1,2] cognitive view of the individual's ability to shape the personal life is described by Viktor Frankl[13,14,15] as being a "forerunner" to existential psychiatry and existential psychotherapy.

VIEW OF PEOPLE

In contrast to Freudian theory, which stresses the competitive nature of people, cognitive theorists and practitioners have consistently described people as collaborators, equals, fellow human beings, and cooperators in life.[2,10,22] The cognitive model of social work practice generally views people as neither good nor bad but as creative beings who can decide how to live their life.[22] Cognitive theorists and social work practitioners are highly impressed by the individual's ability to utilize thought to identify personal goals and actions and to use these to change the self and the social environment surrounding the self.[18,22,44,45,48,49]

THE PROCESS OF CHANGE

In a cognitive theory approach to social work practice, human change occurs when the social work helper is able to facilitate a cognitive reflection process in which the client identifies, challenges, and changes misconceptions, faulty beliefs, distorted cognitions, and irrational self-talk that have created dysfunctional emotions and behavior.[20,21,23,44,45,50] In most cognitive theory approaches to social work treatment, emotional support given by the helper to the client is considered useful and important but it is not the core aspect of treatment. Also, in a cognitive approach to social work treatment, advocacy and environmental modifications are considered important and useful, but helping the client to identify, challenge, and change cognitive misconceptions remains the central agent of change.[20,45]

In a cognitive approach to social work treatment, the process of helping the client is primarily educational.[20,21] The purpose of treatment is to help the client learn to be his or her own counselor and to use cognitive theory concepts to consistently understand the self and control dysfunctional emotions and behavior.[31] As a result, cognitive practitioners seriously attempt to "empower" their clients by giving them cognitive theory tools for the purpose of mastery, control, and self-help.[6,10,20,38,42,44] Ellis,[10] Beck,[6] and Maultsby[38] outline in detail group-educational programs to supplement casework, counseling, and psychotherapy and specifically address the client's need to learn cognitive intervention skills for self-mastery, empowerment, and control.

SIGNIFICANT OTHERS AND SIGNIFICANT ENVIRONMENTS

Cognitive theorists and cognitive practitioners have a mixed record in terms of understanding the importance of the client's family, significant others, and the social environment. For some early cognitive theorists, it was considered most important to emphasize the human capacity to use rational thinking to overcome problems in the social environment or in the family. As a result, many cognitive theory practitioners have not emphasized social action, environmental modification, family treatment, and/or network interventions. This deficiency in the cognitive theory tradition is not, however, a problem in the Adlerian[1,2] approach to cognitive theory practice.

In the Adlerian approach to cognitive theory practice, the human "life-style" is understood as a set of cognitive beliefs, conceptions, and/or misconceptions that a person accepts about the world, about the self, and about problem-solving in the world.[1,2,22] Life-style cognitions may be understood as cognitive beliefs about the person's self-concept, self-ideal expectations, picture of the world, and ethical conceptions.[1,2,22] In the Adlerian approach to cognitive theory, beliefs, conceptions, misconceptions, and self-talk are learned primarily through a person's social experiences and interactions with his or her family and family of origin.[22] As a result, the family and the social environment often are targets for intervention in Adlerian treatment.[22]

TIME IN COGNITIVE THEORY PRACTICE

For most cognitive theorists and cognitive theory practitioners, the past is not extremely important. For Ellis,[10] Beck,[6] Maultsby,[38] and Tosi,[42] the present moment is the most important part of time because it is when change can and does occur. For Ellis,[10] Tosi,[42] and Maultsby,[38] it is a technical mistake to spend a great deal of time with a client reflecting on the past. For these cognitive practitioners,[10,38,42] what matter most are the self-talk, misconceptions, and cognitive distortions that the client is using in the present to create dysfunctional emotions and behavior, and the healthier ideas, beliefs, and self-talk that could be used in the here and now to improve affect and behavior.

Adlerian cognitive theory practitioners have a somewhat different idea about time and its importance in the treatment process. For Adler[1,2] and many Adlerian practitioners,[22] it is helpful to talk about the past with a client because it gives the practitioner insight into the cognitions, thoughts, beliefs, and/or misconceptions used by the client in the present to create problematic feelings and behavior. This Adlerian view of time resulted in one of the first projective tests (the Early Recollection Test) developed in the mental health professions.[22]

A third view of time is held by cognitive-existential practitioners.[30] In the cognitive-existential view,[28,29,30] the future, the present, and the past are all important. In the cognitive-existential approach to the helping process, it is the function of the practitioner to help the client use cognition and reflection to find and make use of the meanings and meaning potentials in life.[13,14,15,27] Specifically, the cognitive-existential practitioner facilitates client thought and reflection in a way that helps the client to "notice" meaning potentials in the future, to "actualize" such meaning potentials in the present moment, and to recollect, remember, and "honor" meaning potentials previously actualized and deposited in the past.[13,14,15,27,28,29,30,48,49]

SOCIOCULTURAL AND ETHNIC SENSITIVITY

Cognitive theory practitioners have consistently noted that irrational beliefs, self-talk, and misconceptions are generally learned and reactive to social and cultural experiences.[10] As a result, cognitive practitioners understand that race, class, and gender experience may well have an impact upon client beliefs and cognitions. Still, as Ellis,[10] Maultsby,[38] and Tosi[42] all note, there is no demonstrated association or correlation between race, class, gender, and irrational thinking. Most cognitive practitioners agree that all classes, races, and genders are capable of irrational thinking rather equally.[10,38,42] The cognitive treatment tradition would be improved by the implementation of research studies focusing upon race, class, and gender in the cognitive theory treatment process.

COGNITIVE THEORY TREATMENT

As noted previously, the principal therapeutic goal in cognitive theory social work practice is to help the client identify, challenge, and change the misconceptions, faulty beliefs, disturbed thinking, and irrational self-talk that create dysfunctional feelings and behavior. In a recent publication, Judith Beck[6] summarizes ten useful treatment principles of the cognitive approach to social work treatment:

1. Cognitive treatment is based upon an evolving formulation of the client and client problems in cognitive terms.
2. Cognitive treatment requires a sound therapeutic treatment relationship.
3. Cognitive treatment is based upon collaboration with the helper and active participation by the client.
4. Cognitive treatment is problem focused and goal oriented.
5. Cognitive treatment emphasizes the present.
6. Cognitive treatment is educational and hopes to teach the client to be his or her own helper.
7. Cognitive treatment attempts to be time limited when possible.
8. Cognitive treatment interviews are structured.
9. Cognitive treatment teaches clients to identify, evaluate, and respond effectively to dysfunctional thoughts and beliefs.
10. Cognitive treatment uses a variety of treatment techniques to help the client change thinking, feelings, and behavior.[6]

THE TREATMENT RELATIONSHIP IN COGNITIVE SOCIAL WORK PRACTICE

In cognitive theory practice, the relationship between client and helper is an important part of the treatment process.[6] The treatment relationship allows the client to learn and gives him or her an opportunity to view the self and the world in different ways.[6,29,39]

The treatment relationship can be used in two major ways as a powerful tool for helping the client change cognitive misconceptions that result in dysfunctional emotions and behavior. First, the supportive element in the treatment relationship gives the client a message about the social worker's opinion of his or her capacity for growth, ability to function in a healthy way, and value as a human being. When the social worker takes time to be with the client, shows interest in the client as a person, and responds to the client with empathy and concern, the social worker is frequently giving the client quite a different message regarding his or her importance as a person than the client usually receives from him- or herself or from others. According to Raimy,[39] low self-esteem is an emotional response resulting primarily from the client's negative misconceptions about the self. This cognitive process can be challenged or interrupted when the social worker demonstrates the belief that the client is important by providing respect, support, and encouragement during the treatment process. Raimy[39] has labeled such behavior "positive regard" and has shown that such feelings, actions, and beliefs on the part of the professional helper are often a primary curative factor in the process of human change.

A second way in which the treatment relationship can be used to help the client change misconceptions is by focusing on and examining distortions in the relationship between the client and the worker. As Raimy[39] and others have noted, during the treatment process the client may often begin to ascribe to the professional helper many attitudes, ideas, feelings, and motivations that do not, in reality, originate with the worker. Such distortions are often a result of the client's misconceptions about how a significant other "should" think, feel, and behave toward him or her. If the client has positive feelings about the self, he or she will expect others to act accordingly. If the client's idea of self is negative, he or she will project negative feelings, thoughts, and behaviors about him- or herself onto others. Examining the relationship between the worker and the client can bring into the client's awareness many of his or her misconceptions about the self and how he or she expects to be treated by others. Such misconceptions are then subject to the possibility of change through cognitive review. This can often be facilitated either by teaching the client how to check out such assumptions with significant others, such as the caseworker, as they occur in the present, or by helping the client identify how such patterns of distortion and misconception began, through a discussion of the client's developmental experiences.[28,29,39] Cognitive theory practitioners do not generally use the terms "transference" and "countertransference." Cognitive theory practitioners view such phenomena as cognitive distortions that disrupt encounter and the treatment relationship.[6,10,24,39] The Freudian view of transference and countertransference is not accepted by most cognitive practitioners.[31,46]

The following section will provide an overview of many of the treatment techniques that can be used in cognitive social work practice. All of the following treatment techniques depend upon a good treatment relationship in order to be useful and effective.

CLARIFYING INTERNAL COMMUNICATION

Clarification of internal communication is a frequently used procedure in cognitive theory social work that is effective, in this author's opinion, primarily because it provides feedback to the client about what the client is thinking and telling the self. In this way, the social work helps the client develop a better understanding of many of the misconceptions and irrational beliefs that are hidden in the client's verbalizations both to him- or herself and to others. Again, when such misconceptions are brought to the client's awareness, they become available for change through cognitive review.

In the following illustration, a social worker uses clarification of internal communication to help the mother of a ten-year-old boy develop insight into a hidden assumption that prevents her from providing more effective direction to her son.

MOTHER: He's terrible.

CASEWORKER: In what specific way is he terrible?

MOTHER: He won't do what I say. I want him to pick up his toys, and he starts screaming.

CASEWORKER: Then what do you say?

MOTHER: Sometimes nothing. I get upset.

CASEWORKER: What does your silence mean in that situation? What could it mean?

MOTHER: I don't know. I guess I feel guilty.

CASEWORKER: Guilty?

MOTHER: Yes. I don't know. . . . I don't feel . . . It's hard for me to punish him. I've made a lot of mistakes and it hasn't been easy for him. So, you know . . . I feel guilty about punishing him.

CASEWORKER: What kind of people make mistakes?

MOTHER: [Silence] *Failures.*

CASEWORKER: You think you are a failure?

MOTHER: [Silence] Yes. Often.

EXPLANATION

Explanation is another treatment procedure that can be used to help the client change misconceptions. In cognitive social work treatment, "explanation" is a term used for a set of treatment techniques aimed at teaching the client Ellis's[10] ABC model of how emotions work. They help the client to identify and discover the misconceptions he or she is using to create dysfunctional emotions, and to challenge and change misconceptions and irrational ideas. The following illustration gives a more specific idea of how explanation can be used by cognitive social work practitioners to help the client change.

Mrs. Smith was referred for mental health services by her caseworker at a child welfare agency. Mrs. Smith was listless, slept a great deal during the day, felt depressed, had periodic outbursts of anger, and was becoming phobic about leaving her house. The referring caseworker was considering temporarily removing Mrs. Smith's only child from the home.

In their first interview, the clinical social worker and Mrs. Smith were able to develop some initial trust. The client stated that her goal for treatment was to stop feeling so depressed. The worker explained to Mrs. Smith that probably one of the reasons she was not able to stop feeling depressed was that she did not know much about how emotions worked and about what might help. The worker and Mrs. Smith agreed to a contract whereby the worker would teach the client how emotions worked and some strategies she could use to decrease her depression. Mrs. Smith agreed to attend treatment sessions regularly and to do the homework that the worker assigned.

The clinical worker then began explaining the ABC emotional analysis model. Part of the conversation was as follows:

SOCIAL WORKER: If I told you a bomb was under your chair, how would you feel?
MRS. SMITH: I'd laugh.
SOCIAL WORKER: You wouldn't be afraid?
MRS. SMITH: No, because I wouldn't believe you.
SOCIAL WORKER: Good. You see, it's what you believe or think that causes how you feel. A is what I told you about the bomb, the event. B is what you believed and told yourself about the event. C, how you feel, depends on B, what you believe.

Once Mrs. Smith realized that, "in theory," emotions are caused by thoughts and beliefs, the social worker explained how to use a written homework form to help discover and challenge the misconceptions that she frequently used to create and maintain her depression.

WRITTEN HOMEWORK

Written homework is often a useful way for clients who can read and write to learn how to use the Ellis[10] ABC theory of emotions to identify, challenge, and change misconceptions and irrational self-talk. The following written homework form was developed by Maultsby[38] and is often a helpful part of the cognitive theory practice process.

A: What is the event?

B: What are my misconceptions about the event, or what could I be thinking to cause my feelings?

C: How do I feel?

D1: Is my description of A accurate?

D2: Are my Bs rational? If not, challenge them.

E: What new emotion will result from D1 and D2?

This form is used both as part of the explanation treatment procedure and as a format for emotional fractionalization, that is, it helps the client break down a complex emotional sequence into a more understandable problem.[10,20,21,23,38]

EXPERIENTIAL LEARNING

Experiential learning used as a procedure for challenging and changing cognitive misconceptions is best explained by the cognitive dissonance principle. Cognitive dissonance refers to human beings' tendency to change attitudes and beliefs that do not seem congruent with their behavior, actions, or style of life.[21] When using the principle of cognitive dissonance as a way of changing misconceptions, the cognitive practitioner attempts to set up a treatment situation that will help the client engage in specific behaviors that are incongruent with the client's misconceptions. As the client engages in such behaviors, he or she will tend to change the misconceptions.[21] Many common treatment techniques may be based in part on the use of experiential learning and the principle of cognitive dissonance, including assertiveness training, group therapy socialization experiences, role prescription, psychodrama, modeling, role playing, and task assignments.[10]

PARADOXICAL INTENTION

Paradoxical intention is a cognitive restarting technique developed by Viktor Frankl.[13,14,15] The technique is used most appropriately when the client has developed a specific unpleasant behavior that is often triggered by anxiety about the possible occurrence of the same behavior. For example, one of this author's clients, a usually medically stabilized epileptic, would frequently worry about having a seizure at a business meeting in front of his peers. The client's anxiety about this possibility would, in fact, trigger a seizure. Using paradoxical intention, the author instructed the client to try to have a seizure at the beginning of every business meeting to get it out of the way. The fact that the client was then unable to do so helped him stop thinking about how awful a seizure would be, and as a result, no further seizures occurred in this situation. The prescription of the symptom challenged the client's misconceptions about having no way to control it, decreasing the anticipatory anxiety that triggered the seizures.

In this author's view, it is important to use paradoxical intention only in situations of anticipatory anxiety.[27] The technique should never be used to challenge suicidal ideation and should not be used when symptoms have a physical basis.[13,27] It is also this author's view that paradoxical intention should be used "with" the client, not "on" the client, and that the client should be fully informed about this treatment technique before it is used.[27]

DYNAMIC AND EXISTENTIAL REFLECTION
TREATMENT ACTIVITIES

Dynamic and existential reflection treatment activities are cognitive restructing activities[27,28,29,30] based upon Lantz's understanding of the philosophical concepts of Gabriel Marcel.[33,34,35] They are used in a cognitive-existential approach to social work practice to help the client notice, actualize, and honor the meanings and meaning potentials in his or her life.[27,28,33,34,35]

Gabriel Marcel[33,34,35] distinguishes two kinds of human thought, "dynamic" and "existential" reflection. In Marcel's view,[33,34] both kinds of thought are necessary and valid when properly used. Dynamic reflection (which predominates in science and technology) should be used to focus upon problems and problem solving, and existential reflection (which is more characteristic of philosophy, religion, art, meditation, and prayer) is the means by which we facilitate the discovery of meanings and meaning potentials in human life.[27,28,29,30,33,34,35]

Dynamic reflection is problem-solving reflection that aims at knowledge that is verifiable, objective, experimental, and abstract.[33,34] An important feature of dynamic reflection is the separation of the reflector from the object of reflection.[34,35] In dynamic reflection, thought is directed at confronting, reducing, and breaking down problems.

Because dynamic reflection is directed toward the development of knowledge that is objective and verifiable, it is abstract and includes a "minimized" relationship between the thinker and the object of thinking.[27,28,33,34] Dynamic reflection puts the material world in a spotlight and "pushes" the world to answer questions.[27,34] Dynamic reflection is different from existential reflection in that it is directed at breaking down and solving problems, whereas existential reflection is the way to discover connection, unity, wholeness, meanings, and meaning potentials.[27,28,35] In cognitive-existential social work practice, dynamic reflection is best utilized to help clients develop problem-solving strategies that can help them actualize and make use of the meanings and meaning potentials discovered through existential reflection.[27,28,29,30]

Gabriel Marcel[33,34,35] does not criticize dynamic reflection but is adamant in his criticism of its misuse. For Marcel,[33,34] dynamic reflection has allowed and encouraged us to use technology and abstraction to manipulate our world, gain knowledge, and solve many problems. Marcel's[33,34,35] critical observations about the misuse of dynamic reflection highlight the moral and meaning confusions that result when dynamic reflection is "imperialistic" and "judges" all knowledge and truth only by objective and abstract criteria.

For Marcel,[33,34,35] dynamic reflection is used to gain clarity about problems through verification and objectification, whereas existential reflection is used to gain a deeper, richer, wider, and more inclusive understanding of the meanings and meaning potentials of human existence. Existential reflection is the path toward the awareness of meanings and meaning potentials in life.[33,34,35]

The specific mechanics of existential reflection are difficult to present in an exact and systematic fashion.[28] One aspect of existential reflection is "disbelief" in the complete adequacy of dynamic reflection, which then results in an attempted "recovery" of meanings and of the unity of experience that is distorted by abstract and dynamic thought.[24,25,26,28,29,30,33,34] Here, Marcel[33,34,35] is pointing out that abstract thought and the manipulative and experimental aspects of dynamic reflection are "reductionistic" and can cloud the meanings of human existence. Marcel[33,34] believes that whenever dynamic reflection reduces loves, life, friendship, faith, prayer, commitment, fidelity, encounter, courage, joy, and other manifestations of meaning to experiences that can be understood "clearly" or "systematically" or "experimentally," existential reflection must and will "rise up" to correct the "blindness" of dynamic reflection.

A second aspect of existential reflection is its capacity to help us discover and participate in the "unmeasurable" meanings and meaning potentials of life in a serious, sensitive, and "rigorous" fashion.[24,27,33,34] Existential reflection includes discovery through participation instead of distant observation, encounter instead of the subject-object split, and concrete involvement in daily life rather than distant and disengaged abstraction.[27,30,33,34,35] Existential reflection is practiced in the presence of meaning potentials, during participation in what is being contemplated, and with personal connection to what is being recollected and experienced.[27,33,34] Existential reflection allows us to discover the meanings and meaning potentials to be found in friendship, love, art, literature, drama, meditation, recollections, celebration, poetry, music, testimony, and the "I-Thou" dialogue.[27,33,34,35] In this author's view, existential reflection is the way to rediscover and recollect meaning potentials that have been deposited in the past and to discover those in the future that can be actualized in the here and now.[24,25,26,27,28] Existential reflection recollects meanings deposited in the past and notices meaning potentials available in the future, while dynamic reflection helps us actualize meaning potentials in the present.[25,29,30]

CASE VIGNETTES

The following two case illustrations are provided to give the reader a taste of how cognitive theory can be used in the practice of social work. The first case illustrates a rather classical, Ellis–Beck style of using cognitive theory, with an adult man worried about his mother. The second case provides a clinical example of how the Adlerian approach to cognitive theory social work practice was helpful to a graduate student.

MR. A

Mr. A was referred to the mental health center by a caseworker at the Welfare Department, where he had applied for a nursing home placement for his mother. In an interview with the department caseworker, the client talked about his depression, his difficulty sleeping, and how terrible he felt about having to apply for assistance. The caseworker accurately assessed Mr. A's acute reactive depression and referred him to the mental health center for cognitive theory social work treatment.

INTERVIEW ONE:

At the same interview, Mr. A, who was fifty-two, employed, and married with five children, said his family doctor had told him his mother needed to be placed in a nursing home because she required twenty-four-hour nursing care. Mr. A had then appealed to the Welfare Department. He felt terrible. He felt that receiving welfare was "bad" and a son should never "put his mother out." He felt guilty and depressed about taking such a step, as he was "the first person in the family to ever do such a thing." Mr. A said he was worried, had started missing work, and was drinking too much.

The social worker at the mental health center helped Mr. A to realize that his mother did need nursing home care, that he did need to apply for assistance, and that it was doubtful that these things would change. The worker asked Mr. A whether he wanted to feel better even if things didn't change. Mr. A said that he needed to get over this because he had "a wife and children to take care of," and that he would do whatever was necessary. The worker then told the client that he felt it might take about ten interviews for Mr. A to get over his depression, and that Mr. A would have to "work at it very hard." The worker asked whether he could tape record the rest of the session, and Mr. A agreed. At this point, the worker explained to Mr. A how emotions work, using the Ellis[10] ABC emotional analysis framework, with examples different from Mr. A's situation. When the worker was sure the client understood the theory, he explained that Mr. A's depression was the result of what he was telling himself (that he was "bad," a "terrible person," "the first rotten egg in the family," and "a failure as a son, as a man should live up to all of his financial responsibilities"). The worker challenged each of Mr. A's irrational ideas and beliefs. At the end of the interview, Mr. A said that he felt better, and that he had been telling himself some "crazy stuff." The worker told Mr. A he would probably slip back into the irrational self-talk, and suggested that at least ten times a day, Mr. A should go over the rational self-analysis (RSA) homework sheet that the worker had filled out. The worker also asked Mr. A to take the tape-recorded interview with him and play it several times a day. Mr. A was asked to return in three days. The initial interview lasted two hours.

INTERVIEW TWO:

At the second interview, Mr. A said he felt "a lot better." On a couple of occasions, he had begun to feel low, but had gone over his homework sheet and had repeated the rational thoughts to himself. He had listened to the tape of the previous interview and found it helpful. The rest of the session was spent reviewing and repeating the discussion in the first session, and reviewing the homework.

INTERVIEW THREE:

Mr. A came to the third interview somewhat depressed. He had made plans to move his mother into a nursing home the next day and was worried about how she would react. He hoped she wouldn't cry or "make a scene." The worker helped Mr. A to complete an RSA homework sheet using his mother's crying as the event section. At the end of the interview, Mr. A thought he would be able to handle the nursing home move. An appointment was set for the next week.

INTERVIEW FOUR:

Mr. A said that the move had gone well and he had realized that his mother had a right to cry if she wanted to. He believed he had done the right thing for her; he felt sad that it had to happen, but not depressed. He was going to work every day, had stopped drinking, and no longer believed he was a failure. The worker suggested that Mr. A start applying his new insights and ideas in other areas of his life, and asked him to do homework on problems other than his mother's situation and to bring the homework sheets with him the next week.

INTERVIEWS FIVE, SIX, AND SEVEN:

The next three interviews were spent on rational principles to help Mr. A in other areas of his life. He said he often "got down on himself" about bills and tended to take responsibility for all family problems onto his own shoulders. As a result of his new insights, he was able to ask his wife and children for more help. His children started earning money for their own minor expenses, and Mr. A started requiring the children to do more around the house. He no longer was afraid of "emotional reactions" from his family.

TERMINATION INTERVIEW:

Mr. A said that he felt things were much better and that he no longer needed to come for social work treatment. The worker explained that because Mr. A had a long-term habit of putting himself down, it would help if he continued to do written homework.

The worker called Mr. A six months after termination. Mr. A said that "everything was fine" and that he was still doing homework.

FRED

Fred was a thirty-two-year-old graduate student of business administration who requested social work treatment after the termination of a relationship with a girlfriend whom he had wanted to marry. His major complaints included depression, problems with sleep, poor appetite, studying difficulties, and the development of an obsessive-compulsive hand-washing ritual. Fred stated that he was frightened that he would "lose his mind." He was worried that his present "condition" would cause him to "drop out of school." Fred and the worker agreed that the initial goals for treatment would be to help Fred overcome his depression, remain in graduate school, and function effectively as a student.

PSYCHOSOCIAL HISTORY:

Fred was the eldest of three children, and the only boy, born to a doctor and his wife. He was eight when the first of his two sisters was born. Fred graduated from high school and college, worked for a period of time, and then returned to graduate school. He was married for approximately two years but had no children. After he and his wife divorced, Fred "felt like a failure" and experienced depression.

Fred viewed his father as "demanding perfection and excellence." He did well in high school and college, but believed that his father was not proud of him. Fred remembered feeling "cheated" when his first sister was born. One of Fred's early recollections was of helping his father to paint a fence and being told to stop because, as Fred recalled, "I wasn't doing it right."

LIFE-STYLE ASSESSMENT:

One way of understanding Fred is to view him as a young man who experiences strong feelings of inferiority. These feelings seem to stem from three major life-style themes. The first could be called the "living for a dominant other" theme. In this style of life, the individual accepts the evaluations of significant others as the total evidence upon which his or her own evaluation of the self is based. This often results in severe depression. Fred seemed to live for his father, his teachers, and the women in his life.

Fred's second major life-style theme was a low self-concept and high expectations as a part of the self-ideal. Fred seemed to have accepted that his father viewed him as inadequate and as not living up to "standards." Whether or not Fred's father actually communicated this message was not as important as the fact that Fred believed that he did, and had internalized that message.

Fred's third major life-style theme was the development of obsessive-compulsive compensation mechanisms to fend off feelings of inferiority. Over the years, Fred had developed a compulsive style of working and studying to fend off the possibility of failure. Unfortunately, this had also prevented him from enjoying study or work. After the breakup with his girlfriend, Fred developed an obsessive hand-washing ritual. This ritual served to provide Fred with a reason to avoid people and his work at school. The ritual may be understood as a sort of "side show"[12] that gave Fred a reason to avoid continued functioning. It protected him from additional inferiority feelings by providing an excuse for failure ("I couldn't do my work because of my symptoms, but I could have done this work if I did not have symptoms").

TREATMENT APPROACH:

During the first ten weeks of treatment, Fred was seen by the social worker twice a week. This was to maximize support and encourage Fred, who was grieving over the loss of his girlfriend, to continue in graduate school even though he felt depressed. Fred was also encouraged to do a half-hour of strenuous physical exercise before he went to bed. This, combined with the worker's support, helped Fred to sleep at night.

During the fourth social work treatment session, the worker said that he considered the hand-washing ritual to be a very intelligent way for Fred to protect himself from further damage to his self-esteem by providing an excuse for his failure at school (Fred was not going to classes because he could not wash his hands in class). The worker presented this interpretation as evidence of Fred's creativity, intelligence, and coping ability, and he wondered out loud whether Fred really needed or wanted to use this approach. This interpretation "made sense" to Fred; the "unconscious use" of the symptom stopped, and Fred returned to classes.

During the initial sessions, the worker helped Fred put into words the attitudes, beliefs, and assumptions that he had about himself as a result of the breakup with his girlfriend. Putting such assumptions into words creates a feedback loop that can help the client to recognize misconceptions and reorganize his or her thinking. As his attitudes were put into words, Fred was able to start reorganizing his thinking. A significant decrease in anxiety and depression occurred. By the tenth week of treatment, Fred was working well in school, was no longer feeling depressed, and wanted to discuss termination.

During the termination discussion, the social worker said that termination seemed appropriate because Fred had achieved the goals agreed upon during the initial treatment interview. The worker also said that Fred could benefit from continued treatment by trying to change his tendency to rely on others for his self-esteem and to set up unrealistic expectations for himself in his daily life. Fred was asked to return in three weeks to give the worker his decision about whether to stop or continue treatment. Fred opted for long-term social work treatment that focused upon helping to change some of his basic life-style patterns. Family assessment, early recollections, and dream interpretations were utilized to help Fred understand and reorganize his cognitive life-style assumptions and to help him develop more social interests. At the follow-up evaluation two years later, Fred reported no depression. He felt more comfortable with himself and had learned to take it easy and enjoy the "little things." He had married, had a baby, done well at his job, and was on the board of directors of a social service organization.

TREATMENT MODALITIES

The two previous clinical illustrations demonstrate the use of cognitive theory during individual social work treatment. In addition to individual treatment,[1,3,6,10,17,20,21,32,38,39,42,46,50] cognitive theory has been used in group treatment,[2,3,6,10,16,38,42] marital treatment,[2,3,6,10,25,27,28,29,32] and family treatment.[2,3,6,10,27,28,32] According to Judy Beck,[6] cognitive theory has had good results in all treatment modalities. Cognitive theory is especially useful in support groups in theme-centered groups in which the educational aspect of the treatment theory can be enhanced by group process.[6,22] Lantz[27] has presented considerable evaluation data demonstrating that cognitive-existential treatment is effective in marital and family treatment.

INDICATIONS AND CONTRAINDICATIONS

Cognitive treatment practice has been extremely well researched in a variety of treatment settings and with a variety of clients and clinical problems. According to Judy Beck,[6] cognitive theory has been shown to be especially useful in the treatment of depression, anxiety, substance abuse, and personality disorders. Cognitive theory practice is most effective with clients who have learned cognitive misconceptions and irrational thoughts.[6,10] Cognitive theory can also be used with good results as an adjunctive, existential treatment when the client is suffering with schizophrenia, biochemical depression, and/or organic mental conditions.[21] Cognitive theory should not be used as the only treatment for victims of violence. In such situations, cognitive theory is used "after" the victim of violence has been protected from the abusive person.[27]

PRACTICE APPLICATIONS

Cognitive theory can be utilized in a great number of social work practice settings. Cognitive theory social work practice has been found useful in mental health, crisis intervention, child welfare, public assistance, family service, health care, substance abuse, settlement house, and private practice settings.[6,7,9,17,20,21,22,27,31,41,43,44,47,50] Cognitive theory is compatible with social work values and can be adapted for use with a wide variety of client service requests.[6,21,32,46]

PROSPECTS

The future is hard to predict. Still, it is this author's prediction that cognitive theory will be found to be more and more useful by social work practitioners as the years go by. Cognitive theory is a flexible theory that can be adapted for use in a variety of social work settings. It can also be utilized in either short-term or long-term treatment.[6] As a result, cognitive theory practitioners often adjust well in the managed care environment.[6] Cognitive theory is compatible with existential social work, feminist social work, constructionist social work, narrative social work, and communication theory social work practice. Cognitive theory should continue to provide the social work profession with excellent practice principles and treatment activities that many generations of young social workers looking for a service orientation that is flexible and that works will appreciate, value, and use.

REFERENCES

1. Adler, A. (1959). *Understanding Human Nature.* New York: Premier Books.
2. Adler, A. (1963). *The Practice and Theory of Individual Psychology.* Patterson, NJ: Littlefield.
3. Beck, A. (1976). *Cognitive Theory and the Emotional Disorders.* New York: International Universities Press.

4. Beck, A. (1988). *Love is Never Enough*. New York: Harper and Row.
5. Beck, A., & Greenberg, R. (1974). *Coping with Depression*. Bala Cynwyd, PA: Beck Institute for Cognitive Therapy and Research.
6. Beck, J. (1995). *Cognitive Therapy: Basics and Beyond*. New York: Guilford Press.
7. Berlin, S. (1980). "A Cognitive-Learning Perspective for Social Work." *Social Service Review* 54, 537–555.
8. Chatterjee, P. (1984). "Cognitive Theories and Social Work Practice." *Social Service Review* 58, 63–80.
9. Combs, T. (1980). "A Cognitive Therapy for Depression: Theory, Techniques and Issues." *Social Casework* 61, 361–366.
10. Ellis, A. (1962). *Reason and Emotion in Psychotherapy*. New York: Stuart.
11. Epstein, L. (1980). *Helping People: The Task-Centered Approach*. St. Louis: Mosby.
12. Furst, J. (1954). *The Neurotic—His Inner and Outer Worlds*. New York: Citadel Press.
13. Frankl, V. (1955). *The Doctor and the Soul*. New York: Vintage.
14. Frankl, V. (1959). *Man's Search for Meaning*. New York: Simon and Schuster.
15. Frankl, V. (1969). *The Will to Meaning*. New York: New American Library.
16. Glasser, W. (1965). *Reality Therapy*. New York: Harper and Row.
17. Goldstein, H. (1981). *Social Learning and Change: A Cognitive Approach to Human Services*. Columbia: University of South Carolina Press.
18. Goldstein, H. (1984). *Creative Change: A Cognitive-Humanistic Approach to Social Work Practice*. New York: Methuen.
19. Krill, D. (1978). *Existential Social Work*. New York: Free Press.
20. Lantz, J. (1975). "The Rational Treatment of Parental Adjustment Reaction to Adolescence." *Clinical Social Work Journal* 3, 100–108.
21. Lantz, J. (1978). "Cognitive Theory and Social Casework." *Social Work* 23, 361–366.
22. Lantz, J. (1980). "Adlerian Concepts, A Caseworker's Review." *Clinical Social Work Journal* 8, 188–197.
23. Lantz, J. (1981). "Depression and Social Interest Tasks." *Journal of Individual Psychology* 31, 113–116.
24. Lantz, J. (1989). "Meaning in Profanity and Pain." *Voices* 25, 34–37.
25. Lantz, J. (1990). "Existential Reflection in Marital Therapy with Vietnam Veterans." *Journal of Couples Therapy* 1, 81–88.
26. Lantz, J. (1993). "Existential Reflection and the Unconscious Ought." *Voices* 29, 50–55.
27. Lantz, J. (1993). *Existential Family Therapy: Using the Concepts of Viktor Frankl*. Northvale, NJ: Jason Aronson, Inc.
28. Lantz, J. (1994). "Primary and Secondary Reflection in Existential Family Therapy." *Contemporary Family Therapy* 16, 315–327.
29. Lantz, J. (1994). "Marcel's Availability in Existential Psychotherapy with Couples and Families." *Contemporary Family Therapy* 16, 489–501.
30. Lantz, J. (1995). "Frankl's Concept of Time: Existential Psychotherapy with Couples and Families." *Journal of Contemporary Psychotherapy* 25, 135–144.
31. Lantz, J., and Werk, K. (1976). "Short Term Casework: A Rational-Emotive Approach." *Child Welfare* 55, 29–38.
32. Lazarus, A. (1981). *The Practice of Multimodal Therapy*. Baltimore: John Hopkins University Press.
33. Marcel, G. (1951). *Homo Viator*. Chicago: Henry Regnery Press.
34. Marcel, G. (1956). *The Philosophy of Existence*. New York: Citadel Press.
35. Marcel, G. (1963). *The Existential Background of Human Dignity*. Cambridge: Harvard University Press.
36. May, R. (1979). *Psychology and the Human Dilemma*. New York: W. W. Norton.
37. May, R. (1983). *The Discovery of Being*. New York: W. W. Norton.

227

38. Maultsby, M. (1975). *Help Yourself to Happiness.* New York: Institute for Rational Living.
39. Raimy, V. (1975). *Misunderstandings of the Self.* San Francisco: Jossey-Bass.
40. Reid, W. (1978). *The Task Centered System.* New York: Columbia University Press.
41. Snyder, V. (1975). "Cognitive Approaches in the Treatment of Alcoholism." *Social Casework* 56, 480–498.
42. Tosi, D. (1974). *Youth Towards Personal Growth: A Rational-Emotive Approach.* Columbus, OH: Charles C. Merrel.
43. Weiner, H., and Fox, S. (1982). "Cognitive-Behavioral Therapy with Substance Abusers." *Social Casework* 63, 564–567.
44. Werner, H. (1965). *A Rational Approach to Social Casework.* New York: Association Press.
45. Werner, H. (1982). *Cognitive Therapy: A Humanistic Approach.* New York: Free Press.
46. Werner, H. (1986). "Cognitive Therapy." In Turner, F. (ed.), *Social Work Treatment.* New Yokr: Free Press.
47. Witkin, S. (1982). "Cognitive Clinical Practice." *Social Work* 27, 389–395.
48. Yalom, I. (1980). *Existential Psychotherapy.* New York: Basic Books.
49. Yalom, I. (1989). *Love's Executioner.* New York: Basic Books.
50. Zastrow, C. (1981). "Self-Talk: A Rational Approach to Understanding and Treating Child Abuse." *Social Casework* 62, 182–185.

Reading 10
Cognitive Assessment

COGNITIVE ASSESSMENT: ISSUES AND METHODS

ZINDEL V. SEGAL

BRIAN F. SHAW

There are a thousand thoughts lying within a man that he does not know till he takes up the pen to write.
 —Henry Esmond *by William Makepeace Thackery*

While Thackery's advice may have been intended for the earnest young authors of his day, his observation rings equally true to those involved in the present day enterprise of cognitive assessment. As those involved in this field will recognize, however, the complexities associated with the assessment of cognitive processes only start to surface once the thoughts have been written down or collected. This chapter will address a number of conceptual and methodological issues relevant to the practice of cognitive assessment. An attempt will be made to answer questions regarding what is actually being measured by cognitive assessment, what are the potential threats to the accurate and reliable report of cognitive events, and what type of cognitive content we are most interested in knowing about. Finally, with this last question in mind, a resource list of currently available instruments to assess anxiety and depressive disorders will be presented and evaluated.

DEFINITIONAL ISSUES AND LEVEL OF ANALYSIS

Implicit in the thinking behind this chapter is a view of human cognitive functioning derived from an information processing perspective. Within this model, humans are portrayed as actively seeking, selecting, and utilizing information (both internal and external) in the process of constructing the mind's view of reality (Gardner, 1985; Merluzzi, Rudy, & Glass, 1981; Neisser, 1976). Such activity is an essential feature of the cognitive system and is thought to produce varied contents at different levels of operation (Anderson, 1985). While the passage of information through the system is conceived of as both a synthetic and reciprocal process (Neisser, 1976), most

39

of the attention in the literature seems directed at three distinct levels of analysis. Cognitive structures, processes, and products have been identified by Hollon and Kriss (1984) and others (Arnkoff & Glass, 1982; Ingram, 1984; Turk & Salovey, 1985) as representing the principles or framework through which knowledge about the world is organized, how this framework guides ongoing processing, and what the most accessible products of this processing are.

An illustrative case of the interface of this typology and clinical theory can be found by examining the cognitive model of depression (Beck, Rush, Shaw, & Emery, 1979). This model specifies the operation of cognitive factors at a number of different levels that are then used to explain various features of the disorder. For example, consider the construct of cognitive structures. Beck (1967) has postulated the existence of maladaptive self-schemata that serve as mnemonic representations of the depressed person's negative view of self. One source of information used to assess the self-schema derives from attempts to map out relatively enduring dysfunctional attitudes regarding the contingencies for self-worth that are assumed to reflect schematic content. Another level of assessment directs attention to the putative characteristic style of information processing in depression. The observation that depressed patients selectively attend to negative information may be seen as a function of the individual's self-schema that facilitates the efficient processing of schema-congruent (negative) information (Kuiper, Olinger, MacDonald, & Shaw, 1985). Beck (1967) refers to the various biases of information processing as cognitive distortions (e.g., selective abstraction, arbitrary inference). Cognitive products are considered as the end results or output of the information processing stream (Hollon & Kriss, 1985) and are thought to correspond to the "automatic thoughts" or negative self-statements that are largely accessible to the individual and are often the focus of assessment on self-statement inventories (e.g., Automatic Thoughts Questionnaire; Hollon & Kendall, 1980).

Two points from the preceding example are worthy of more comment. First, as the level of analysis moves from cognitive factors that are more accessible to those that are less readily accessible, (e.g., self-schema), our reliance on inference increases. Hollon & Bemis (1981) explain this by invoking the linguistic based concepts of "surface" and "deep" structure representations. According to this view, the assessment of surface structure content is more observable and corresponds to the propositional type of content most questionnaires and inventories attempt to measure. Deep structure is not as uniformly propositional and hence not as easily captured by the majority of paper and pencil cognitive assessment formats. As a result, deeper structure content is more often endorsed than produced spontaneously, with the endorsement itself reflecting an inferred relationship between the material and its deep structure representation. Second, by specifying the level of cognition we are most interested in, our efforts can be maximized by choosing the assessment format most compatible with that level of analysis (Hollon & Bemis, 1981; Meichenbaum & Cameron, 1981).

PROCESS AND METHODS OF COGNITIVE ASSESSMENT

Cognitive assessment can be organized in terms of seven categories: the assessment of imagery, attributions, beliefs, self-efficacy expectations, cognitive style, self-statements, and *in vivo* thought-sampling (Kendall & Korgeski, 1979). These approaches cut across all three cognitive domains—the structures, processes, and products outlined earlier.

Choosing a particular method of cognitive assessment is best conceived of as a theory guided process (Segal & Shaw, 1986). The type of cognition to be studied and its relationship to performance reflect a specification of the cognitive conceptualization of the disorder utilized by the clinician. Similarly, the existence of a number of different instruments that perform similar functions has led some authors to suggest that what is needed is a framework of cognitive assessment procedures that will facilitate the matching of assessment needs with available methods (Kendall & Hollon, 1981). One such approach has been presented by Glass and Arnkoff (1982). They organize the methods of cognitive assessment according to two dimensions: temporality and degree of structure. The temporal classification examines when the assessment was administered relative to the occurrence of the thoughts one is interested in studying. The resulting scheme yields a continuum of assessment procedures ranging from concurrent evaluations to retrospective evaluations. Figure 2.1 indicates the placement of some of the more common measures on this continuum and provides a brief description of each. Recordings of spontaneous speech have been employed in a number of studies purportedly assessing subject's actual self-talk. These recordings can be taken unobtrusively or following specific instructions. They represent verbal behavior that can then be transcribed and coded into categories (Kendall & Hollon, 1981). This format is one of the most concurrent methods for assessing private speech, yet the investigator is limited to the subject's verbalizations and can never be fully certain that silences are synonymous with the lack of cognitive processing. The free association method as it is used in psychoanalysis also meets the concurrence criterion since patients are asked to verbalize their thoughts as they experience them throughout the therapy session (Bowers & Meichenbaum, 1984).

Think aloud procedures require subjects to provide a continuous monologue of their thoughts during the performance of a specific task. The exact wording of the think aloud instructions may well influence the content of the protocol (Ericsson & Simon, 1984) yet most instructions capture the spirit of this request by Duncker (1926) to his subjects:

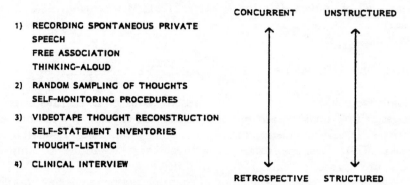

SPECIFIC TECHNIQUES

1) RECORDING SPONTANEOUS PRIVATE
   SPEECH
   FREE ASSOCIATION
   THINKING-ALOUD

2) RANDOM SAMPLING OF THOUGHTS
   SELF-MONITORING PROCEDURES

3) VIDEOTAPE THOUGHT RECONSTRUCTION
   SELF-STATEMENT INVENTORIES
   THOUGHT-LISTING

4) CLINICAL INTERVIEW

Figure 2.1. Contuiuum of temporal and structural dimensions of cognitive assessment (adapted from Glass & Arnkoff, 1982).

I am not primarily interested in your final solution, still less in your reaction time, but in your thinking behavior, in all your attempts, in whatever comes to your mind, no matter whether it is a good or less good idea or a question. Be bold. I do not count your wrong attempts, therefore speak them all out.

At the next level on the continuum we find methods such as random sampling of thoughts and techniques for self-monitoring. The former procedure attempts to provide an unbiased estimate of cognitive frequencies by requesting subjects to record their current thoughts when cued (either in person or by a portable mechanical device) at random intervals. This procedure enables data to be gathered over relatively long periods of time in the subject's own milieu, at intervals that are not contingent on the occurrence of any particular environmental events (Hurlburt, 1979). Newton and Barbaree (in press), for example, utilized *in vivo* random sampling to assess pain related thoughts in a population of chronic headache sufferers. They report a significant shift in appraisal processes and coping strategies following a cognitive-behavioral treatment program for headaches.

With self-monitoring procedures the individual is asked to record the occurrence of specific thoughts in a particular stimulus situation or at a particular time. Their utility lies in the fact that they maximize the probability of gathering clinically relevant information concerning important but possibly infrequent situations. In headache research for example, the experience of pain is a salient event that serves as an internal signal to begin self-monitoring; therefore, cognitive samples are collected during this period (Newton & Barbaree, in press). However, a number of problems reflecting concerns regarding reactivity, social desirability and evaluation apprehension (Nelson, 1977) inherent in self-monitoring procedures in general do exist.

Videotape thought reconstruction allows a subject to reconstruct his or her train of thought by viewing a videotape of an actual or roleplayed problematic situation. Subjects may be asked to think aloud while watching themselves, or alternatively, to record the occurrence of specific cognitive events (Genest & Turk, 1981). With respect to temporality, these procedures are classified as more retrospective than techniques discussed earlier since their aim is to facilitate the subject's "re-living" and reporting of a prior experience, as opposed to reporting on the original experience while it is occurring. A methodology related to videotape thought reconstruction is thought listing, where the subject is asked to report what thoughts he or she experienced while being in a particular stimulus situation. This procedure is more constrained than think aloud methods since the assessment takes place once the subject is out of the situation. The method can be likened to videotape thought reconstruction without the videotape. Cacioppo and Petty (1981) distinguish between listings that examine (1) thoughts elicited by the stimulus situation, (2) general thoughts about the situation or problems, and (3) all thoughts that occurred while subjects anticipated and/or attended to the stimulus. Thoughts can then be coded and scored on a number of dimensions that are of interest to the investigator. Segal and Marshall (1985), using such a procedure in a study of incarcerated sex offenders found that negative self-evaluative thoughts bore a stronger relation to poor heterosexual social skill than did task-referent thoughts, regardless of valence.

Endorsement methods such as self-report inventories or questionnaires contain a predetermined set of thoughts that subjects are asked to rate with respect to whether or not they had experienced the specific thought in the assessment situation, as well as its frequency of occurrence (Kendall & Hollon, 1981). Such instruments have been developed to assess cognitive contents particular to a number of domains such as depression (Hollon & Kendall, 1980), assertion (Schwartz & Gottman, 1976), social anxiety (Glass, Merluzzi, Biever, & Larson, 1982), chronic headaches (Newton & Barbaree, in press) and pedophilia (Abel, Becker, Cunningham-Ratner, Rouleau, & Kaplan, 1984). Finally, the clinical interview can be used as a retrospective cognitive assessment tool, in which case the therapist will ask the client to recall a recently upsetting situation and then recount what he or she was thinking and feeling at the time (Glass & Arnkoff, 1982).

Cognitive assessment procedures may also be organized on the basis of structure, wherein the extent to which the assessment imposes its own limits or format on the individual determines its placement on this continuum (see Figure 2.1). Structured assessments offer the benefits of economy, ease of scoring and administration, as well as a greater potential for standardization across studies (Meichenbaum & Cameron, 1981). The trade-off, however, is against a potentially richer data source and the investigator's ability to uncover unexpected information about unpredicted relationships (Genest & Turk, 1981). Deciding on the degree of structure in an assessment often requires the specification of the extent to which the individual's ongoing cognitive activity can be "punctuated" while still providing an accurate picture of its flow. This concern is introduced by Glass & Arnkoff (1982), who point out that as structure is added, the demand characteristics of the assessment also increases.

While think aloud procedures have an appeal due to their provision of the unaltered flow of subjects' thoughts, the instructions given to subjects to "think aloud" are consequential (Cacioppo & Petty, 1981) and can result in the reporting of varying contents. The rationale for videotape thought reconstruction is that providing subjects with a record of their performance will yield a richer description of what the person was thinking at the time, due to the enhancement of memory functions (Genest & Turk, 1981). Yet it is also possible that subjects are reporting what they guess they could have been thinking in the situation, rather than reporting on the basis of a visual and auditory aided re-experience of the event (Meichenbaum, 1977; Nisbett & Wilson, 1977).

It has long been the consensus within the field that a convergent operations approach is optimal (Webb, Campbell, Schwartz, & Sechrest, 1966). Such an approach minimizes the drawbacks of relying on any one format alone and, if dissimilar measures produce similar findings, construct validity increases (Kendall, 1984; Meichenbaum & Cameron, 1981). As our discussion is now moving into the area of psychometrics, we will turn our focus to questions of threats to the validity of the assessment process.

THREATS TO THE VALIDITY OF COGNITIVE ASSESSMENT

The proliferation of research aimed at explicating cognitive factors in various populations has led to the development of numerous new assessment tools for this express purpose. Thus, it is very important not to lose sight of the fact that methodology is no substitute for validity. At a theoretical level, cognitive assessment endeavours to demonstrate that the self-report of cognitive experience generated by the subject is the result of a patterned and consistent model, albeit idiosyncratic, of information processing. This systematic approach is in contrast to the same self-report generated by an essentially random, individual process that tells us nothing about the way in which an individual's cognitive experience is patterned, much less about the utility of our assessment.

Ericsson and Simon (1984) suggest three criteria that verbal reports should meet if they are to be validly used to infer underlying cognitive processes. The relevance criterion specifies that verbalizations should be relevant to the given task or performance. To be considered pertinent, verbalizations should be logically consistent with those that have just preceded them, and the memory criterion states that some of the information attended to during the situation will be remembered. The authors then go on to illustrate how these criteria can be used as validity checks on verbal protocols:

First, if a verbalization describes a situation that the subject can perceive directly, its correspondence with the stimulus can be checked. Second, its relevance to the task and to plausible steps toward a solution (as determined by task analysis) can be assessed. Third, its consistency with just previously verbalized information presumed to be in STM (short term memory) can be checked. Finally, whenever there is reason to believe that verbalized information will be committed to memory, its presence in memory can be tested by subsequent demands for recall or recognition. (p. 172)

Assumptions regarding the temporal and situational stability of cognitive contents impact on the validity of the assessment process by portraying these contents according to models that do not capture their inherent variability (Kendall, 1982). Arguing against the notion of cognitive intransience (the belief that people think the same things in the same situations at all times), Hollon and Bemis (1981) point out that the burden of proof falls on the assessor to demonstrate that this stability of thinking is, in fact, real. By way of illustration, let us take the case of self-efficacy versus attribution assessment. The assessment of self-efficacy expectations dictates that the rating of the particular behavioral item be taken just prior to performance (Bandura, 1977), in this way providing the investigator with an index of self-efficacy specific to the assessment session. Measuring attributions involves asking individuals to provide their explanations for the causes of events in their lives usually at a point farther removed in time from the actual event. While in the case of self-efficacy ratings we have access to the individual's beliefs at the time of performance, applying this same model to measuring attributions would require that "a retrospectively recalled attribution of job loss to bad luck was indeed the attribution made *at the time* the job was actually lost" (Hollon & Bemis, 1981, p. 150; emphasis added). This type of verification is rarely sought.

Situational instability is another reason why the assumption of cognitive intransience seems to be ill founded. Perhaps the best illustration of this phenomenon can be seen in the differences between thoughts elicited by imagining a stressful situation in the therapist's office as opposed to the thoughts elicited by the situation *in vivo* (Hollon & Bemis, 1981; Kendall, 1982). Data from a study by Last, Barlow, and O'Brien (1985) makes this point forcefully. In an attempt to assess the congruence between three cognitive measures of anxiety these authors compared an *in vivo* think aloud procedure performed with subjects in a shopping mall to a thought-listing procedure that was administered after the *in vivo* assessment. Their final measure was an imaginal cognitive assessment task. Last *et al.*, (1985) found little congruence between the *in vivo*, think-aloud procedure and the thought-listing protocol that was taken when subjects were no longer in the situation they dreaded. Their conclusion that there was little evidence of a direct one-to-one correspondence between these two measures underlines the need to take situationally induced variance into account when deciding at what point in time and where the assessment process will take place.

Questions regarding the construct validity of cognitive assessment focus not on the prediction of a criterion or the match between the content of a test and a specific domain, but rather on the ability of the test itself to measure the cognitive processes of interest (Ghiselli, Campbell & Zedeck, 1981). This issue particularly applies to questionnaire or self-report formats that supply the subject with a particular content. He or she is then asked to provide ratings on dimensions such as presence or absence, frequency, or degree of belief in the cognitions. The best example of this format is the self-statement inventory, which as Kendall (1984) points out is one of the most popular formats for assessing self-talk. The question of content validity should not be confused with concerns regarding construct validity, for while we can establish that the self-statements of which the inventory is composed are a representative sample of what people in general think in the assessment situation, we are less clear on what actual meaning an endorsement of one of these statements carries for the individual. Furthermore, meaning checks or inquiries are rarely conducted in conjunction with the administration of self-statement inventories (Arnkoff & Glass, 1982; Kendall, 1982), leaving us with the assumption that self-statements have the same personal meanings for all individuals involved. One step towards remediation can be found in the "degree of belief" ratings that some inventories require in addition to the usual frequency tallies (e.g., Automatic Thoughts Questionnaire, Hollon & Kendall, 1980).

Glass and Arnkoff (1982) provide a cogent critique of the assumption of an isomorphic relationship between cognition and its representation on self-statement inventories. They list four possibilities that reflect different processes underlying item endorsement. One possibility is that subjects who report having a thought "very frequently" may be indicating the impact or the importance of the thought to them, and not necessarily its frequency. This concern is problematic for most self-statement inventories, since scores usually reflect a simple tally of items endorsed. The second possibility is that a translation process is occurring on the part of the subjects, whereby the idiosyncratic or fragmented thoughts the subject experiences in the situation are translated into grammatically correct sentences as they appear on the inventory. Alternatively, a decision to endorse a thought may reflect the view that the thought matches one's view of oneself, rather than the actual experience of that specific thought. For example, a woman who sees herself as poorly skilled at solving math problems may endorse an item such as "I'm no good at math so why even try" for an exam anxiety questionnaire, because it corresponds to her self-image rather than because she necessarily had the thought.

A final possibility is that endorsement may reflect the translation of affective experiences into a language-based format. While a subject who is in a highly aroused state may or may not be aware of any ongoing cognitive activity, self-statement inventories may provide the opportunity for converting this experience into a linguistic representation of the event. In this sense, the subject may endorse a thought such as "I'm really getting worked up about this" without necessarily having experienced it at the time (Glass & Arnkoff, 1982).

The preceding sections were meant to raise some of the issues that are current concerns in the field of cognitive assessment. While no definitive answers to these questions are as yet forthcoming, there does seem to be agreement that more methodological studies are needed to examine how best to conduct cognitive assessment (Kendall, 1984; Meichenbaum & Cameron, 1981). In addition, the integration of cognition with affect is an area that will hopefully receive more research interest in the near future (Greenberg & Safran, 1984; Segal & Shaw, 1986). Having raised these points, we move now to an examination of the various methods of assessing cognition within the respective domains of anxiety and depression.

COGNITIVE ASSESSMENT OF ANXIETY

That the phenomenology of anxiety is predominantly cognitive has not been overlooked by a number of theorists who posit a significant role for maladaptive cognitions in the development and maintenance of anxiety disorders (Beck & Emery, 1985; Ellis, 1962). Cognitive assessment is, therefore, especially suited to this domain, yet cannot be considered as a sufficient description until it is integrated with the other response modes (behavioral, physiological) characteristic of anxiety (Nelson, Hayes, Felton, & Jarrett, 1985; Nietzel & Bernstein, 1981). In fact, the synchrony or lack thereof between the various response modes is an issue in its own right, but one which is elaborated more fully elsewhere (e.g., Mavissakalian & Barlow, 1981; Rachman & Hodgson, 1974).

The cognitive assessment of anxiety disorders is a relatively recent development and so it is encouraging to note that the range of measures in this area covers both micro (e.g. self-efficacy) and macro (e.g. articulated thoughts during simulated interaction) levels of analysis. While most of the instruments reflect applications of self-report methodology to a particular cognitive target (e.g., self-statements), others are more closely linked to a model of dysfunction, and assess theory specific contents (e.g. based on the cognitive model of anxiety, assessing the degree of threat or perceived danger). The following section describes and critically evaluates a number of these measures with the intent being to provide the reader with enough information to allow him or her to decide on the utility of using these instruments in his or her assessment context.

Questionnaires that purport to measure some of the general cognitive features of anxiety have been used for some time. While the routine use of a standard test battery offers the advantage of comparability to previously published research using these measures, their relative lack of specificity and cumbersome format (e.g. true–false endorsements) often requires the administration of other measures to tap more differentiated cognitive content. The Fear of Negative Evaluation (FNE) Scale (Watson & Friend, 1969) is a 30-item, true–false questionnaire designed to measure the degree of apprehension about receiving social disapproval by others in social situations, whereas the Social Avoidance and Distress (SAD) Scale (Watson & Friend, 1969) uses a similar format with 28 items, to measure the experience of distress and discomfort in social situations. Both scales show good internal consistency with KR-20 reliabilities for the FNE and SAD being .94 for both measures. Test–retest reliabilities are reported as .78 and .68 for the FNE and SAD over a 1-month interval. As a way of broadening the subject's range of response on these scales, some authors have suggested adopting a 5-point response format ranging from "never" to "always" as an alternative to the true–false version of these scales (Bellack, 1979; Glass et al., 1982).

Another general cognitive assessment measure that has been used with anxiety populations is the Irrational Beliefs Test (IBT: Jones, 1969). This 100-item self-report inventory asks subjects to indicate the degree to which they endorse certain beliefs. Items such as "I want everyone to like me" or "I can't stand to make changes" are rated on a 5-point scale. The measure itself shows adequate concurrent validity and internal consistency. A recent factor analysis of the IBT yielded 10 factors that closely match specific beliefs characteristic of those addressed in rational–emotive therapy (Lohr & Bonge, 1982). Scores from the three measures previously described have also been used to categorize subjects into extreme groups (e.g., high vs. low irrational types, high vs. low socially anxious types), thereby utilizing the scales as independent variables in a particular research design. Yet, the implied homogeneity of groups chosen on the basis of having scored in the same upper quartile of a self-report inventory can be questioned (Arkowitz, 1977; Bellack, 1979). Perhaps application of these measures for purposes of classification should be limited to initial screenings.

Another concern about the IBT expressed by Smith and colleagues (Smith, 1982; Smith & Zurawski, 1983) is that the IBT actually measures anxiety and general distress (e.g., neuroticism) rather than irrational beliefs per se. Their work was conducted with a student sample and requires replication with a clinical population. Furthermore, the IBT may not be specific to anxiety disorders as it has also been correlated with depression (Cash, 1984; Nelson, 1977). A more differentiated assessment of cognitive content is provided by self-statement inventories that sample content specific to particular problem areas, and are constructed to reflect the typical types of thoughts that subjects in the situation of interest may experience. Heterosexual social anxiety is the focus of the Social Interaction Self-Statement Test (SISST: Glass *et al.*, 1982), in which subjects are asked to rate 15 positive and 15 negative thoughts (1 = hardly ever had the thought to 5 = very often had the thought) after participating in a live heterosexual social interaction. Split-half reliability of the SISST, based on odd versus even items, is .73 for the positive and .86 for the negative scale. Concurrent validity, as evidence by correlations with other measures of social anxiety, is stronger for the negative self-statements than for the positive ones (negative scale with SAD = .74, with FNE = .58; positive scale with SAD = −.57, with FNE = −.32) using a written stimulus presentation format (Zweig & Brown, 1985). This pattern of functional asymmetry between positive and negative thoughts has been replicated using the SISST with other populations (Segal & Marshall, 1985) and has been suggested as a feature of the relationship between self-statements and affect in general (Safran, 1983). Given that a recent review of cognitive interventions for social anxiety reported that few studies actually assessed cognitive variables (Glass & Merluzzi, 1981), and that those that did often relied on a single measure, the SISST may help to bolster cognitive assessment efforts in this area.

The role of self-statements in assertiveness is relevant to this discussion since high anxiety levels are one of the explanatory constructs that have been proposed to account for nonassertive behavior (Galassi & Galassi, 1979). Schwartz and Gottman (1976) developed the Assertive Self-Statement Test (ASST), which asks subjects to rate on a 5-point scale the frequency of occurrence of 16 positive and 16 negative assertive responses. The self-statements represent thoughts that are believed to facilitate or inhibit the refusal of an unreasonable request and as such represent a more detailed elaboration of cognitive content associated with a specific behavioral performance. Fiedler and Beach (1978) have adopted a different perspective, in that their interest lies in measuring the types of consequences subjects believe are associated with refusal behavior, rather than just positive or negative self-statements. Their Subjective Probability of Consequences Inventory (SPCI) lists positive and negative consequences that could result from complying with or refusing an unreasonable request. The SPCI was constructed by choosing items based on clinical experts' consensual validation of representative consequences. Bruch, Haase, and Purcell (1984) report that both the ASST and SPCI show adequate internal reliability and that the factor structure of the ASST is more complex than was initially assumed, whereas the factor structure of the SPCI corresponds more closely to the dimensions originally outlined by Fiedler and Beach (1978).

Cognitive assessment of agoraphobia is the focus of a self-statement inventory developed by Chambless, Caputo, Bright, and Gallagher (1984).

This measure consists of thoughts concerning negative consequences of experiencing anxiety, and its 14 items were generated through interviews with agoraphobic clients as well as during imaginal and *in vivo* exposure sessions. Each item on their Agoraphobic Cognitions Questionnaire (ACQ) is rated on a 5-point scale ranging from (1) "thought never occurs" to (5) "thought always occurs," and clients are asked to judge the frequency of thoughts when they are in an anxious state. Reliability data show good test-retest stability ($r = .86$) but low internal consistency (Cronbach alpha $= .48$). Validity analyses have shown this scale to be sensitive to treatment-induced changes as well as being able to discriminate the scores of an agoraphobic and normal control sample. Together with its companion scale, the Body Sensations Questionnaire (BSQ: Chambless *et al.*, 1984), which measures physical sensations associated with autonomic arousal, the ACQ represents the first step towards a comprehensive cognitive assessment for agoraphobia. By considering both cognitions and sensations, assessment efforts will be more finely tuned to cognitive conceptualizations of agoraphobia (Goldstein & Chambless, 1978), which stress the fact that catastrophic thinking about anxiety in agoraphobic clients is often precipitated by arousal-mediated internal cues.

Moving away from self-statement inventories, we find a number of alternative structured measures of thought that have been employed in the cognitive assessment of anxiety. Some of these instruments are simply scales that have been devised to measure constructs suggested by the cognitive model of anxiety (Beck & Emery, 1985), whereas others have been generated in different domains.

Consistent with the cognitive model of anxiety, a number of authors have assessed the constructs of perceived danger or the overestimation of personal risk as the salient cognitive processes in anxiety. Butler and Mathews (1983) asked subjects to fill out separate questionnaires requiring interpretations of ambiguous scenarios, rating 20 threatening items in terms of their subjective cost to the subject (e.g., "how bad would it be for you"), and rating a number of positive and negative items in terms of their subjective probability of occurrence. Anxious subjects interpreted the ambiguous material as more threatening and rated the subjective cost of the threatening events as higher than did a control group of nonanxious subjects. Anxious subjects also tended to think that negative events were more likely to happen to them than to someone else. While it is difficult to attribute a high degree of specificity to these findings, since a control group of depressed patients scored similarly on two of these scales, the anxiety group was characterized by inflated estimations of threat and personal risk. Williams (1985) describes a measure of perceived danger, defined as a subject's perception of the probability of a negative event occurring given a specific performance. This measure is quantified as a likelihood or probability rating from 0% ("believe it is not possible") to 100% ("believe it is certain"). He reports that perceived danger ratings did not correlate with behavioral test performance before treatment ($r = .07$), but did correlate significantly after treatment ($r = .56$). Two additional measurement areas are anticipated anxiety, which refers to the degree of anxiety subjects think they would experience if they were to perform a specific task, and perceived self-efficacy, which addresses subjects' beliefs that they can perform a specific task and their confidence in those beliefs (Bandura, 1977). The strength of self-efficacy assessment lies in its operational specification of the behaviors to be measured. Subjects are provided with a series of specific behaviors and asked to rate whether they believe they can perform these behaviors, as well as how confident they are of their judgment, on a scale ranging from 10 to 100. Anticipated anxiety is rated using a 0–10 scale for each specific behavioral task described. In comparing these two indices, Williams (1985) points out that self-efficacy tends to be more accurate in predicting behavior, whereas anticipated anxiety ratings are superior in predicting performance-related anxiety. Given that the correlations between anticipated anxiety and behavior range from .40 to .80 across different studies, Williams (1985) goes on to suggest that perhaps self-efficacy is the major cognitive mediator of phobic avoidance behavior, whereas anticipated anxiety serves the same function for phobic anxiety.

Less structured formats for the cognitive assessment of anxiety have ranged from attempts to sample thinking during *in vivo* (Last *et al.*, 1985) or simulated (Davison, Robins, & Johnston, 1983) anxiety-arousing situations, to the random sampling of thoughts experienced by anxious individuals (Hurlbert & Sipprelle, 1978). Thought-listing has been used in a number of studies where the aim has been to record subjects' thoughts immediately following *in vivo* performance. Last *et al.* (1985), for example, had agoraphobics report what was going through their minds during an exposure session conducted at a shopping mall, while Segal and Marshall (1985) asked rapists to recall what their thoughts were in conjunction with an interaction they just had with an attractive female.

Thought-sampling was employed by Williams and Rappoport (1983) in their research comparing cognitive- and exposure-based treatments for agoraphobia. Subjects were provided with a beeper that would activate periodically, thus cueing the individual to record whatever he or she was thinking about on a tape recorder. The assessments had high ecological validity, as they were taken during behavioral tests of driving capability. A related approach was used by Sewitch and Kirsch (1984), who provided subjects with small booklets in which subjects were instructed to try and recall what thoughts or feelings they were experiencing each time they felt anxious or uptight within a specified 24-hour interval.

The popularity and appeal, due to high face validity, of the two general methodologies described above should not lead to complacency regarding the type of data produced by each approach. In a direct comparison of thought-listing with thinking aloud for the assessment of math anxiety, Blackwell, Galassi, Galassi, and Watson (1985) conclude that different procedures may reveal different cognitive contents. On the basis of using these two methods to assess thinking associated with solving a set of math problems, the authors point out that "think aloud and thought-listing are not equivalent either in the data they produce or in the effects they have on subjects" (p. 409). It seems that the former approach yields relatively more cognitions related to problem solving, whereas the latter format is superior for accessing evaluative processes and other non-problem-solving thought. Findings such as these serve to illustrate the problems of comparability and reactive potential associated with different cognitive assessment measures and point to the need for further research addressing the effects of such method variance.

While the majority of material covered in this section has described efforts at measuring these cognitive aspects of anxiety within the individual's awareness, attempts have also been made to assess the "deep" structure representations of anxious individuals; processes that are inferred from behavior (Landau, 1980; Rudy, Merluzzi, & Henahan, 1982). Rather than focus on the actual cognitive content that subjects are able to report in the assessment situation, these studies aim at a level of analysis that describes the operation of certain cognitive processes or structures, thought to play a key role in the experience of anxiety (Goldfried & Robins, 1983; Segal & Hood, 1985). Multidimensional scaling has been used by a number of investigators in an attempt to map the semantic structure of social anxiety (Goldfried, Padawer, & Robins, 1984; Rudy & Merluzzi, 1984). Similarity ratings on a given dimension for a set of objects serve as the input, in this approach, and yield proximity scores. The output produced is a spatial representation that reflects the data structure, so that the more dissimilar subjects' ratings are, the farther apart they will be represented on a spatial map. In this way, similarity ratings as represented by geometric distance are thought to reflect psychological space, and offer a view of the "deep" structure of a chosen data base (Merluzzi & Rudy, 1982).

Goldfried et al. (1984) used multidimensional scaling with a sample of socially anxious college males and found that they weighted the dimension of "chance of being evaluated" the highest with respect to the likelihood of generating anxiety, while giving lower weights to dimensions of "intimacy" and "academic relevance." Nonanxious males, on the other hand, weighted "intimacy" twice as heavily as "chance of being evaluated," suggesting a possible difference in the saliencies that stand out for these two groups when confronted by an opportunity for heterosexual interaction. Huber and Altmaier (1983) report using a different methodology to investigate the self-statement system of snake phobics. Phobic and nonphobic controls were asked to record their thoughts associated with an avoidance task and these were subsequently rated on a number of dimensions by two trained graduate students. Results indicated that while phobics and non-phobics did not differ in the content of their self-statement systems, the organization of these systems was different for each group. The degree of threat, as a content variable, was equal among the two groups whereas the salience of threat at either end of the dimension (snake will bite vs. snake will not bite) was stronger in the phobics' self-statements.

Finally, Mathews and his colleagues (Butler & Mathews, 1983; MacLeod, Mathews, & Tata, 1986; Mathews & MacLeod, 1985) propose that activation of schemata biased towards the processing of information related to personal danger is characteristic of anxiety states. Mathews and MacLeod (1985), for example, used the Stroop Color-Naming task and found that anxious subjects took longer than controls in color-naming words with a threatening (disease, coffin) as opposed to a neutral (welcome, holiday) content. Studies utilizing other measures derived from cognitive science, such as the degree of visual capture associated with a particular stimulus (MacLeod *et al.*, 1986), have reported findings in a similar direction—namely that anxious subjects are more vigilant for or distracted by threat-related stimuli than are normal controls. The authors interpret these results as supporting the existence of cognitive "danger" schemata, which when activated bias information processing at a preattentive level. Whether this bias is perceptual or attentional in nature, it is thought to play an important role in the maintenance of the disorder, since it has an impact on the interpretations that individuals make at a later point in the information-processing stream.

Before leaving this section and moving on to the cognitive assessment of depression, it is important to consider a number of issues that interface with both domains. While cognitive assessment efforts in anxiety are a more recent development than those in depression, it is equally accurate to characterize both endeavours as still in their infancy. As a result, more work is needed to refine and evaluate the measures that exist in these already method-rich areas (Meichenbaum & Cameron, 1981; Segal & Shaw, 1986). Scoring criteria for thought-listing or think-aloud protocols are a good example of an area where the injection of some degree of regularity in the dimensions or attributes scored would aid comparability among investigations. Similarly, the increasing attention being paid to cognitive structures or "deeper" levels of processing would benefit from a focus on resolving some of the definitional issues surrounding the operation of these constructs. When descriptions of processing along schematic (Segal, Hood, Shaw, & Higgins, 1986), semantic-structural (Goldfried, Padawer, & Robins, 1984) or superordinal (Huber & Altmaier, 1983) construct lines, for example, have their maximal meaning solely for the investigators involved and few others in the field, then terminological clarification at both a conceptual and operational level becomes a necessity (Segal & Hood, 1985).

Readers should also bear in mind the close relationship between anxiety and depression symptoms. Up to 90% of patients report both symptoms of anxiety and depression (Brier, Charney, & Heninger, 1984; Dobson, 1985; Fawcett & Kravitz, 1983; Hamilton, 1981; Swinson & Kirby, 1987). Most researchers have set out to differentiate the various syndromes of anxiety and depression using diagnostic systems or symptom inventories. Dobson (Dobson, 1985; Shaw & Dobson, 1981), using an interactive model of life events and traits tired to differentiate the disorders using a self-report measure to evaluate the subjects' self-descriptive responses to various stressful situations. Investigators have only recently made attempts to document the relative contribution of anxiety-related and depression-related cognitions within an individual diagnosed as suffering from an anxiety and/or depressive disorder. Considerable work is needed to clarify the value of cognition and cognitive processes for the differentiation of these disorders. Acknowledging that their resolution will no doubt be a gradual process, we now move on to consider the cognitive assessment of depression.

COGNITIVE ASSESSMENT OF DEPRESSION

Most of the cognitive assessment measures of depression are paper and pencil instruments designed to capture either the content of the patients' thinking or their underlying attitudes or beliefs. Other significant efforts have addressed the manner in which depressed patients process information, particularly of self-referent descriptions or feedback from task performances (Shaw & Dobson, 1981). Few investigators have concerned themselves with thought-listing or think-aloud procedures although the recall (reconstruction) of automatic thoughts or self-statements in specific situations is widely employed in the clinical interview format (Beck et al., 1979.

Our review of depression measures will capitalize on previous reviews of this subject matter (Hammen & Krantz, 1985; Rush, 1983; Shaw & Dobson, 1981) and provide a selective reporting. Our choice of measures is meant to illustrate categories of cognitive assessment with particular reference to the clinical utility and the psychometric evaluations of the measure. The majority of our efforts in this section will be spent on a review of self-report measures of the cognitive changes that accompany depression. Later we shall go on to discuss neomentalistic strategies (Paivio, 1975), particularly those addressing the self-schema construct to assess cognitive change. Along with a review of the various measures the reader can consult Tables 2.1, 2.2, and 2.3 for the scores of depressed patients on selected cognitive assessment instruments.

The Dysfunctional Attitude Scale (DAS) was designed by Weissman and Beck (Weissman, 1979; Weissman & Beck, 1978) to identify the relatively stable set of attitudes associated with depressive disorders. It is now clear that these attitudes are relevant to several psychopathological conditions although the actual DAS score may differentiate various groups (Dobson & Shaw, 1986; Hollon, Kendall, & Lumry, 1986). As dysfunctional attitudes are thought to reflect prepotent self-schemata, the DAS has been proposed as one measure of cognitive vulnerability to major depressive disorder (cf. Olinger, Kuiper, & Shaw, 1987; Olinger, Shaw, & Kuiper, 1987). The DAS is a self-report inventory available in three forms. The original 100-item inventory (DAS-T) is only occasionally employed in research studies. From the DAS-T, two 40-item parallel forms (DAS-A and DAS-B) have been derived, with the former being the most commonly used. Patients indicate the degree to which they agree or disagree with the stated attitudes on a 7-point scale. The scores range from 100 to 700, while on the DAS-A and DAS-B the range is from 40 to 280.

The DAS items are typically stated as contingencies concerning approval from others, prerequisites for happiness or perfectionistic standards; for example, "It is difficult to be happy unless one is good looking, intelligent, rich and creative"; "People will probably think less of me if I make a mistake"; and "If someone disagrees with me, it probably indicates he or she does not like me."

Weissman (1979) developed the DAS on a sample of college students and more recently, Oliver and Baumgart (1985) evaluated all three forms in a sample of adult hospital workers and their spouses. A psychometric study with a nonselected normative sample remains to be completed. The DAS has been widely researched on depressed and psychiatric control patients. In the Oliver and Baumgart (1985) study the mean score on the DAS-T was 296 ($SD = 75$), while according to Weissman (1979) the mean total score for students using either the DAS-A or the DAS-B was 117.7 ($SD = 26.8$). Depressed patients typically receive scores of 150 ($SD = 40$). Both short forms of the DAS have good internal consistency and stability over time, with coefficient alphas ranging from .89 to .92 and a test–retest correlation of .84 over an 8-week period (Weissman, 1979). Oliver and Baumgart (1985) reported alpha coefficients of .90, .85, and .81 for the DAS-T, DAS-A, and DAS-B respectively. Their 6-week test–retest reliability for the DAST was .73 ($N = 43$).

One area of controversy in the research concerns the stability of DAS scores in samples of depressed patients. Some investigators report a relatively stable pattern of DAS scores, while others find a marked change in scores. The concurrent validity of the DAS has been tested in several studies but there have been few evaluations of construct validity. It is expected that the DAS would have moderate correlations with measures of depressive severity and with measures of negative automatic thoughts, or cognitive distortions. For example, in three studies (Dobson & Shaw, 1986; Hamilton & Abramson, 1983; O'Hara, Rehm, & Campbell, 1982) the DAS correlations with the Beck Depression Inventory (BDI) were in the moderate range (i.e., 40-.65). Riskind, Beck, and Smucker (1983) found that the DAS remained significantly correlated with the Hopelessness Scale ($r = .22$) and a self-concept test ($r = -.15$), with the effects of depression severity partialled out. The DAS correlates .52 with the Cognitive Bias Questionnaire and with the Automatic Thoughts Questionnaire, both of which are state-dependent measures of depressive cognitions (Hollon *et al.*, 1986). While the DAS discriminates groups of depressed and psychiatric control patients, it is not specifically associated with a major depressive disorder. Patients with generalized anxiety disorder, anxorexia nervosa, panic disorder or dysthymia may manifest abnormal DAS scores (Dobson & Shaw, 1986). In addition, it is notable that approximately 15% of depressed patients do not have abnormally high (i.e., at least one standard deviation above the mean) scores (Hamilton & Abramson, 1983).

The DAS has been employed to evaluate attitudes hypothesized to change as a function of cognitive therapy of other treatments of depression. Several studies have found the DAS to be a sensitive measure of clinical improvement. Keller (1983) found that DAS scores were useful to predict the outcome of a cognitive therapy treatment. Simons, Garfield, and Murphy (1984) reported that the DAS scores were lowered following *either* cognitive therapy or pharmacotherapy for depression. Silverman, Silverman, and Eardley (1984) also noted a significant reduction in the DAS scores following pharmacotherapy. The stability of the DAS scores of depressed patients following a remission of the depression is a matter of some controversy. Eaves and Rush (1984), Dobson and Shaw (1986), and Isaacs and Silver (1980) observed a reduction in DAS scores associated with a reduction in depressive symptoms, but found that remitted depressed patients continue to have abnormally high scores. Reda, Carpiniello, Secchiaroli, & Blanco (1985) used a shortened form of the DAS (NB a 37-item version that was neither Form A nor Form B) to evaluate depressed inpatients. Sixty patients were tested originally, and 30 of these were retested at a 1-year followup. Patients were treated with drugs (typically, amitriptyline and, when indicated, a benzodiazepine), but *not* with psychotherapy. They found a parallel reduction in the Hamilton Rating Scale (the HRSD) and the DAS total scores in both the acute and the follow-up phases. At discharge from hospital when the depression had remitted, the DAS scores of the depressed group did not differ from a group of 60 normal controls. These investigators identified specific, persistent, dysfunctional assumptions that continued to be endorsed even at follow-up. These included: "I feel well only when I have complete control over the situation"; "Turning to someone else for advice or help is an admission of weakness"; and "I should be able to please everybody." The pattern reflected a cognitive style with the following elements: (1) a pessimistic view of life; (2) a need for complete control; (3) overvaluing the judgements of others; and (4) a view that personal problems should be solved rapidly and independently. In contrast, other investigators (Hamilton & Abramson, 1983; Silverman *et al.*, 1984; Simons *et al.*, 1984) observed that the DAS scores returned to normal as the depression remitted. These disparate results may be accounted for in part by the definition of remission and the time of retesting. Many of the studies (e.g., Dobson & Shaw, 1986; Hamilton & Abramson, 1983; Eaves & Rush, 1984) tested patients shortly after the remission, when patients no longer met depression diagnostic criteria but still had some symptoms of the disorder (i.e., the depression had not been completely resolved). Nevertheless, it is clear that dysfunctional attitudes abate with a range of treatments; a change in DAS scores is by no means specific to cognitive therapy.

The DAS may also be useful in the prediction of future depressive symptomatology in remitted depressed patients (Rush, Weissenberger, & Eaves, 1986; Simons, Murphy, Levine & Wetzel, 1986). Furthermore, the DAS has been used in several studies as an independent variable, to identify subjects who are assumed to have a cognitive vulnerability to depression (Kuiper *et al.*, 1985; Kuiper & Olinger, 1986).

The DAS has been factor analyzed in a number of investigations. Originally, Weissman (1979) used factor analysis on the DAS-T to devise the two parallel short forms. Olinger *et al.* (1987), in a study of college students, reported two factors, one involving a concern for performance evaluation and another a need for approval. Oliver and Baumgart (1985) found four factors from both the DAS-A and DAS-B in their study of adult volunteers. Unfortunately, the two-factor structure from the DAS-A and the DAS-B differed with the exception of a need for approval factor. This factorial incongruence is a concern that led these authors to conclude that the shortened forms cannot replace the DAS-T. (See Table 2.1 for comparative data of reviewed and related studies.)

Several conceptual questions may be raised about the use of the DAS. First, are dysfunctional attitudes meaningful reflections of the self-schema? Some authors (Beck, 1967; Rush, 1983) equate the two constructs, while our position is that different aspects of the patient's cognitive organization are tapped by the self-schema and dysfunctional attitude constructs. Second, what are the most theoretically and clinically meaningful methods of scoring the DAS? Weissman (1979) used a total score from either of the 40-item short forms of the test to quantify the severity of dysfunctional attitudes endorsed by the individual. It is expected that most subjects will endorse some dysfunctional attitudes to various degrees. From a theoretical viewpoint, is it more meaningful to consider the total score on the DAS or some other metric, such as the proportion of attitudes that are held in an extreme (presumably rigid) fashion? Clinically, an individual with a few dysfunctional attitudes held in an extreme and inflexible degree may be more vulnerable and/or more difficult to treat. In addition we must remain uncertain about the scoring until we obtain more information on the relationship between dysfunctional attitudes and vulnerability to psychopathology. A third question about the DAS is how stable the total scores on

Table 2.1. Dysfunctional Attitude Scale

Study	Sample	Pre		Post		Pre- and Post-Period (Days)
		$\bar{x}$	SD	$\bar{x}$	SD	
Simons, Garfield, & Murphy (1984)	70 RDC Depressed Outpatients	158.9	29.0	119.8	—	112
Isaacs & Silver (1980)	38 RDC-Depressed Outpatients (12 were age 60 or older)	150.6	—	—	—	N/A
Rapp (1985)	100 RDC-Depressed Patients (74 Inpatients)	150.3	37.4	—	—	N/A
Hamilton & Abramson (1983)	20 RDC-Depressed Patients	148.5	46.8	116.6	27.7	17
Eaves & Rush (1984)	31 RDC-Depressed Female Outpatients (26 Outpatients)	162.8	43.8	132.4	38.3	74
Dobson & Shaw (1986)	35 RDC-Depressed Inpatients	146.8	41.3	136.8[a]	34.6	60
Silverman, Silverman, & Eardley (1984)	35 DSM-III-Depressed Outpatients	147.5	—	113.3	—	
Silverman, Silverman, & Eardley (1984)	63 DSM-III-Unipolar Depressed Patients	N/A		123.4	29.2	
Blackburn & Smyth (1985)	10 Remitted RDC-Depressed Patients	N/A				
Keller & Haase (1984)	19 DSM-III-MDD Patients	146.8	32.0	N/A		
Blackburn & Jones (in press)	72 RDC-Depressed Patients (62 Major, 10 Minor)	147.7	4.1[b]	—	—	
	29 Recovered Depressed Patients	—	—	127.7	5.4[b]	120

[a]n = 15 at post. [b]standard error.

58

250

the DAS are, as well as how stable the specific items of the test are. Theoretically, dysfunctional attitudes are assumed to be more stable than other measures of cognition, such as the frequency of negative automatic thoughts or the probability of negatively biased recall of information. During a major depressive episode it has been generally observed that most patients exhibit abnormally high scores on the DAS (i.e., greater than 140), yet it is still unclear whether these DAS scores remain abnormal once the episode has remitted.

The Cognitive Bias Questionnaire (CBQ: Hammen & Krantz, 1983; Krantz & Hammen, 1979) is a self-report measure consisting of six stories, three with primarily a social/interpersonal theme and three with primarily an achievement/competence theme. Each story is followed by four multiple-choice questions (one story has only three questions) designed to reflect the central character's feelings, thoughts, and expectations. Each question, in turn, has four response options, constructed along two dichotomous and crossed dimensions: (1) depressed versus nondepressed responses (note: depression refers to dysphoria, not the syndrome of depression), and (2) distorted versus nondistorted responses, in terms of logical inference. An example of a depressed/distorted response to a situation involving the first thoughts following an election loss is "feel bad and imagine I've lost by a landslide" (Krantz & Hammen, 1979, p. 613).

Researchers and clinicians focus on the depressed/distorted category, since it is this category that is the most relevant to Beck's (1967) cognitive theory of depression. In the original validation Krantz and Hammen (1979) studied two clinical samples, 29 unipolar depressed patients meeting the Research Diagnostic Criteria (RDC: Spitzer, Endicott, & Robins, 1978) for a major depressive episode, and 10 RDC depressed male inpatients. They reported means (standard deviations in parentheses) of 4.3 (3.5) and 7.0 (4.4) of depressed distortions respectively in the two samples. Norman, Miller, & Klee (1983) reported means of 3.3 (3.0) and 2.6 (1.9) from a group of 30 (24 females) primary depressed inpatients and a group of 30 (13 females) secondarily depressed inpatients.

In two student samples studied, Krantz and Hammen (1979) reported coefficients of internal consistency (alphas) to be .62 and .69. These modest alpha coefficients may reflect the heterogeneous nature of the cognitive distortion construct (Hammen & Krantz, 1985), which was based on the initial observations of depressed patients reported by Beck (1970). Distortions such as arbitrary inference, overgeneralization, and selective abstraction do describe quite different biases in information processing. Test-retest correlations across 4 to 8 weeks were acceptable ($r = .48$ and $r = .60$). To date, no tests of the reliability of the CBQ have been reported with a clinically depressed sample.

The construct validity of the CBQ was demonstrated in two clinical samples (Krantz & Hammen, 1979; Norman et al., 1983). The correlation between the CBQ depressed/distorted score and the Beck Depression Inventory were significant (e.g., $r = .46$ with the full scale, $r = .50$ with the adult factor, and $r = .47$ with the retardation factor of the BDI). The BDI–CBQ depressed/distortion score correlations in student samples have been consistent and significant (see Blaney, Behar, & Head, 1980; Frost & MacInnis, 1983).

It is by no means clear whether the CBQ changes are specific to depression, however. As Hammen and Krantz (1985) have stated, the concept of cognitive biases is a complex one and there has been little work on the discriminant validity of the CBQ. Krantz and Hammen (1979) noted differences between depressed and nondepressed psychiatric patients in the predicted direction, although Norman *et al.* (1983) could not differentiate primary from secondary depressed samples using the CBQ.

Another potentially significant problem for the CBQ is its lack of sensitivity (Rush, 1984), since the depressed/distorted response constitutes only 6 of the 23 responses available to subjects. Nevertheless, the CBQ is sensitive to changes in mood following induction procedures with students (Goodwin & Williams, 1982; Riskind & Rholes, 1984). Future studies are needed to evaluate the CBQ's sensitivity, specificity, and stability in clinical samples.

The Automatic Thoughts Questionnaire (ATQ: Hollon & Kendall, 1980) is a 30-item self-report test designed to assess the frequency and the intensity of negative automatic thoughts typically associated with depression (Beck, 1976). Clinically, this test may be useful to identify changes in the content of thinking, although it is not clear whether depressed patients can reliably estimate the frequency of their negative thinking in a week (Coyne & Gotlib, 1983). The items are face-valid and are rated on a 5-point scale from "not at all" (1) to "all the time" (5), based on the occurrence of such thoughts in the past week. Using a 5-point scale, ratings of the degree of belief in each thought are also included.

The ATQ does not control for either social desirability or acquiescence (Jackson, 1970). The test has consistently been shown to have strong internal consistency with Cronbach alpha in the 0.90's across different samples (Dobson & Breiter, 1983; Harrell & Ryan, 1983; Hollon & Kendall, 1980; Rapp, 1985).

The ATQ has reasonable test–retest reliability, providing that the person's severity of depression has not changed. It seems clear that the ATQ is a state-dependent measure that is significantly related to the severity of depression. Correlations with the BDI (Beck, Ward, Mendelson, Mock, & Erbaugh, 1961) and other measures of depression severity (i.e., Hamilton Rating Scale for Depression [HRSD], SCL-90 Depression) tend to be high. For example, Dobson and Shaw (1986) reported an ATQ–BDI correlation of .84 and an ATQ–HRSD correlation of .80.

The ATQ has strong construct validity with acceptable to high correlations with several other measures of cognitive content. One factor analytic study reported four factors: (1) personal maladjustment and desire for change, (2) negative self-concept and expectations, (3) low self-esteem, and (4) helplessness and giving up (Hollon & Kendall, 1980). These factors are all consistent with the cognitive theory of depression (Beck, 1967).

To interpret the ATQ results, one can use the following guidelines. The mean ATQ frequency in a combined sample of depressed patients (inpatients and outpatients) is approximately 104 with standard deviations in the range of 26. When the depression remits, scores in the range of 67 (standard deviation of 24) can be expected. With this range of scores the ATQ is clearly a sensitive cognitive measure of change in depression. Early studies (e.g., Dobson & Shaw, 1986; Hollon *et al.*, 1986) reveal that the ATQ can discriminate depressed from other psychiatric groups, although more work on this issue is needed.

No concurrent validity data have been reported comparing other measures of automatic thoughts (e.g., using the Daily Record of Dysfunctional Thoughts in Beck *et al.*, 1979) and the ATQ. Rush (1984) questioned the face validity of the specific items for depressed patients, given that the ATQ was developed with college students. This concern is somewhat lessened now that several clinical studies have produced results similar to the college student studies. (See Table 2.2 for studies examining the ATQ in clinical samples).

The Cognitive Response Test (CRT: Watkins & Rush, 1983) is a self-report sentence-completion type of measure that uses an unstructured format for subjects to report their automatic thoughts. Originally validated as a 50-item questionnaire, the form in use today has 36-items. The completed sentences are scored into one of four categories: rational responses, irrational–depressed, irrational–nondepressed, and unscorable. Example items include "Lately my work has become more and more demanding. I think _____" and "When I consider being married, my first thought is _____." The irrational-depressed scale is of most theoretical and practical interest. Interestingly, the CRT-36 scores are signficantly affected by the severity of depression but not neuroticism (Wilkinson & Blackburn, 1981), indicating a greater specificity for the CRT than other tests. On the negative side, the CRT accounted for a relatively small amount of the variance of the BDI (36%; a BDI–CRT correlation of .60) compared to other measures of cognitive bias. This scale differentiated a sample of depressed from nondepressed subjects in four studies (Dobson & Shaw, 1986; Simons *et al.*, 1984; Watkins & Rush, 1983; Wilkinson & Blackburn, 1981). The CRT is scored by raters who are guided by a standardized scoring manual. The interrater reliabilities have been reported to range from .72 to .88. Rush (1984) pointed out that while the CRT avoids the "transparency problems" of fixed-choice tests, it

Table 2.2. Automatic Thoughts Questionnaire

Study	Sample	Pre		Post		Pre- and Post-Period (Days)
		$\bar{x}$	SD	$\bar{x}$	SD	
Simons, Garfield, & Murphy (1984)	70 RDC-Depressed Outpatients	108.5	21.9	62.3	—	
Eaves & Rush (1984)	31 RDC-Depressed Females	110.9	26.6	50.7	23.7	74
Dobson & Shaw (1986)	35 RDC-Depressed Inpatients	93.3	29.7	88.3[a]	23.7	60
Rapp (1985)	100 RDC-Depressed Patients (74 Inpatients and 26 Outpatients)	105.9	27.8	—	—	
Blackburn, Jones, & Lewin (1986)	72 Depressed Patients	82.5	3.9[b]	—	—	
	(64 Inpatients and 8 Outpatients)			42.4	5.1[b]	>120

[a]retest on 15 Ss only [b]standard error.

is more time-consuming to score. Clinically, it is expected that depressed patients will obtain scores around 10.2, with a standard deviation of 4.9. When the depression remits, scores range around 5.0, with a standard deviation of 3.2.

The Cognitive Style Test (CST: Wilkinson & Blackburn, 1981) is a self-report, fixed-response measure of cognitive style. The CST was rationally designed to reflect Beck's (1967) theory, as well as the reformulated learned helplessness theory (Abramson, Seligman, & Teasdale, 1978). The authors also based their thinking on the notion that there are multiple causal pathways to depression (Akiskal & McKinney, 1975). Subjects respond to 30 vignettes of everyday events designed to address Beck's (1967) cognitive triad (negative views of self, world, and future). Each part of the triad is represented by five pleasant and five unpleasant situations. For each situation subjects choose one of four responses that receive scores on a 0 to 3 scale. Numerical indices are derived for the degree of negative interpretation of pleasant events, of unpleasant events, and of the combination of the two events. Examples of responses reflecting a depressed cognitive style are:

1. A person you admire tells you that he or she likes people like you. Response: He or she is being sarcastic. (3)
2. You go out socially with some people you have just met, but the evening is not very enjoyable. Response: They didn't like me. (3)

Clearly, the first event is pleasant while the second is unpleasant. High scores on the CST reflecting a depressed cognitive response are obtained if the subject makes external attributions (or negative interpretations) for pleasant events and internal attributions (or positive interpretations) for unpleasant events. The test controls for acquiescence but not social desirability.

Test–retest reliability was established over an interval of 16 days in a small sample of normal subjects. Split-half reliability was 0.68. The CST scales regarding total, pleasant, and unpleasant events differentiated depressed subjects from normal and recovered depressed subjects. The CST total score mean was 54.9 ($SD = 10.3$) for the depressed group, while the normal and recovered depressed samples had means of 36.7 (6.4) and 32.0 (5.4) respectively. Notably, Wilkinson and Blackburn (1981) report that the CST is affected by both depression severity and the level of neuroticism. On the positive side, the CST has good concurrent validity (e.g., the correlations with the CRT-36 (irrational–depressed scale was .67). The CST-BDI correlation was 0.68, while the correlation between the CST and a measure of neuroticism (the Middlesex Hospital Questionnaire (MHQ: Crown & Crisp, 1970)) was .59.

The CST may prove to be a useful measure of cognitive bias relevant to several psychopathological disorders. It is unlikely to be specific to major depression. More work on the psychometric properties of the CST is needed.

Notably, Blackburn, Jones, and Lewin (1986) revised the CST to make it more suitable for a middle-aged target population by changing some of the stimulus situations and clarifying the response options. The resulting measure provides scores for five subscales: pleasant events, unpleasant events, events relating to the self, the world, and the future, as well as a total score. They demonstrate high internal consistency, and strong concurrent validity using the revised scale.

The Hopelessness Scale (HS: Beck, Weissman, Lester, & Trexler, 1974) is a 20-item, self-report test designed to measure the person's negative expectancies about future events. Theoretically, the measure taps the negative view of the future proposed by Beck (1967) as one of the central constructs of depression. Example items include "I might as well give up because I can't make things better for myself" and "The future seems dark to me."

Acquiescence is controlled for by keying patient responses in a true-false format (11 of the 20 items are keyed as true). HS scores are expected to fluctuate with subjects' changing negative expectations about coping with life stressors or attaining valued outcomes. The HS is a state-dependent measure like the ATQ and CBQ.

The item-total correlations of the HS range from .39 to .76. The internal consistency was high (coefficient alpha = .93). Mendonca, Holden, Mazmanian, and Dolan (1983) cautioned that the high degree of internal consistency was attributable to a negative desirability set. They pointed to the importance of separating hopelessness from the tendency to view one's condition unfavourably in a crisis situation. These investigators observed that crisis patients often obtained high hopelessness scores when in interview they were anxious and/or depressed but "not particularly hopeless." Furthermore, they found the HS to be more sensitive to a socially undesirable response set than to the degree of suicidal behavior. This work demonstrates an important caution in the use of the HS and may serve as a motive to develop other measures of hopelessness.

The HS correlates significantly with the BDI (r's range from .68 to .84) and with clinical ratings of hopelessness ($r = .60$ to .74) (Minkoff, Bergman, Beck, & Beck, 1973). The construct validity of the HS has been further demonstrated by significant relationships with the Cognitive Style Test ($r = .64$) and the Cognitive Response Test irrational–depressed subscale ($r = .57$). Wilkinson and Blackburn (1981) and Keller and Haase (1984) found the HS–DAS relationship to be significant ($n = 19$, $r = .66$).

The HS scores differentiate depressed from recovered depressed and normal subjects (Wilkinson & Blackburn, 1981). The HS is also a sensitive measure of treatment outcome with depressed patients treated by either pharmacotherapy or cognitive therapy (Rush, Beck, Kovacs, Weissenburger, & Hollon, 1982).

Perhaps, most importantly, hopelessness as measured by the HS has been shown to be a predictor of suicidal ideation (Beck, Steer, Kovacs, & Garrison, 1985). Early studies found that the intensity of suicidal intent was more highly correlated with hopelessness than depression (Minkoff *et al.*, 1973). More recently, the Beck *et al.* (1985) study found that the HS score differentiated a group of suicidal ideators who eventually died by suicide from ideators who did not. A cutoff score of 9 on the HS separated the completer from the noncompleter group. The major problem with this finding from a practical perspective, however, is that there was a 88.4% false positive rate with this cutoff. Nevertheless, it seems reasonable to increase clinical concern and further assessment for suicidal ideation when patients have high HS scores. (See Table 2.3 for clinical samples using the Hopelessness Scale.)

The Attributional Style Questionnaire (ASQ: Peterson, *et al.*, 1982) is designed to detect the negatively biased attributions found in depression. Subjects are presented with twelve hypothetical situations, six with good outcomes and six with bad outcomes. The themes of affiliation and achievement concern are also balanced across the situations.

The subject is asked to imagine him- or herself in each situation and then to describe the major cause of the event. The subject is then asked to rate whether the cause is due to (1) internal versus external reasons; (2) stable versus unstable factors, and (3) global versus specific factors. These dimensions reflect the reformulated learned helplessness theory (Abramson, *et al.*, 1978). The affiliation and achievement subtypes are typically more difficult to separate consistently than the good and bad outcome grouping. Five-week, test–retest correlations are moderate, ranging from .67 to .70 for good outcomes and .64 to .67 for bad (Golin, Sweeny, & Schaeffer, 1981; Peterson *et al.*, 1982). Examples of good outcome situations are "You do a project that is highly praised" and "Your spouse (boyfriend/girlfriend) has been treating you more lovingly." Examples of bad outcome situations are "You can't get all of the work done that others expect of you" and "You meet a friend who acts hostilely toward you."

The internal consistency of the ASQ is problematic, with alphas for good outcomes ranging from .44 to .58 and those for bad outcomes ranging from .46 to .69 (Peterson *et al.*, 1982). If the internality, stability, and globality dimensions are combined to form a composite good or bad outcome score, the alphas are acceptable (.75 and .72, respectively). For the assessment of attributional biases, the differences between depressed and nondepressed subjects are only found with the bad outcomes (Seligman, Abramson, Semmel, & von Baeyer, 1979). Some investigators get around this problem by aggregating the two scales (see, e.g., Hamilton & Abramson, 1983). Hammen and Krantz (1985) have indicated that the relationship between ASQ scores and depressed mood, while significant, is quite modest (mean $r = .21$ with the bad outcomes composite score). Another

Table 2.3. Hopelessness Scale

Study	Sample	Pre		Post		Pre- and Post-Period (Days)
		$\bar{x}$	SD	$\bar{x}$	SD	
Hamilton & Abramson (1983)	20 RDC-Depressed Inpatients	10.2	7.4	4.1	4.9	17
Keller & Haase (1984)	19 DSM-III-MDD Volunteers	9.6	4.9	—	—	
Blackburn, Jones, & Lewin (1986)	72 RDC-Depressed Patients (64 Inpatients and 8 Outpatients)	11.4	0.6[a]	6.0	1.1[a]	

[a]standard error.

258

problem with the ASQ is that subjects present a different pattern of attributions on the ASQ compared to their causal explanations for stressful life events or for laboratory tasks (Miller, Klee, & Norman, 1982).

Like the DAS, the ASQ may identify a subset of depressed patients who are vulnerable to future episodes. Some investigators observed that the ASQ behaves in a state-like manner, while others noted a more trait-like style. Zimmerman, Coryell, and Corenthal (1984) compared ASQ scores in major depressed patients who either did or did not meet criteria for melancholia. The ASQ did not differentiate between these subtypes. Hamilton and Abramson (1983) and Dobson and Shaw (1986) observed that the ASQ was basically a state-dependent measure of depression, while Eaves and Rush (1984) reported a stability of ASQ scores between periods of the episode and periods of remission. They noted that the ASQ decreased somewhat as the depression remitted but still remained abnormally high.

Adding to this controversy is the recent study by Winters and Neale (1985). They tested 16 remitted unipolar depressed outpatients on the pragmatic inference task, a measure of attributional bias. This measure was proposed as less sensitive than the ASQ to a self-presentation bias. The task differs from the ASQ in that (1) both success and failure are embedded in each story, (2) subjects are required to answer questions about facts and inferences not related to causality, and (3) the task is presented as a nonspecific memory task (Winters & Neale, 1985, p. 284). Their important finding was that the remitted depressed patients were found to retain "depressive-like cognitions." Winters and Neale argued that the Hamilton and Abramson (1983) findings are subject to a self-presentation bias (presumably a positive bias) before discharge. More research is needed to clarify the stability of any attributional biases following a depressive episode.

There are several other cognitive assessment measures relevant to the study of depression. Since these measures were judged to lack important reliability or validity data or were viewed as preliminary for other reasons, we shall describe them only in passing. The Cognitions Questionnaire (Fennell & Campbell, 1984) was designed to assess a cognitive style that would reflect a cognitive vulnerability to depression. Like the ASQ, eight scenarios were developed, with subjects' responses following each description. These responses tape the emotional impact, attribution of causality, generalization across time, generalization across situations, and perceived uncontrollability. Unfortunately, while the scale is sensitive to the depressed state, no evidence of an enduring vulnerability based on this measure has been shown. Munoz (1977) in collaboration with Lewinsohn designed three questionnaires to detect negative cognitions. These scales (the Subjective Probability Questionnaire, the Personal Beliefs Inventory and the Cognitive Events Schedule) are dependent upon depressed mood but are neither antecedents of nor sequels to depression (Lewinsohn, Steinmetz, Larson, & Franklin, 1981).

The Self-Control Schedule (SCS: Rosenbaum, 1980) is a 36-item questionnaire designed to evaluate the use of cognitions to control emotional responses (e.g., depression, anger, anxiety, pain), the use of problem-solving strategies, the ability to delay gratification, and the sense of self-efficacy. Sample items tapping these various dimensions include "When I plan to work, I remove all the things that are not relevant to my work" and "I often find it difficult to overcome my feelings of nervousness and tension without any outside help." The SCS was not developed as a specific measure of cognition in depression but rather was meant to assess the broad construct of self-control or learned resourcefulness. As it turns out, however, the SCS has been useful in some studies of depression. The internal reliability of the SCS is acceptable, ranging from .78 to .88. Test–retest reliability over a 4-week period was good ($r = .86$). As noted by Hammen and Krantz (1985), little information exists on the validity of the SCS for the measurement of self-control processes in depression. In fact, Rude (1983) reported nonsignificant correlations with two measures of depression severity (SCS–BDI correlation was $-.08$ and the SCS–Dempsey-30 correlation was $-.28$).

The most intriguing finding with the SCS to date was presented by Simons, Lustman, Wetzel, and Murphy (1985). These investigators treated 35 unipolar depressed patients with either cognitive therapy or pharmacotherapy. The SCS was the single best predictor variable in treatment outcome (percent change in Beck Depression Inventory scores). The higher the SCS score, the better the response to cognitive therapy but the worse the response to medication. Subjects who had low scores on the SCS responded better to medication than to cognitive treatment.

The Crandell Cognitions Inventory (CCI: Crandell & Chambless, 1981) is a 34-item scale developed to assess the frequency of negative cognitions in depression. In this respect it is simlar to the ATQ, perhaps one of the reasons accounting for its limited use.

The Cognitive Error Questionnaire (CEQ: Lefebvre, 1981) is another instrument that has received little attention. Patterned after the CBQ (Krantz & Hammen, 1979) the CEQ consists of 24 short vignettes. Subjects indicate their likely responses in the situations and raters evaluate these responses for cognitive distortions. While the CEQ differentiates depressed from control subjects, the raters could not distinguish the various cognitive distortions specified by Beck *et al.* (1979).

The Self-Verbalization Questionnaire (Missel & Sommer, 1983) is a 38-item measure describing 19 everyday situations. Each situation has either a positive or negative outcome and patient responses (positive, negative, or externally attributed) are scored. Depressed patients exhibit a bias of more negative than positive self-verbalizations.

Thus far we have reported on a variety of self-report measures of cognitive assessment in depression. We now turn to assessments of depression based on models of memory and social cognition. There is a substantial literature on the cognitive functioning of depressed patients. Much of this literature concerns deficits in memory functioning and/or attentional processes (see Shaw & Dobson, 1981; Miller, 1975). In this chapter we concern ourselves with information processing as it reflects on the cognitive theories of depression. This literature includes studies on self-schema and personal constructs.

Beck (1967; Beck *et al.*, 1979) proposed that a negative self-schema becomes prepotent in depression, thereby biasing information processing in two ways. The depressed patients' views of their current experiences, their future, and their recall of past events are thoughts that are affected by the dominance of a negative self-schema. The schema construct refers to cognitive structures of organized prior knowledge, abstracted from experience with specific instances (see Fiske & Linville, 1980). Schemas guide the processing of new information by directing attention to schema-congruent material. In addition, they affect the retrieval of stored information by increasing the accessibility of schema-related memories. Beck's original notion was that the development of depression involved the activation of a primitive cognitive organization of the self. These negative self-schemata were elicited by life event stressors. The main theme of the person's experience was a sense of loss from the personal domain, the areas of his or her life that were the most meaningful. This stress diathesis model puts a negative self-schema in a central position for the development and maintenance of major depression.

The vulnerability of the depression-prone individual is the result of these enduring negative concepts. Though schemata may be latent at a given time, they are activated by particular kinds of experiences and consequently, may lead to a full-blown depression (Beck & Rush, 1978, p. 238).

The measurement of self-schema remains an enduring challenge for the field. There continues to be some conceptual confusion about which cognitive variables reflect self-schema. Mostly, however, the problems have been in the measurement of the construct. Beck (1967) viewed dysfunctional attitudes—as measured, for example, by the DAS—as reflecting the negative self-schema. Depression-prone persons were seen as judging their self-worth in terms of their acceptability by others (an approval-seeking style), by achievements, or by other external events. They were seen as rigid and extreme in the way that they endorsed various dysfunctional attitudes. As a result, when the approval-seeking or achievement contingencies were not met, these individuals experienced a significant loss attributable to their own unworthiness. Clinically, these attitudes were reflected by the theme that others wouldn't respect or care for the person if they knew what the depressed person was really like. Thus, one method consistent with cognitive theory to determine negative self-schema was indirectly via his or her dysfunctional attitudes.

An alternate method of detecting negative self-schema has emerged from investigators of social cognition, a field that applies methods of cognitive psychology, particularly information-processing paradigms, to evaluate socially-relevant phenomena (see, e.g., Kuiper & Higgins, 1985). Information processing paradigms typically involve testing the patient's memory for self-descriptive adjectives. In addition, several studies employ reaction time to determine the efficiency with which patients recognize or recall this information.

Our review here will not attempt to cover all of the different methodologies addressing self-schema in depression. Instead, we will selectively attend to some of the most widely researched paradigms and present examples of newer methodologies pursuing similar objectives.

The first experimental work on the self-schema of depressed patients was completed by Davis (Davis 1979a, 1979b; Davis & Unruh, 1981). He employed the incidental recall paradigm proposed by Rogers, Kuiper, and Kirker (1977), which in turn was based on the depth-of-processing model of Craik and Lockhart (1972). Essentially, this paradigm requires subjects to rate adjectives according to questions tapping structural, phonemic, schematic, or self-referent dimensions. For example, the self-referent task is to rate whether a personally relevant adjective (e.g., sincere, loyal) describes the subject. The prediction was that self-referent adjectives in the Rogers *et al.* (1977) study would be processed at a deeper level and that this would be evidenced by superior recall for this material.

Davis (1979b) tested depressed patients and concluded that "a self-schema is not an active agent in the encoding of personal information in depression" (p. 107). He based this conclusion on data that showed that depressed subjects recalled significantly fewer self-referent adjectives than controls. Other investigators have criticized this conclusion because of the disproportionate number of positively valenced adjectives in the list (Derry & Kuiper, 1981; Ingram, Smith, & Brehm, 1983). Davis and Unruh (1981) pursued this line of research, using the same set of adjectives to evaluate the subjective organization of depressed patients. Again, the conclusion was that the self-schema of patients who had been depressed for less than 1 year was "not a strong organizer of personal information" (p. 126).

In contrast, Roth and Rehm (1980), using a different but comparable memory paradigm, tested depressed male inpatients and nondepressed controls. They employed equal numbers of positive and negative adjectives and found that the two groups did not differ in either their recognition or their recall. The major problem with this study is that the time of exposure to each adjective was not controlled (Bradley & Matthews, 1983).

Derry and Kuiper (1981) have extended this early work by employing the depth of processing paradigm with both depressed and nondepressed content adjectives. They found that depressed patients exhibited enhanced recall for negative self-referent adjectives, despite having endorsed equal numbers of negative and positive adjectives as self-referent. In addition, the depressed subjects were as efficient as normal controls and nondepressed psychiatric controls in processing the self-referent information. This bias was viewed as supporting Beck's (1967) cognitive model, while demonstrating the existence of a negative self-schema. Research in this area continued with attempts to detect a similar processing bias in nondepressed subjects identified as vulnerable according to the DAS. (Kuiper et al., 1985). It does not appear, however, that this methodology is sensitive enough to detect a cognitively vulnerable individual. Recent evidence using this paradigm revealed that the ratio balance between positive to negative self-referent words during the episode changes once the depression remits (Dobson & Shaw, 1986). Furthermore, the possibilities for the replication of Derry and Kuiper's (1981) recall findings are drawn into question.

Bradley and Matthews (1983) designed an experiment similar to Derry and Kuiper (1981). "Recall and processing time for self and other referent adjectives was studied in clinically depressed patients and in matched controls" (p. 175). As in other studies, they found that depressed patients rate more negative adjectives as being self-descriptive. This finding may bias the results, since "yes"-rated words are likely to be recalled more easily. To control for this possibility, a covariance analysis removed the influence of decision frequency. Results indicated that depressed subjects recalled more negative than positive words when this material was presented as self-referent. Notably, if the information was presented with a general focus or in relation to other people, the bias was not observed. The negative bias in recall was not influenced by more severe or more prolonged depression in this study. This finding is somewhat discrepant with other studies of Kuiper and his colleagues (e.g., Kuiper & Derry, 1982), who found mildly depressed subjects to exhibit less of a negative bias in their recall pattern.

There are other methods of assessing self-schema in depression. One intriguing development is the use of the Stroop (1938) color-naming task as adapted by Warren (1972). In this procedure, subjects are presented with a list of three semantically related words (e.g.: cow, horse, chicken). They are then asked to name the ink color of a fourth word (the target word), which varies in its semantic relatedness to the list (e.g.: pig, crow, table). When the target word is closely related in meaning to the list words, subjects exhibit longer latencies in color naming. The explanation of this effect is that response competition occurs when a meaning structure is accessed. Several investigators are using this procedure to explore accessibility effects in depression (Gotlib & McCann, 1984) and the structural basis of self-schemata (Segal et al., 1986).

Another method used to assess self-schema is known as the behavioral example recall procedure (e.g., Hammen, Marks, Mayol, & de Mayo, 1985; Markus, 1977). The assumption of this method is that "schema consistent information will be relatively accessible in memory compared with schema noncongruent information and can be used to index the strength of a schema for that information" (Hammen *et al.*, 1985, p. 310). Subjects are asked to list specific examples of events that actually occurred within the past month. They follow instructions to provide examples of times when they felt bad about themselves, good about themselves, helpless, and critical (or guilty). Raters then evaluate each example for consistent themes such as the schema subtypes of dependent or achievement-oriented individuals.

Up to this point we have discussed efforts to assess self-schema in depression in some detail. There are, of course, other methods to assess cognition in depression but as with the self-report measures we shall only describe these briefly. Depressed subjects have consistently been shown to manifest an increased probability of recalling sad memories compared to happy ones (Fogarty & Hemsley, 1983). This method of assessment requires subjects to recall past real-life experiences associated with 20 stimulus words (e.g., ice, wood, letter, house). None of the stimulus words are self-referent. Subjects indicate whether or not they can recall a specific event (associated with the word but not a word association), and if so, are asked to describe the event in enough words to be used as a prime later on. Depressed patients recall a greater percentage of unhappy compared with happy memories (Lishman, 1972; Lloyd & Lishman, 1975), yet this measure like so many others is likely state-dependent, returning to "normal" when the depression remits (Fogarty & Hemsley, 1983).

The final method of cognitive assessment for depression that we shall review is the Role Construct Repertory Test (Kelly, 1955). Again, this test will not be reviewed in detail; the interested reader may refer to recent work by Neimeyer (1985). Basically, the technique is designed to assess the organization of cognitive structure along various dimensions used by the subject rather than imposed by the experimenter. Prior to computer-aided scoring, the method was difficult to utilize because of the time for administration and analysis. Space & Cromwell (1980) tested depressed, psychiatric control, and normal subjects with the repertory grid test. Depressed patients had more mixed (positive & negative) self-descriptions than other patients, and tended to view themselves as different from others.

In summary, research on depression has resulted in a range of measures addressing the content, process, and "deep structure" of cognition. It remains to be seen whether cognitive variables are important markers of a vulnerability to depression. The clinician has many ways to assess cognitive changes during a depressive episode. Depending on his or her particular theoretical concerns, measures of cognition may be taken prior to, during, and following treatment. Most measures discussed in this chapter will be useful indicators of improvement. On the other hand, it is not easy to determine the cognitive changes that are uniquely influenced by cognitive-behavioral treatments. At present it seems that any treatment (or, for that matter, time alone) that serves to alter the state of depression will also result in substantial cognitive changes.

Cognitive therapists (e.g., Beck *et al.*, 1979) have proposed that altering the cognitive dysfunction associated with affective and/or anxiety disorders provides a powerful means of treating these disorders. The evidence to date supports this proposal. It is not clear, however, whether cognitive therapies alter the likelihood of future episodes by reducing the individual's vulnerability to the disorder. It would be a significant breakthrough in our field if it could be shown (1) that there are enduring cognitive characteristics that differentiate those who have had the disorder from those who have not, (2) that cognitive-behavioural therapies have a specific (if not unique) impact on these characteristics, and (3) that changing the vulnerable characteristics of depressed cognition influences the probability of future episodes. For now, it will suffice to say that the cognitive assessment of depressive and anxiety disorders has developed to the point that clinicians are relatively well served.

ACKNOWLEDGMENTS

The authors would like to acknowledge Anne Simons, John Rush, Ivy Blackburn, Kevin Keller, Stephen Rapp, Nick Kuiper, and Joan Olinger for providing current data on a number of measures described in this chapter. We would also like to thank Jane Burnie, Doreen Vella, and Debi Wilson for their assistance in the preparation of this manuscript. Dr. Segal is a Medical Research Council of Canada Fellow. This work was supported in part by grants from the Laidlaw Foundation and the Canadian Psychiatric Research Foundation.

REFERENCES

Abel, G. G., Becker, J. V., Cunningham-Ratner, J., Rouleau, J. L., & Kaplan, M. (1984). The treatment of child molesters. *Treatment Manual*, Emory University, Atlanta.

Abramson, L. Y., Seligman, M. E. P., & Teasdale, J. D. (1978). Learned helplessness in humans: Critique and reformulation. *Journal of Abnormal Psychology, 87*, 102–109.

Akiskal, H. S., & McKinney, W. T. (1975). Overview of recent research in depression. *Archives of General Psychiatry, 32*, 285–305.

Anderson, J. R. (1985). *Cognitive psychology and its implications* (2nd ed.). New York: W. H. Freeman.

Arkowitz, H. (1977). Measurement and modification of minimal dating behavior. In M. Hersen, R. M. Eislen, & P. M. Miller (Eds.), *Progress in behavior modification* (Vol. 5). New York: Academic Press.

Arnkoff, D. B., & Glass, C. R. (1982). Clinical cognitive constructs: Examination, evaluation, and elaboration. *Advances in Cognitive Behavioral Research and Therapy*, Vol. 1. New York: Academic.

Bandura, A. (1977). Self-efficacy: Toward a unifying theory of behavioral change. *Psychological Review, 84*, 191–215.

Beck, A. T. (1967). *Depression: Clinical, experimental and therapeutic aspects*. New York: Harper & Row.

Beck, A. T. (1976). *Cognitive therapy and the emotional disorders.* New York: International Universities Press.

Beck, A. T., & Emery, G. (1985). *Anxiety disorders and phobias.* New York: Basic Books.

Beck, A. T., & Rush, A. J. (1978). Cognitive approaches to depression and suicide. In G. Serban (Ed.), *Cognitive defects in development of mental illness.* New York: Brunner/Mazel.

Beck, A. T., Rush, A. J., Shaw, B. F., & Emery, G. (1979). *Cognitive therapy of depression.* New York: Guilford.

Beck, A. T., Steer, R. A., Kovacs, M., & Garrison, B. S. (1985). Hopelessness and eventual suicide: A 10-year prospective study of patients hospitalized with suicidal ideation. *American Journal of Psychiatry, 142,* 559–563.

Beck, A. T., Ward, C. H., Mendelson, M., Mock, J., & Erbaugh, J. (1961). An inventory for measuring depression. *Archives of General Psychiatry, 4,* 561–571.

Beck, A. T., Weissman, A., Lester, D., & Trexler, L. (1974). The measurement of pessimism: The Hopelessness Scale. *Journal of Consulting and Clinical Psychology, 42,* 861–865.

Bellack, A. S. (1979). Behavioral assessment of social skills. In A. S. Bellack & M. Hersen (Eds.), *Research and practice in social skills.* New York: Plenum.

Blackburn, I. M., Jones, S. & Lewin, R. J. P. (1986). Cognitive style in depression. *British Journal of Clinical Psychology, 25,* 241–252.

Blackburn, I. M., & Smythe, P. (1985). A test of cognitive vulnerability in individuals prone to depression. *British Journal of Clinical Psychology, 24,* 61–62.

Blackwell, R. T., Galassi, J. P., Galassi, M. D., & Watson, T. E. (1985). Are cognitive assessment methods equal? A comparison of think aloud and thought listing. *Cognitive Therapy and Research, 9,* 399–413.

Blaney, P. H., Behar, V., & Head, R. (1980). Two measures of depressive cognitions: Their association with depression and with each other. *Journal of Abnormal Psychology, 89,* 678–682.

Bowers, K. S., & Meichenbaum, D. (1984). *The unconscious reconsidered.* New York: Wiley.

Bradley, B., & Matthews, A. (1983). Negative self-schemata in clinical depression. *British Journal of Clinical Psychology, 22,* 173–181.

Breir, A., Charney, D. S., & Heninger, G. R. (1984). Major depression in patients with agoraphobia and panic disorder. *Archives of General Psychiatry, 41,* 1129–1135.

Bruch, M. A., Haase, R. F., & Purcell, M. J. (1984). Content dimensions of self-statements in assertive situations: A factor analysis of two measures. *Cognitive Therapy and Research, 8,* 173–186.

Butler, G., & Mathews, A. (1983). Cognitive processes in anxiety. *Advances in Behavior Research Therapy, 5,* 51–62.

Cacioppo, J. T., & Petty, R. E. (1981). Social psychological procedures for cognitive response assessment: The thought-listing technique. In T. V. Merluzzi, C. R. Glass, & M. Genest (Eds.), *Cognitive assessment.* New York: Guilford Press.

Cash, T. F. (1984). The Irrational Beliefs Test: Its relationship with cognitive–behavioral traits and depression. *Journal of Clinical Psychology, 40,* 1399–1405.

Chambless, D. L., Caputo, G. C., Bright, P., & Gallagher, R. (1984). Assessment of fear in agoraphobics: The body sensations questionnaire and the agoraphobic cognition questionnaire. *Journal of Consulting and Clinical Psychology, 52,* 1090–1097.

Coyne, J. C., & Gotlib, I. H. 1983). The role of cognition in depression: A critical appraisal. *Psychological Bulletin, 94,* 472–505.

Craik, F. M., & Lockhart, R. S. (1972). Levels of processing: A framework for memory research. *Journal of Verbal Learning and Verbal Behaviour, 11,* 671–684.

Crandell, C. J., & Chambless, D. L. (1981, November). *A validation of an inventory for measuring depressive thoughts.* Toronto: Paper presented at the Annual Meeting of the Association for Advancement of Behavior Therapy.

Crown, S., & Crisp, A. H. (1970). *Manual of the Middlesex Hospital Questionnaire (MHQ)*. Barnstaple, Devon: Psychological Test Publication.

Davis, H. (1979a). Self-reference and the encoding of personal information in depression. *Cognitive Therapy and Research, 3,* 97–110.

Davis, H. (1979b). The self-schema and subjective organization of personal information in depression. *Cognitive Therapy and Research, 3,* 415–425.

Davis, H., & Unruh, W. R. (1981). The development of the self-schema in adult depression. *Journal of Abnormal Psychology, 90,* 125–133.

Davison, G. C., Robins, C., & Johnston, M. K. (1983). Articulated thoughts during simulated situations: A paradigm for studying cognition in emotion and behavior. *Cognitive Therapy and Research, 7,* 17–40.

Derry, P. A., & Kuiper, N. A. (1981). Schematic processing and self-reference in clinical depression. *Journal of Abnormal Psychology, 90,* 286–297.

Dobson, K. S. (1985). The relationship between anxiety and depression. *Clinical Psychology Review, 5,* 307–324.

Dobson, K. S., & Breiter, H. J. (1983). Cognitive assessment of depression: Reliability and validity of three measures. *Journal of Abnormal Psychology, 92,* 107–109.

Dobson, K. S., & Shaw, B. F. (1986). Cognitive assessment with major depressive disorders. *Cognitive Therapy and Research, 10,* 13–29.

Duncker, K. (1926). A qualitative (experimental and theoretical) study of productive thinking (solving of comprehensible problems). *Pedagogical Seminary, 33,* 642–708.

Eaves, G., & Rush, A. J. (1984). Cognitive patterns in symptomatic and remitted major depression. *Journal of Abnormal Psychology, 93,* 31–40.

Ellis, A. (1962). *Reason and emotion in psychotherapy.* New York: Lyle Stuart.

Ericsson, K. A., & Simon, H. A. (1984). *Protocol analysis.* Cambridge, MA: MIT Press.

Fawcett, J., & Kravitz, H. M. (1983). Anxiety syndromes and their relationship to depressive illness. *Journal of Clinical Psychiatry, 44,* 8–11.

Fennell, M. J. V., & Campbell, E. A. (1984). The Cognitions Questionnaire: Specific thinking errors in depression. *British Journal of Clinical Psychology, 23,* 81–92.

Fiedler, R., & Beach, L. R. (1978). On the decision to be assertive. *Journal of Consulting and Clinical Psychology, 46,* 537–546.

Fiske, S., & Linville, P. (1980). What does the schema concept buy us? *Personality and Social Psychology Bulletin, 6,* 543–557.

Fogarty, S. J., & Hemsley, D. R. (1983). Depression and the accessibility of memories. A longitudinal study. *British Journal of Psychiatry, 142,* 232–237.

Frost, R. D., & MacInnis, D. J. (1983). The Cognitive Bias Questionnaire: Further evidence. *Journal of Personality Assessment, 47,* 173–177.

Galassi, J. P., & Galassi, M. D. (1979). Modification of heterosocial skills deficits. In A. S. Bellack & M. Hersen (Eds.). *Research and Practice in Social Skills.* New York: Plenum.

Gardner, H. (1985). *The mind's new science: A history of the cognitive revolution.* New York: Basic Books.

Genest, M., & Turk, D. C. (1981). Think-aloud approaches to cognitive assessment. In T. V. Merluzzi, C. R. Glass, & M. Genest (Eds.), *Cognitive assessment.* New York: Guilford.

Ghiselli, E. E., Campbell, J. P., & Zedeck, S. (1981). *Measurement theory for the behavioral sciences.* San Francisco: Freeman.

Glass, C. R., & Arnkoff, D. B. (1982). Think cognitively: Selected issues in cognitive assessment and therapy. In P. C. Kendall (Eds.). *Advances in cognitive-behavioral research and therapy, (Vol. 1).* New York: Academic.

Glass, C. R., & Merluzzi, T. V. (1981). Cognitive assessment of social evaluative anxiety. In T. V. Merluzzi, G. R. Glass, & M. Genest (Eds.), *Cognitive Assessment.* New York: Guilford.

Glass, C. R., Merluzzi, T. V., Biever, J. L., & Larsen, K. H. (1982). Cognitive assessment of social anxiety: Development and validation of a self-statement questionnaire. *Cognitive Therapy and Research, 6,* 37-55.

Goldfried, M. R., & Robins, C. (1983). Self-schema, cognitive bias, and the processing of therapeutic experiences. In P. C. Kendall (Ed.), *Advances in cognitive-behavioral research and therapy.* New York: Academic.

Goldfried, M. R., Padawer, W., & Robins, C. (1984). Social anxiety and the sematnic structure of heterosocial interactions. *Journal of Abnormal Psychology, 93,* 86-97.

Goldstein, A. J., & Chambless, D. L. (1978). A reanalysis of agoraphobia. *Behavior Therapy, 9,* 47-59.

Golin, S., Sweeny, P. D., & Schaeffer, D. E. (1981). The causality of causal attributions in depression: A cross-lagged panel correlation analysis. *Journal of Abnormal Psychology, 90,* 14-22.

Goodwin, A. M., & Williams, J. M. G. (1982). Mood induction research: Its implication for clinical depression. *Behaviour Research and Therapy, 20,* 373-382.

Gotlib, I. H., & McCann, C. D. (1984). Construct accessibility and depression: An examination of cognitive and affective factors. *Journal of Personality and Social Psychology, 47,* 427-439.

Greenberg, L. S., & Safran, J. D. (1984). Integrating affect and cognition: A perspective on the process of therapeutic change. *Cognitive Therapy and Research, 8,* 559-578.

Hamilton, M. (1981). Depression and anxiety: A clinical viewpoint. In M. Hamilton & J. B. Bakker (Eds.). *Psychiatry in the 80's: Ideas, Research, Practice.* Exerpta Medica.

Hamilton, E. W., & Abramson, L. Y. (1983). Cognitive patterns and major depressive disorder: A longitudinal study in a hospital setting. *Journal of Abnormal Psychology, 92,* 173-184.

Hammen, C. L., & Krantz, S. E. (1983). Effects of success and failure on depressive cognitions. *Journal of Abnormal Psychology, 85,* 577-586.

Hammen, C. L., & Krantz, S. E. (1985). Measures of psychological processes in depression. In E. E. Beckham & W. R. Leber (Eds.). *Handbook of Depression: Treatment, Assessment and Research.* Homewood, IL: Dorsey Press.

Hammen, C., Marks, T., Mayol, A., & de Mayo, R. (1985). Depressive self-schemas, life stress and vulnerability to depression. *Journal of Abnormal Psychology, 94,* 308-319.

Harrell, T. H., & Ryan, N. B. (1983). Cognitive-behavioral assessment of depression: Clinical validation of the Automatic Thoughts Questionnaire. *Journal of Consulting and Clinical Psychology, 51,* 721-725.

Hollon, S. D., & Bemis, K. M. (1981). Self-report and the assessment of cognitive functions. In M. Hersen & A. S. Bellack (Eds.), *Behavioral assessment: A practical handbook.* New York: Pergamon.

Hollon, S. D., & Kendall, P. C. (1980). Cognitive self-statements in depression: Development of an automatic thoughts questionnaire. *Cognitive Therapy and Research, 4,* 383-396.

Hollon, S. D., Kendall, P. C., & Lumry, A. (1986). Specificity of depressotypic cognitions in clinical depression. *Journal of Abnormal Psychology, 95,* 52-59.

Hollon, S. D., & Kriss, M. R. (1984). Cognitive factors in clinical research and practice. *Clinical Psychology Review, 4,* 35-76.

Huber, J. W., & Altmaier, E. M. (1983). An investigation of the self-statements of phobic and nonphobic individuals. *Cognitive Therapy and Research, 7,* 355-362.

Hurlburt, R. T. (1979). Random sampling of cognitions and behavior. *Journal of Research in Personality, 13,* 103-111.

Hurlburt, R. T., & Spirelle, C. N. (1978). Random sampling of cognitions in alleviating anxiety attacks. *Cognitive Therapy and Research, 2,* 165-169.

Ingram, R. E. (1984). Toward an information processing analysis of depression. *Cognitive Therapy and Research, 5,* 443-478.

Ingram, R. E., Smith, T. W., & Brehm, S. S. (1983). Depression and information processing: Self-schemata and the encoding of self-referent information. *Journal of Personality and Social Psychology, 45,* 412–420.

Isaacs, K., & Silver, R. J. (1980, November). *Cognitive structure in depression.* Toronto: Paper presented at the annual meeting of the Association for Advancement of Behavior Therapy.

Jackson, D. N. (1970). A sequential system for personality scale development. In C. D. Spielberger (Ed.), *Current topics in clinical and community psychology.* New York: Academic.

Jones, R. G. (1969). A factored measure of Ellis's irrational belief system. (Doctoral dissertation, Texas Technological College, 1968). *Dissertation Abstracts International, 29,* 4379B–4380B.

Keller, K. E. (1983). Dysfunctional attitudes and cognitive therapy for depression. *Cognitive Therapy and Research, 7,* 437–444.

Keller, E. K., & Hasse, R. F. (1984). The relationship of dysfunctional attitudes to depression and hopelessness in a depressed community sample. *British Journal of Cognitive Psychotherapy, 2,* 61–66.

Kelly, G. A. (1955). *The psychology of personal constructs.* New York: Norton.

Kendall, P. C. (1982). Behavioral assessment and methodology. In C. M. Franks, G. T. Wilson, P. C. Kendall, & K. D. Brownell (Eds.). *Annual review of behavior therapy* (Vol. 8). New York: Guilford.

Kendall, P. C. (1984). Behavioral assessment and methodology. In C. M. Franks, G. T. Wilson, K. D. Brownell, & P. C. Kendall (Eds.), *Annual review of behavior therapy* (Vol. 9). New York: Guilford.

Kendall, P. C., & Hollon, S. D. (1981). Assessing self-referent speech: Methods in the measurement of self-statements. In P. C. Kendall & S. D. Hollon (Eds.), *Assessment strategies for cognitive-behavioral interventions.* New York: Academic.

Kendall, P. C., & Korgeski, G. P. (1979). Assessment and cognitive-behavioral interventions. *Cognitive Therapy and Research, 3,* 1–21.

Krantz, S., & Hammen, C. L. (1979). Assessment of cognitive bias in depression. *Journal of Abnormal Psychology, 88,* 611–619.

Kuiper, N. A., & Derry, P. A. (1982). Depressed and nondepressed content self-reference in mild depressives. *Journal of Personality, 50,* 67–79.

Kuiper, N. A., & Higgins, E. T. (1985). Social cognition and depression: A general integrative perspective. *Social Cognition, 3,* 1–15.

Kuiper, N. A., & Olinger, L. J. (1986). Dysfunctional attitudes and a self-worth contingency model of depression. In P. C. Kendall (Ed.), *Advances in cognitive-behavioral research and therapy, Vol. 5.* New York: Academic.

Kuiper, N. A., Olinger, L. J., MacDonald, M. R., & Shaw, B. F. (1985). Self-schema processing of depressed and nondepressed content: The effects of vulnerability to depression. *Social Cognition, 3,* 77–93.

Landau, R. J. (1980). The role of semantic schemata in phobic word interpretation. *Cognitive Therapy and Research, 4,* 427–434.

Last, C. G., Barlow, D. H., & O'Brien, G. T. (1985). Assessing cognitive aspects of anxiety: Stability over time and agreement between several methods. *Behavior Modification, 9,* 72–93.

Lefebvre, M. (1981). Cognitive distortion and cognitive errors in depressed psychiatric and low back pain patients. *Journal of Consulting and Clinical Psychology, 49,* 517–525.

Lewinsohn, P. M., Steinmetz, J. L., Larson, D. W., & Franklin, J. (1981). Depression-related cognitions: Antecedent or consequence? *Journal of Abnormal Psychology, 90,* 213–219.

Lishman, W. A. (1972). Selective factors in memory: Part 2: Affective disorders. *Psychological Medicine, 2,* 121–138.

Lloyd, G. G., & Lishman, W. A. (1975). Effect of depression on the speed of recall of pleasant and unpleasant experiences. *Psychological Medicine, 5,* 173–180.

Lohr, J. M., & Bonge, D. (1982). The factorial validity of the Irrational Beliefs Test: A psychometric investigation. *Cognitive Therapy and Research, 6,* 225–230.

MacLeod, C., Mathews, A., & Tata, P. (1986). Attentional bias in emotional disorders. *Journal of Abnormal Psychology, 95,* 15–20.

Markus, H. (1977). Self-schema and processing information about the self. *Journal of Personality and Social Psychology, 35,* 63–78.

Mathews, S. A., & MacLeod, C. (1985). Selective processing of threat cues to anxiety states. *Behaviour Research and Therapy, 23,* 563–569.

Mavissakalian, M., & Barlow, D. H. (1981). Phobia: An overview. In M. Mavissakalian & D. H. Barlow (Eds.), *Phobia: Psychological and pharmacological treatment.* New York: Guilford.

Meichenbaum, D. (1977). *Cognitive-behavior modification: An integrative approach.* New York: Plenum.

Meichenbaum, D., & Cameron, R. (1981). Issues in cognitive assessment: An overview. In T. V. Merluzzi, C. R. Glass, & M. Genest (Eds.), *Cognitive assessment.* New York: Guilford.

Mendonca, J. D., Holden, R. D., Mazmanian, D., & Dolan, J. (1983). The influence of response style on the Beck Hopelessness Scale. *Canadian Journal of Behavioral Science, 15,* 237–247.

Merluzzi, T. V., & Rudy, T. E. (1982, August). *Cognitive assessment of social anxiety: A "surface" and "deep" structure analysis in social anxiety: Social, personality, and clinical perspectives.* Paper presented at the American Psychological Association, Washington, DC.

Merluzzi, T. V., Rudy, T. E., & Glass, C. R. (1981). The information-processing paradigm: Implications for clinical science. In T. V. Merluzzi, C. R. Glass, & M. Genest (Eds.), *Cognitive Assessment.* New York: Guilford.

Miller, W. R. (1975). Psychological deficit in depression. *Psychological Bulletin, 2,* 238–260.

Miller, I. W., Klee, S. H., & Norman, H. W. (1982). Depressed and nondepressed inpatients' cognitions of hypothetical events, experimental tasks and stressful life events. *Journal of Abnormal Psychology, 91,* 78–81.

Minkoff, K., Bergman, E., Beck, A. T., & Beck, R. (1973). Hopelessness, depression, and attempted suicide. *American Journal of Psychiatry, 130,* 455–459.

Missel, P., & Sommer, G. (1983). Depression and self-verbalization. *Cognitive Therapy and Research, 7,* 141–148.

Munoz, R. F. (1977). Cognitive approach to the assessment and treatment of depression. Unpublished doctoral dissertation, University of Oregon.

Neimeyer, R. A. (1985). Personal constructs in clinical practice. In P. C. Kendall (Ed.), *Advances in cognitive-behavioral research and therapy, Vol. 4.* New York: Academic.

Neisser, V. (1976). *Cognition and reality: Principles and implications of cognitive psychology.* San Francisco: Freeman.

Nelson, R. D. (1977). Methodological issues in assessment and self-monitoring. In J. D. Cone & R. P. Hawkins (Eds.), *Behavioral assessment: New directions in clinical psychology.* New York: Brunner/Mazel.

Nelson, R. D., Hayes, S. C., Felton, J. L., & Jarrett, R. B. (1985). A comparison of data produced by different behavioral assessment techniques with implications for models of social-skills inadequacy. *Behaviour Research and Therapy, 23,* 1–11.

Newton, C. R., & Barbaree, H. E. (in press). Cognitive changes accompanying headache treatment: The use of a thought-sampling procedure. *Cognitive Therapy and Research.*

Nietzel, M. T., & Bernstein, D. A. (1981). Assessment of anxiety and fear. In M. Hersen & A. S. Bellack (Eds.), *Behavioral assessment: A practical handbook.* New York: Pergamon.

Nisbett, R. E., & Wilson, T. D. (1977). Telling more than we can know: Verbal reports on mental processes. *Psychological Review, 84,* 231-259.

Norman, W. H., Miller, I. W., & Klee, S. H. (1983). Assessment of cognitive distortion in a clinically depressed population. *Cognitive Therapy and Research, 7,* 133-140.

O'Hara, M. W., Rehm, L. P., & Campbell, S. B. (1982). Predicting depressive symptomatology: Cognitive behavioral models and post-partum depression. *Journal of Abnormal Psychology, 91,* 457-461.

Olinger, L. J., Kuiper, N. A., & Shaw, B. F. (1987). Dysfunctional attitudes and stressful life events: An interactive model of depression. *Cognitive Therapy and Research, 11,* 25-40.

Olinger, L. J., Shaw, B. F., & Kuiper, N. A. (1987). Nonassertiveness and vulnerability to depression: A cognitive perspective. *Canadian Journal of Behavioural Science, 19,* 40-49.

Oliver, J. M., & Baumgart, E. P. (1985). The Dysfunctional Attitude Scale: Psychometric properties and relation to depression in an unselected adult population. *Cognitive Therapy and Research, 9,* 161-168.

Paivio, A. (1975). Neomentalism. *Canadian Journal of Psychology, 29,* 263-291.

Peterson, C., Semmel, A., von Baeyer, C., Abramson, L., Metalsky, G., & Seligman, M. E. P. (1982). The Attributional Style Questionnaire. *Cognitive Therapy and Research, 6,* 287-299.

Rachman, S., & Hodgson, R. (1974). 1. Synchrony and desynchrony in fear and avoidance. *Behaviour Research and Therapy, 12,* 311-318.

Rapp, S. R. (1985, November). *Cognitive and behavioral patterns among depressive subtypes.* Paper presented at the Association for Advancement of Behavior Therapy. Houston, TX.

Reda, M. A., Carpiniello, B., Secchiaroli, L., & Blanco, S. (1985). Thinking, depression, and antidepressants: Modified and unmodified depressive beliefs during treatment with amitriptyline. *Cognitive Therapy and Research, 9,* 135-144.

Riskind, J. H., Beck, A. T., & Smucker, M. R. (1983, December). *Psychometric properties of the Dysfunctional Attitude Scale in a clinical population.* Paper presented at the meeting of the World Congress of Behavior Therapy, Washington, D.C.

Riskind, J. H., & Rholes, W. S. (1984). Cognitive accessibility and the capacity of cognitions to predict future depression: A theoretical note. *Cognitive Therapy and Research, 8,* 1-12.

Rogers, T. B., Kuiper, N. A., & Kirker, W. S. (1977). Self-reference and the encoding of personal information. *Journal of Personality and Social Psychology, 35,* 677-688.

Rosenbaum, M. (1980). A schedule for assessing self-control behaviors: Preliminary findings. *Behavior Therapy, 11,* 109-121.

Roth, D., & Rehm, L. P. (1980). Relationships among self-monitoring processes, memory and depression. *Cognitive Therapy and Research, 4,* 149-157.

Rude, S. S. (1983). *An investigation of differential response to two treatments of depression.* Unpublished doctoral dissertation, Stanford University.

Rudy, T. E., & Merluzzi, T. V. (1984). Recovering social-cognitive schemata: Descriptions and applications of multidimensional scaling for clinical research. In P. C. Kendall (Ed.), *Advances in cognitive-behavioral research and therapy.* Orlando, FL: Academic.

Rudy, T. E., Merluzzi, T. V., & Henahan, P. T. (1982). Construal of complex assertive situations: A multidimensional analysis. *Journal of Consulting and Clinical Psychology, 50,* 125-137.

Rush, A. J. (1983). Cognitive therapy for depression. In M. Zales (Ed.), *Affective and schizophrenic disorders: New approaches to diagnosis.* New York: Brunner/Mazel.

Rush, A. J. (1984, March). *Measurement of the cognitive aspects of depression.* Paper presented at the NIMH Workshop on Measurement of Depression. Honolulu, HI.

Rush, A. J., Beck, A. T., Kovacs, M., Weissenburger, J., & Hollon, S. D. (1982). Comparison of the effects of cognitive therapy and pharmacotherapy on hopelessness and self-concept. *American Journal of Psychiatry, 139,* 862-866.

Rush, A. J., Weissenberger, J., & Eaves, G. (1986). Do thinking patterns predict depressive symptoms? *Cognitive Therapy and Research, 10,* 225–236.

Safran, J. D. (1983). The functional asymmetry of negative and positive self-statements. *The British Journal of Clinical Psychology, 21,* 223–224.

Schwartz, R., & Gottman, J. (1976). Toward a task analysis of assertive behavior. *Journal of Consulting and Clinical Psychology, 44,* 910–920.

Segal, Z. V., & Hood, J. (1985, June). *Measures of self-schema in depression: A construct in search of a structure.* Paper presented at the Society for Psychotherapy Research Meeting, Evanston, IL.

Segal, Z. V., Hood, J. E., Shaw, B. F., & Higgins, E. T. (1986). *A structural analysis of the self-schema construct in major depression.* Manuscript submitted for publication.

Segal, Z. V., & Marshall, W. L. (1985). Heterosexual social skills in a population of rapists and child molesters. *Journal of Consulting and Clinical Psychology, 53,* 55–63.

Segal, Z. V., & Shaw, B. F. (1986). Cognition in depression: A reappraisal of Coyne and Gotlib's critique. *Cognitive Therapy and Research, 10,* 671–694.

Seligman, M. E. P., Abramson, L., Semmel, A., & von Baeyer, C. (1979). Depressive attributional style. *Journal of Abnormal Psychology, 88,* 242–248.

Sewitch, T. S., & Kirsch, I. (1984). The cognitive content of anxiety: Naturalistic evidence for the predominance of threat-related thoughts. *Cognitive Therapy and Research, 8,* 49–58.

Shaw, B. F., & Dobson, K. S. (1981). Cognitive assessment of depression. In T. V. Merluzzi, C. R. Glass, & M. Genest (Eds.), *Cognitive assessment.* New York: Guilford.

Simons, A. D., Garfield, S. L., & Murphy, G. E. (1984). The process of change in cognitive therapy and pharmacotherapy for depression: Changes in mood and cognition. *Archives of General Psychiatry, 41,* 45–51.

Simons, A. D., Lustman, P. J., Wetzel, R. D., & Murphy, G. E. (1985). Predicting response to cognitive therapy of depression: The role of learned resourcefulness. *Cognitive Therapy and Research, 9,* 79–90.

Simons, A. D., Murphy, G. E., Levine, J. L., & Wetzel, R. D. (1986). Cognitive therapy and pharmacotherapy for depression. *Archives of General Psychiatry, 43,* 43–48.

Silverman, J. S., Silverman, J. A., & Eardley, D. A. (1984). Do maladaptive attitudes cause depression? *Archives of General Psychiatry, 41,* 28–30.

Smith, T. W. (1982). Irrational beliefs in the cause and treatment of emotional distress: A critical review of the Rational-Emotive model. *Clinical Psychology Review, 2,* 505–522.

Smith, T. W., & Zurawski, R. M. (1983). Assessment of irrational beliefs: The question of discriminant validity. *Journal of Clinical Psychology, 39,* 976–979.

Space, L. G., & Cromwell, R. L. (1980). Personal constructs among depressed patients. *The Journal of Nervous and Mental Disease, 168,* 150–518.

Spitzer, R. L., Endicott, J., & Robins, E. (1978). *Research Diagnostic Criteria (RDC) for a selected group of functional disorders.* New York: Biometrics Research.

Stroop, J. R. (1938). Factors affecting speed in serial verbal reactions. *Psychological Monographs, 50,* No. 225.

Swinson, R., & Kirby, M. (1987). The differentiation of anxiety and depressive syndromes. In B. F. Shaw, Z. V. Segal, T. M. Vallis, & F. E. Cashman (Eds.), *Anxiety disorders: Psychological and biological perspectives.* New York: Plenum.

Turk, D. C., & Salovey, P. (1985). Cognitive structures, cognitive processes, and cognitive-behavior modification: 1. Client issues. *Cognitive Therapy and Research, 9,* 1–17.

Warren, R. E. (1972). Stimulus encoding and memory. *Journal of Experimental Psychology, 94,* 90–100.

Watkins, J., & Rush, A. J. (1983). The cognitive response test. *Cognitive Therapy and Research, 7,* 425–436.

Watson, D., & Friend, R. (1969). Measurement of social-evaluative anxiety. *Journal of Consulting and Clinical Psychology, 33,* 448–457.

Webb, E. J., Campbell, D. T., Schwartz, R. D., & Sechrest, L. (1966). *Unobtrusive measures: Non-reactive research in the social sciences.* Chicago: Rand McNally.

Weissman, A. N. (1979). *The Dysfunctional Attitude Scale: A validation study.* Unpublished dissertation. University of Pennsylvania.

Weissman, A. N., & Beck, A. T. (1978). *Development and validation of the Dysfunctional Attitude Scale: A preliminary investigation.* Paper presented at the Annual Meeting of the American Educational Research Association. Toronto, Canada.

Wilkinson, I. M., & Blackburn, I. M. (1981). Cognitive style in depressed and recovered depressed patients. *British Journal of Clinical Psychology, 20,* 283–292.

Williams, S. L. (1985). On the nature and measurement of agoraphobia. In M. Hersen, R. M. Eisler, & P. M. Miller (Eds.), *Progress in behavior modification.* New York: Academic.

Williams, S. L., & Rappoport, A. (1983). Cognitive treatment in the natural environment for agoraphobics. *Behavior Therapy, 14,* 299–313.

Winters, K. C., & Neale, J. M. (1985). Mania and low self-esteem. *Journal of Abnormal Psychology, 94,* 282–290.

Zimmerman, M., Coryell, W., & Corenthal, C. (1984). Attribution style, the Dexamethasone Suppression Test and the diagnosis of melancholia in depressed inpatients. *Journal of Abnormal Psychology, 93,* 373–377.

Zweig, D. R., & Brown, S. D. (1985). Psychometric evaluation of a written stimulus presentation format for the Social Interaction Self-Statement Test. *Cognitive Therapy and Research, 9,* 285–296.

Reading 11
Character and Schema Change

Character and Schema Change

Character refers to the learned, psychosocial influences on personality. Because character is essentially learned, it follows that it can be changed through such processes as psychotherapy. Largely because of the influence of Freud and his followers, psychotherapy and psychiatric treatment focused almost exclusively on the dimension of character to the point at which personality essentially became synonymous with character. Character forms largely because of the socialization process, particularly regarding cooperativeness, and the mirroring process that promotes the development of self-concept and a sense of purpose in life (i.e., self-transcendence and self-responsibility). Character can be assessed both by structured interview and by self-report inventories. On the Temperament Character Inventory (Cloninger, 1993), character is measured by three character dimensions: cooperativeness, self-directedness—also called self-responsibility—and self-transcendence. Healthy personality reflects plus positive or elevated scores on these three dimensions, whereas personality disorders reflect negative or low scores on them. Furthermore, individuals with low scores on one or more of the character dimensions and increased dysregulation of one or more of the temperament dimensions typically experience either considerable distress or impairment in life functioning or both. For example, the borderline personality disorder would likely rate high in two temperament dimensions but low in character dimensions of self-directedness and cooperation.

Schema

Another way of specifying the characterological component of personality is with term *schema*. Whether in the psychoanalytic tradition (Horowitz, 1988; Slap & Slap-Shelton, 1981) or the cognitive therapy tradition (Beck, 1964; Young, 1994), schema refers to the basic beliefs individuals use to organize their view of self, the world, and the future. Although the centrality of schema has historically been more central to the cognitive tradition and the cognitive-behavioral tradition than to the psychoanalytic tradition, this apparently is changing (Stein & Young, 1992). Schema and schema change and modification strategies are central to this book. The remainder of this chapter reviews some different conceptualizations of schema and then describes several different schemas useful in clinical practice.

Adler first used the term *schema of apperception* in 1929 to refer to the individual's view of self and the world. For Adler, psychopathology reflected the individual's "neurotic schema" (Adler, 1956, p. 333) and these schemas were central to the individual's life-style. Recently, the use of the term *schema* and *schema theory* has emerged as central in the various subdisciplines of cognitive science, as well as by various psychotherapy schools' (Stein & Young, 1992) convictions. This section describes the psychodynamic and cognitive-behavioral traditions of schemas.

Psychodynamic Tradition

Whereas classical psychoanalysts focused on libidinal drives, modern analysts have focused instead on relational themes, emphasizing the self, the object, and their interaction, while a number of ego psychology and object relations theorists have emphasized schema theory. Many have contributed to the development of schema theories in the psychoanalytic tradition (Eagle, 1986; Horowitz, 1988; Inderbitzin & James, 1994; Slap & Slap-Shelton, 1981; Wachtel, 1982).

A representative example of these theories is the model described by Slap and Slap-Shelton (1991). They described a schema model that contrasts with the structural model devised by Freud and refined by the ego psychologists, and that they contend better fits the clinical data of psychoanalysis than the structural model. Their schema model involves the ego and sequestered schema. The ego consists of many schemas that are loosely linked and integrated with one another and relativity accessible to consciousness. These schemas are based on past experience but are modified by new experience. This process forms the basis of adaptive behavior. Se-

20

questered schemas are organized around traumatic events and situations in childhood that were not mastered or integrated by the immature psyche of the child. These schema remain latent and repressed. To the extent that these sequestered or pathological schemas are active, current relationships may be cognitively processed according to these schemas, rather than treated objectively by the more adaptive schemas of the ego. Essentially, current situations cannot be perceived and processed in accord with the reality of the present event but rather as replications of unmastered childhood conflict.

Treatment consists of helping the patient to describe, clarify, and work through these sequestered, pathological schema. These schemas are exposed to the client's nature, adaptive ego to achieve integration. Patients are helped to recognize how they create and recreate scenarios that reopen their pathologic schemas. The repeated demonstration and working through of the traumatic events that gave rise to the pathological schemas engenders a greater degree of self-observation, understanding, and emotional growth.

Cognitive-Behavioral Tradition

Like the psychodynamic tradition, the cognitive-behavioral tradition is quite heterogeneous. Common to this tradition is the belief that behavior and cognitions influence each other. Approaches within this tradition include stress-inoculation and self-instructional training (Meichenbaum, 1977), rational emotive therapy (Ellis, 1979), and cognitive therapy (Beck, 1976). Because cognitive therapy has taken the lead in articulating schema theory in the cognitive-behavioral tradition, it will be highlighted.

The Basics of Cognitive Therapy. Cognitive therapy is a relatively recent therapeutic approach developed by a University of Pennsylvania psychiatry professor, Aaron Beck (1976). Although Beck was trained as a psychoanalyst, he was greatly influenced by the work of Adler, Horney, and Rank. Accordingly, there are influences of these cognitively oriented approaches in his system. Beck believes that cognitive processes influence behavior and that overt behavior and emotional expression can be changed by cognitive interventions. Specifically, cognitive therapy aims at altering underlying assumptions that influence a patient's perceptual view, which leads to negative automatic beliefs and dysfunctional cognitions on which behavior is based. In cognitive therapy, the clinician helps the patient to understand and then to modify *automatic thoughts, dysfunctional cognitions,* and *core maladaptive schemas.* Examples of automatic thinking are over-

generalization, selective abstraction, minimal evidence, personalization, magnification, and dichotomized or "either-or" thinking, such as "I'll never be good enough" and "People are only nice to you to gain an advantage." Schemas are the silent, core assumptions based on the patient's early experiences that determine the content of cognitions. They form the basis for evaluating, categorizing, and distorting experiences. These thoughts often involve arbitrary conclusions based on what Beck calls automatic thinking.

The treatment process in cognitive therapy is relatively straightforward: The clinician engages the patient as a collaborator in examining her dysfunctional cognitions and how they might be altered. Typically, the patient is asked to keep a daily record of dysfunctional thoughts. The clinician's role is to challenge these dysfunctional cognitions, the automatic thinking they engender, as well as the schemas that underlie them, so that they can be replaced with more functional cognitions. By modeling this process, the clinician teaches the patient to be able to discover and challenge dysfunctional patterns and to develop more adaptive patterns of thinking and behaving. If treatment is successful, the patient is on her way to becoming her own therapist. Essentially, then, the clinician's role is that of a coach or guide, rather than an expert or guru. A variety of cognitive restructuring techniques, as well as role playing, cognitive rehearsal and other cognitive-behavioral interventions are used. Homework or other between-session assignments are commonly prescribed. Medication may be used in combination with individual cognitive therapy sessions. Other modalities such as group, family, or couples interventions might also be integrated or serve as the primary modality.

Cognitive therapy was originally developed for the treatment of major depression. Over time, it has been adapted for the treatment of the anxiety disorders, substance disorders, psychotic disorders, as well as for the personality disorders. Usually, the course of treatment for depression and anxiety disorders would be 12–20 sessions, whereas treatment of personality disorders could take a year or more (Beck & Freeman, 1990).

Schema Theory in Cognitive Therapy. Beck introduced the schema concept with reference to depression (Beck, 1964) over 30 years ago, when he described the cognitive triad of depression as negative views of the self, the world, and the future. He describes schemas by types: cognitive, affective, motivational, instrumental, or control schemas. Of these, the most clinically useful are the cognitive schemas regarding self-evaluation and world view or evaluation of others. Beck's colleagues have greatly extended schema theory, specifically with regard to personality disorders (Beck, Freeman, & Associates, 1990; Young, 1990). Young articulated the concept of early maladaptive schemas (EMS) and has described several core schemas commonly noted in individuals with personality disorders. Furthermore, he has developed an assessment instrument for eliciting EMS.

Schema Assessment

There are various ways of assessing schemas. Basic to a schema is the individual's self-view and world view. From an Adlerian perspective, schemas are central to an individual's lifestyle (Adler, 1956). Lifestyle, as well as schemas, can be assessed with a semi-structured interview that includes the elicitation of early recollections or early memories. The process begins by asking the patient: "What is your earliest memory?" or "Think back as far as you can and tell me the first thing you remember." An early recollection must be distinguished from a report. An *early recollection* is a single, specific event that is personally remembered by the individual, whereas a *report* can be an event that occurred more than once or for which the patient was told about the event by another, or by seeing it in a photo, home movie, or video. Additional memories from early and middle childhood are then elicited. From these memories the clinician searches for patterns related to the patient's view of self, that is, "I am strong, defective, unloved," and the patient's view of the world: "The world puts too many demands on me, is a scary place, is unfair." These views can be summarized and interpreted to reveal the individual's lifestyle themes or schemas (Eckstein, Baruth, & Mahrer, 1992). The case studies in Chapters 8 and 9 illustrate how early recollections are interpreted as schemas.

In the cognitive therapy tradition, schemas are typically identified or derived from the interview process (Beck, Freeman, & Associates, 1990). Young (1994) briefly described his approach to schema identification: The evaluation interview is critical in identifying schemas. In this interview, the clinician elicits presenting symptoms and problems and attempts to formulate a connection between specific symptoms, emotions, life problems, and maladaptive schemas.

During the course of inquiry about life events and symptoms, the clinician endeavors to develop hypotheses about patterns or themes. Issues of autonomy, connectedness, worthiness, reasonable expectations, and realistic limits are probed to ascertain if any of these present significant problems for the patient. It can be quite useful to inquire about "critical incidents" by asking the patient to describe a situation or incident that they consider indicative of their problem (Freeman, 1992). The clinician listens for specific triggers, patterns indicative of schemas, and specific be-

havioral, emotional, and cognitive responses. As themes and patterns emerge, the clinician formulates them in schema language, that is, view of self and view of the world and others. Because schemas are predictable and recurring phenomenon they can be "triggered" in the interview through imagery and discussing upsetting events in past or present. This process of triggering confirms the clinician's hypothesis about the presence of a specific schema.

In addition, Jeffrey Young and Gary Brown have developed a 123-item self-report instrument for assessing 15 common maladaptive schemas called the Schema Questionnaire (Young, 1994). This questionnaire has been validated on both clinical and nonclinical populations (Schmidt et al., 1995).

Schema Change

From a cognitive therapy perspective, schema change is the domain of what has come to be called *schema-focused cognitive therapy*. This approach involves a collaborative process in which the clinician and patient endeavor to understand and alleviate long-term characterological problems. It uses many of the intervention strategies and tactics of short-term cognitive therapy, but it also incorporates a variety of interpersonal and experiential intervention strategies and tactics that assist patients in reexperiencing and distancing themselves from early childhood traumas and wounds.

Schema change involves three steps: (a) identify maladaptive schemas; (b) establish the goal of treatment, that is, the level of schema change; and (c) develop an intervention strategy to accomplish this goal.

Schemas are identified by taking a patient's detailed history and by the Schema Questionnaire (Young, 1994). The purpose is to ascertain the developmental roots of these maladaptive schemas.

The second step is to establish the goal of treatment in terms of degree or level of schema change. Beck et al. (1990) identified schema change in terms of a continuum or levels of change ranging from maximum schema changes to minimal schema change. Four levels can be described.

The first level is *schema reconstruction*. It involves identifying faulty schemas and replacing them with more functional schemas. An example of successful schema reconstruction would be a paranoid personality disordered individual who was transformed into a more trusting person (Beck et al., 1990). Such total change may not be possible or feasible in that not all dysfunctional schemas can be restructured nor are all patients capable of undergoing such major change. Although many clinicians might look to this level of change as the ideal therapeutic goal, it can seldom be achieved (Freeman & Davison, 1997).

The second level is *schema modification*. It is analogous to rehabilitating a house and involves identifying schemas and modifying rather than replacing them. An example of schematic modification would involve modification of the schema: "I must always have others around if I'm going to survive" to "I must generally have others around for me to survive." Although the schema has not changed completely, the absolutistic nature of it is greatly modified (Freeman & Davison, 1997).

The third level is *reinterpretation*. This involves helping the patient to use an existing schema in a more prosocial way. For example, an excitement-seeking schema would be reframed as potentially adaptive rather than simply maladaptive. Rather than manifesting only in potentially dangerous behavior, the patient could be helped to use it prosocially. For instance, the patient could be helped to identify occupational choices or other social outlets that are in line with the schema (Freeman & Davison, 1997).

The fourth level is *schema camouflage*. Interventions at this level do not directly impact on the schema. Most treatment interventions, particularly within a short-term therapy, will be focused on schema modification and reinterpretation. With more impaired individuals, schematic camouflage will also be used. For example, a parasuicidal borderline personality disordered individual could be helped to make a non-suicide contract and call a help-line when a self-destruction schema is experienced (Freeman & Davison, 1997).

The third step is to develop a treatment strategy for accomplishing this goal. When schema restructuring or modification is the goal, an important part of this strategy involves educating patients as to how their maladaptive schemas arose and are maintained. The schema restructuring and modification change process usually also involves a "life review." While constructing the life review, the patient provides evidence that supports the schema as well as evidence that contradicts it. These schemas are tested through predictive experiments, guided observation, and reenactment of early schema-related incidents. A variety of emotive, interpersonal, behavioral, and cognitive techniques are used. Young (1994) detailed these schema reconstruction change interventions in his book, *Cognitive Therapy for Personality Disorder: A Schema-Focused Approach*.

Through the cognitive analysis of life evidence, patients become able to distance themselves, rather than being overidentified with and controlled by the "voice" of the schemas. Only then can schemas be viewed as something they've learned through repeated indoctrination by early caregivers, siblings, and peers rather than as something inherent in themselves. Finally, these patients become more able to notice and remember counterschema data about themselves and their social experiences (Bricker, Young, & Flanagan, 1993).

☐ Description of Common Maladaptive Schemas

A promising development in Cognitive Therapy is Schema-Focused Cognitive Therapy (Bricker, Young, & Flanagan, 1993; Young, 1994). Fifteen maladaptive schema have been articulated based on clinical experience and research on the Schema Questionaire. Each of these schemas is briefly described.

Abandonment/Instability

The essential feature of this schema is the belief that significant others will not or cannot provide ongoing nurture, emotional support, strength, or protection because they are emotionally unstable and unreliable, or because they might die or abandon the patient in favor of someone else. This schema develops because of parental inconsistency in meeting the child's emotional needs. Parental separation, divorce, or other experiences of loss or abandonment such as illness or deaths of close relatives or peers can influence the internalization of this schema. Finally, individuals with this schema typically cling to relationships because of their exaggerated fears of being left alone or abandoned.

Abuse/Mistrust

The essential feature of this schema is the belief that others will hurt, abuse, humiliate, manipulate, or take advantage of one. The fear of others' violent outbursts can also be part of this schema. Others' negative behaviors are perceived as intentional or the result of extreme and unjustifiable negligence. This schema develops as a result of early childhood experiences of abuse from parents or siblings: physical, emotional, or sexual. Finally, individuals with this schema tend to be hypervigilant and accusatory of others' motives.

Emotional Deprivation

The essential feature of this schema involves the core belief that one's desire for a normal degree of emotional support will not be met by others. Individuals who have internalized this schema tend to feel deprived of nurturance, protection, or empathy. Deprivation of nurturance involves an absence of attention, affection, and warmth from others. Absence of strength, direction, or guidance from significant others leads to deprivation of protection. In the absence of understanding, listening, self-disclosure, or mutual sharing of feelings and experiences with others, these individuals experience deprivation of empathy. These individuals have usually experienced some emotional neglect in early childhood. They may present as cold, demanding, or withholding, and tend to choose significant others who are unwilling or unable to provide emotional support.

Functional Dependence/Incompetence

The essential feature of this schema involves the core belief of being unable to handle everyday responsibilities competently or without considerable help from others. Such everyday responsibilities include minor decisions, hassles, chores, and tasks that constitute an average day. The schema develops when parents fail to encourage or allow a sense of independence, self-sufficiency, or competence in the child. Consequently, they ask for help and reassurance in what they do, while making wrong decisions or exercising bad judgment when they are expected to function independently. Not surprisingly, they choose significant others on whom they can be dependent.

Vulnerability to Harm and Illness

The essential feature of this schema involves an exaggerated fear that major disaster will strike at any time and that one is unable to protect oneself from disaster. These disasters can include financial, medical, criminal, or natural catastrophic events. This schema develops in the context of overly protective parents who continually communicate that the world is dangerous and life is unpredictable. Accordingly, these individuals present with a host of unrealistic fears and are frequently diagnosed with anxiety disorders.

Enmeshment/Undeveloped Self

The essential feature of this schema is the core belief that excessive emotional closeness and involvement with significant others can only occur at the expense of full individuation and normal social development. This schema often involves the belief that the enmeshed individual cannot sur-

vive or be happy without the constant support or presence of the other. Enmeshed individuals often feel that they are fused with the other. As such they find it difficult to experience a sense of individual identity or inner direction. They will feel smothered when around the enmeshed other but will feel emptiness or panic when left alone. This schema develops within the context of an enmeshed family. Subsequently, these individuals find it extremely difficult to individuate and functionally separate from that family or enmeshing others.

Defectiveness/Shame

The essential feature of this schema involves the core belief that one is inwardly defective or flawed. As a result, these individuals believe they must be fundamentally unlovable or unacceptable. Consequently, they experience a deep sense of shame concerning their perceived inadequacies and constantly fear exposure and further rejection by significant others. This schema tends to develop in the context of constant criticism, devaluation, or rejection by parents. Subsequently, these individuals are hypersensitive and expect blame and rejection from others. They tend to be self-critical and exaggerate their own defects, while avoiding situations requiring self-disclosure and the risks associated with intimacy.

Social Undesirability/Alienation

The essential feature of this schema is the core belief that one is outwardly undesirable to, or different from, others. Individuals with this schema tend to belief that they are ugly, sexually undesirable, socially inept, or low in status. They feel self-conscious and insecure in social situations and subsequently become alienated or isolated from others. Therefore, they are likely to conclude that they are not part of any group or community. This schema usually develops in the context of repeated criticism of one's appearance, social behavior, or being treated differently than others. Subsequently, these individuals tend to feel more comfortable when alone because social circumstances trigger self-consciousness or pressure to pretend they are enjoying themselves.

Failure to Achieve

The essential feature of this schema is the belief that one will inevitably fail or that one's capacity to achieve is inferior to one's peers. Corollary beliefs include the perception that one is inadequate, untalented, or ignorant. This schema tends to develop in the context of parental criticism usually involving invidious comparisons with siblings or peers. It can also arise when parents fail to provide sufficient encouragement, direction, or support. Subsequently, these individuals perceive they have failed in comparison to others even when their performance meets or exceeds that of others.

Subjugation

The essential feature of this schema is the surrender of control over one's own decisions and preferences to others. The purpose of this self-surrender is to avoid anger, retaliation, or abandonment. Subjugated individuals perceive their desires are neither valid nor important to others. Not surprisingly, this perception often leads to anger at those who subjugate. This schema usually develops in the context of domineering or controlling parents who punish, threaten, or withdraw from the child for expressing needs or wants. Subsequently, these individuals present as overly compliant or underassertive who avoid conflict and confrontation at all cost.

Self-Sacrifice/Overresponsibility

The essential feature of this schema involves a voluntary but excessive focus on meeting the needs of others at the expense of one's own needs. Such self-sacrifice and overresponsibility is motivated by a desire to spare others pain, to maintain a connection with others who are perceived as more needy, to avoid guilt, or to gain self-esteem. While self-sacrifice results from sensitivity to the pain of others, it often leads to a feeling that one's own needs are not being met and to resentment of those for whom one sacrifices. This schema tends to develop in the context of an emotionally needy parent who expects or requires the child to assume a caretaker role at a very early age. Guilt is a prominent feature of this schema. Subsequently, these individuals place the needs of others before their own and tend to overextend and over commit themselves.

Emotional Inhibition

The essential feature of this schema involves excessive inhibition of emotions and impulses. These individuals anticipate that the expression of

emotions and impulses will invariably result in loss of self-esteem, embarrassment, abandonment, or harm to self or others. This schema develops in the context of parents who promote the value of emotional control and discourage the expression of affect, particularly anger. Subsequently, these individuals appear cold and nonspontaneous and are also quite uncomfortable around displays of positive affect. Not surprisingly, they tend to choose significant others who are also controlled and rigid, or who are highly emotive so they can vicariously experience some emotional freedom.

Unrelenting/Unbalanced Standards

The essential feature of this schema is the relentless striving to meet the high flown expectations of oneself at the expense of happiness, spontaneity, health, and satisfying interpersonal relationships. It often includes unrealistic expectations of others. Individuals who have internalized this schema place undue emphasis on following strict personal rules of behavior or morality, and ignore their basic needs for gratification and enjoyment. They may also value status, money, achievement, or recognition over inner peace and harmony. This schema tends to develop in the context of parents with extremely high standards of achievement or moral superiority, and who make their love and approval dependent on task accomplishment. Subsequently, these individuals may be quite accomplished and successful, but also suffer from anxiety, depression, or stress-related complaints or disorders. Not surprisingly, these individuals tend to choose significant others who will also be highly critical of them or whom they can criticize and demand perfection.

Entitlement/Self-Centeredness

The essential feature of this schema is the belief that one is entitled to whatever one wants irrespective of the cost to others or of what might be regarded as unreasonable. This schema is likely to develop in the context of parents who overindulge or who do not encourage the child to develop self-responsibility. Alternatively, this schema can develop as a compensation for feelings of deprivation, social undesirability, or defectiveness. Subsequently, individuals who develop this schema tend to be self-centered and have an exaggerated view of themselves and their rights. They also tend to have significant empathic deficits and tend to treat others carelessly.

Insufficient Self-Control/Self-Discipline

The essential feature of this schema is the belief that it is extremely difficult to exercise sufficient self-control or frustration tolerance in the process of achieving personal goals or refraining from impulsive behaviors or emotional outbursts. This schema tends to develop in the context of parents who failed to model self-control, to set limits, or to adequately discipline the child. Alternatively, the schema can develop as a result of intolerable feelings of insecurity or tension arising from an unstable home environment. Subsequently, these individuals exhibit problems of impulsivity and aggressivity and have considerable difficulty delaying gratification.

☐ Summary

Traditionally, character, which is conceptualized as the learned, psychosocial component of personality, has been the focus of psychodynamically oriented psychotherapies. Today, the term *schema* is being used to operationalize the characterological component of personality. Although the construct of schema is used by both psychodynamic clinicians and cognitive therapy clinicians, it is the schema-focused approach to cognitive therapy that has developed a systematic approach to the treatment of the personality disorders. In this approach, the clinician works collaboratively with the patient to assess and then modify maladaptive schemas. This chapter has described 15 maladaptive schemas that are commonly observed in personality disordered individuals.

Reading 12
Behavior Theory and Social Work Treatment

BEHAVIOR THEORY AND SOCIAL WORK TREATMENT

Barbara Thomlison and Ray Thomlison*

Behavioral social workers practice in nearly every type of organization and environment and with a variety of populations, problems, and issues requiring change. Extensive behavioral literature illustrates the compatibility of behavior theory with social work values and treatment. Most important, the outcome research studies demonstrate the effectiveness of behavior therapy in contemporary social work problems and practice. A review of the empirical research in social work and related fields of service identifies behavioral elements in social work interventions with individuals, couples, families, small groups, and communities (Thomlison. 1984a). As well, the application of single-system research designs to the evaluation of social work practice has taken on significant prominence (Thyer & Boynton Thyer, 1992). These developments suggest that the impact of behavior therapy on social work practice has been more than a passing interest of the past two decades. The literature addresses the theory, application. monitoring, and practice of behavior therapy in social work. This chapter is therefore written with two primary objectives in mind: (1) to inform social work practitioners of the origins and development of behavioral social work and of its basic assumptions, conceptual framework, procedures. and techniques and (2) to illustrate common applications of behavioral theory to social work practice. As well, the writers hope to inspire social workers to integrate social learning theory and behavioral therapy into their social work treatment model.

DEVELOPMENT OF BEHAVIORAL SOCIAL WORK

Behavior therapy† refers to the systematic application of techniques intended to facilitate behavioral changes that are based principally, but not exclusively, on the con-

*The authors wish to thank Cathryn Bradshaw for her invaluable research assistance in the preparation of this chapter.
†Some argue that the concepts of behavior therapy and behavior modification are differentially applied (Wilson. 1990). For the purposes of this chapter we prefer behavior therapy but the concepts will be used synonymously.

ditioning theories of learning. It may be argued that it is more appropriate to refer to the behavior therapies than to imply that a single method of behavior therapy exists. Behavior therapy is, however, characterized by multiple theories and techniques, in the same way as other "therapies" such as psychotherapy, marital therapy, and family therapy.

Behavioral practice traces its beginnings to the first quarter of this century in the work of Ivan Pavlov on respondent or classical conditioning; of Thorndike. Hull, Watson, and B. F. Skinner on operant conditioning; and of Bandura on social learning theory (Franks et al., 1990). The contributions of Pavlov and Skinner are well documented in both the behavioral and social work literature and need only be mentioned here. It is important to recognize that these two founders of modern behavior therapy identified and studied two distinct behavioral processes.

Pavlov's studies of the salivation reflex of dogs are familiar to most students of human behavior. The basic experimental procedure for the learning process involved placing food within the view of the dog. Salivation was elicited and the relationship between the unconditioned stimulus (food) and the unconditioned response (salivation) was established. An arbitrary event for example, a bell, was then established to occur at the same time as the presentation of the food. Over a number of such pairings, the bell (the conditioned stimulus) took on the power to elicit the response of salivation (the conditioned response). This behavioral learning process is referred to as respondent conditioning and remains the fundamental theoretical explanation for a variety of anxiety and phobic disorders in contemporary behavior therapy (Thomlison, 1984b).

Skinner's contribution to behavior therapy was initially motivated by a different set of objectives than those of Pavlov. Skinner was dedicated to the scientific study of human behavior. While he did not deny the possibility of the internal mechanisms postulated by other theorists, he argued that human behavior could be empirically investigated only through the measurement of observable behavior. He expressed the belief underlying his approach as follows: "If we are to use the methods of science in the field of human affairs, we must assume that behavior is lawful and determined. We must expect to discover that what an individual does is the result of specifiable conditions and that once these conditions have been discovered, we can anticipate and to some extent determine one's actions" (Skinner, 1953, p. 6). It is necessary to understand that this commitment to science set relatively stringent requirements on the pursuit of knowledge within the behavioral school, not the least of which was the need to develop techniques of measurement compatible with the exploration of human behavior.

True to his commitment, Skinner evolved one of the most empirically based theories of human behavior and set the foundation for contemporary behavior therapy. At the heart of this Skinnerian theory was the concept of reinforcement. The operant (or voluntary) behavior of an individual could be increased in frequency if it was positively or negatively reinforced. Alternatively, the frequency of a behavior could be decreased by either administering punishment or withholding reinforcement; this latter process was referred to as extinction. In other words, the essence of the Skinnerian or operant model of human behavior relied heavily upon an understanding of the environmental (behavioral) events that preceded and/or followed the behavior(s) under scrutiny. This theoretical explanation of human behavior has been refined and elaborated as a result of clinical experience and research. Importantly, however, the interaction between behavior and the events the precede and follow it remains the foundation of most contemporary behavior therapy.

Cognitive behavioral approaches are also regarded as part of the behavioral paradigm and are illustrated by the contributions of Beck (1976), Ellis (1989), and Meichenbaum (1977). Cognitive approaches have developed directly from behavior theory, but because they are considered to contain distinct ideas, they are discussed in a separate chapter in this textbook (see chapter 5).

It was not until the late 1960s, when psychodynamic theories came under attack, that behavioral approaches appeared in social work. Much of the impetus for the development of behavior therapy as applied to social work was provided by the practice and research contributions of Bruce Thyer (1987a, 1988, 1989, 1990, 1991, 1992). Other significant initial contributors were Ray Thomlison (1972, 1981, 1982, 1984a, 1984b), for work on the applications of behavior theory to marital problems and phobic disorders and on its effectiveness for clinical social work practice; Richard Stuart (1971, 1977), for work on the application of behavior theory to delinquency, marital problems, and weight management; Sheldon Rose (1981), for behavior therapy conducted in groups; and Eileen Gambrill (1977, 1983, 1994), for work with clinical problems. Current contributors to the single-system research designs are identified in a bibliography compiled by Thyer and Boynton Thyer (1992).

BASIC ASSUMPTIONS AND PRINCIPAL CONCEPTS

Several assumptions about behavior underlie behavior therapy. All behavior is assumed to be learned and can be both defined and changed. Problems are formulated as undesirable behavior that can be understood through systematic exploration and modified through specific behavioral techniques. Thus, personal and social problems are translated into behavior that is observable, measurable, and changeable. Change occurs by rearranging "contingencies of reinforcement," that is, by altering what happens before and after the specified behavior. Behaviorists believe that behavioral change is brought about by changing environmental events and reinforcement by significant others in the environment, as well as by the enhanced perception of self that comes from acquiring new behavior. Behavior therapy acknowledges that there are a large number of reinforcing and aversive events that can be operative in any given behavioral exchange. Identifying current and alternative stimuli is essential. By changing the contingencies of reinforcement, the behavior that needs to be changed can be extinguished or other behavior can be conditioned to replace it. The learning and changing of behavior can be understood using social learning theory.

ELEMENTS OF SOCIAL LEARNING THEORY

Social learning theory comprises three major elements: target behaviors, antecedents, and consequences (Bandura, 1976). First are those behaviors that are the focus of the behavioral analysis. These are often identified during the period of assessment as undesirable, problematic, or a behavior that needs to be changed. When behaviors become the focus for change they are referred to as the "target behaviors." The other elements are those behaviors or environmental events that precede the problematic or target behaviors. These are referred to as "antecedent behaviors" or "events." Events that follow behavior are called "consequences." They are often identified as the controlling or maintaining conditions for the problem behaviors. These behaviors serve as the focus of the behavioral assessment. The interaction of these three elements is described in the ABC behavior therapy paradigm and is represented in Figure 3–1.

It must be noted that this paradigm serves to label one exchange in an ongoing sequence of exchanges between people. In order for the social worker to determine the antecedents and consequences, a decision as to the problem or target behavior must first be made. With this target behavior in mind, the social worker identifies those events or behaviors that precede or follow the target behavior. This identification process is usually done by direct observation by the social worker or by client self-report. This process is known as "behavioral analysis" and is considered essential to effective behavior therapy.

A common parent–child behavioral exchange can serve to illustrate the application of this social learning paradigm to a behavior therapy assessment and change program. Mr. S. complains that his child, Josh, will "never do what he is told." One of the concerns is that Josh will not come to the dinner table when he is called. The presenting situation, as explained by Mr. S., is shown in Table 3–1.

In order to assess the behavior further, it is generally necessary to examine the nature of the consequences that might be provided for Josh. Behavioral consequences differ in terms of quality and purpose. Some are of a positive (pleasing) nature, while others are of a negative (displeasing) variety. The former category is referred to as "positive consequence" and is employed to increase the occurrence of a behavior. The latter category is usually referred to as "punishment" and is frequently observed when a parent attempts to prevent the recurrence of an undesired behavior by spanking the child, that is, by physical punishment. While the use of physical punishment as a consequence is acknowledged as a means of decreasing the frequency of a behavior, it is viewed among behavioral social workers as an unacceptable means of altering behavior. In addition to humanitarian reasons, physical punishment is generally considered unacceptable because in many instances it suppresses a behavior without providing an alternative, more desirable behavior. Behavior therapy requires that any

FIGURE 3–1 THE A-B-C BEHAVIOR THERAPY PARADIGM

Antecedent Event(s) ⟶ Behavior ⟶ Consequence(s)

(A) (B) (C)

Table 3–1
Illustration of A-B-C Paradigm

	Antecedents (A)	Behavior (B)	Consequences (C)
Behavioral Analysis of Presenting Situation	Mr. S. calls Josh several times to the table. There is an escalation of threats and yelling when Josh does not immediately respond	Josh ignores his father's first requests but eventually presents himself angrily at the table and begins to eat	Father is silent and appears angry
Behavior Change Contract	Mr. S. makes one verbal request in a pleasant tone for Josh to come to the table	Josh comes to the table when called	When Josh arrives at the table as requested, Mr. S. verbally praises Josh and places a check mark on Josh's tally sheet
			If Josh chooses not to respond to his father's request, Mr. S. will begin eating alone, ignoring Josh's absence. Josh will forego the opportunity for his father's praise and tangible, positive acknowledgment for this dinner time

agreed-upon behavioral change must be defined in terms of desired increased frequency by the participants. This requires that all parties to a behavioral change define what behaviors are desired, not simply what is undesired. This is often a difficult requirement, as it is almost always easier to tell someone to stop doing something that is undesirable than to ask them to engage in a desired behavioral alternative. The use of positive consequences to increase desirable behavior is the strength of the social learning approach to behavior therapy. The research in the clinical arena strongly supports the use of positive consequences as a means of facilitating desired behavior. Few would find this an unacceptable research finding and, indeed, might see it as axiomatic. Interestingly, however, it is not always easy to put this principle into practice. For example, Mr. S. may feel that if Josh would do what he was told, then all would be okay, but until Josh changes Mr. S. feels he cannot give Josh any positive messages or praise. Unfortunately, Josh and his father have reached a stalemate such that, even if they agree that change is desirable, it is difficult because they are into a "coercive exchange" (Patterson & Reid, 1970).

Attempting to control another person's behavior by command and threat is familiar to most of us. In many instances, however, it has the effect demonstrated by Josh and his father. The commands and threats escalate until finally the child complies in order to terminate the threats and/or yelling. By the time the child obeys the parent's command, the parent has become agitated enough to lose any motivation to acknowledge, in positive terms, the child's compliance. This coercive process can be conceptualized using the following Skinnerian notions: a "negative reinforcement process," that is, the termination of a behavior (threats) upon occurrence of the desired behavior (compliance); an "extinction process," that is, the withholding of a positive reinforcer upon the occurrence of the desired behavior (compliance); and a "positive reinforcement process," that is, Mr. S. achieves what he set out to get (compliance).

In other words, when Josh did do as he was asked, for example, sit down at the table, his father chose to ignore his compliant behavior. On the other hand, Mr. S. achieved his objective and to some degree was positively reinforced, except for the feelings of frustration and anger. The difficulty is that one person (Josh) is being negatively reinforced and the other (Mr. S.) is being positively reinforced. This behavioral exchange will therefore be strengthened and can be predicted to increase in frequency unless an alternative exchange can be identified and practiced by both.

In order to help Josh and his father alter their undesirable interaction, the social worker will need to devise a program by which the father can give a clear cue, or instruction, to Josh and positive consequences if Josh complies by arriving at the dinner table at the desired time. Intervention requires that a target behavior for desired change be clearly identified. In this case, such a target might be labelled "Josh coming to the table when called." New antecedents or instructions would be identified, as well as new consequences for this new target behavior. An agreement to change might well be formalized as a contractual statement detailing the new behavioral target, its antecedents, and its consequences (see Table 3–1).

This brief example serves to demonstrate the basic procedures of assessment and intervention in accordance with the A-B-C paradigm. While the overall behavior therapy program would require a more detailed assessment and a more comprehensive intervention strategy, behavior and its controlling antecedents and consequences remain the focus of this approach.

ELEMENTS OF COGNITIVE THEORY

Returning briefly to the developmental history of behavior therapy, there has always been some question raised, both within and outside the behavioral school, regarding the place of human "internal mental" or cognitive processes. Essentially, there is considerable interest in the role of cognition in shaping behavior. For example, the relatively potent technology of systematic desensitization used in the treatment of anxiety reactions and phobic disorders has always depended heavily on a classical learning theory explanation. However, the actual procedures of desensitization developed by Joseph Wolpe require the anxiety-ridden client to learn a relaxation response that is then called forth in association with mental images of the client's anxiety-provoking situations. Simply speaking, the client is instructed to imagine a hierarchy of increasingly anxiety-provoking scenes while in a state of relaxation. This reliance on visual imagery to facilitate the therapeutic process has lent considerable support to the exploration of the place of cognition in behavioral change. An analysis of the literature since 1979 demonstrates an increasing emphasis on cognitions within the behavioral field (Dobson et al., 1992). For some, this seems to be the next logical phase of development for behavior therapy, while for others it represents a basic violation of the principles underlying empirically based behavior therapy.

The debate regarding the place of cognitions in behavior therapy centers on several assertions by traditional behaviorists. Some theorists, such as Skinner (1988) and Wolpe (1989), argue that behavior therapy has been sidetracked through the inclusion of cognitively based techniques and principles. They propose that a reliance on cognitions in behavior therapy has led to a general abandonment of individualized behavior analysis in favor of treating classes of problems. It has also been stated that the empirical nature of behavior therapy has been eroded through the inclusion of feelings and thoughts that are inaccessible to direct, external observation. Finally, analysis of research data comparing behavior therapy and cognitive and/or cognitive-behavioral therapy outcomes indicate that, in general, outcomes are not improved through the addition of cognitive components to behavior therapy (Sweet & Loizeaux, 1991; Wolpe, 1989). For example, Sweet and Loizeaux (1991) reported that eighty-three percent of the forty clinical outcome studies used in their analysis demonstrated that "no more beneficial outcome was achieved by adding therapy modules that specifically attended to cognitive-semantic variables" (p. 176). However, the efficacy of treatment methods tended to vary according to type of problem. When follow-up versus immediate post-treatment results were considered, cognitive-behavior interventions seemed to offer longer-lasting results.

Whatever the final resolution of this debate, there is no doubt that a cognitively based behavior therapy has developed, one that is quite compatible with social work practice. In its broadest definition, cognition incorporates many of the elements of human thought processes characteristically of concern to social work. These include the processes by which information (input) from the environment is translated, considered, integrated, stored, retrieved, and eventually produced as some form of personal activity (output). Cognitive-behavior practitioners have selected and explored certain cognitive elements in behavior change. In a consideration of cognitive-behavior modification, Robert Schwartz (1982) identified the following elements of cognitive theory used in behavior modification:

1. *information processing:* the acquisition, storage and utilization of information; encompassing attention, perception, language and memory;
2. *beliefs and belief systems:* ideas, attitudes and expectations about self, others and experience;
3. *self statements:* private monologues that influence behavior and feelings; and
4. *problem-solving and coping:* conceptual and symbolic processes involved in arriving at effective responses to deal with problematic situation (Schwartz, 1982, p. 269).

Cognitive-behavior therapy is the result of a concerted effort to integrate two important theories of human functioning: behavior and cognitive. It should offer a viable alternative to those social workers who have been attracted to the behavioral focus of behavior therapy but have felt that it did not adequately deal with the individual's internal processes.

BEHAVIORAL SOCIAL WORK PRACTICE

Behavioral approaches to assessment, intervention, implementation, and evaluation share a number of characteristics with the basic social work problem-solving process. The goals of behavioral social work treatment are to increase desirable behaviors and reduce undesirable behaviors in order that the client can improve his or her day-to-day and moment-to-moment functioning. Relationship skills form the foundation of work with clients, just as it does in other areas of social work treatment. The basic behavioral assessment method is used to analyze the client's problem and assist in a plan of change by developing appropriate behavioral change goals. Behavioral interventions have been applied and evaluated with increasing sophistication and success and provide the most effective strategies for dealing with common client problems. The selection of a specific intervention is based on the assessment process, during which presenting problems are translated into observable behaviors. Then, specification of behavior techniques and strategies to be followed are detailed in a treatment contract that addresses the client's problems and circumstances.

Conducting a behavioral assessment requires a focus on the here and now of the problem, as well as on current environmental factors related to the problem behavior. Also, a clear description of the intervention is provided, along with concrete ways to measure progress. Building on client strengths while developing new skills and increasing the knowledge base is another characteristic of behavioral intervention. Generally, the etiology of the behavior is not investigated, nor is the provision of a diagnostic label pursued. Both of these are deemed stigmatizing and uninformative (Gambrill, 1994). Much of the behavioral research literature utilizes diagnostic labels (for example, agoraphobia, attention deficit disorder, post-traumatic stress syndrome) in describing the problem behavior under investigation. This has resulted from the integration of behavior assessment methods with traditional psychiatric diagnostic classifications. This practice has been criticized as promoting a neglect of individual differences (Gambrill, 1994; Wolpe, 1989) and potentially masking outcome differences between types of intervention (Eifert et al., 1990).

The major behavior therapy techniques include: (1) cognitive-behavioral procedures such as cognitive restructuring, self-instructional training, thought stopping, and stress inoculation training; (2) assertiveness training; (3) systematic desensitization and variants of this procedure such as eye-movement desensitization, procedures involving strong anxiety evocation (e.g., flooding and paradoxical intention), and operant-conditioning methods (e.g., extinction and positive or negative reinforcement); and (4) aversion therapy. Each of these approaches deserves a depth of exploration that space does not permit here. However, texts on behavior therapy and practice provide descriptions of the application of these procedures and their effectiveness (Franks et al., 1990; Granvold, 1994; Sundel & Sundel, 1993; Thomlison, 1984b, 1986; Thyer, 1992; Wolpe, 1990). These methods can be applied to practice with individuals, couples, families, groups, and communities. The choice of a specific intervention method should be based on a careful assessment of client needs and the empirically determined effectiveness of specific procedures.

GENERAL APPROACH TO BEHAVIORAL ASSESSMENT AND INTERVENTION

Behavior therapy provides a planned systematic approach to social work intervention. Indeed, there are specific stages through which all behavior therapy must proceed. While there are a range of activities that are specific to each of the different behavior therapy approaches, there is also a basic set of general procedures that serve as a framework. It is important to remember, however, that this framework is essentially a summary of a behavior therapy approach and is based primarily on the social learning paradigm. The following procedural outline is based on the authors' practice and research with married couples, children, and families. Since much of clinical social work practice is carried out within the context of the family, the outline is presented as an approach to working with the family system.

Beyond the procedural steps identified here, it is important to emphasize that behavioral social workers bring a strong sense of importance to building a positive therapeutic relationship early in the contact with the client system and actively involving the client as much as possible in each step of the assessment and intervention. The importance of this relationship building is not to be underestimated as it establishes trust, rapport, and necessary support to the analysis and management of problem behavior. Once the client system is engaged through the relationship, behavioral procedures can occur. A behavioral assessment to determine the client's problem is the next step.

ASSESSMENT PROCEDURES

This section outlines ten procedures during a behavioral assessment. The objective is to define as clearly as possible the problems or events for change and the desired outcome.

1. Compilation of the problematic behavior inventory.
    (a) Begin by asking one member of the family group to identify the perception of the problems that have resulted in the meeting.
    (b) Clarify these perceived problems by asking for behaviorally specific examples. Most perceived problems can be translated into statements of who does what to whom within what context.
    (c) As each family member offers his or her perception of the problem, there is a high probability that the ensuing discussion will stimulate disagree-

ments among family members. It is important to observe who disagrees with whom, and over what behavioral statements. Therefore, these interchanges must be allowed to occur; however, they can become counterproductive to the objective of the assessment. When this occurs, the social worker should intervene, requesting the family members to terminate the debate yet acknowledging that differences of opinion are expected. Assure all family members that their perceptions of the problems are important and that each member will have an opportunity to present personal views.

2. Identify priority behavioral problems and their maintaining conditions.

    (a) Attempt to identify the antecedent events of at least those behaviors that arouse the highest level of intensity of feeling among family members. Antecedent events are those conditions existent immediately prior to the occurrence of the target behavior (e.g., what other members of the family are doing or not doing prior to the occurrence of an undesired behavior).

    (b) Identify the consequences of those problem behaviors that elicit the more intense family feelings. Identify the consequences of those events that occur after a target behavior (e.g., what other family members do after one of the problem behaviors has occurred).

3. Identify the contingencies existent for the provision of consequences, that is, what rules appear to govern the conditions under which these consequences are provided (e.g., when a child is or is not reprimanded, or when privileges are or are not withdrawn.

4. Identify recurrent behavior patterns in the exchanges among family members. Observe and record behavioral exchanges (e.g., coercive exchanges, shouting, avoidance responses, excessive demands, etc.).

5. Secure a commitment from all members of the family system, ensuring that they wish to work toward change. This commitment should state clearly: (a) that they will work as a unit on these family problems and (b) that they, as individuals, will work toward behavioral change. At this point in the assessment procedure, the social worker should be able to demonstrate to the family the interconnections among their individual behaviors: when one individual behaves, all family members respond in some manner. That is, behaviors do not occur in isolation. For example, when the adolescent repeatedly violates a curfew, the resultant parent-youth conflict affects all members of the family.

6. Begin to identify possible behavior targets for change. The target behaviors should be desirable behaviors and the objective to increase their frequency. This identification is often assisted by asking each family member to answer two questions: How could you behave differently to make this a happier family? How would you like to see others behave to make this a happier family? These questions may be given as homework assignments, with each family member asked to provide as many answers as possible to each question. The social worker should point out that this assignment is a challenge, as it requires the identification of desired behaviors. Individuals are more often accustomed to identifying what behaviors they do not like to see, as opposed to those they prefer.

7. On the basis of the family's homework assignment, discuss possible appropriate behavioral targets for change.
   (a) Select behaviors that are to be increased in frequency in order to maximize the opportunities for positive consequences.
   (b) Select behaviors that appear to be most relevant to this family's definition of its own happiness.
   (c) Select behaviors that are incompatible with undesirable (problematic) behaviors.
   (d) For each child, select at least one behavior that is "low risk" for change. A "low-risk behavioral target" is one that can be easily attained by the child and that, if performed without positive reinforcement (a violation of the change contract), will not jeopardize the growing trust of the child. An example of a child's low-risk target behavior change might be combing the hair in the morning or cleaning up after dinner each evening.
   (e) Attempt to select behaviors that are commonly identified by family members (e.g., mealtime behavior, family get-togethers, tidying up cooperatively, playing with all siblings).
   (f) Remember that a behavior must be observable to all. It is therefore necessary to explicate the indicators of some behaviors in order to minimize debate over whether they have actually occurred. For many parents, the behavior called "cleaning up her room" is a desired behavior change objective. Interestingly, what appears to be a very clear behavior leaves a great deal open to individual interpretation. It is therefore necessary to pinpoint specific behaviors such as picking up clothes, placing them in the appropriate locations, making the bed, placing trash in appropriate containers, etc.
8. Allow time for all family members to present their concerns and their support for the target behaviors. Certain behavior choices will elicit strong feelings from some family members. Negotiation must take place before selected behaviors are settled upon and must always take place within the spirit of the agreement or commitment to change. If one or more family members wishes to reevaluate this commitment in light of the selected targets for change, this request must be honored. Such reevaluation may have to take place within the context of the consequences of no change; that is, all persons have a right not to be required to change. There are, however, certain consequences of not changing. What are they for the individual and the family?
9. When target behaviors have been agreed upon, set the conditions for a baseline measure.
   (a) Before instructing the family to change, request that the parents monitor the frequency of occurrence of the target behaviors. This will allow for some baseline behavior frequency measures. These measures should be recorded and can be used at a later date to assess ongoing behavioral changes within the family.
   (b) Appoint the parents monitors of the behavior targets. Give them a tally sheet and instructions to record the frequency of each target behavior.

10. During the assessment phase, the social worker may identify problems with an individual or with the couple that require specific attention. On occasion, the assessment may indicates that the change process should be focused on the couple rather than on the child. Behavioral intervention is compatible with the assessment in progress. With the couple's agreement, the intervention may be temporarily suspended in light of the recognized need to concentrate on the couple's problems.

IMPLEMENTATION PROCEDURES

The implementation phase of a behavioral therapy program is marked by the identification of new contingencies between identified behaviors and their consequences. To this point the focus has been on the appropriate targeting of behaviors for change. When a program for change is to be implemented, a "contingency contract" might be formulated in order to facilitate a systematic, cooperative effort on the part of the family.

1. Clearly identify the target behaviors that have been agreed upon as the focus for change.
2. Establish new antecedent events for each of these target behaviors.
3. Establish new consequences that are to be provided for each occurrence or nonoccurrence of a targeted behavior.
4. Formulate a written contract specifying the following:
    (a) The target behaviors for change and their pinpointed elements.
    (b) New antecedents; if these are to be instructions, specify by whom they are to be given.
    (c) New positive consequences; these might include check marks and/or tokens provided upon behavioral occurrence, as well as social reinforcers such as affection and praise.
    (d) Specify what is to happen if there is a violation of the contract; that is, if a behavior does not occur or an undesired behavior occurs, it must be clear what others in the family are to do. For example, if a target behavior focuses on good dinner table behavior and one or more of the children violate this agreement, all family members must be clear about what is to happen.
    (e) Specify those positive consequences that are to act as bonus reinforcers, particularly when certain behavioral objectives are accomplished. For example, it is often helpful to include special privileges, such as family outings, as bonus reinforcers of a designated behavioral achievement, such as a target behavior that occurs at the desired level for a period of one week or more.
    (f) Specify those in the family unit who are to be responsible for recording the frequency of behavioral occurrences. This is usually one or both of the parents. These tally records are important in communicating to family members the degree and intensity of change.

(g) Contracts may be written in a variety of ways, but they must all state who does what to whom under what conditions. Many different examples of contracts may be found in the literature.

5. It is necessary to follow up with a series of telephone calls to ensure that the program has been implemented. In addition, these telephone calls provide the opportunity for members of the family, particularly the parents, to ask any questions that might have arisen as a result of implementing the program for change. These calls need not take long and should be limited to the pragmatics of the program implementation. Any conflict among family members reported at this time should be directed back to the family for resolution. If resolution is not possible, the persons in charge of recording should make note of the nature of the conflict and the context in which it occurs. This will be dealt with at the next meeting with the social worker.

6. Difficulties in implementing the program are inevitable. These problems usually pertain to such things as tally recording, differences in target behavior definition, and lack of "cooperation" on the part of certain family members. In order to deal with these problems, the social worker must remember that the contract is the reference point. Once agreed to, all problems must relate back to the original document. Changes in the contract must be negotiated by all members of the family. Remember that all problems related to implementation of and adherence to a contract for family interactional modification may eventually have to be related back to the original commitment to change agreed to by the family during the assessment period.

7. Each interview with the family after implementation should begin with an examination of the tally recording provided by the family members. Where change is evident in these data, the social worker must provide positive reinforcement by acknowledging the change and the hard work of all family members.

8. Discussion must then shift to problems arising between sessions. These discussions may address more general aspects of the family's functioning, and special techniques such as role playing, modelling, and behavioral rehearsal may be introduced in an effort to assist the family in dealing with these problems.

9. Since much of the family's energy goes into problem-solving and conflict resolution, the social worker must spend time on these areas of family life. One of the advantages of having required the family to negotiate a contingency contract is that they have experienced successful problem solving and negotiation. Examples derived from that process can be utilized in the ongoing problem-solving and conflict resolution training.

10. Where the monitoring of change indicates that little if any change is taking place, it is necessary to examine certain aspects of the program design. Depending on the area in which the program is failing, it will be necessary to consider changes in target behavior, consequences, or violations. It is often necessary to assess whether people are in fact following through on the re-

quirements of the contract. For example, it might be that a parent has agreed to read a bedtime story for successful achievement of a behavioral objective during the day, but fails to deliver.

11. When target behaviors have been achieved at the desired level of frequency, identify new behaviors for change or move toward termination of the behavioral therapy program.

TERMINATION PROCEDURES

1. Together with the family system, evaluate progress in relation to the objectives of the contract.

2. If the decision is to terminate, set the conditions for behavioral maintenance.

3. Behavioral maintenance requires the social worker to review with the family the basic learning principles identified during the modification of the target behavior (e.g., positive consequences versus punishment).

4. Instruct the family to continue the tally recording over the next four weeks but without the regularly scheduled appointments.

5. Set up an appointment for four weeks from the last interview for the purposes of termination and follow-up.

FOLLOW-UP PROCEDURES

The follow-up interview should assess whether or not the behavioral changes have been maintained. If they have not been maintained at a level consistent with the expectations of the social worker and/or the family, it will be necessary to reinstitute the program structure. If, on the other hand, the social worker and family feel that the behavioral changes have been maintained within desired parameters, termination may take place. Termination, of course, does allow for the family to contact the social worker at any point in the future when they feel the necessity.

From the perspective of clinical evaluation, it is important that the social worker analyze the results of the behavioral change program. Further, it is helpful for the social worker to contact family members at three-month and six-month intervals to ascertain the degree to which the behavioral changes have been maintained.

PRINCIPAL APPLICATIONS IN SOCIAL WORK TREATMENT

The diverse applications of behavior theory in social work practice can only be briefly highlighted in this chapter. Given the quantity of behavioral articles in social work journals and textbooks, behavioral social work has been characterized as a "major school of practice" (Thyer, 1991, p. 1). In a survey of clinical social workers, one-third of the practitioners who participated preferred a behavioral approach in their practice (Thyer, 1987a). Social workers have found behavioral interventions most influential when applied to disorders such as anxiety, depression, phobias, addictions, sexual dysfunction, and relationship distress. A number of misconceptions about behavior therapy continue to persist and may account for why some social workers do not employ behavioral strategies in their practice. A few of the most common myths held by social workers and other professionals about behavior therapy are that it ignores client feelings and is applicable to simple rather than complex problems, and that it overrelies on aversive techniques and is limited to symptom alleviation rather than treatment of root problems (Acierno et al., 1994b; Franks et al., 1990; Thyer, 1991).

Because behavior therapy has been applied to clients who have severely debilitating or difficult-to-treat conditions, ethical considerations play a prominent role in behavior therapy. Many programs have established protective mechanisms, such as treatment review processes, to address the issues of utilizing aversive procedures, determining appropriate individualized assessment and intervention, as well as keeping written records and assessment checklists and questionnaires (Sundel & Sundel, 1993).

During the past two decades, one of the most important areas of behavioral practice to emerge has been that of dealing with parenting, parent training, and child management and skill acquisition. With the help of the basic A-B-C paradigm, many childhood problems have been reconceptualized as behavioral problems resulting from interactional exchanges between children and parents. By systematically altering these exchanges in the context of behavior therapy, it has repeatedly been demonstrated that both parental and child behavior can be altered toward their desired objectives (Dangel et al., 1994; Graziano & Diament, 1992; Sundel & Sundel, 1993).Typical child problems addressed using behavioral techniques include noncompliance, chore completion, enuresis, eating disorders, interrupting, fire setting, sleep problems and bedtime anxieties, and hyperactivity (Butterfield & Cobb, 1994). Conduct disorders or antisocial behaviors in children have received considerable clinical and research attention in the past decade. Behavioral techniques have been demonstrated as effective in changing these behaviors (Christophersen & Finney, 1993; Doren, 1993; Jensen & Howard, 1990; Kazdin, 1990). It has been estimated that three to five percent of school-age children have attention deficit-hyperactivity disorder (ADHD), which has been identified as a risk factor in conduct disturbance and antisocial behavior (DuPaul et al., 1991). Social workers encounter these children and adolescents within the program contexts of child welfare, foster care, incarceration, therapeutic day programs, and residential and school-based programs (Meadowcroft et al., 1994).

Home-based interventions with families and children have developed as the preferred treatment setting for many multifactor child and parent-related problems. The focus is on family interaction supported by the social learning model. Maltreatment or risk of maltreatment of children by primary caretakers has become a focus of in-home intervention. Problem-solving and skills training for parents usually include child management skills, anger management, and parent issues involving substance abuse, communication difficulties, and social isolation (Gambrill, 1994; Hodges, 1994).

Since the late 1950s, the treatment of choice for many professionals working with anxiety- and phobic-disordered clients has been Joseph Wolpe's systematic desensitization (1990). Clients suffering the inhibitory effects of phobic disorders have been the subjects of a great deal of effective intervention by behavior social workers. Combined with the basic systematic desensitization, new cognitive-behavioral approaches are promising even more effective outcomes. In fact, it is now to the point where a social worker would be hard-pressed to make an argument for an alternate treatment method for any of the phobic disorders.

Couple counselling is another area where social workers frequently utilize a behavioral approach. Jacobson (1992) asserts that behavioral interventions are the most widely investigated treatment for couple problems. Communication, conflict management, and problem-solving skills building are the most common behavioral interventions used. Behavioral procedures have been demonstrated to be effective with a multitude of problems, circumstances, and populations in diverse settings. Indeed, behavioral social work treatments have been found to be superior to other treatment approaches to social skills training, phobias, hyperactivity and, developmental problems of children and adults.

EDUCATION AND TRAINING FACTORS

Training for behavior therapy occurs in a variety of educational contexts. The content, format, and objectives of behavior training vary widely (Alberts & Edelstein, 1990). Social work curricula generally provide an overview of behavioral change principles and techniques but not detailed training (Thyer & Maddox, 1988). There are some social work educational programs that offer electives in behavioral social work practice. Thyer (1991) reports there over sixty published textbooks on behavioral social work and most social work textbooks present practice information on behavioral social work treatment. Many organizations, treatment settings, and programs offer behavioral training to social workers, foster parents, and in-home family support workers. Given the efficacy of behavioral methods and their extensive application to social work practice, an argument can be made for the inclusion of behavioral social work practice in the core curriculum in social work education.

CULTURALLY COMPETENT BEHAVIORAL PRACTICE

It is only relatively recently that concern for the needs of culturally different groups has received attention among behavior therapists. Behavior theory, like many contemporary practice theories, draws on Western cultural values, assumptions, and philosophy. In reality, both clients and behavioral social workers are racially diverse. Efforts to offer culturally competent therapy are very much affected by the political, social, and economic power and status of each group. Additionally, barriers exist in terms of access to and participation in therapy for different racial and ethnic groups. Barriers include philosophical and value differences, language, as well as individual and organizational structures associated with Western helping systems (Corcoran & Vandiver, 1996).

Working with culturally different individuals involves recognizing diversity in the perspectives and behavior of individuals. Different cultural groups develop their own patterns of coping strategies. Many of the techniques used by Western trained behavioral social workers may employ strategies that conflict with the values, beliefs, and family traditions of a particular cultural group. For example, the understanding of time is critical to the concept of shaping, reinforcement schedules, and extinction. This concept may be understood differently by those who view time in other ways. As well, what constitutes problematic behavior, help-seeking behavior, and inappropriate behavior is interwoven with the Western perspective on the person and what behaviors, thoughts, and feelings make up the person. Many behavioral social workers argue, however, that the principles underlying behavior cross the boundaries of culture. The main concern is whether the assumptions underlying the principles of learning are universally accepted. This needs further exploration. For example, the definition of a positive reinforcer, as an event that increases behavior frequency, does not appear to be culturally determined, but a specific positive reinforcer, such as TV watching, may work in one culture but not in another.

It is therefore very important for behavioral social workers at the beginning of assessment to understand how family and the individuals who constitute family are defined in a given culture, and to recognize that individuals make different choices based on the culture. If social workers mislabel behavioral interactions, their interventions can compound rather than resolve parenting dilemmas or other problematic behaviors. Therefore, interventions should be carefully sculpted to the client's cultural orientation and preferences. It requires modification of existing interventions and understandings of behavior, so that they are grounded in local understandings (Landrine & Klonoff, 1995).

Many social workers are beginning to ask what the cultural determinants and parameters of behavior therapy are. It is suggested that organizations in culturally specific and diverse communities should ensure that the social work staff be diverse and have a high level of self-awareness and openness. The ability to do a cultural self-assessment is also essential. Behavioral social workers must keep in mind that individuals develop problem-solving styles that fit their culture and values, and therefore solutions must fit the cultural attributes of culturally different populations. Most of the existing knowledge about diversity has not been developed by behavior therapists. Therefore, the creation of multicultural interventions is only beginning. In summary, research on the relationship between cultural competencies, behavior theory, and outcomes is largely absent or inappropriate for culturally specific situations.

SELECTED CONCERNS IN BEHAVIORAL PRACTICE

The social work literature once reflected numerous concerns about the use of behavior therapy in social work practices. Many of these earlier concerns appear to have abated. For illustrative purposes, the following concerns reflect the current practice literature.

1. For those who want "insight" or a "talking" psychotherapy, this approach is not appropriate. It is action oriented and leans heavily on an educative focus for client change.
2. The focus is on behavior/cognitive change and generally requires a structured approach to change by both client and therapist. Some social workers feel this is inappropriate or restrictive.
3. Some nonprofessionals and professionals misunderstand or misrepresent the approach, seeing it as very simple and as a quick fix for complex problems. The usual sources of such misunderstanding are inappropriately designed child management programs that rely on aversive methods of "punishment" for undesired behavior, often coupled with the unsystematic use of "rewards" for compliant behavior. Such interventions are devoid of the elements of behavior analysis and the systematic use of behavioral techniques essential for successful behavioral change.
4. The behavior therapies are often thought to be derived from a homogeneous theory, when in fact they are made up of numerous theories of behavior with an array of optional intervention strategies and techniques. Many social workers fail to understand that differential approaches are often available for specific problems identified through the process of behavioral assessment. Such matching of technique to problem is criticized by some therapists as contrived and as treating the symptom rather than the cause. Differential applications relate to the problem and are guided by the behavioral analysis of the conditions under which the problem behavior occurs.
5. Some behavioral techniques appear on the surface to be insensitive to the client. For example, the use of imagery and/or confrontation with fear-producing events is viewed as causing undue anxiety and discomfort to the client.

EMPIRICAL BASE

In general, the effectiveness of the various strategies is increasingly a concern for social work practitioners. Much of the literature supporting the relative success of various therapies depends on anecdotal material from the case reports of social workers. Many of these accounts are unidimensional and relatively few are based on empirical findings that use before and after measures and that establish clear relationships between the therapeutic intervention and client change.

In contrast, behavior therapies have a built-in opportunity for data collection by both social workers and clients. Behavioral procedures involve the systematic application of specific techniques intended to facilitate observable behavior change. Measurement of change is therefore an integral part of behavior therapy. This emphasis on problem assessment and concrete indicators of progress has led to the extensive development and use of standardized measures. One example of a widely utilized behavioral measure is the Achenbach Child Behavior Checklist (Achenbach, 1991). The empirical literature reports extensive research data demonstrating the effectiveness of behavioral approaches to many client problems. Indeed, behavior therapy has championed the use of single-system research design (Gambrill, 1994; Hersen, 1990; Thyer & Boynton Thyer, 1992), as well as studies in group outcome research (Barrios, 1990; Kazdin, 1989).

Many behavioral treatments have progressed to the advanced stage where they can be implemented on a presciptive basis with children and adults. This is a highly desirable opportunity for improving social work clinical practice. Prescriptive interventions are standardized treatments that have been empirically validated for use with precisely defined populations and problems under clearly defined conditions. This maturity and richness in the empirical literature is the result of decades of clinical application of behavioral interventions and rigorous research in such areas as anxiety disorders, phobic disorders, and marital problems. The development of behavioral interventions for other problematic behaviors is still in its infancy and as yet has not developed strong empirical validation. It should be noted that for some problems, behavior therapy is routinely and effectively used in conjunction with pharmacotherapy (e.g., some depressions, attention deficit-hyperactivity disorder, obsessive-compulsive disorder). The *Handbook of Behavior Therapy with Children and Adults* (Ammerman & Hersen, 1993) includes pharmacological approaches commonly combined with behavioral approaches. Table 3–2 provides a selective sampling of research studies and literature reviews that appraise the effectiveness of behavior therapy in producing individual change for a wide range of problems.

Behavior approaches to group work have a recognized place in social work primarily due to the excellent ongoing work of Rose (1981). Gambrill (1983), Tolman and Molidor (1994), and others. (Gambrill, 1983) have used the behavioral approach successfully with a variety of groups including adults and children (Gamble et al., 1989; Tallant et al., 1989; Thyer, 1987b; Van Der Ploeg-Stapert & Van Der Ploeg, 1986). Group work often focuses on teaching assertive behaviors and other interpersonal skills. It has been utilized extensively in the treatment of depression, eating disorders, parent and child skills training, and addictions. Tolman and Molidor (1994) reviewed group work within social work practice throughout the 1980s. They note that 69 percent of the articles reviewed had a cognitive-behavioral orientation. Child social skills training and other behavior problems of children and adolescents were the most frequently targeted fields of social work practice research utilizing behavioral group work (Jenson & Howard, 1990; Zimpfer, 1992).

Finally, applications of behavior therapy principles to community practice have been somewhat more limited but have not been ignored. Importantly, however, there are numerous examples of community projects based on behavioral principles reported in the literature (Mattaini, 1993; O'Donnell & Tharpe, 1990; Rothman & Thyer, 1984). The behavioral interventions employed are the same as those utilized for individual change (for example, modelling, feedback, contingency management).

Table 3–2
Selective Summary of Behavior Therapy Effectiveness

Problem Area	Effectiveness Research*
Addictions	Acierno, Donohue, & Kogan, 1994; Goldapple & Montgomery, 1993; Hall, Hall, & Ginsberg, 1990; Lipsey, & Wilson, 1993; Peyrot, Yen, & Baldassano, 1994; Polansky & Horan, 1993; Sobell, Sobell, & Nirenberg, 1988
Anxiety disorders	Acierno, Hersen, & Van Hasselt, 1993; Beck & Zebb, 1994; Emmelkamp & Gerlsma, 1994; Lipsey & Wilson, 1993; Rachmann, 1993; Van Oppen, De Haan, Van Balkom, Spinhoven, Hoogdin, & Van Dyck, 1995
Autism	Celiberti & Harris, 1993; Ducharme, Lucas, & Pontes, 1994; McEachin, Smith, & Lovaas, 1993; Scheibman, Koegel, Charlop, & Egel, 1990
Child maltreatment	Gambrill 1983; Finkelhor & Berliner, 1995; Gaudin, 1993; Meadowcroft, Thomlison, & Chamberlain, 1994; Wekerle & Wolfe, 1993; Wolfe, 1990; Wolfe & Wekerle, 1993
Conduct disorders	Bramlett, Wodarski, & Thyer, 1991; Christophersen & Finney, 1993; Dumas, 1989; Kazdin, 1990; Lochman & Lenhart, 1993; Maag & Kotlash, 1994; Magen & Rose, 1994; Raines & Foy, 1994
Couple problems	Granvold, 1994; Epstein, Baucom & Rankin, 1993; Halford, Sanders, & Behrens, 1994; Hahlweg & Markman, 1988; Lipsey & Wilson, 1993; Montang & Wilson, 1992; O'Farrell, 1994; Thomlison, 1984a
Depression	Beach, Whisman, & O'Leary, 1994; Frame & Cooper, 1993; Hoberman & Clarke, 1993; Norman & Lowry, 1995; Rohde, Lewinsohn, & Seeley, 1994
Developmental disabilities	Feldman, 1994; Hile & Derochers, 1993; Kirkham, 1993; Nixon & Singer, 1993; Thomlison, 1981; Underwood & Thyer, 1990
Eating disorders	Garner & Rosen, 1990; Isreal, 1990; Kennedy, Katz, Neitzert, Ralevski, & Mendlowitz, 1995; Lipsey & Wilson, 1993; Morin, Winter, Besalel, & Azrin, 1987; Saunders & Saunders, 1993; Smith, Marcus, & Eldridge, 1994; Wilson, 1994
Family violence	Edleson & Syers, 1990; 1991; Faulkner, Stoltenberg, Cogen, Nolder, & Shooter, 1992; Peled & Edleson, 1992; Tolman & Bennett, 1990
Gerontology	Fisher & Carstensen, 1990; Hersen & Van Hasselt, 1992; Nicholson & Blanchard, 1993; Widner & Zeichner, 1993
Juvenile delinquency	Bank, Marlowe, Reid, Patterson, & Weinrott, 1991; Hagan & King, 1992; Hawkins, Jensen, Catalano, & Wells, 1991; Lipsey & Wilson, 1993; Meadowcroft, Thomlison, & Chamberlain, 1994; Zimpfer, 1992
Pain management	Biederman & Schefft, 1994; Gamsa, 1994; Holroyd & Penzien, 1994; Lipsey & Wilson, 1993; Subramanian, 1991; 1994
Phobic disorders	Donohue, Van Hasselt, & Hersen, 1994; King, 1993; Mersch, 1995; Newman, Hofman, Trabert, Roth, & Taylor, 1994; Turner, Beidel, & Cooley-Quille, 1995
Post-traumatic stress	Caddell & Drabman, 1993; Corrigan, 1991; Foy, Resnick, & Lipovosky, 1993; Richards, Lovell & Marks, 1994; Saigh, 1992
Psychosis	Liberman, Kopelowicz, & Young, 1994; Lipsey & Wilson, 1993; Morrison & Sayers, 1993; Scotti, McMorrow, & Trawitzki, 1993; Tarrier, Beckett, Harwood, Baker, Yusupoff, & Ugarteburu, 1993
Sexual deviance	Camp & Thyer, 1993; Hanson, Steffy, & Gauthier, 1993; Marshall, Jones, Ward, Johnston, & Barbaree, 1991; Kaplan, Morales, & Becker, 1993; Marques, Day, Nelson, & West, 1994
Sleep disturbances	Lichstein & Riedel, 1994; Minde, Popiel, Leos, & Falkner, 1993
Stress management	Dubbert, 1995; Lipsey & Wilson, 1993

*When possible, review articles and research directly applicable to social work practice were selected.

Some of the problem areas addressed in behavioral community practice have been increasing the level and quality of community participation and decreasing undesirable community practices (Mattaini, 1993).

Overall, and relative to other approaches, behavior therapy has an attractive record of success with a wide variety of human problems. However, several gaps in knowledge and research of behavior therapy are noted in the literature. These gaps include maintaining and generalizing behavioral changes and determining which behavioral approaches work most effectively with which kind of problem in what context. Maintenance refers to the durability of the behavioral change over time; generalization refers to behavioral change in contexts different from the one in which the intervention took place. Strategies to enhance both maintenance and generalization need to become part of any behavioral change program and to be validated through empirical research (Gambrill, 1994; Kendall, 1989; Whisman, 1990). Critical variables that predict which clients will benefit from which intervention procedures can be identified not only by looking at those clients for whom a specific behavioral procedure is effective but also by considering those clients who fail to improve from the treatment (Goldfried & Castonguay, 1993; Steketee & Chambless, 1992). The quality of prediction will improve if a number of common methodological problems are addressed.

PROSPECTUS

Behavior therapy, as it has been presented here, comprises a variety of distinctly different approaches to facilitating behavioral and, in some cases, cognitive changes. It has been developed from a strong commitment to planned and systematic assessment, a distinct strength over other therapeutic models of change. Intervention strategies evolve from the prescriptive approach to assessment within a context of empirical inquiry, primarily utilizing nominal and ratio level of measurement to establish frequency and duration of problems. Its impact on social work practice continues to be felt both directly in clinical practice and indirectly in practice areas such as task-centered approaches, as well as single-system designs in research. Behavior therapy has been demonstrated to be effective in most areas of social work practice. For some large and complex problems such as those of crack addicts and autistic children, the theory is considered underdeveloped (Jordan & Franklin, 1995, p. 21). However, for the majority of problems encountered by social workers, empirical support for behavior therapy as an effective therapeutic intervention is well established and most argue behavior theory is the most advisable therapeutic option. There is little doubt that its place within social work practice has been assured. It is our sincere hope that social workers will understand the contribution behavior theory will make to quality assurance in social work practice.

APPENDIX

BASIC ASSUMPTIONS AND PRINCIPLES

Contingencies of reinforcement	Reinforcing and aversive stimuli
Target behaviors	Antecedent behaviors
Consequences	Behavioral analysis
Coercive exchange	Negative reinforcement process
Positive reinforcement process	Extinction process
A-B-C paradigm	Information processing
Beliefs and belief systems	Self statements
Problem solving and coping	

BEHAVIORAL ASSESSMENT AND INTERVENTIONS

Behavior inventory	Behavioral exchanges
Contingencies	Low-risk behavioral target
Homework assignments	Negotiation
Observable	Baseline measure
Commitment to change	Tokens
Contingency contract	Bonus reinforcers
Social reinforcers	Tally records
Recording	Modelling
Role playing	Problem-solving activity
Behavioral rehearsal	Monitoring of change
Conflict resolution	Behavioral maintenance clinical evaluation
Evaluate progress	
Maintaining conditions	

REFERENCES

Achenbach, T. M. (1991). Manual for the child behavior checklist/4–18 and 1991 profile. Burlington, VT: Department of Psychiatry, University of Vermont.

Acierno, R., Donohue, B., & Kogan, E. (1994a). Psychological interventions for drug abuse: A critique and summation of controlled studies. *Clinical Psychology Review 14*, 417–440.

Acierno, R., Hersen, M., & Van Hasselt, V. (1993). Interventions for panic disorder: A critical review of the literature. *Clinical Psychology Review 13*, 561–578.

Acierno, R., Hersen, M., Van Hasselt, V., & Ammerman, R. (1994b). Remedying the Achilles heel of behavior research and therapy: Prescriptive matching of intervention and psychopathology. *Journal of Behavior Therapy and Experimental Psychiatry 25*, 179–188.

Alberts, G. M., & Edelstein, B. A. (1990). Training in behavior therapy. In A. Bellack, M. Hersen, and A. Kazdin (Eds.), *International Handbook of Behavior Modification and Therapy* (pp. 213–226). New York: Plenum Press.

Ammerman, R. T., & Hersen, M. (Eds.) (1993). *Handbook of Behavior Therapy with Children and Adults: A Developmental and Longitudinal Perspective.* Boston: Allyn and Bacon.

Bandura, A. (1976). *Social Learning Theory.* Englewood Cliffs, NJ: Prentice-Hall.

Bank, L., Marlowe, J. H., Reid, J. B., Patterson, G. R., & Weinrott, M. R. (1991). A comparative evaluation of parent-training interventions for families of chronic delinquents. *Journal of Abnormal Child Psychology 19*, 15–33.

Barrios, B. (1990). Experimental design in group outcome research. In A. Bellack, M. Hersen, and A. Kazdin (Eds.), *International Handbook of Behavior Modification and Therapy* (pp. 151–174). New York: Plenum Press.

Beach, S. R., Whisman, M. A., O'Leary, K. D. (1994). Marital therapy for depression: Theoretical foundation, current status, and future directions. *Behavior Therapy 25*, 345–372.

Beck, A. (1976). *Cognitive Therapy and the Emotional Disorders.* New York: International Universities Press.

Beck, J. G., & Zebb, B. J. (1994). Behavioral assessment and treatment of panic disorder: Current status, future directions. *Behavior Therapy 25*, 581–612.

Biederman, J. J., & Schefft, B. K. (1994). Behavioral, physiological, and self-evaluative effects of anxiety on the self-control of pain. *Behavior Modification 18*, 89–105.

Bramlett R., Wodarski, J. S., & Thyer, B. A. (1991). Social work practice with antisocial children: A review of current issues. *Journal of Applied Social sciences 15*, 169–182.

Butterfield, W. H., & Cobb, N. H. (1994). Cognitive-behavioral treatment of children and adolescents. In D. K. Granvold (Ed.), *Cognitive and Behavioral Treatment: Methods and Applications* (pp. 63–89). Pacific Grove, CA: Brooks/Cole Publishing Company.

Caddell, J. M., & Drabman, R. S. (1993). Post-traumatic stress disorder in children. In R. Ammerman and M. Hersen (Eds.), *Handbook of Behavior Therapy with Children and Adults: A Developmental and Longitudinal Perspective* (pp. 219–235). Boston: Allyn and Bacon.

Camp, B. H., & Thyer, B. A. (1993). Treatment of adolescent sex offenders: A review of empirical research. *Journal of Applied Social Sciences 17*, 191–206.

Celiberti, D. A., & Harris, S. L. (1993). Behavioral interventions for siblings of children with autism: A focus on skills to enhance play. *Behavior Therapy 24*, 573–599.

Christophersen, E. R., & Finney, J. W. (1993). Conduct disorder. In R. Ammerman and M. Hersen (Eds.), *Handbook of Behavior Therapy with Children and Adults: A Developmental and Longitudinal Perspective* (pp. 251–262). Boston: Allyn and Bacon.

Corcoran, K., & Vandiver, V. (1996). *Maneuvering the Maze of Managed Care.* New York: Free Press.

Corrigan, P. W. (1991). Social skills training in adult psychiatric populations: A meta-analysis. *Journal of Behavior Therapy and Experimental Psychiatry 22*, 203–210.

Dangel, R. F., Yu, M., Slot, N. W., & Fashimpar, G. (1994). Behavioral parent training. In D. K. Granvold (Ed.), *Cognitive and behavioral treatment: Methods and applications* (pp. 108–122). Pacific Grove, CA: Brooks/Cole Publishing Company.

Dobson, K. S., Beamish, M., & Taylor, J. (1992). Advances in behavior therapy: The changing face of AABT conventions. *Behavior Therapy 23*, 483–491.

Donohue, B. C., Van Hasselt, V. B., & Hersen, M. (1994). Behavioral assessment and treatment of social phobia: An evaluative review. *Behavior Modification 18*, 262–288.

Doren, D. M. (1993). Antisocial personality disorder. In R. Ammerman and M. Hersen (Eds.) *Handbook of Behavior Therapy with Children and Adults: A Developmental and Longitudinal Perspective* (pp. 263–276). Boston: Allyn and Bacon.

Dubbert, P. M. (1995). Behavioral (lifestyle) modification in the prevention of hypertension *Clinical Psychology Review 15*, 187–216.

Dumas, J. E. (1989). Treating antisocial behavior in children: Child and family approaches. *Clinical Psychology Review 9*, 197–222.

Ducharme, J. M., Lucas, H., & Pontes, E. (1994). Errorless embedding in the reduction of severe maladaptive behavior during interactive and learning tasks. *Behavior Therapy 25* 489–502.

DuPaul, G. J., Guevremont, D. C., & Barkley, R. A. (1991). Attention deficit-hyperactivity disorder in adolescence: Critical assessment parameters. *Clinical Psychology Review 11*. 231–245.

Edleson, J. L., & Syers, M. (1990). Relative effectiveness of group treatments for men who batter. *Social Work Research and Abstracts 26*, 10–17.

Edleson, J. L., & Syers, M. (1991). The effects of group treatment for men who batter: An 18-month follow-up study. *Research on Social Work Practice 1*, 227–243.

Eifert, G. H., Evans, I. M., & McKendrick, V. G. (1990). Matching treatments to client problems not diagnostic labels: A case for paradigmatic behavior therapy. *Journal of Behavior Therapy and Experimental Psychiatry 21*, 163–172.

Ellis, A. (1989). Overview of the clinical theory of rational-emotive therapy. In R. Grieger & J. Boyd (Eds.), *Rational-Emotive therapy: A Skills Based Approach.* New York: Van Nostrand Reinhold.

Emmelkamp, P. M., & Gerlsma, C. (1994). Marital functioning and the anxiety disorders. *Behavior Therapy 25*, 407–430.

Epstein, N., Baucom, D. H., & Rankin, L. A. (1993). Treatment of marital conflict: A cognitive-behavioral approach. *Clinical Psychology Review 13*, 45–57.

Faulkner, K., Stoltenberg, C. D., Cogen, R., Nolder, M., & Shooter, E. (1992). Cognitive-behavioral group treatment for male spouse abusers. *Journal of Family Violence, 7*, 37–55.

Feldman, M. A. (1994). Parenting education for parents with intellectual disabilities: A review of outcome studies. *Research in Developmental Disabilities 15*, 299–302.

Finkelhor, D., & Berliner, L. (1995). Research on the treatment of sexually abused children: A review and recommendations. *Journal of the American Academy of Child and Adolescent Psychiatry 34*, 1–16.

Fisher, J. E., & Carstensen, L. L. (1990). Behavior management of the dementias. *Clinical Psychology Review 10*, 611–629.

Foy, D. W., Resnick, H. S., & Lipovsky, J. A. (1993). Post-traumatic stress disorder in adults. In R. Ammerman and M. Hersen (Eds.), *Handbook of Behavior Therapy with Children and Adults: A Developmental and Longitudinal Perspective* (pp. 236–248). Boston: Allyn and Bacon.

Frame, C. L., & Cooper, D. K. (1993). Major depression in children. In R. Ammerman and M. Hersen (Eds.), *Handbook of Behavior Therapy with Children and Adults: A Developmental and Longitudinal Perspective* (pp. 57–72). Boston: Allyn and Bacon.

Franks, C. M., Wilson, G. T., Kendall, P. C., & Foreyt, J. P. (1990). *Review of Behavior Therapy: Theory and Practice.* Vol. 12. New York: Guilford Press.

Gamble, E. H., Elder, S. T., & Lashley, J. K. (1989). Group behavior therapy: a selective review of the literature. *Medical Psychotherapy An International Journal 2*, 193–204.

Gambrill, E. D. (1977). *Behavior Modification: A Handbook of Assessment, Intervention, and Evaluation.* San Francisco: Jossey-Bass.

Gambrill, E. D. (1983). Behavioral intervention with child abuse and neglect. In M. Hersen, R. Eisler, and P. Miller (Eds.), *Progress in Behavior Modification* (pp. 1–56). New York: Academic Press.

Gambrill, E. D. (1994). Concepts and methods of behavioral treatment. In D. K. Granvold (Ed.), *Cognitive and Behavioral Treatment: Methods and Applications* (pp. 32–62). Pacific Grove, CA: Brooks/Cole Publishing Company.

Gamsa, A. (1994). The role of psychological factors in chronic pain. Part I: A half century of study. *Pain 57*, 5–15.

Garner, D. M., & Rosen, L. W. (1990). Anorexia nervosa and bulimia nervosa. In A. Bellack, M. Hersen, and A. Kazdin (Eds.), *International Handbook of Behavior Modification and Therapy* (pp. 805–817). New York: Plenum Press.

Gaudin, J. M., Jr. (1993). Effective interventions with neglectful families. *Criminal Justice and Behavior 20*, 66–89.

Goldapple, G. C., & Montgomery, D. (1993). Evaluating a behaviorally based intervention to improve client retention in therapeutic community treatment for drug dependency. *Research on Social Work Practice 3*, 21–39.

Goldfried, M. R., & Castonguay, L. G. (1993). Behavior therapy: Redefining strengths and limitations. *Behavior Therapy 24*, 505–526.

Granvold, D. K. (Ed.). (1994). *Cognitive and Behavioral Treatment: Methods and Applications*. Pacific Grove, CA: Brooks/Cole Publishing Company.

Graziano, A. M., & Diament, D. M. (1992). Parent behavioral training: An examination of the paradigm. *Behavior Modification 16*, 3–38.

Hagan, M., & King, R. P. (1992). Recidivism rates of youth completing an intensive treatment program in a juvenile correctional facility. *International Journal of Offender Therapy and Comparative Criminology 36*, 349–358.

Hahlweg, K., & Markman, H. J. (1988). Effectiveness of behavioral marital therapy: Empirical status of behavioral techniques in preventing and alleviating marital distress. *Journal of Consulting and Clinical Psychology 56*, 440–447.

Halford, K. K., Sanders, M. R., & Behrens, B. C. (1994). Self-regulation in behavioral couples' therapy. *Behavior Therapy 25*, 431–452.

Hall, S. M., Hall, R. G., & Ginsberg, D. (1990). Cigarette dependence. In A. Bellack, M. Hersen, and A. Kazdin (Eds.), *International Handbook of Behavior Modification and Therapy* (pp. 437–448). New York: Plenum Press.

Hanson, R. K., Steffy, R. A., & Gauthier, R. (1993). Long-term recidivism of child molesters. *Journal of Consulting and Clinical Psychology 61*, 646–652.

Hawkins, J. D., Jenson, J. M., Catalano, R. F., & Wells, E. A. (1991). Effects of a skill training intervention with juvenile delinquents. *Research on Social Work Practice 1*, 107–121.

Hersen, M. (1990). Single-case experimental designs. In A. Bellack, M. Hersen, and A. Kazdin (Eds.), *International Handbook of Behavior Modification and Therapy* (pp. 175–212). New York: Plenum Press.

Hersen, M., & Van Hasselt, V. B. (1992). Behavioral assessment and treatment of anxiety in the elderly. *Clinical Psychology Review 12*, 619–640.

Hile, M. G., & Derochers, M. N. (1993). The relationship between functional assessment and treatment selection for aggressive behavior. *Research in Developmental Disabilities 14*, 265–274.

Hoberman, H. M., & Clarke, G. N. (1993). Major depression in adults. In R. Ammerman and M. Hersen (Eds.), *Handbook of Behavior Therapy with Children and Adults: A Developmental and Longitudinal perspective* (pp. 73–90). Boston: Allyn and Bacon.

Hodges, V. G. (1994). Home-based behavioral interventions with children and families. In D. K. Granvold (Ed.), *Cognitive and Behavioral Treatment: Methods and Applications* (pp. 90–107). Pacific Grove, CA: Brooks/Cole Publishing Company.

Holroyd, K. A., & Penzien, D. B. (1994). Psychosocial interventions in the management of recurrent headache disorders. Part I: Overview and effectiveness. *Behavioral Medicine 20*, 53–63.

Isreal, A. C. (1990). Childhood obesity. In A. Bellack, M. Hersen, and A. Kazdin (Eds.), *International Handbook of Behavior Modification and Therapy* (pp. 819–830). New York: Plenum Press.

Jacobson, N. S. (1992). Behavioral couple therapy: A new beginning. *Behavior Therapy 23*, 493–506.

Jenson, J. M., & Howard, M. O. (1990). Skills deficits, skills training, and delinquency. *Children and Youth Services Review 12*, 213–228.

Jordan, C., and Franklin, C. (1995). *Clinical Assessment for Social Workers: Quantitative and Qualitative Methods.* Chicago: Lyceum.

Kaplan, M. S., Morales, M., & Becker, J. V. (1993). The impact of verbal satiation of adolescent sex offenders: A preliminary report. *Journal of Child Sexual Abuse 2*, 81–88.

Kazdin, A. E. (1989). *Behavior Modification in Applied Settings* (4th ed.). Homewood, IL: Dorsey.

Kazdin, A. E. (1990). Conduct disorders. In A. Bellack, M. Hersen, and A. Kazdin (Eds.), *International Handbook of Behavior Modification and Therapy* (pp. 669–706). New York: Plenum Press.

Kendall, P. C. (1989). The generalization and maintenance of behavior change: Comments, considerations, and the "no-cure" criticism. Behavior Therapy 20. 357–364.

Kennedy, S. H., Katz, R., Neitzert, C. S., Ralevski, E., & Mendlowitz, S. (1995). Exposure with response treatment of anorexia nervosa-bulimic subtype and bulimia nervosa. *Behaviour Research and Therapy 33*, 685–689.

King, N. J. (1993). Simple and social phobias. *Advances in Clinical Child Psychology 15*, 305–341.

Kirkham, M. A. (1993). Two-year follow-up of skills training with mothers of children with disabilities. *American Journal on Mental Retardation 97*, 509–520.

Landrine, H., & Klonoff, E. (1995). Cultural diversity and the silence of behavior therapy. *The Behavior Therapist 18*(10), 187–189.

Liberman, R. P., Kopelowicz, A., & Young, A. S. (1994). Biobehavioral treatment and rehabilitation of schizophrenia. *Behavior Therapy 25*, 89–107.

Lichstein, K. L., & Riedel, B. W. (1994). Behavioral assessment and treatment of insomnia: A review with an emphasis on clinical applications. *Behavior Therapy 25*, 659–588.

Lipsey, M. W., & Wilson, D. B. (1993). The efficacy of psychological, educational, and behavioral treatment. *American Psychologist 48*, 1181–1209.

Lochman, J. E., & Lenhart, L. A. (1993). Anger coping intervention for aggressive children: Conceptual models and outcome effects. *Clinical Psychology Review 13*, 785–805.

Maag, J. W., & Kotlash, J. (1994). Review of stress inoculation training with children and adolescents. *Behavior Modification 18*, 443–469.

Magen, R. H., & Rose, S. D. (1994). Parents in groups: Problem solving versus behavioral skills training. *Research on Social Work Practice 4*, 172–191.

Marques, J. K., Day, D. M., Nelson, C., & West, M. A. (1994). Effects of cognitive-behavioral treatment on sex offender recidivism: Preliminary results of a longitudinal study. Special Issue: The assessment and treatment of sex offenders. *Criminal Justice and Behavior 21*, 28–54.

Marshall, W. L., Jones, R., Ward, T., Johnston, P., & Barbaree, H. E. (1991). Treatment outcome with sex offenders. *Clinical Psychology Review 11*, 465–485.

Mattaini, M. A. (1993). Behavior analysis and community practice: A review. *Research on Social Work Practice 3*, 420–447.

McEachin, J. J., Smith, T., & Lovaas, O. I. (1993). Long-term outcome for children with autism who receive early intensive behavioral treatment. *American Journal on Mental Retardation 97*, 359–372.

Meadowcroft, P., Thomlison, B., & Chamberlain, P. (1994). A research agenda for treatment foster family care. *Child Welfare* (special issue) *(73)5*, 565–581.

Meichenbaum, D. (1977). *Cognitive Behavior Modification*. New York: Plenum Press.

Mersh, P. P. A. (1995). The treatment of social phobia: The differential effectiveness of exposure *in vivo* and the integration of exposure *in vivo*, rational emotive therapy and social skills training. *Behavioural Research and Therapy 33*, 259–269.

Minde, K., Popiel, K., Leos, N., & Falkner, S. (1993). The evaluation and treatment of sleep disturbances in young children. *Journal of Child Psychology and Psychiatry and Allied Disciplines 34*, 521–533.

Montang, K. R., & Wilson, G. L. (1992). An empirical evaluation of behavioral and cognitive-behavioral group marital treatments with discordant couples. *Journal of Sex and Marital Therapy 18*, 255–272.

Morin, C. M., Winter, B., Besalel, V. A., & Azrin, N. H. (1987). Bulimia: A case illustration of the superiority of behavioral over cognitive treatment. *Journal of Behavior Therapy and Experimental Psychiatry 18*, 165–169.

Morrison, R. L., & Sayers, S. (1993). Schizophrenia in adults. In R. Ammerman and M. Hersen (Eds.), *Handbook of Behavior Therapy with Children and Adults: A Developmental and Longitudinal Perspective* (pp. 295–310). Boston: Allyn and Bacon.

Newman, M. G., Hofman, S. G., Trabert, W., Roth, W. T., & Taylor, C. B. (1994). Does behavioral treatment of social phobia lead to cognitive changes? *Behavior Therapy 25*, 503–517.

Nicholson, N. L., & Blanchard, E. B. (1993). A controlled evaluation of behavioral treatment of chronic headache in the elderly. *Behavioral Therapy 24*, 395–408.

Nixon, C. D., & Singer, G. H. (1993). Group cognitive-behavioral treatment for excessive parental self-blame and guilt. *American Journal on Mental Retardation 97*, 665–672.

Norman, J., & Lowry, C. E. (1995). Evaluating inpatient treatment for women with clinical depression. *Research on Social Work Practice 5*, 10–19.

O'Donnell, C., & Tharpe, R. (1990). Community intervention guided by theoretical development. In A. Bellack, M. Hersen, and A. Kazdin (Eds.), *International Handbook of Behavior Modification and Therapy* (pp. 251–266). New York: Plenum Press.

O'Farrell, T. J. (1994). Marital therapy and spouse-involved treatment with alcoholic patient. *Behavior Therapy 25*, 391–406.

Patterson, G., & Reid, J. (1970). Reciprocity and coercion: Two facets of social systems. In C. Neuringer and J. Michael (Eds.), *Behavior Modification in Clinical Psychology* (pp. 133–177). New York: Appleton-Century-Crofts.

Peled, E., & Edleson, J. L. (1992). Multiple perspectives on group work with children of battered women. *Violence and Victims 7*, 327–346.

Peyrot, M., Yen, S., & Baldassano, C. A. (1994). Short-term substance abuse prevention in jail: A cognitive behavioral approach. *Journal of Drug Education 24*, 33–47.

Polansky, J., & Horan, J. J. (1993). Psychoactive substance abuse in adolescents. In R. Ammerman and M. Hersen (Eds.), *Handbook of Behavior Therapy with Children and Adults: A Developmental and Longitudinal Perspective* (pp. 351–360). Boston: Allyn and Bacon.

Rachmann, S. (1993). A critique of cognitive therapy for anxiety disorders. *Journal of Behavior Therapy and Experimental Psychiatry 24*, 279–288.

Raines, J. C., & Foy, C. W. (1994). Extinguishing the fires within: Treating juvenile firesetters. *Families in Society 75*, 595–607.

Richards, D. A., Lovell, K., & Marks, I. M. (1994). Evaluation of a behavioral treatment program. *Journal of Traumatic Stress 7*, 669–680.

Rohde, P., Lewinsohn, P. M., & Seeley, J. R. (1994). Response of depressed adolescents to cognitive-behavioral treatment: Do differences in initial severity clarify the comparison of treatments? *Journal of Consulting and Clinical Psychology 62*, 851–854.

Rose, S. (1981). Cognitive behavioural modification in groups. *International Journal of Behavioural Social Work and Abstracts 1*(1), 27–38.

Rothman, J., & Thyer, B. A. (1984). Behavioral social work in community and organizational settings. *Journal of Sociology and Social Welfare 11*, 294–326.

Saigh, P. A. (1992). The behavioral treatment of child and adolescent posttraumatic stress disorder. *Advances in Behaviour Research and Therapy 14*, 247–275.

Saunders, R. I., & Saunders, D. N. (1993). Social work practice with a bulimic population: A comparative evaluation of purgers and nonpurgers. *Research on Social Work Practice 3*, 123–136.

Scheibman, L., Koegel, R. L., Charlop, M. H., & Egel, A. L. (1990). Infantile autism. In A. Bellack, M. Hersen, and A. Kazdin (Eds.), *International Handbook of Behavior Modification and Therapy* (pp. 763–789). New York: Plenum Press.

Schwartz, R. (1982). Cognitive-behavior modification: A conceptual review. *Clinical Psychology Review 2*, 267–293.

Scotti, J. R., McMorrow, M. J., & Trawitzki, A. L. (1993). Behavioral treatment of chronic psychiatric disorders: Publication trends and future directions. *Behavior Therapy 24*, 527–550.

Skinner, B. F. (1953). *Science and Human Behavior.* New York: Macmillan.

Skinner, B. F. (1988). The operant side of behavior therapy. *Journal of Behavior Therapy and Experimental Psychiatry 19*, 171–179.

Smith, D. E., Marcus, M. D., & Eldredge, K. L. (1994). Binge eating syndromes: A review of assessment and treatment with an emphasis on clinical application. *Behavior Therapy 25*, 635–658.

Sobell, L. C., Sobell, M. B., & Nirenberg, T. D. (1988). Behavioral assessment and treatment planning with alcohol and drug abusers: A review with an emphasis on clinical application. *Clinical Psychology Review 8*, 19–54.

Steketee, G., & Chambless, D. L. (1992). Methodological issues in prediction of treatment outcome. *Clinical Psychology Review 12*, 387–400.

Stuart, R. B. (1971). Behavioral contracting with families of delinquents. *Journal of Behavior Therapy and Experimental Psychiatry 2*, 1–11.

Stuart, R. B. (Ed.). (1977). *Behavioral Self Management: Strategies, Techniques, and Outcomes.* New York: Brunner/Mazel.

Subramanian, K. (1991). Structured group work for the management of chronic pain: An experimental investigation. *Research on Social Work Practice 1*, 32–45.

Subramanian, K. (1994). Long-term follow-up of a structured group treatment for the management of chronic pain. *Research on Social Work Practice 4*, 208–223.

Sundel, S., & Sundel, M. (1993). *Behavior Modification in the Human Services* (3rd ed.). Newbury Park, CA: Sage.

Sweet, A. A., & Loizeaux, A. L. (1991). Behavioral and cognitive treatment methods: A critical comparative review. *Journal of Behavior Therapy and Experimental Psychiatry 22*, 159–185.

Tallant, S., Rose, S. D., & Tolman, R. M. (1989). New evidence for the effectiveness of stress management training in groups. Special Issue: Empirical research in behavioural social work. *Behavior Modification 13*, 431–446.

Tarrier, N., Beckett, R., Harwood, S., Baker, A., Yusupoff, L., & Ugarteburu, I. (1993). A trial of two cognitive-behavioral methods of treating drug-resistant residual psychotic symptoms in schizophrenic patients. Part I: Outcome. *British Journal of Psychiatry 162*, 524–532.

Thomlison, R. J. (1972). *A Behavioral Model for Social Work Intervention with the Marital Dyad.* Unpublished doctoral dissertation. Toronto: University of Toronto.

Thomlison, R. J. (1981). Behavioral family intervention with the family of a mentally handicapped child. In D. Freeman and B. Trute (Eds.), *Treating Families with Special Needs* (pp. 15–42). Ottawa: Canadian Association of Social Workers.

Thomlison, R. J. (1982). Ethical issues in the use of behavior modification in social work practice. In Shankar Yelaja (Ed.), *Ethical Issues in Social Work.* Springfield, IL: Charles B. Thomas.

Thomlison, R. J. (1984a). Something works: Evidence from practice effectiveness studies. *Social Work 29,* 51–56.

Thomlison, R. J. (1984b). Phobic disorders. In Francis Turner (Ed.), *Adult Psychopathology: A Social Work Perspective* (pp. 280–315). New York: Free Press.

Thomlison, R. J. (1986). Behavior therapy in social work practice. In Francis Turner (Ed.), *Social Work Treatment: Interlocking Theoretical Approaches* (pp. 131–155). New York: Free Press.

Thyer, B. A. (1987a). Behavioral social work: An overview. *Behavior Therapist 10,* 131–134.

Thyer, B. A. (1987b). Community-based self-help groups for the treatment of agoraphobia. *Journal of Sociology and Social Welfare 14,* 135–141.

Thyer, B. A. (1988). Radical behaviorism and clinical social work. In R. Dorfman (Ed.), *Paradigms of Clinical Social Work* (pp. 123–148). New York: Guilford Press.

Thyer, B. A. (1989). Introduction to the special issue. *Behavior Modification 13*(4), 411–414.

Thyer, B. A. (1990). Single-system research designs and social work practice. In L. Sherman and W. J. Reid (Eds.), *Advances in Clinical Social Work Research* (pp. 33–37). Silver Spring, MD: National Association of Social Workers Press.

Thyer, B. A. (1991). Behavioral social work: It is not what you think. *Arete 16,* 1–9.

Thyer, B. A. (1992). Behavior therapies for persons with phobias. In K. Corcoran (Ed.), *Structuring Change. Effective Practice for Common Client Problems* (pp. 31–71). Chicago: Lyceum.

Thyer, B. A., and Boynton Thyer, K. (1992). Single-system research designs in social work practice: A bibliography from 1965 to 1990. *Research on Social Work Practice. 2,* 99–116.

Thyer, B. A., & Maddox, M. K. (1988). Behavioral social work: Results of a national survey on graduate curricula. *Psychological Reports 63,* 239–242.

Tolman, R. M., & Bennett, L. W. (1990). A review of quantitative research on men who batter. *Journal of Interpersonal Violence 5,* 87–118.

Tolman, R. M., & Molidor, C. E. (1994). A decade of social work group work research: Trends in methodology, theory, and program development. *Research on Social Work Practice 4,* 142–159.

Turner, S. M., Beidel, D. C., & Cooley-Quille, M. R. (1995). Two-year follow-up of social phobics with social effectiveness therapy. *Behaviour Research and Therapy 33,* 553–555.

Underwood, L., & Thyer, B. A. (1990). Social work practice with the mentally retarded: Reducing self-injurious behaviors using non-aversive methods. *Arete 15,* 14–23.

Van Der Ploeg-Stapert, J. D., & Van Der Ploeg, H. M. (1986). Behavioral group treatment of test anxiety: An evaluation study. *Journal of Behavior Therapy and Experimental Psychiatry 17,* 255–259.

Van Oppen, P., De Haan, E., Van Balkom, A., Spinhoven, P., Hoogduin, K., & Van Dyck, R. (1995). Cognitive therapy and expose *in vivo* in the treatment of obsessive compulsive disorder. *Behaviour Research and Therapy 33,* 379–390.

Wekerle, C., & Wolfe, D. A. (1993). Prevention of child physical abuse and neglect: Promising new directions. *Clinical Psychology Review 13,* 501–540.

Whisman, M. A. (1990). The efficacy of booster maintenance sessions in behavior therapy: Review and methodological critique. *Clinical Psychology Review 10,* 155–170.

Widner, S., & Zeichner, A. (1993). Psychologic interventions for elderly chronic patients. *Clinical Gerontologist 13,* 3–18.

Wilson, G. T. (1994). Behavioral treatment of obesity: Thirty years and counting. *Advances in Behavior Research and Therapy 16,* 31–75.

Wolf, M., Philips, E., Fixsen, D., Braukmann, C., Kirigin, K., Willner, A., & Schumaker, J. (1976). Achievement Place: The teaching family model. *Child Care Quarterly 5,* 92–103.

Wolfe, D. A., & Wekerle, C. (1993). Treatment strategies for child physical abuse and neglect: A critical progress report. *Clinical Psychology Review 13*, 473–500.

Wolfe, V. V. (1990). Sexual abuse of children. In A. Bellack, M. Hersen, and A. Kazdin (Eds.), *International Handbook of Behavior Modification and Therapy* (pp. 707–730). New York: Plenum Press.

Wolpe, J. (1989). The derailment of behavior therapy: A tale of conceptual misdirection. *Journal of Behavior Therapy and Experimental Psychiatry 20*, 3–15.

Wolpe, J. (1990). *The Practice of Behavior Therapy* (4th ed.). New York: Pergamon Press.

Zimpfer, D. G. (1992). Group work with juvenile delinquents. *Journal for Specialists in Group Work 17*, 116–126.

Reading 13
Conduct Disorder and the Development of Antisocial Behavior

Conduct Disorder
and the Development
of Antisocial Behavior

Conduct disorder has a unique place among the psychopathologies. Not only is the development of the individual with this disorder disrupted, but along the way enormous costs are borne by society and the victims of antisocial acts. Therefore, it is not surprising that more attention has been paid to understanding the development of conduct disorder than any other childhood psychopathology.

Definition and Characteristics

DSM-IV defines **conduct disorder** (CD) as "a repetitive and persistent pattern of behavior in which either the basic rights of others or major age-appropriate societal norms or rules are violated." (See Table 9.1.) Conduct problems may occur in four categories: *aggression toward others, destruction of property, deceitfulness or theft,* and serious *rule violations*.

Severity is specified as *mild* (few conduct problems beyond those necessary to make the diagnosis, and those present cause only minor harm to others); *moderate* (an intermediate number and severity of problems); and *severe* (many conduct problems *or* their effect causes considerable harm to others). DSM-IV further differentiates between conduct problems with a *childhood onset* (prior to age 10) or *adolescent onset* (absence of criteria characteristic of CD prior to age 10), which is an important distinction, as we shall see.

Problem Behavior versus Conduct Disorder Misbehavior is part of normal development, as we know. Therefore, our first task is to determine when behavior problems warrant a diagnosis of CD. DSM-IV specifies that the category should be used only in cases in which the behavior is symptomatic of an *underlying dysfunction in the person* rather than being a reaction to the immediate social environment. DSM-IV suggests that in order to make this judgment the clinician should consider the *social and economic context* in which problem behavior occurs. For example, aggressive behavior may

189

Table 9.1   DSM-IV Criteria for Conduct Disorder

A repetitive and persistent pattern of behavior in which either the basic rights of others or major age-appropriate societal norms or rules are violated, during which at least three of the following are present in the past 12 months:

Aggression to people and animals

(1) Often bullies, threatens, or intimidates others

(2) Often initiates physical fights

(3) Has used a weapon that can cause serious physical harm to others (e.g., a bat, brick, broken bottle, knife, gun)

(4) Has stolen while confronting a victim (e.g., mugging, purse snatching, extortion, armed robbery)

(5) Has been physically cruel to people

(6) Has been physically cruel to animals

(7) Has forced someone into sexual activity

Destruction of property

(8) Has deliberately engaged in fire setting with the intention of causing serious damage

(9) Has deliberately destroyed others' property (other than by fire setting)

Deceitfulness or theft

(10) Has broken into someone else's house, building, or car

(11) Often lies or breaks promises to obtain goods or favors or to avoid obligations (i.e., "cons" others)

(12) Has stolen items of nontrivial value without confronting a victim (e.g., shoplifting, but without breaking and entering; forgery)

Serious violations of rules

(13) Often stays out at night despite parental prohibitions, beginning before 13 years of age

(14) Has run away from home overnight at least twice while living in parental or parental surrogate home (or once without returning for a lengthy period)

(15) Is often truant from school, beginning before 13 years of age

Reprinted with permission from the Diagnostic and Statistical Manual of Mental Disorders, Fourth Edition. Copyright 1994 American Psychiatric Association.

have arisen out of a need for survival in immigrant youth from war-torn countries. Therefore, some youths' misbehavior might represent an adaptation to a deviant environment, rather than a mental disorder. Some concern has been expressed, however, about whether this guideline is sufficient to prevent misdiagnosis of behaviorally troublesome but otherwise normal youth (Richters & Cicchetti, 1993). (See Box 9.1.)

Prevalence   *Prevalence* rates are difficult to pinpoint. (Our review follows Hinshaw and Anderson, 1996, except where noted.) Reported prevalence rates for normative children and adolescents range widely from study to study, from as low as 1 percent to as high as 10 percent. A well-conducted large-scale study in Canada (Offord, Boyle, & Racine, 1991) used DSM criteria to define the disorder. For children ages 4 to 11, the investigators found rates of 6.5 percent for boys and 1.8 percent for girls. For youth 12 to 16 years old, percent rates were 10.4 for boys and 4.1 for girls.

CD is even more prevalent in *clinical samples*: referrals for conduct problems, aggressiveness, and antisocial behavior make up about one-third to one-half of all child and adolescent cases. Because they are observable and are disturbing to others, as Weisz and Weiss (1991) note, conduct problems are among the most "referable" forms of childhood disorder.

Gender Differences   Gender differences are significant. The diagnosis of CD is about four times more common in boys than in girls.

Typologies of Conduct Disorder

Childhood Onset versus Adolescent Onset

As noted above, DSM-IV distinguishes between two types of CD. *Childhood-onset* CD, also termed "life-course persistent" CD (Moffitt, 1993) or "aggressive-versatile" CD (Loeber, 1988), is associated with overt aggression and physical violence and tends to be accompanied by multiple problems, such as neuropsychological deficits, inattention, impulsivity, and poor school performance. It occurs most often in males and is predicted by antisocial behavior in parents and disturbed parent–child relationships. The childhood-onset type is the one most likely to show persistence across the life span.

Adolescent-onset CD, also termed "adolescence-limited" CD (Moffitt, 1993) or "nonaggressive-antisocial" CD (Loeber, 1988), is characterized by

Box 9.1   **"Mark Twain Meets DSM-IV"**

Consider a school-age boy who is habitually truant from school, defies authority, runs away from home, consorts with criminals, and engages in smoking, drinking, and using foul language. Is this a conduct-disordered child, a future criminal, a fledgling psychopath? Not in this case, according to Richters and Cicchetti (1993), for this is a description of a boy named Huckleberry Finn, one of Mark Twain's most well-known creations.

Although developmental psychopathology emphasizes the continuum between normative and pathological development, diagnostic labels require that we place some boundary

between them. Nowhere is there more controversy over where the line should be drawn than in the diagnosis of conduct disorder. The behavioral criteria for the CD diagnosis are extremely wide-ranging, from shoplifting and truancy to murder and rape. While some forms of antisocial activity are in the behavioral repertoire of many of us (even if we have sufficient moxie to avoid being caught), others are outside the normal pale and suggest a psychopathological disturbance.

Richters and Cicchetti are concerned about the ease with which the CD criteria can be applied to children. They point out that some of the best-

loved characters in fiction, such as Huckleberry Finn—and even such real-life characters as Huck's creator, Mark Twain—could be considered deserving of the CD label. Clearly it is important to identify those youths who are emotionally disturbed and whose behavior presages more trouble to come. However, Richters and Cicchetti argue that it is equally important not to pathologize youth who might get into trouble because of characteristics—such as nonconformity, independent-mindedness, and "mischeevousness"—that represent potential sources of resiliency in the long term.

---

normal early development and less severe behavior problems in adolescence, particularly in the form of violence against others. In contrast to the higher prevalence of childhood-onset CD in males, adolescent-onset youth are just as likely to be female (Fergusson, Lynskey, & Horwood, 1996). Fewer comorbid problems and family dysfunctions are seen in comparison to the childhood-onset type.

Moffitt and colleagues (1996) have demonstrated that there are different developmental predictors and consequences of these two subtypes. Longitudinal data were obtained in New Zealand from a representative sample of males who were assessed every two years from ages 3 to 18. The investigators were able to establish a number of ways in which youth with childhood-onset CD could be distinguished from their "late-blooming" peers. A *difficult temperament* at age 3 was a predictor of childhood-onset CD, as was an early history of *aggressiveness* and antisocial behavior. In adolescence, in contrast to other youth, the early starters were more likely to describe themselves as *self-seeking, alienated, callous* toward others, and *unattached* to families. They were also more likely to have committed a *violent crime*: early starters were disproportionately

convicted of such offenses as assault, rape, and use of a deadly weapon. Further, few of those on the childhood-onset pathway evidenced recovery—less than 6 percent avoided developing conduct problems in adolescence.

Troubled youth may seek a sense of belonging and acceptance in an antisocial peer group.

Box 9.2

Case Examples of Conduct Disorder: Social Mimicry versus Psychopathy

Eleven-year-old Angelo was required by the judge to get psychological help or be confined in the juvenile correctional center. The judge was lenient because Angelo was the only member of his gang to get caught breaking into and robbing a corner grocery store. He was caught because he was obviously a not-too-bright follower who was doing what he was told. Yet his loyalty to the gang far outweighs any sense of wrongdoing. And for good reason. School has been an endless series of humiliations and failures. He was passed from grade to grade primarily because he was not a troublemaker, and his teachers be-

came tired of calling him on the carpet for making mistakes and handing in sloppy homework.

His family is large and poor, and while they fight a good deal, they also have a sense of cohesion. The father is a laborer who is hired and fired according to the state of the economy. He is a bitter man who demands respect from his children but sees no reason for them to be good citizens in a society which has treated him so shabbily. His mother—a stressed, careworn woman—prays to the Virgin every night to help her children and wonders where she will get the strength to get through another day. So it is the

gang that gives Angelo a sense of belonging, of sharing, of being valued. While his slowness makes him the goat, the leader has taken a liking to him, and Angelo's fondest dream is to one day become a leader himself.

Mark, another 11-year-old, is a lively, assured, nice-looking, all-American-type boy. Except that, for the past two years, he has been breaking into and robbing houses in the wealthy suburb where he lives. After a robbery was discovered, Mark would show up and offer to help put the house back in order. His manner was one of sincere concern, and he asked for no favors in return. He was

Moffitt (1993) argues that in contrast to their early developing peers, the majority of those with adolescent-onset CD do not deserve a diagnosis at all. Their behavior is best explained as a product of "*social mimicry*," in that they imitate the antisocial actions of others in order to gain status in the peer group. As they reach adulthood, as they have more opportunities to gain status in legitimate ways, their conduct problems generally desist. (Consider the case of Angelo in Box 9.2.)

Destructive/Nondestructive and Overt/Covert

More recent empirical research has pointed to another important distinction, this one based not on age of onset but on the kinds of acts perpetrated by the youth. Frick and colleagues (1993) conducted a meta-analysis of data from 60 factor-analytic studies involving more than 28,000 children. They identified two dimensions on which children's behavior could be distinguished. One dimension concerned whether misbehavior was *destructive* (cruelty to others, assault) or *nondestructive* (swearing,

breaking rules). The second dimension concerned whether behavior problems were *overt* (hitting, fighting, bullying) or *covert* (lying, stealing, destroying property), a distinction that has reliably been made in a number of studies.

Taking these two dimensions into account, the investigators were able to identify four subtypes of conduct-disordered youth, depending on the kind of misbehavior in which they engaged (see Figure 9.1, pg. 194). These were labeled *oppositional* (overt and nondestructive), *aggressive* (overt and destructive), *property violations* (covert and destructive), or *status violations* (covert and nondestructive).

Frick and colleagues (1993) also found that these types could be differentiated in terms of *age of onset*. Those who were primarily oppositional were identified by parents by as early as 4 years of age. Aggressive children, in contrast, demonstrated problems after their sixth year. Those who engaged in property violations showed an average age of onset of about 7½ while those whose misbehavior took the form of status violations had an average age of onset of about 9.

finally caught because a careless remark revealed that he knew an item had been stolen before the owner had mentioned it to anyone outside her family.

Mark is bright, enterprising, and capable beyond his years. But he is also a daredevil in the extreme. He was the youngest boy in his class to smoke marijuana and drink alcohol. He charmed his way into being taught how to drive a car and then bribed the gardener into letting him drive at breakneck speed on the back roads. He enjoys luring younger boys into joining him in venturing into forbidden places—a liquor store, an adult bookstore, an abandoned building—because he likes being in command. While other boys are sporadically attracted to Mark's daring and charm, his friendships are short-lived. In school he is restless and inattentive, except in shop, where his interests and skills make him the top student. He is a master of the sincere lie—looking the teacher straight in the face. One of his teachers said, "I just can't reach him. I could beat him or plead with him or cuddle him, and it just wouldn't matter."

Mark's father, a successful surgeon, has little time for his family during the week but enjoys being with his son on weekends. In his eyes, Mark can do no wrong. Even the robberies were extenuated: "Wild colts make good horses." Mark's mother is a kind and loving woman but lacking in resources. Early on she perceived Mark's disregard for her prohibitions concerning dangerous objects and activities, and she did not know what to do about his constant lying. Affection and reasoning gave way to angry shouts and finally to whippings. Mark was determined not to cry; he sensed that if she could not hurt him, she would be powerless. He was right, and the whippings gave way to resignation and withdrawal.

Psychopathy

An additional category has been necessitated by recent research on **psychopaths** (sometimes referred to as sociopaths). Hare (1996) has found that, among those with antisocial behavior, there is a subset who exhibit psychopathic personality traits. These include *callousness* (a lack of remorse, empathy, or guilt), *egocentricity, superficial charm, impulsivity, shallow emotions, manipulativeness*, and an *absence of meaningful relationships*. Psychopaths are individuals who commit antisocial acts against others not out of necessity—they do not rob because they are poor or strike out at others to defend themselves—but because they derive pleasure from hurting or manipulating other people. They exhibit a lack of awareness of other people as fellow human beings deserving of consideration or compassion. They are, in short, "without conscience" (Hare, 1993). (Consider the case of Mark in Box 9.2.)

Hare believes that ordinary antisocial behavior and psychopathy have different developmental origins. For example, while antisocial behavior *without* psychopathy is predicted by childhood adversity, psychopathy *alone* is not. This has led Hare to suspect that psychopathy derives from an innate predisposition. For example, brain scan imagery shows that psychopaths process information about emotions differently than do nonpsychopaths. Ordinarily, when people process information about emotionally meaningful words such as "love," the frontal cortex is activated, showing that the information is being processed at a deep level and many complex associations are being made. In contrast, the processing of a word with little emotional significance, such as "lamp," will not be associated with frontal activity. However, psychopaths process words having to do with feelings and relationships at the same shallow level that they do words about inanimate objects (Williamson, Harpur, & Hare, 1991). Consequently, Hare hypothesizes, psychopathy may have its origins in the "hard wiring" of the brain.

Can children be psychopaths? Evidence is accumulating that psychopathic youth can be identified (Lynam, 1997). For example, Frick and associates (1994) developed a child version of Hare's device for detecting psychopathic traits, the Psychopathy

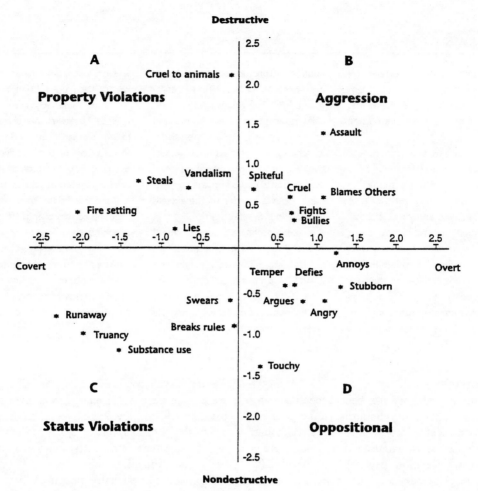

Figure 9.1   Meta-Analytic Factor Analysis of Child Conduct Problems.

Source: Frick et al., 1993

Checklist. Just as with Hare's studies of adults, they found two separate dimensions of behavior, one concerned with antisocial behavior, termed *impulsivity/conduct problems* and the other reflecting *callousness/unemotionality*. Consistent with the adult research, psychopathic traits in children and adolescents are related to the violence of their offenses and are predictive of the likelihood that they will reoffend (Forth, Hart, & Hare, 1990). Further, consistent with Hare's hypothesis about the distinct etiology of psychopathy, Wootton and colleagues (1997) found that ordinary conduct problems in children were predicted by ineffective parenting whereas psychopathic callousness/unemotionality was not.

Comorbidity

CD frequently co-occurs with other disturbances. (Here we follow Hinshaw and Anderson, 1996, excepted where noted.) *Attention-deficit hyperactivity disorder* (ADHD) and *oppositional-defiant disorder* (ODD) are the diagnostic categories most commonly associated with CD. Youths with comorbid ADHD and CD also are among the most disturbed. They display higher rates of physical aggression, more persistent behavior problems, poorer school achievement, and more rejection from peers than the "pure" CD type.

Learning disorders are associated with CD, particularly reading disorder. In some youth, learning problems may lead to frustration, oppositional attitudes, and misbehavior in school, and thus to a diagnosis of CD. However, as we saw in Chapter 6, the weight of the evidence argues that learning disorders do not lead to CD, but rather that a third variable accounts for the relationship between them. *ADHD* youth are overrepresented amongst those who have both conduct and learning disorders, and it may be the overlap of these disorders with ADHD that accounts for their co-occurrence.

Depression is highly correlated with CD. As we saw in Chapter 7, Capaldi's (1992) longitudinal research suggests that antisocial behavior in boys leads to academic failures and peer rejection, which lead, in turn, to depression. Comorbid depression and CD is of particular concern in that it is disproportionately associated with suicide. Finally, CD also co-occurs with *substance abuse* and may be a precursor to it, as we discuss in Chapter 11.

There is a *gender difference* in that comorbidity is most common in girls. Although girls develop CD less often than boys overall, when they do it is more likely to take a comorbid form (Loeber & Keenan, 1994). In particular, while *depression and anxiety* frequently occur in conduct-disordered youth, girls demonstrate higher rates of comorbidity with these internalizing problems. As we saw in our discussion of depression (Chapter 7), these different comorbidities might in fact represent different subtypes of CD.

Developmental Course

There is a high degree of *continuity* in conduct-disordered behavior. Large-scale epidemiological studies in the United States and other countries have established stability from preschool age to middle childhood (Campbell, 1997), from childhood to adolescence (Lahey et al., 1995), from adolescence to adulthood (Farrington, 1995), and, most impressively, from infancy to adulthood (Newman et al., 1997). Thus, the developmental course is a persistent one, and the prognosis poor. For example, Fergusson, Horwood, and Lynskey (1995) found that, over a two-year period, only 14 percent of children diagnosed with CD evidenced remission.

Researchers also have looked more closely at the developmental unfolding of problem behavior. Generally, a sequential progression is found such that one form of problem behavior virtually always occurs before the emergence of another. Relying on reconstructive data, Loeber and colleagues (1992) found an *"invariant sequence"* across development: from *hyperactivity-inattention* to *oppositional* behavior, and then to *conduct problems*. Combining Loeber's research with other work on the precursors

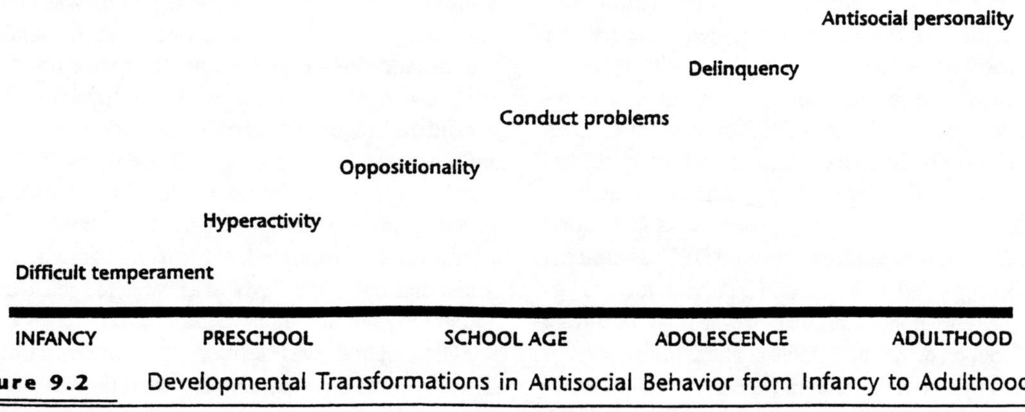

Figure 9.2   Developmental Transformations in Antisocial Behavior from Infancy to Adulthood.

and sequelae of conduct problems, we can construct a developmental model tracing the sequencing of behavior problems from difficult temperament in the early years to antisocial personality in adulthood. (See Figure 9.2.)

As youth progress through this sequence, they tend to maintain their prior antisocial behaviors; therefore, because behaviors are retained rather than replaced, the developmental progression is better described as one of *accretion* rather than succession. However, the fact that this sequence exists does not mean that all individuals are fated to go through all the steps. On the contrary, while most individuals progress to different stages of increasing seriousness of antisocial behavior, few progress through all of them.

On the other hand, as Loeber and Stouthamer-Loeber (1998) note, *discontinuity* in CD also can be found. For example, some studies show desistance rates from preschool to schoolage of about 25 percent. Although it appears that these are youth with less serious behavior problems, little is known about the factors that account for their ceasing their antisocial behavior. However, as longitudinal research on the precursors and consequences of CD has emerged, distinct developmental pathways have been identified over the life span, which we describe next.

Early Childhood: Pathways from ADHD to Conduct Disorder

As noted above, a number of studies have confirmed the link between CD and ADHD (Lahey et al., 1995). Symptoms of ADHD appear to increase the risk for childhood-onset CD, to be associated with more severe behavior problems, and to result in greater resistance to change. Thus, ADHD propels youth to an earlier onset of behavior problems, which is predictive, in turn, of a longer-lasting antisocial career.

ADHD does not lead irrevocably to CD, however. Only those children whose ADHD symptoms are accompanied by *antisocial behavior* such as aggression and noncompliance are at risk for future CD (Loeber & Keenan, 1994). Thus, in this case it appears that ADHD potentiates early conduct problems, hastening them on the way to full-blown CD.

Middle Childhood: Pathways from Oppositionality to Conduct Disorder

ODD, as described in Chapter 5, is characterized by persistent age-inappropriate displays of anger and defiance. While ODD and CD share some similar behavioral features and risk factors, the two syndromes can be distinguished from one another. As Figure 9.1 shows, large-scale meta-analyses of children's problem behavior reveal a unique factor comprising the kind of overt, nondestructive behaviors that define ODD. ODD also emerges earlier in development than CD, with an average age of onset of 6 years for oppositionality as compared to 9 years for conduct problems (Loeber et al., 1992).

Loeber and colleagues (1993) found that CD was almost universally preceded by ODD. In addition, the most severely disturbed children were likely to retain features of oppositionality in addition to acquiring CD symptoms (Lahey et al., 1995). Therefore, there is convincing evidence for a developmental progression from ODD to CD.

Late Childhood and Adolescence: Divergent Pathways

Loeber and colleagues (1993) used prospective data from a longitudinal study of high-risk boys in order to investigate the *developmental pathways* predictive of later problem behavior. Basing their thinking on previous research differentiating CD along the dimensions of overt/covert and destructive/nondestructive, they derived three distinct types (see Figure 9.3).

The first identified was the *authority conflict* pathway. The behavior of these youths was characterized by defiance, stubborn and oppositional behavior, and rule violations such as truancy and running away. While disruptive, these behaviors were considered to be less serious because they did not inflict direct harm on others. Those whose behavior escalated in the authority conflict pathway tended to have continual conflicts with adults, but they were not likely to develop other forms of aggressive and antisocial behavior. They also were the least likely to become labeled delinquent.

The second was termed the *covert* pathway. These youths engaged in minor and nonviolent acts such as shoplifting, joyriding, and vandalism. Esca-

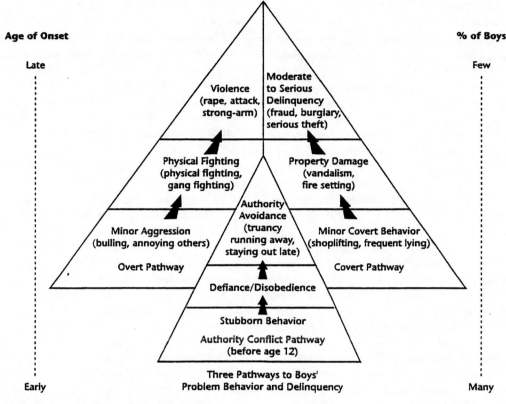

Figure 9.3   Developmental Pathways to Conduct Disorder.

Source: Loeber and Keenan, 1994

lation in this pathway involved progressing to more serious forms of property crime and theft in later adolescence but was rarely associated with violence or more severe kinds of antisocial behavior.

The third, the *overt* pathway, was composed of children who exhibited aggression early in childhood. Escalation in this pathway was associated with progression from aggression to fighting to more serious assaults and violence against others. The overt pathway was linked to high rates of criminal offenses in adolescence. In addition, these youths were likely to add covert forms of aggression to their repertoire as their careers proceeded. *Dual overt/covert* pathway youth were more likely to become delinquents; however, the worst outcomes were seen in *triple-pathway* youth—those who showed a combination of overt and covert aggression, as well as authority conflict.

Loeber and Stouthamer-Loeber (1998) point out that not all youth who demonstrate conduct problems have a childhood history of aggression and antisocial behavior. Thus, in this developmental period arises the *adolescent-onset*, or late-onset, type. These youths have been neglected in previous studies of developmental psychopathology, perhaps because their numbers are fewer, but also perhaps because, by the time they have begun acting out in adolescence, they are not distinguishable from their early-onset peers. Therefore, attention to the youth's early developmental history is imperative to accurate identification of these subtypes. In contrast to the undercontrolled, early onset conduct-disordered child, these may be "overcontrolled offenders" in whom problem behavior is sparked by emotional distress.

Late Adolescence: Pathways to Antisocial Personality and Criminality

Two conclusions can be drawn from the research linking CD to adult *antisocial personality disorder* and criminal behavior. First, *looking backward*, we find that antisocial adults almost without exception met the criteria for CD earlier in their development. However, one of the criteria for the diagnosis of antisocial personality disorder is onset of problem behavior before age 15, so this is a link that is structured into the diagnostic criteria. Secondly, *looking forward*, we find that only a minority of conduct-disordered youths go on to develop the chronic and disabling patterns characteristic of the adult diagnosis.

The characteristics predictive of those who do go on to develop antisocial personality disorder include early age of onset and diverse, persistent conduct problems in childhood, including aggression and antisocial behavior. As we have seen previously, *age of onset* is one of the most significant predictors of the subsequent seriousness of antisocial behavior. Children with early onset have both a higher level of disruptive behavior and progress more rapidly to more serious problems (Loeber et al., 1992). There is clear evidence that those who begin their antisocial activities before the teenage years will continue to commit a large number of offenses at a high rate over a long period of time.

A landmark study by Magnusson and Bergman (1990) provides a unique glimpse into the sequences leading up to the development of CD in late adolescence. They utilized a remarkable longitudinal data set—3,244 male children drawn from a Swedish community and followed from childhood to adulthood. Some of the findings were to be expected: boys with no problems at 13 years of age had few problems as adults, while aggression and hyperactivity predicted later criminality. It was the *multiple-problem boys* who became disturbed adults: about half those with four to five problems became criminals, for example. The unexpected finding was that none of the variables—even aggression—predicted adult antisocial behavior by themselves. It was only when aggression was accompanied by *hyperactivity* that it predicted criminality, and only as poor peer relations were accompanied by several other problem behaviors that it also became predictive.

In sum, aggression is a risk factor for the development of antisocial personality disorder in adulthood. However, while aggression may be stable, Magnusson and Bergman found that aggression predicts criminal behavior in adulthood when it is accompanied by hyperactivity or is part of multiple problems. The further an individual has progressed along a path of antisocial behavior, the more likely continuity will be demonstrated.

Discontinuity   Not all aggressive youth go on to become antisocial adults. While most adult antisocial behavior is rooted in childhood, only half of the at-risk children grow up to be antisocial adults (Loeber & Hay, 1997). It is also important to understand the factors that account for this discontinuity. With this in mind, Kolvin and coworkers (1989) conducted a longitudinal study of the *protective factors* shielding high-risk boys from adult delinquency. They found that a number of factors were important and that they played different roles in different developmental periods. For the first five years, good parental care, positive social circumstances, and few adverse experiences (e.g., accidents) were protective. Protective factors in the preadolescent period included parental supervision, absence of developmental delays, relatively good intelligence and academic achievement, easy temperament, good peer relations and prosocial activities. More recently, Hoge, Andrews, and Leschied (1996) compiled a virtually identical list of protective factors in adolescence.

Gender Differences in Developmental Pathways

It is notable that almost all of the longitudinal studies cited have been based exclusively on males. What about *female* developmental trajectories? Because most CD appears in boys, the greater attention focused on males is justified to some extent. However, only by including girls in the research can we determine whether or not they are at reduced risk or have a different developmental course.

Of interest is the fact that girls are underrepresented amongst virtually all of the disorders that co-occur with—or are precursors to—CD, including oppositional defiance, ADHD, and learning dis-

Relational aggression.

orders. Various theoretical perspectives have been offered to explain this gender difference, summarized by Eme and Kavanaugh (1995). Some have argued that males are more biologically vulnerable to neuropsychological deficits that might underlie all these disorders. Others point to socialization factors, including parental reinforcement of aggressive behavior in boys and nurturance in girls, same-sex role modeling of aggression, and the peer group, which enforces sex-role stereotypic behavior such as an assertive-dominant style in males. Others hypothesize that girls misbehave in less overt ways. For example, while boys are more likely than girls to engage in physical aggression, girls engage in *relational aggression*: attempting to hurt others by ridiculing them, excluding them from the peer group, withdrawing friendship, and spreading rumors (Crick & Grotpeter, 1995).

Conduct-disordered girls and boys also tend to be identified on the basis of different kinds of behavior problems. Fighting and theft are the most frequent reasons for referring boys, while *covert antisocial activities* such as truancy are more often the cause for concern about girls (Zahn-Waxler, 1993).

Gender also appears to be a factor in *age of onset*. While boys and girls tend to go through the same sequence of behavior problems in the progression toward CD, these misbehaviors have a later onset in girls than in boys. Antisocial behavior usually starts at age 8 to 10 for boys, while for girls it generally does not appear until age 14 to 16 (Kazdin, 1997a).

Developmental factors also come into play in other gender-differentiated ways. For example, *sex-ual maturation* is a powerful predictor of antisocial behavior for girls. Girls who develop early tend to engage in more norm-violating behavior, such as staying out late without parental permission, cheating on exams, being truant, taking drugs, and having unprotected sex (Simmons & Blyth, 1987). The reason for this appears to be that early maturing girls spend more time with older peers who involve them precociously in risk-taking behavior, as we will explore further when we discuss peer influences.

Despite these gender differences in prevalence, there is also evidence that, for those girls who do develop CD, the *continuity* is equivalent to that seen in boys. Bardone and colleagues (1996) found that among girls, CD at age 15 predicted antisocial behavior, substance dependence, and poor achievement in young adulthood.

Etiology

The Intrapersonal Context

As we have seen, there is a continuum between normalcy and psychopathology, and deviations in fundamental developmental processes underlie many disorders. Therefore, to better understand what has gone awry in the development of those children who come to be labeled "conduct-disordered," it will be helpful to review what is known about some of the major developmental variables underlying problem behavior: aggression, self-control, perspective taking, and interpersonal problem solving.

Aggression CD is a syndrome or complex of behaviors; therefore, aggression does not define it any more than a sad mood defines depression. Indeed, aggression is part of normal development, and there is no reason for assuming that a "hothead" or a "scrapper" has CD if other aspects of his or her personality are proceeding apace. However, aggression is a major part of the picture of CD and accounts for the symptoms that raise the most concern in those who attempt to intervene with antisocial youth. Therefore, it is important to consider the natural course of aggression and its role in normative and pathological development.

Olweus's (1979) landmark review of sixteen longitudinal studies of aggression in boys sets the stage. Olweus concludes that there is a substantial degree of *continuity* in aggression over time; indeed, it seems to be as stable as intelligence. He summarizes the findings with a simple formula: the younger the subject and the longer the interval of time between evaluations, the less the stability. Thus, over the same interval of time, a 2-year-old's aggressiveness will vary more than that of a 10-year-old; and at any given age, predictability decreases with the passage of time. By the time a boy is 8 or 9, there is a substantial correlation with aggressive patterns ten to fourteen years later; by 12 to 13 years of age, the stability is even higher for the next 10 years and is a powerful predictor of later aggression.

The stability of aggressive behavior in the face of development and environmental variation leads Olweus to conclude that it arises from an inherent tendency or motivational system within the individual. In other words, rather than reacting to environmental provocation, highly aggressive children may actively seek out conflicts in order to express their impulses.

Loeber (1991) summarizes research on the factors associated with the *persistence* of aggression. In general, these are early onset; extremely high rates of such behavior; occurrence in more than one setting, such as home, school, and community; and multiple problem behaviors.

What about *discontinuity*—is aggression "outgrown"? Data to answer this question come from Kohn's (1977) five-year longitudinal study of 1,232 preschoolers. Kohn asked teachers to rate aggressive traits in children, including open defiance with teachers, hostility, and aggression with other children. While aggressiveness was highly consistent over the five-year period, the correlation of .36 was sufficiently low to indicate that a good deal of change was also taking place. Analysis of the data revealed that 59 percent of those high in aggressiveness during preschool were no longer disturbed in the fourth grade; moreover, 14 percent of the highest-scoring aggressive children were subsequently among the most well-functioning fourth graders. In contrast, 13 percent of the children whose behavior was positively rated during preschool were now extremely aggressive.

Self-Control   Self-control is essential to normative functioning, and the expectations placed on children to control their impulses increase with age. While we might not be surprised to see a 4-year-old have a temper tantrum on the floor of the grocery store when denied an ice cream cone, such behavior in a 14-year-old would raise a few eyebrows. However, the 4-year-old is still expected to refrain from attacking a sibling in a rage, masturbating in a restaurant, or trying out a new toy hammer on the stereo set. Early socialization of self-control is particularly important because toddlers and preschoolers have a strong desire for immediate gratification of their aggressive, sexual, and exploratory urges, and they tend to be egocentric and self-seeking. However, objective studies confirm that conduct-disordered children evidence a limited ability to delay impulses and tolerate frustration (see Hinshaw and Anderson, 1996).

Kochanska and Aksan (1995) have conducted studies devoted to uncovering the roots of self-control in young children, which they view as an outgrowth of the internalization of parental values (see Chapter 2). The researchers placed young children in a laboratory situation in which they were given time alone in a room with an attractive toy that their mothers had forbidden them to touch; self-control was indicated by their ability to resist the temptation. Those children who showed "committed compliance"—an eager and wholehearted endorsement of their mother's values, as opposed to mere obedience—were those who had experienced the most *mutually positive* affect in the parent–child relationship.

Further, Kochanska's (1997) research has shown that specific parenting styles are optimal for promoting self-control in children with different temperaments. Using longitudinal data, she found that for children assessed as fearful in toddlerhood, a gentle maternal discipline style was most effective. However, for children assessed as fearless, gentleness was not sufficient. Instead, mothers needed to heighten their emotional bond with children in order to foster the motivation to accept and internalize parental values. Therefore, conscience development in temperamentally difficult children, who are at risk for CD, may require the most *intensely involved* and *emotionally available* parenting—the kind they are least likely to receive.

Emotion Regulation   *Emotion regulation* is a specific aspect of self-control that has been implicated in the development of CD (Cole et al., 1996). Children chronically exposed to family adversity, poor parenting, and high levels of conflict, as we saw in Chapter 7, are overwhelmed by strong emotions and receive little help in managing them from stressed and unskilled parents. Therefore, they are at risk for failing to develop adequate strategies for coping with their negative emotions and regulating their expression. Consistent with this idea, research has shown that conduct-disordered children have difficulty managing strong affects, particularly anger, and that children with poor emotion regulation skills are more likely to respond aggressively to interpersonal problems (Eisenberg et al., 1997).

As was pointed out in Chapter 2, however, emotion regulation may involve not only underregulation but also overregulation. A good example of this can be found in Cole, Zahn-Waxler, and Smith's (1994) study. In order to obtain a sample of preschoolers at risk for developing CD, they specifically recruited children who were noncompliant, aggressive, and hard to manage. As expected, at-risk boys were more likely to respond to frustration by directing displays of negative affect to the experimenters, and they had more difficulty managing their anger. Poor emotion regulation, in turn, was related to symptoms of disruptive behavior and oppositionality. For girls, however, *overcontrol* of negative emotions predicted CD symptoms. Attempting to put too tight a lid on anger may cause it simply to spill over at a later time.

Perspective Taking, Moral Development, and Empathy   Piaget (1967) observed that one of the pivotal developments in the transition to middle childhood is decentering; that is, shifting from cognitive egocentrism—in which the world is viewed primarily from the child's own vantage point—to cognitive perspectivism—in which a situation can be seen from the diverse views of the individuals involved and their rights and feelings taken into account. **Perspective taking**, the ability to see things from others' point of view, is fundamental to the development of moral reasoning and empathy, both of which can counter the tendency to behave in antisocial and aggressive ways.

Research attests to the fact that aggressive and conduct-disordered youth are delayed in the development of these cognitive and affective variables. In contrast to their nondelinquent peers, juvenile delinquents are more cognitively immature in their *moral reasoning* (Smetana, 1990). In addition, conduct-disordered youth are less *empathic*, as well as being less accurate in reading the emotions of others when compared to their nondisturbed peers (Cohen & Strayer, 1996). Happe and Frith (1996) go so far as to propose that a conduct-disordered youth's lack of social insight and understanding of other people's mental states is akin to the deficits in *theory of mind* seen in autistic children. Accordingly, conduct-disordered youth tend to misperceive the motives of others and to exhibit distortions in their reasoning about social situations, both of which increase the likelihood that they will respond in an aggressive manner. We next turn to these social cognitive dimensions underlying problem behavior.

Social Cognition   Eron and Huesmann (1990), in musing about the stability of aggression across time and generations, state: "The frightening implication of this intractable consistency is that aggression is not situation specific or determined solely by the contingencies. The individual carries around something inside that impels him or her to act in a characteristically aggressive or nonaggressive way" (pp. 152–153). They conclude that underlying aggression are *cognitive schemata*: scripts for interpreting and responding to events that are derived from past experiences and are used to guide future behavior.

Some evidence suggests that children with CD have distinctive *social-information processing* styles (Crick and Dodge, 1994). For example, aggressive children misattribute aggressive intent to others when in an ambiguous situation, are insensitive to social cues that might help them more correctly interpret others' intentions, and respond impulsively on the basis of their faulty assumptions. In addition, these children are able to generate few alternatives for solving interpersonal problems, and they have positive expectations of the outcomes of aggression.

These social-information processing patterns have also been shown to account for the relationship between early experiences of maltreatment and later childhood aggression (Dodge et al., 1995). Harsh and abusive parenting appears to instill in children a generalized belief that others are hostile and have malicious intent toward them, an assumption that is verified each time they engage in negative exchanges with parents, peers, and others. Therefore, children come to internalize their experiences of family violence in ways that are deeply ingrained in their personalities and behavioral repertoires, replete with complex cognitive rationales that insure consistency in their behavior.

Selman and Schultz (1988) have proposed a model of the cognitive developmental processes underlying the ability to resolve interpersonal problems without resorting to aggression. Parallel to Kohlberg's stages of morality, the development of *interpersonal negotiation strategies* (INS) proceeds from lower to higher levels of cognitive complexity and comprehensiveness. Selman and Schultz delineate four stages of INS, which have both a thinking (cognitive) and a doing (action) component. (See Table 9.2.) The stages progress from physical aggression or withdrawal at Stage 0, to assertive ordering or submissive obedience at Stage 1, to persuasion and deference at Stage 2, and, finally, to collaboration at Stage 3.

Another contribution to understanding the cognitive basis for children's aggression and behavior problems has been made by Shure and Spivack (1988). They delineate the following cognitive components to *interpersonal problem solving* (IPS): a sensitivity to human problems, an ability to imagine alternative courses of action, an ability to conceptualize the means to achieve a given end, consideration of consequences, and an understanding of cause and effect in human relations.

There is a developmental unfolding of the components related to IPS. In the preschool period, *generating alternative solutions* to problems such as, "What could you do if your sister were playing with a toy you wanted?" is the single most significant predictor of interpersonal behavior in a classroom setting. Children who generate fewer alternatives are rated by their teachers as disruptive, disrespectful, and defiant, and unable to wait to take turns. In middle childhood, alternative thinking is still related to classroom adjustment, while *means–end thinking*

Table 9.2   Selman and Schultz's INS

Stage 0: Impulsive. The strategies are primitive—for example, based on fight or flight—and show no evidence of perspective taking. Either extremes of aggressiveness (e.g., "Tell him to screw off!") or passivity (e.g., "Just do what he says!") would be at this level.

Stage 1: Unilateral. Strategies here show an awareness of the other person's point of view and of the conflict that exists, but strategies are based on assertions of the child's needs or wants (e.g., "Tell him you are not going to show up") or simple accommodation (e.g., "He's the boss, so you've got to do what he says").

Stage 2: Self-reflective and reciprocal. Strategies are now based on reciprocal exchanges, with an awareness of the other party's point of view. However, negotiations are designed to protect the interests of the child: for example, "He'll help the boss out this time, and then the boss will owe him one."

Stage 3: Collaborative. The child or adolescent is now able to view the situation objectively, taking his or her own and the other person's perspective into account and recognizing that negotiations are necessary for the continuity of the relationship: for example, "The boss and he have to work it out together, so they might as well talk out their differences."

Source: Selman and Schultz, 1988.

emerges as an equally important correlate. For instance, when presented with the problem of a boy's feeling lonely after moving to a new neighborhood, the well-adjusted child can think not only of different solutions but also of ways to implement the solutions and overcome the obstacles involved, such as saying, "Maybe he could find someone who liked to play Nintendo like he does, but he'd better not go to a kid's house at suppertime or his mother might get mad!" Again, impulsive and inhibited children are deficient in these cognitive skills.

The data on adolescence are meager but suggest that means–end thinking and alternative thinking continue to be correlated with good adjustment. The new component to IPS involves *considering consequences* or weighing the pros and cons of potential action: "If I do X, then someone else will do Y and that will be good (or bad)." Thus the developing child is able to utilize progressively advanced cognitive skills to solve interpersonal problems.

The Interpersonal Context: Family Influences

Attachment   Insecure attachments with parents in infancy have been linked prospectively to pre-school behavior problems such as hostility, oppositionality, and defiance. However, insecure attachment relationships predict elementary school aggression in girls but not boys, and these predictions are influenced by a number of other factors related to family adversity and environmental stress. As Greenberg, Speltz, and Deklyen (1993) conclude, the research to date has not established a direct effect of attachment on antisocial behavior, although a poor parent–child relationship is a clear risk factor for the development of psychopathology in general.

Family Discord   First, looking at whole-family processes, we find that family discord is fertile soil for producing antisocial acting out, especially in boys (Shaw et al., 1994). In particular, children exposed to *family violence* are more likely to develop behavior problems (Jouriles et al., 1996). Children exposed to violence in the home also start delinquent careers at an earlier age and perpetrate more serious offenses (Kruttschnitt & Dornfeld, 1993). Further, the children are often the targets of their parents' aggression; e.g., youths with CD are more likely to have been victims of *child maltreatment* (Dodge et al., 1994).

CD is also associated with nonviolent forms of *interparental conflict* (Cummings & Davies, 1994b) and *divorce* (Emery & Kitzmann, 1995). However, it is not coming from a "broken home" per se that leads to child behavior problems, but rather the turmoil and disruptions in parent–child relationships surrounding marital dissolution that increase the likelihood of antisocial acting out, as we explore in more detail in Chapter 14.

Boys growing up in *single-parent* households are also at risk. Vaden-Kiernan and colleagues (1995) found that, once family income, neighborhood, and earlier aggressive behavior were taken into account, boys with a father or father-figure in the home were less likely to be rated as aggressive than boys in mother-only families. No such relationship between family type and aggression was found for girls. On the other hand, there is evidence that boys are rarely juvenile delinquents in mother-alone families if the mother has good parenting skills and the parent–child relationship is a supportive one (McCord, 1990). Again, it is not the family structure that matters so much as the emotional quality of relationships within the family.

Family stress also increases the likelihood of CD. Children who develop behavior problems are more likely to come from families that have experienced more negative life events, daily hassles, unemployment, financial hardship, moves, and other disruptions. In addition, the family members of disruptive children have few sources of social support and engage in chronic conflict with others in the community (McMahon & Estes, 1997). However, it may be that family stress is not a direct cause of antisocial behavior but rather that it acts as an amplifier of other problematic parent–child relationship processes (Dishion, French, & Patterson, 1995).

Parent Psychopathology   Parental *substance abuse*, especially in fathers, is predictive of CD in children. *Maternal depression* has also been linked to child conduct problems, as well as a number of other kinds of maladjustment (Cummings & Davies, 1994a).

The most powerful parent-related predictor of CD in children is parent *antisocial personality disorder*, which increases both the incidence and the persistence of the CD. For example, Lahey and colleagues (1995) conducted a four-year prospective study of 171 children diagnosed with CD. Parental antisocial personality disorder was correlated with CD at the first assessment and, in combination with boys' verbal intelligence, predicted the continuation of conduct problems in later development. How does parent personality translate into child behavior problems? This question concerns us next.

Harsh Parenting and the Intergenerational Transmission of Aggression   There is strong evidence for the *intergenerational transmission* of aggression. Aggression is not only stable within a single generation but across generations as well. Eron and Huesmann (1990) conducted a 22-year prospective study, compiling data on 82 participants when they were 8 and 30 years of age, as well as collecting information from their parents and 8-year-old children. Strong associations were seen between grandparents', parents', and children's aggressiveness. The correlation between the aggression parents had shown at age 8 and that displayed by their children was remarkably high (.65), higher even than the consistency in parents' own behavior across the lifespan.

While the mechanisms responsible for the continuity of this behavior are not clear, Eron and Huesmann believe it is learned through *modeling*. As noted above, children who have antisocial parents are exposed to models of aggressive behavior, including interparental violence and child maltreatment. However, the aggression need not be so extreme in order to provide a model. For example, adult antisocial behavior is predicted by *harsh punishment* received as a child (Eron & Huesmann, 1990). In adulthood, those punished harshly as children were more likely endorse using severe discipline in child rearing—in fact, their responses to parenting style questionnaires were strikingly similar to the ones given by their own parents 22 years earlier.

Corresponding results have been obtained regarding the relationship between *spanking* and child aggression. Straus, Sugarman, and Gile-Sims (1997) followed a nationally representative sample of over 800 children ages 6 to 9 over a two-year period and found that spanking was associated with increased aggression and antisocial behavior. Childhood corporal punishment also increases the risk that men will become spousal batterers in adulthood (Straus & Yodanis, 1996). In sum, through their observations of their own parents, children learn that the rule governing interpersonal relationships is "might makes right."

Parenting Inconsistency   Other research indicates that it is not only the severity of parental discipline but also a pattern of *parental inconsistency*—an inconsistent mix of harshness and laxness—that is related to antisocial acting out. Laxness may be evidenced in a number of ways: lack of supervision, parents being unconcerned with the children's whereabouts, absence of rules concerning where the children can go and whom they can be with. These are parents who, when phoned by researchers and asked, "It is 9 P.M.; do you know where your child is right now?" do not know the answer (Forgatch, 1994).

Coercion Theory   Patterson, Reid, and Dishion (1992) have carried out an important program of research on the family origins of conduct disorder. Based on social learning theory, they set out to investigate the factors that might train antisocial behavior in children. They found that parents of antisocial children were more likely than others to *positively reinforce* aggressive behavior—for example, by regarding it as amusing. They also observed that these parents exhibited inconsistent outbursts of anger and punitiveness, and made harsh threats with no follow-through, both of which were ineffectual in curbing negative behavior. On the other side of the coin, children's prosocial behavior was either ignored or reinforced noncontingently. Therefore, the investigators conclude that CD is initiated and sustained in the home by maladaptive parent–child interactions.

Patterson's most important contribution was to analyze the interactions of antisocial children and their parents in terms of what he calls coercive family processes. By **coercion**, Patterson means negative behavior on the part of one person that is supported or directly reinforced by another person. These interactions are transactional and reciprocal; they involve both parent and child, whose responses to one another influence each other's behavior. For example, Patterson notes that the families of normal and CD children have different ways of responding to each other. When punished by parents, CD children are twice as likely as normal children to persist in negative behavior. This is because their family members tend to interact through the use of *negative reinforcement*. Unlike punishment, in which an unpleasant stimulus is applied in order to decrease a behavior, negative reinforcement increases the likelihood of a behavior by removing an unpleasant stimulus as the reward.

To illustrate this concept, consider the scenario presented in Figure 9.4. Who is reinforcing whom? Calvin has learned that if he behaves aversively

Figure 9.4   Coercion.

when his father says no, he can get his way—his father has inadvertently *positively reinforced* him for misbehaving. His father, in turn, has been *negatively reinforced* for giving Calvin what he wants when he misbehaves—he is rewarded by the fact that the child ceases his misbehavior.

Calvin's father has fallen into what Patterson calls the *"reinforcement trap"*: he obtains a short-term benefit at the expense of negative long-term consequences. The trap is that by giving in, he has ended Calvin's immediate negative behavior but has inadvertently increased the likelihood that he will behave the same way in the future. Through the reinforcement trap, children are inadvertently rewarded for aggressiveness and the escalation of coercive behavior, and parents are rewarded for giving in by the relief they experience when children cease their obstreperousness. However, the parents pay a heavy price. Not only are their socializing efforts negated, but their children's behavior will become increasingly coercive over time.

Transactional Processes   Another significant aspect to Patterson's observations is that they involve *transactional* processes between parents and children, such that they affect and shape one another's behavior. A number of investigators agree. For example, Campbell (1997) has observed the relationship between parenting stress and preschool children's aggressiveness and noncompliance. She infers

a bidirectional process whereby the stressed mother becomes more restrictive and negative when trying to cope with her impulsive, noncompliant child; this, in turn, makes the child more difficult to handle.

On a similar note, Dumas, LaFreniere, and Serketich (1995) studied the interactions between mothers and their children, who were categorized as being socially competent, anxious, or aggressive. Surprisingly, they found that aggressive children and their mothers overall shared a positive emotional tone. However, in comparison to other dyads, aggressive children were more likely to use *aversive control techniques*, and their mothers were more likely to *respond indiscriminately* and to *fail to set limits* on their children's more extreme forms of coercion. Thus, they conclude, both parents and young children are active agents in the interaction and reciprocally influence one another.

Others take a different view of who is in the driver's seat. Lytton (1990) describes a provocative experiment that tested the hypothesis that problematic parenting is a functioning of children's behavior. The investigators observed mothers of conduct-disordered and normative boys interacting with their own sons, an unrelated conduct-disordered boy, or an unrelated well-behaved child. As hypothesized, all mothers were more negative and demanding with conduct-disordered boys, with the highest rates of negativity displayed by mothers of antisocial children when interacting with their own sons.

However, when interacting with a normative child, mothers of conduct-disordered children behaved like any other mother. Lytton points to this study, as well as to evidence indicating that some children have a constitutional bias to be aggressive, difficult to manage, and underresponsive to rewards and punishments, in order to argue that we should not underestimate the child's contribution to aversive parent–child relationships.

In general, while attending to the child's contribution is a healthy antidote to parent-blaming, the prevailing opinion seems to be that transactional parent–child processes are more likely to provide an accurate explanation than is either a child-only focus or a parent-only focus (Dodge, 1990).

A Developmental Perspective on Parenting and Conduct Disorder

Shaw and Bell (1993) reviewed the available evidence in support of various parenting contributions to the development of antisocial behavior and constructed a speculative transactional account of how they might each come into play over the course of development.

During the first stage of life, from birth to 2 years of age, Shaw and Bell propose that the most important factor is likely to be *maternal responsiveness*. Through inconsistent and neglectful caregiving, nonresponsive mothers may contribute to the development of irritable, impulsive, and difficult infants, as well as to an insecure attachment. In the second stage, from 2 to 4 years, *parental demandingness* is hypothesized to take on greater importance. Rather than forming a "goal-directed partnership" based on mutual negotiation and compromise, the mothers of future antisocial children are more likely to initiate coercive and punitive patterns of exchange, which, in turn, contribute to children's further noncompliance and negativism. In the third stage, from 4 to 5 years, the most important factor is *parental inconsistency* or laxness in discipline. At this stage, as children begin to transfer the oppositional and coercive patterns of exchange learned at home to their peer relationships and school behavior, conduct problems intensify and the consequences become more severe, requiring increasing parental firmness and consistency. Instead, however, the parents of conduct-disordered children are likely to vacillate between ignoring misbehavior and employing—or merely threatening—harsh punishment.

Shaw and colleagues (1996) have just begun to test this developmental model. To date, they have followed a sample of children from infancy to age 5. Consistent with the model, they found that disorganized attachment was a predictor of disruptive behavior during the first year, while from the second year onward, maternal personality problems and parent–child conflicts also contributed.

The Interpersonal Context: Peer Relations

Children with CD are readily identified by peers. They are argumentative, easily angered, resentful, and deliberately annoying to others (Kazdin, 1997a). As early as the preschool period, habitual child aggression is associated with subsequent *peer rejection*, which leads, in turn, to further aggressive behavior (Capaldi & Patterson, 1994; Coie et al., 1995). Aggressive children also gain a *negative reputation* with peers that continues to follow them even when their behavior improves. Therefore, transactions between conduct-disordered children and their peers can contribute to further aggression and problem behavior.

There is another side to the coin, however. By middle childhood, while aggressive children may be avoided by their prosocial agemates, they are apt to be accepted into *antisocial peer groups* that tolerate or even value problem behavior. Antisocial youths spend most of their time in peer groups with no adult supervision, staying out after curfew, "hanging out" on the streets, and engaging in risky behavior. Thus, antisocial youth tend to gravitate toward one another and reinforce one another's behavior.

Consistent with this, Dishion, French, and Patterson (1995) found that peer rejection at age 10 (along with academic failure) predicted involvement with antisocial peers at age 12, more so than did parental discipline or monitoring practices. Involvement with antisocial peers, in turn, predicts escalating misbehavior (Kupersmidt, Burchinal, & Patterson, 1995). Similarly, Fergusson and Horwood's (1996) longitudinal research showed that association with antisocial peers had a reinforcing and sustaining effect on youth misbehavior from childhood to adolescence. Notably, one of the characteristics that accounted for the 12 percent of their sample of disruptive children who did not go on to develop adolescent CD was their lower rates of affiliation with delinquent peers.

Peer factors can be seen clearly in the development of CD during late childhood and adolescence in girls. As noted previously, *early sexual maturation* is a powerful predictor of antisocial behavior for females. Although at first blush sexual maturation might be assumed to be a strictly biological factor, the onset of menarche has important social implications. Puberty results in noticeable secondary sexual characteristics, such as breast development, which, for the first girl in her class to need a bra, can be a source of teasing from same-sex peers and unwanted sexual attention from males. In fact, evidence suggests that peer relations mediate the link between sexual maturation and norm violation. Early maturing girls attract the attention of older males who engage in norm-violating behavior and, in turn, involve the girls precociously in risk-taking behaviors and sexual activity (Simmons & Blyth, 1987). Late maturers evidence similar behavioral problems after they biologically "catch up" with their early maturing peers.

The mediating role of *heterosexual peer relationships* was made explicit by Caspi and coworkers (1993), who followed 297 girls from childhood to adolescence. They found that early maturation was only a risk factor for girls who attended mixed-sex schools. Those who attended all-female schools were not exposed to the social influences that made early maturation a predictor of conduct problems for other girls. In turn, CD in girls is related to a high risk for *teenage pregnancy* (Zoccolillo, 1997). Thus, it appears that peer modeling of antisocial behavior and increased pressure for sexual relations from males account for the effects of biological maturation on girls' behavior.

Not all children and youth are equally susceptible to peer influences, however. Vitaro and colleagues (1997) followed a sample of almost 900 boys from age 11 to age 13. Based on teacher reports, they typologized boys and their friends as moderately disruptive, highly disruptive, or conforming. Moderately disruptive boys who associated with disruptive peers engaged in more delinquent behavior as time went on. However, friends appeared to have no impact on the development of behavior problems in highly disruptive or conforming boys. For these latter two groups of youth, *intrapersonal characteristics* seem to be steering their development—in a positive direction when associated with prosocial skills but in a negative direction when associated with antisocial traits.

In sum, research on the influence of peers indicates that they are a contributing factor but not a determining one. Two different processes seem to be at work, which we might term "pushing" versus "pulling." While early aggression may cause a child to be pushed away by prosocial peers, positive attachments to antisocial peers may pull a youth in the direction of engaging in escalating misbehavior. This latter influence may be particularly important for understanding adolescent-onset CD. In fact, association with *antisocial peers* has a direct effect on delinquency only in the *adolescent-onset type*, while *parent socialization* is a more significant causal factor in the *child-onset* form of the disorder. For adolescent-onset conduct-disordered youth, then, antisocial peer influences appear to be essential, while for early onset youth the picture is more complicated.

The Superordinate Context

A number of superordinate factors are associated with the risk of CD. In particular, children growing up in communities marked by *poverty* and *violence* are more likely to develop antisocial behavior and CD (Osofsky, 1995). Impoverished inner-city children in the United States are routinely exposed to shocking degrees of violence: by age 5 most have seen a shooting, and by adolescence one-third have witnessed a murder (Bell & Jenkins, 1993). Chronic exposure to violence may desensitize children to these experiences. For example, Lorion and Satzman (1993) found that fifth- and sixth-grade children living in high-crime neighborhoods described the shootings, police raids, and dead bodies they had seen in blasé terms, as "nothing special." Further, the gang and drug culture of the inner cities offer few alternatives to youths, who feel they must join in, in order to survive.

Additionally, Kasen, Johnson, and Cohen (1990) found that a *school environment* characterized by a high degree of conflict (fighting, vandalism, defiant students, and teachers unable to maintain order) was related to an increase in CD over a two-year period.

At a larger social level, the *media* may also play a role in promoting—and even glamorizing—antisocial behavior. Violence has become a mainstay of American television and movies, is perpetrated by heroes as much as by villains, and is seldom met with negative consequences (Eron & Huesmann, 1990). Instead, the lesson is largely communicated that violence is an effective method of solving problems and will be rewarded. Research bears out the relationship between television violence and children's behavior. Children with strong preferences for viewing violent television programs are more aggressive than their peers, and laboratory studies also show that increased viewing of aggressive material leads to subsequent increases in aggressive behavior. Further, longitudinal studies also show that children who prefer violent television programs during elementary school engage in more violent and criminal activity as adults (Eron et al., 1996).

Further insights into specific cultural influences have also been offered, particularly regarding the role of *masculine socialization* in the development of male aggression. For instance, Cohen and colleagues (1996) describe the masculine ethic of the American South as a "culture of honor," which requires that males use physical force in order to defend against perceived insults to their own or their family's reputation. The investigators demonstrated this empirically by instructing a confederate to purposely bump into male research participants and to make a profane and personally disparaging comment. While Northerners were relatively unaffected by the insult, those participants who originated from the South were more likely to feel that their masculinity was threatened, to show heightened physiological arousal and signs of distress, to be more cognitively primed for aggression, and to be more likely to retaliate with violent behavior. The investigators interpret this response as a product of social learning, such that their cultural upbringing leads Southern men to experience interpersonal problems as threats to masculine honor that must be defended through physical aggression.

In sum, opportunities for learning antisocial behavior—and reinforcements for engaging in it—abound in the school, neighborhood, and the culture at large.

The Organic Context

Recent attention has been drawn to the possibility of uncovering organic factors underlying the development of CD. While much of this research is still in progress, and little of it is definitive, a number of suggestive leads have been identified.

One of the best predictors of conduct problems in children is parental criminality or antisocial behavior, especially when research focuses on fathers and sons. This may well be due to a *genetic* factor; however, environmental explanations cannot be ruled out. In general, there is evidence for both (Pike et al., 1996). For example, Ge and colleagues (1996) collected data on biological and adoptive parents of adolescents adopted at birth. Antisocial behavior in biological parents was significantly related to the aggressiveness of children adopted out of the home, providing evidence for a genetic influence. However, the adoptive parents' parenting practices also predicted children's aggression, suggesting that environmental influences also exist.

A shortcoming of the genetic research is that most of it has not attended to the subtypes of CD that have emerged as so important in our review of the literature. While adolescent-onset conduct problems show little evidence for continuity across the generations, evidence for heritability has been demonstrated for the childhood-onset version of the disorder (Frick & Jackson, 1993). On a similar note, Edelbrock and associates (1995) found a significant heritability quotient for overt aggression in twins, but not for covert, nonaggressive behavior problems.

Psychophysiological indicators also set early onset, aggressive, and undersocialized youth apart from their peers. These children demonstrate lower overall autonomic arousal, demonstrated by low heart rate and galvanic skin response. Youth with low heart rates are likely to fight and bully others at school, and are more likely to become violent adults. Low autonomic arousal leads to stimulation-seeking and behavioral undercontol on the one hand, and diminished reactivity to punishment on the other. Quay (1993) hypothesizes that these children have an *underactive behavioral inhibition system*, leading to impulsive responding, heightened reactivity to reward, and an insensitivity to aversive stimuli.

A number of *biochemical* correlates have also been investigated (Hinshaw & Anderson, 1996). Testosterone is a likely candidate because of its relation to aggression in animals. However, research on humans indicates that such hormonal differences are not sufficient to account for aggressive and antisocial behavior, although they may serve a mediating role in individual responses to environmental circumstances. Low levels of serotonin and cortisol also have been linked to aggression in children, although it is worth noting that these deficits have also been identified as factors in the development of a quite different disorder, depression.

Moffit and Lynam (1994) propose that underlying the development of both CD and ADHD are neuropsychological dysfunctions associated with a *difficult temperament*, which predisposes children to impulsivity, irritability, and overactivity. Consistent with this, Newman and colleagues (1997) found that children who showed a difficult, undercontrolled temperamental type at age 3 were more likely to be rated as antisocial in adulthood. However, other longitudinal research indicates that the link between aggression and difficult temperament is not a direct one; instead, it is mediated by family factors (see McMahon and Estes, 1997).

Those pursuing research in the organic domain argue that the existence of biological factors in no way rules out or discounts the importance of social and psychological influences. In fact, there is a general appreciation of the complex *interplay* between psychology and biology. For example, Moffit and Lynam (1994) posit that neuropsychological dysfunctions may have a complex indirect relationship with conduct problems, such as through increasing children's vulnerability to stress. In contrast, Lahey and coworkers (1993) argue that stressful childhood experiences may become transformed into conduct problems through the changes they cause in neuropsychological activity. In a similar vein, Richters and Cicchetti (1993) propose that chronically violent environments might act on the autonomic nervous system in ways that promote underreactivity and the propensity toward disordered behavior. As with the other psychopathologies we have studied, there has been a progression from the "either/or" debates of the past to a new perspective of "yes, and . . ." regarding the relationship between nature and nurture.

Integrative Developmental Model

Patterson and his colleagues have been studying and theorizing about the origins of child conduct problems for over two decades. They provide an integrative developmental model based partly on research and partly on their own observations and experience. (Our presentation is based on Dishion, French, and Patterson, 1995; Patterson, DeBaryshe, and Ramsey, 1989; Patterson, Reid, and Dishion, 1992; and Capaldi and Patterson, 1994.)

The process of "growing" a conduct-disordered youth takes place in a series of hierarchical stages that build upon and elaborate one another, consistent with the organizational hypothesis of developmental psychopathology. (See Figure 9.5). The process begins with a host of risk factors, some of which are in place before the birth of the child. These include low socioeconomic status, living in a high-crime neighborhood, family stress, antisocial parents, and the parents' own history of being reared by unskilled caregivers. However, these risk factors do not directly lead to antisocial behavior. Rather, their effect is mediated by family variables: the basic training camp for antisocial behavior is the home.

The first stage begins in early childhood and involves *poor parental discipline strategies*, with initial coercive interactions escalating into increasingly punitive exchanges. Other poor parent management skills include little involvement and monitoring of children, inconsistency, lack of contingent positive reinforcement, and an absence of effective strategies for solving problems. The products of these dysfunctional family interactions are antisocial, socially incompetent children with low self-esteem.

The next stage occurs in middle childhood when children enter school, where their antisocial behavior and social incompetence result in *peer rejection*

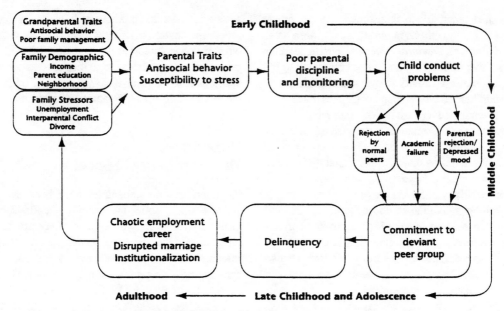

Figure 9.5   Patterson's Model of Conduct Disorder.

Source: Adapted from Patterson, DeBaryshe, and Ramsey, 1989; Patterson, Reid, and Dishion, 1992; and Capaldi and Patterson, 1994

and *poor academic performance*. Failures in these important developmental tasks also contribute to a *depressed mood*. Further, children who chronically bring home negative reports from teachers are more likely to experience *conflicts with parents*, and to be rejected by them.

In adolescence, these youths are drawn to a *deviant peer group* that has a negative attitude toward school and authority and is involved in *delinquency* and substance abuse. These delinquent peers support further problem behavior. As development proceeds, adolescents with an antisocial lifestyle are more likely to have similar difficulties in adulthood, including a *chaotic employment career*, a *disrupted marriage*, and *institutionalization* for crimes or mental disorder. In late adolescence and adulthood, the "assortative mating" process increases the likelihood that antisocial individuals will form relationships with partners with similar personalities and conduct problems. As stressed, unskilled, and antisocial individuals form families and have children of their own, the *intergenerational cycle* is complete.

Intervention

The continuity of CD from childhood to adulthood indicates that this is a psychopathology that becomes entrenched in early development and has long-lasting consequences. Further, other individuals and society pay a high price, in terms of both personal suffering and the dollars-and-cents costs of violence, property destruction, theft, and incarceration. Thus, there is an urgent need for prevention and treatment. Yet the multiple roots of CD—cognitive and affective dysfunctions within the child, psychopathology and discord within the family, encouragement from similarly disordered peers and society at large—present major obstacles to success in both undertakings. As Eron and Huesmann (1990) state, intervention with CD "will take all the knowledge, ingenuity, talent, and persistence we can muster" (p. 154).

In a recent review of the empirical literature, Kazdin (1997b) identified four treatments that seem to be the most promising for CD: parent management training, interpersonal problem-solving skills training, functional family therapy, and multisystemic therapy. We describe these next.

Behavioral Therapy: Parent Management Training

Parent management training (PMT) is one of the most successful and best-documented behavioral programs. PMT was developed by Patterson (see Forgatch and Patterson, 1998) based on his model of maladaptive parent–child relationships as central to the etiology of CD. PMT focuses on altering the interactions between parent and child so that prosocial rather than coercive behavior is reinforced. As the name implies, this is accomplished by training the parents to interact more effectively with the child, based on the principles of social learning theory. Parents learn to implement a number of behavior modification techniques, including the use of *positive reinforcement* for prosocial behavior and the use *mild punishment* such as the use of a "time-out" chair. This is a technique with a large body of empirical research behind it, and we will describe it in more detail when we discuss intervention in Chapter 17.

Cognitive-Behavioral Therapy: Social Problem-Solving Skills Training

As noted above, Shure and Spivack (1988) found that conduct-disordered children show poor problem-solving skills when faced with interpersonal problems. Consequently, their focus in intervention is on helping children to develop *interpersonal problem-solving skills* such as *generating alternative solutions* to problems, *anticipating the consequences* of their behavior, and *planning* and approaching problems in a step-by-step fashion. Structured games and stories are used to practice these skills, and they are progressively applied to more real-life situations. This technique is also described in more detail in Chapter 17.

Systemic Family Therapy

Functional family therapy (FFT) integrates behavioral, cognitive, and systemic perspectives (Alexander & Parsons, 1982). As the name implies, behavior problems are viewed in the context of the functions they serve in the family. For example, misbehaving may be the only way that children can get needs for structure or intimacy met, or may be the only way that children can de-triangulate themselves from a troubled family system. (See Chapter 1.) Consistent with Minuchin's family systems approach, the goal of therapy is to help family members communicate and problem-solve in ways that allow them to meet these needs more satisfactorily. Although relatively few studies have been carried out to assess the effectiveness of FFT, those that do exist demonstrate a consistent positive outcome (Alexander, Holtzworth-Munroe, & Jameson, 1994).

Multisystemic Therapy

Multisystemic therapy (MST) is the fourth treatment recommended by Kazdin for intervention with CD, and it is certainly the most comprehensive (Henggeler & Bourdin, 1990). MST takes to heart the lesson learned by previous investigators—namely, that there are multiple roots of antisocial behavior. While focused on the family system and grounded in family systems theory, the treatment is individualized and flexible, offering a variety of interventions depending on the special needs of the particular child. Thus, treatment may focus on family disharmony and school underachievement in one case, and lack of social skills and parental unemployment in another. The therapist models an active, practical, and solution-focused approach: "You say you didn't understand the teacher's feedback on Casey's school report? Let's give him a call right now and ask for more information."

Empirical studies show the efficacy of the multisystemic approach with severely conduct-disordered youth (Bourdin et al., 1995). Family communication is improved, with a reduction in family patterns of triangulation and lower levels of conflict between parents and children and between parents themselves. Follow-up studies have shown that, for as long as 5 years following treatment, youths who receive MST have lower arrest rates than those who receive other forms of treatment.

Prevention

As Kazdin (1997b) notes, prevention efforts need to be as multifaceted and broad-based as are the risk factors for CD. A combination of family management training for parents and interpersonal problem-solving skills training for children has been used to good effect in prevention programs for kindergarteners and at-risk school-age children (McCord et al., 1994; Tremblay et al., 1995). Five, and even ten years later, those who had undergone these programs were achieving better in school and demonstrating less antisocial behavior than untreated youth.

In the previous five chapters, we have been concerned with disorders whose symptoms lie somewhere along the continuum between normal and abnormal. Depressed feelings, misconduct, anxiety, oppositionality, and inattentiveness all can be seen in well-functioning individuals across the life span. Our next chapter concerns a disorder which, like autism, lies at the extreme end of the continuum. The pervasive and erratic symptoms of schizophrenia lie far beyond the pale of normal development and thus present a major challenge to our ability to understand and treat the disorder.

Reading 14
Temperament and Style Change

Temperament and Style Change

Temperament refers to the innate, genetic, and constitutional influences on personality. Whereas character and schema reflect the psychological dimension of personality, temperament reflects the biological dimension of personality. This chapter describes the dimensions of temperament in terms of its regulation and dysregulation of behavior. It then briefly provides an overview of skills, skill deficits, and skill training and their role in regulating or modulating the temperament/style dimensions of personality disordered individuals. Finally, 15 intervention strategies useful in this modulation process are described. At least one resource citation is provided for each strategy. Reference is made to these strategies in other chapters of this book.

Cloninger (1993) contended that temperament has four biological dimensions—novelty seeking, harm avoidance, reward dependence, and persistence—whereas character has three quantifiable dimensions: self-directedness or self-responsibility, cooperativeness, and self-transcendence. Other researchers would describe impulsivity and aggressivity as additional dimensions of temperament (Costello, 1996). Harm avoidance or behavioral inhibition can be thought of as inhibition of behavior in response to a stimuli. Thus, the more easily and intensely upset a person is by noxious stimuli, the more likely the person is to avoid it. Reward dependence or behavioral maintenance refers to the ease or difficulty with which a person becomes hooked on pleasurable behavior and the degree to the be-

33

345

havior remains controlled by it. Finally, novelty seeking or behavioral activation is the heritable tendency toward exhilaration in response to novel stimuli or cues that have previously been associated with pleasure or relief of discomfort. In other words, it involves the activation of behavior in response to potentially pleasurable stimuli. Each of these temperament dimensions is putatively related to a neurotransmitter system: dopamine to behavioral activation, serotonin to behavioral inhibition, and norepinephrine to behavioral maintenance (Cloninger, 1993). As noted in Chapter 1, the influence of temperament is reflected in the individual's basic styles: affective style, behavioral/relational style, and cognitive style.

Cloninger noted that temperament and character can be measured with biological markers and self-report instruments. On Temperament Character Inventory (TCI), individuals with increased dysregulation of one or more of the temperament dimensions typically experience considerable distress and impairment in life functioning. For example, according to Cloninger's research (1993) the borderline personality disorder would likely rate as high in novelty seeking and harm avoidance, low in reward dependence, while also rating low on three character dimensions. Just as schema—and its modification—is central to this book, so also is temperament and style—and its modulation.

☐ Skills, Skill Deficits, and Skills Training

Effective functioning in daily life requires mastery of a number of requisite personal and relational skills. Most individuals begin learning these requisite skills in childhood and further refine them throughout the course of adolescence and early adulthood. Some patients have the requisite skills but for conscious or unconscious reasons do not use them. Other patients have never learned or sufficiently mastered these skills. This lack of learning or mastery of a basic requisite skill is called a skill deficit (Lieberman, DeRisi, & Mueser, 1989). It is a basic premise of this book that most personality disordered individuals have skill deficits. Because of these deficits, these individuals experience, to varying degrees, dysregulation of one or more temperament dimensions that cause distress to themselves or others. The three temperament or style dimensions emphasized in this book are affective style, behavioral and relational style, and cognitive style. Over- or undermodulation of one or more of these styles can significantly affect level of symptoms and level of functioning (i.e., GAF). In other words, requisite skills—including coping skills—have the effect of regulating or modulating temperament or style dimensions, whereas skill deficits make it more difficult, if not impossible, to modulate style dimensions.

Recall the case examples in Chapter 1. Both Keri and Cindy presented for treatment following a suicide gesture. Although both had the same diagnosis and level of education, Keri's GAF was 40 (with 71 as the highest in the past year) and Cindy's was 27 (with 42 as the highest in the past year). Keri's high level of premorbid functioning suggested that she had mastered most requisite skills, including coping skills, to achieve her level of success. Cindy, on the other hand, had significant skill deficits, which explains why affective, behavioral/relational, and cognitive styles were so overmodulated.

Clinicians can effectively assist patients in reversing such skill deficits by working with them to acquire the personal and relational skills that they have not previously mastered. These skills can be learned directly in individual sessions through practice, that is, coaching and role playing, and through graded task assignment. When feasible, group treatment settings can be particularly useful for social skills training (Lieberman et al., 1989).

For those personality disordered patients with significant symptomatic distress and who exhibit significant functional impairment, traditional psychotherapeutic interventions are of limited use. However, medication and structured interventions—called *skills training*—are quite effective when temperament dysregulation is present. In addition, these structured interventions are effective when skill deficits and reversing these deficits are indicated.

☐ Structured Treatment Interventions for Personality Disorders

The 15 structured interventions are detailed in Table 3.1. These interventions have been referred to throughout the book. Each intervention is described in a step-wise fashion that illustrates its application in the treatment setting. At least one key reference or resource is provided for each of these interventions so that the reader may pursue additional information on using these effective therapeutic interventions.

Anger Management Training

The purpose of anger management training is to decrease the arousal and expression of hostile affects, while increasing the individual's capacity to tolerate and channel this energy in prosocial ways. This is usually a thera-

TABLE 3.1. Structured Intervention Strategies for Personality Disorders

1. Anger Management
2. Anxiety Management Training
3. Assertiveness Training
4. Cognitive Awareness Training
5. Distress Tolerance Training
6. Emotional Regulation Training
7. Limit Setting
8. Empathy Training
9. Impulse Control Training
10. Interpersonal Skills Training
11. Problem Solving Training
12. Self-Management Training
13. Sensitivity Reduction Training
14. Symptom Management Training
15. Thought Stopping

pist-directed intervention that can be applied in individual- or group-treatment context. It is then practiced and applied by the individual. Collaboration between clinician and the individual tends to increase the individual's motivation and compliance. The intervention proceeds in the following fashion.

First, the clinician instructs the patient in the four sets of factors that determine the response of anger in that patient: (a) high-risk circumstances (external, contextual factors, such as individuals, places, or times of day that can potentially provoke an angry or rageful response in the patient); (b) internal triggering factors (internal factors, such as the patient's feelings, cravings, level of fatigue that render the patient more vulnerable to an angry response); (c) patient self-statements (specific beliefs that can render the patient more vulnerable to an angry response, or that can defuse an angry response); and (d) patient's coping skills that neutralize or exacerbate the effects of these internal and external factors.

Second, the clinician instructs/trains the patient in identifying the four sets of factors, and develops—with the patient—a checklist or form of

the most likely factors for that patient. For example, the clinician asks the patient to describe a recent instance of a response of anger, and assists the patient in indicating the four specific factors. He had gotten stopped for speeding and for driving while under the influence of alcohol: (a) he left a tavern after four drinks and decided to drive home rather than take a cab (high-risk circumstance); (b) he was tired after a stressful day at work and was disinhibited and feeling bad that someone had just broken his car aerial (internal triggering factor); (c) he was thinking: "Why does this stuff always happen to me?" and "Nobody does this to my car and gets away with it" (self-statement); and (d)he is impulsive with a "hair-trigger" temper (coping skills) and speeds off angry and resentful.

Third, the clinician tells the patient to write down each incident in which he felt anger, the four factors, and what he did when he experienced that emotion (i.e., cursed and kicked the side of his car when he noticed the car aerial was broken). The patient then self-monitors these factors and responses between sessions with the form. During subsequent sessions, the clinician and patient review the form. They analyze the factors looking for commonalities and specifying coping skill deficits (i.e., he's mostly likely to be angry and disinhibited when he's tired, been stressed at work, or been drinking).

Fourth, the clinician works with the patient to specify alternatives to these high-risk circumstances (i.e., if he's been drinking he'll take a cab or ask a designated driver to get home). Then, the clinician helps the patient to specify a plan for reducing the various internal triggering factors (i.e., when he's tired and stressed out he can go jogging rather than go to the tavern).

Fifth, the clinician instructs and assists the patient to learn effective, alternative self-statements to cope with anger-provocation (i.e., "It's too bad this happened, but I don't have to go ballistic over it").

Finally, the clinician trains the patient in learning relaxation skills (i.e., controlled breathing and counting to 10 before acting when he sees that his car has been vandalized) and other coping skills such as assertive communication as an alternative to the anger and rageful responses.

Resources

Novaco, R. (1975). *Anger control.* Lexington, MA: Heath/Lexington Books.

Novaco, R. (1984). Stress inoculation therapy for anger control. In P. Keller & L. Ritt (Eds.), *Innovations in clinical practice: A source book* (pp. 214–222). Sarasota, FL: Professional Resource Exchange.

Anxiety Management Training

The purpose of anxiety management training is to decrease the arousal and expression of distressing affects, and to increase the individual's capacity to face and tolerate these affects. This is usually a therapist-directed intervention that can be applied in individual- or group-treatment context. It is then practiced and applied by the individual. Collaboration between clinician and the individual tends to increase the individual's motivation and compliance. The intervention proceeds in the following fashion.

First, the clinician instructs the patient in the determinants of the response of anxiety in that patient: (a) external triggering factors, such as specific individuals or stressful demands that can potentially elicit anxiety in the patient; (b) internal triggering factors, such as physiological responsivity and patient self-statements, that is, specific beliefs that can render the patient more vulnerable to anxiety, or that can neutralize it; and (c) patient's coping skills that neutralize or exacerbate the effects of these internal and external factors.

Second, the clinician instructs the patient in identifying the three sets of factors, and develops—with the patient—a checklist of the most likely factors for that patient. The clinician then asks the patient to describe a recent incidence of anxiety and assists the patient to specify the three specific factors. In the example of performance anxiety, the patient is (a) assigned to give a quarterly business report at a board of directors meeting (external trigger); (b) experienced moderate physiological reactivity during other public presentations: "I feel completely inadequate giving a speech to my superiors." "I know I'm going to screw up, and I'll be so embarrassed" [internal triggers]; and (c) prefaces the presentation by asking the group's indulgence saying she is a better accountant than public speaker (coping skills) and experiences feelings of inadequacy, dry mouth, sweaty palms and heart palpitations while giving the presentation. Alternately, an anxiety survey can be used, and if there are more than one anxiety responses, an anxiety hierarchy survey can be used.

Third, the clinician tells the patient to write down each incident in which she has experienced anxiety, the three factors, and what she did when experiencing that emotion (i.e., she quickly excused herself after giving the report, experienced some relief, but concluded she had failed again). The patient then self-monitors these factors and responses between sessions with the form.

Fourth, during subsequent sessions the clinician and patient review the checklist. They analyze the factors looking for commonalities and specifying coping skill deficit (i.e., she's likely to experience performance anxi-

ety when addressing superiors, although she has no problem giving presentations to peers or inferiors).

Fifth, the clinician works with the patient to consider options when faced with external triggers (i.e., to inquire about submitting a written rather than verbal report, or having a colleague give the presentation, while she is present to field questions on the report).

Sixth, the clinician works with the patient to specify a plan for reducing the various internal triggering factors, that is, learning to reduce physiological reactivity by controlled breathing or other relaxation exercises, and specifying more adaptive self-statements, that is, "My worth as a person and as an employee doesn't depend on how well I can give speeches. This is only one small part of my job"; "I know this material cold—certainly better than anyone on board. I can get through this 5-minute talk and maybe even enjoy it."

Seventh, the clinician trains the patient in learning relaxation skills, such as controlled breathing 10 minutes prior to giving a presentation, and other coping skills as an alternative to the anxiety and self-deprecatory responses. Treatment progress is evaluated based on the patient's increasing capacity to face internal and external triggering factors with more adaptive coping behaviors. The patient's self-report of the absence of, or a significant reduction in, anxiety in such circumstances indicates the treatment has been effective.

Resources

Suinn, R. (1977). Manual: Anxiety management training. CO: Rocky Mountain Behavioral Science Institute.
Suinn, R., & Deffenbacher, J. (1982). The self-control of anxiety. In P. Karoly & F. Kanfer (Eds.), The psychology of self-management: From theory to practice (pp. 132–141). New York: Pergamon.

Assertiveness Training

The purpose of assertiveness training is to increase an individual's capacity for expressing thoughts, feelings, and beliefs in a direct, honest, and appropriate manner without violating the rights of others. More specifically, it involves the capacity to say "no," to make requests, to express positive and negative feelings, and to initiate, continue, and terminate conversations. Lack of assertive behavior is usually related to specific skills deficits, but it is sometimes related to interfering emotional reactions and thoughts. Assertiveness training proceeds in the following fashion.

First, the clinician performs a careful assessment to identify the following: situations of concern to the patient; current assertiveness skills; personal and environmental obstacles that need to be addressed, such as difficult significant others or limited social contexts; and personal and environmental resources that can be drawn on.

Second, the clinician formulates an intervention plan. If appropriate behaviors are available but not performed because of anxiety, the focus may be on enhancing anxiety management skills. Discrimination training is required when skills are available but are not performed at appropriate times. If skill deficits are present, skill training is indicated.

Third, the intervention is introduced. For skill training, the clinician teaches the patient specific skills via modeling, behavioral rehearsal, feedback, and homework. Modeling effective behavior in specific situations is accomplished by using one or more of the following methods: in vivo demonstration of the behavior by the clinician, written scripts, videotapes, audiotapes, or films. In behavior rehearsal, the patient is provided opportunities to practice the given skill in the clinical setting.

Fourth, the clinician provides positive feedback following each rehearsal in which effective verbal and nonverbal reactions are noted and identified. Homework assignments involve tasks that the patient agrees to carry out in real-life contexts.

Fifth, the length of assertion training depends on the domain of social behaviors that must be developed and on the severity of countervailing personal and environmental obstacles. If the response repertoire is narrow, such as refusing requests, and the obstacles minor, only a few sessions may be required. If the behavior deficits are extensive, additional time may be required even though only one or two kinds of social situations are focused on during intervention. Assertiveness training can occur in individual sessions, group therapy, as well as in other small contexts such as support groups and workshops. Sank and Shaffer (1984) provided a detailed four-session assertiveness training module for use in a structured group therapy context.

Resources

Alberti, R. (1978). *Assertiveness: Applications and issues.* San Luis Obispo, CA: Impact Publications.
Sank, L. & Shaffer, C. (1984). *A therapist's manual for cognitive behavior therapy in groups.* New York: Plenum.

Cognitive Awareness Training

The purpose of cognitive awareness training is to reduce narcissistic injury, projective identification, and cognitive distortions. Increased recognition and awareness of distorted thinking and unrealistic expectations can attenuate resulting distress and acting out behaviors. As such, this intervention is particularly useful in the treatment of personality disordered individuals. Although this intervention is clinician-initiated, it is essentially a self-management intervention that the individual must practice sufficiently to achieve some level of mastery. The intervention proceeds in the following fashion.

First, the clinician assesses the nature of the patient's cognitive distress, because the intervention is applied somewhat differently for narcissistic injury and projective identification than it is for cognitive distortions.

Second, assuming that the distress is attributed to narcissistic injury or projective identification, the clinician focuses cognitive awareness training on the social interactions that trigger dysfunctional conflicts. The goal is to understand the relationship between the other's anger-provoking behavior and the individual's own frustrated expectations. This involves specifying what it was about the other's behavior that was frustrating or hurtful, and identifying what expectations were frustrated by the other's behavior. In using this technique, it is essential that the clinician help the individual to distinguish the reasonable aspects of the individual's expectations from the unreasonable aspect(s). Failure to recognize this expectation will be experienced by the individual as a narcissistic injury.

Third, assuming that the distress is attributed to cognitive distortion, the clinician focuses cognitive awareness training on the patient's thoughts and images associated with the onset and escalation of conflict. The clinician inquires about the individual's inner experience when anger begins welling up: What were their thoughts, self-talk, and images of the other person as the argument began to escalate? By monitoring these cognitions, the individual can bring into conscious awareness many irrational thoughts and perceptions that had previously been either out of awareness or vague.

Resource

Novaco, R. (1978). Anger and coping with stress: Cognitive behavioral interventions. In J. Foreyth & D. Rathjen (Eds.), *Cognitive behavior therapy* (pp. 217–243). New York: Plenum.

Distress Tolerance Skill Training

Distress tolerance is the capacity to perceive one's environment without demanding it be different, to experience one's current emotional state without attempting to change it, and to observe one's thought and action patterns without attempting to stop them. Thus, it is the ability to tolerate difficult situations and accept them. Typically, lower functioning individuals with borderline and histrionic personality disorders have difficulty tolerating distress. Distress tolerance training attempts to help the patient to develop skills and strategies to tolerate and survive crises and to accept life as it is in the moment. Among individuals with mood lability and impulsivity, the ability to tolerate distress is a prerequisite for other therapeutic change. This intervention is usually introduced and demonstrated by the clinician. It is then practiced and applied by the individual. As such, it is a self-management intervention. Initially, the clinician may have to cue the individual to apply the technique within and between treatment sessions. The intervention proceeds in the following fashion.

First, the clinician assesses the patient's ability to distract themselves from painful emotional thoughts and feelings, and to soothe themselves in the face of worry, loneliness, and distress. Skill deficits in either or both areas are noted.

Second, based on this assessment, the clinician instructs the patient in one or both of the following essential skills and strategies: distraction and self-soothing methods. If distraction is a basic skill deficit, it becomes the focus of treatment. Distraction techniques include thought stopping, shifting attention by making a phone call, watching television or listening to music, jogging, comparing oneself to others who are less well off, and intense sensations; for example, placing one's hand in a container of ice water or flicking a thick rubber band on one's wrist to produce a painful but harmless sensation intense enough to derail the thought and impulse for wrist-cutting and other self-harmful behaviors.

Third, if self-soothing is a basic skill deficit, it becomes the focus of treatment. Self-soothing techniques include controlled breathing exercises—in which air is drawn in slowly and deeply and then exhaled slowly and completely—savoring a favorite food or snack, and listening to or humming a soothing melody. Acceptance skills include radical acceptance—complete acceptance from deep within, turning the mind toward acceptance—choosing to accept reality as it is, and willingness versus willfulness.

Resources

Linehan, M. (1993a). *Cognitive-behavioral treatment of borderline personality disorder*. New York: Guilford.

Linehan, M. (1993b). *Skill training manual for treating borderline personality disorder*. New York: Guilford.

Emotion Regulation Skill Training

Patients who habitually exhibit emotional lability may benefit from help in learning to regulate their emotions. Emotion regulation skills can be extremely difficult to teach, because emotionally labile patients often believe that if they could only "change their attitude" they could change their feelings. Labile patients often come from environments where others exhibits cognitive control of their emotions, and show little tolerance of the patients' inability to exhibit similar control. Subsequently, labile patients often resist attempts to control their emotions because such control implies that others are right and they are wrong for feeling the way they do. Much of the labile patient's emotional distress is a result of such secondary responses as intense shame, anxiety, or rage to primary emotions. Often the primary emotions are adaptive and appropriate to the context. The reduction of this secondary distress requires exposure to the primary emotions in a nonjudgmental atmosphere. Accordingly, mindfulness to one's own emotional responses is essentially an exposure technique. This intervention typically proceeds in the following fashion.

First, the clinician assesses the patient's overall skill in emotional regulation, and then the subskills of identifying and labeling affects, modulating affects, and mindfulness.

Second, the clinician formulates a plan for reversing the skill deficit(s). Skill training can occur in either an individual- or group-treatment context. Although the skills of emotion regulation can be learned in an individual-treatment context, group context greatly facilitates these efforts. Skill training groups can provide a measure of social support and peer feedback that individual treatment cannot.

Third, the clinician, whether in an individual- or a skill-group context, teaches, models, and coaches the patient(s) in the given subskill of emotional regulation. The first step in regulating emotions is learning to identify and label emotions. Identification of an emotional response involves the ability to observe one's own responses as well as to describe accurately the context in which the emotions occur. Identification is greatly aided if one can observe and describe the event prompting the emotion, can interpret the event that prompts the emotion, can differentiate the phenomenological experience, including physical sensations of the emotion, and can describe its effects on one's own functioning.

Similarly, emotional lability can be attenuated by controlling the events that trigger emotions or by reducing the individual's vulnerability to lability. Patients are more susceptible to emotional lability when they are under physical or environmental stress. Accordingly, patients should be assisted in reducing such stressors by achieving a more balanced lifestyle. This includes appropriate nutrition, sufficient sleep, adequate exercise, reduction of substance use, and increased self-efficacy. Although these targets seem straightforward, making headway on them with labile patients can be exhausting for both patients and clinicians. Work on any of these targets requires an active stance by the patients and persistence until positive effects begin to accrue.

Increasing the number of positive events in one's life is one approach to increasing positive emotions. Initially, this involves increasing daily positive experiences. Subsequently, it means making life changes so that positive events will occur more often.

In addition to increasing positive events, it is also useful to work on being mindful of positive experiences when they occur, and unmindful of worries that the positive experience will end. Mindfulness to current emotions means experiencing emotions without judging them or trying to inhibit them, block them, or distract from them. The assumption is that exposure to painful or distressing emotions, without association to negative consequences, will extinguish their ability to stimulate secondary negative emotions. Whenever a patient already feels "bad," judging negative emotions as "bad" leads to feelings of guilt, anger, or anxiety, which further increases distress intolerance. Frequently, patients can tolerate a painful affect if they can refrain from feeling guilty or anxious about feeling bad in the first place.

Fourth, the clinician works together with the patient to arrange for the patient to practice a given skill(s) both within and outside the treatment context. Within the treatment context, the use of role play can be particularly valuable in reinforcing the patient's newly acquired skill(s). Particular situations and relationships can be targeted for practice outside the treatment context.

Resources

Linehan, M. (1993). *Cognitive-behavioral treatment of borderline personality disorder*. New York: Guilford.
Linehan, M. (1993). *Skill training manual for treating borderline personality disorder*. New York: Guilford.

Limit Setting

Limit setting is an intervention designed to help patients recognize aspects of themselves that are being defended against by resorting to a destructive, outer-directed activity or diversion. Personality disordered individuals often have difficulty maintaining boundaries, as well as appreciating and anticipating the consequences, especially the negative consequences, of their actions. Limit setting is a therapeutic intervention that is quite useful in as well as outside treatment settings. The intervention proceeds in the following fashion.

First, the clinician observes or anticipates one of the following patient behaviors: treatment-interfering behaviors, such as coming late for sessions, missing a session, unnecessarily delaying or failing to make payment; harmful behavior to self or others, including parasuicidal behaviors; inappropriate verbal behavior (e.g., abusive language); dominating treatment by excessive or rambling speech; efforts to communicate with the clinician outside the treatment context (i.e., unnecessary phone calls); inappropriate actions (e.g., hitting or unwanted touching, breaking or stealing items); or failure to complete assigned therapeutic tasks (i.e., homework). For example, a fashionably dressed patient complained of financial hardships and requested a special reduced fee and payment schedule.

Second, the clinician begins implementing limit setting. The clinician begins by setting the limit. The limit is specified in "if ___ then ___" language. It is crucial that the clinician state the limit in a neutral, non-critical tone and non-judgmental language. In the above example, rather than making special concessions to him, the standard fee arrangements were clearly explained. He was told that if he could not afford to be seen at the clinic, the clinician would be sorry but would assist him in finding lower cost treatment

Third, the clinician explains the rationale for the limit. In the above example, it was further explained that allowing him to accumulate a sizable bill would not be in his best interest.

Fourth, the clinician specifies or negotiates with the patient the consequences for breaching the limit. In the above example, that clinician told the patient that if he would fall behind in payments by two sessions, according to clinic policy, he would need to wait until his balance was current before additional sessions would be scheduled.

Fifth, the clinician responds to any breeches of the limit setting. Because patients can and do test limits—whether for conscious or unconscious reasons—more commonly in the early phase of treatment, limit testing should be expected. The clinician should be prepared to respond by confronting and/or interpreting it; enforcing the consequences and discussing the impact of the breech on treatment; or predicting that such testing may reoccur. For example, in the above case, the patient did test the agreement once; the clinician expressed concern but upheld the limit. Thereafter, the patient kept up with his payments and his treatment continued.

Resource

Green, S. (1988). *Limit setting in clinical practice.* Washington, DC: American Psychiatric Press.

Empathy Training

Empathy training is a technique for more directly enhancing the patient's empathic abilities. In empathy training, the patient is asked to think about and then communicate his/her understanding of the feelings and point of view of the other. These understandings are then checked out with the other individual and inaccuracies are corrected. Particular attention is given to the patient's understanding of what he/she has done or said that has aroused hurt feelings in the other, and what the other wishes would have happened instead of what did happen. The technique of empathy training is a powerful tool for interrupting projective identification and splitting. It often leads to greatly increased awareness of the feelings and needs of the other. This, in turn, greatly facilitates constructive negotiation and problem solving. Although there are various approaches to empathy training, the relationship enhancement approach has been demonstrated to be effective with personality disordered individuals, including individuals with narcissistic personality disorder in a relatively short time—three to four sessions—particularly if empathy training takes place in the context of couples sessions. The intervention proceeds in the following fashion.

First, the clinician assesses the nature and extent of the patient's capacity to manifest the three skills of empathy: active listening, accurately interpreting interpersonal cues, and responding empathically.

Second, assuming an empathic deficit (i.e., in one or more of the three skills of empathy), the clinician begins the training by modeling the three skills of empathy. After being continually modeled by the clinician, the patient begins to develop empathic understanding and responding.

Third, the clinician begins to coach the patient on the given skill(s) beginning with non-relationship issues, and then moving to positive feelings before progressing to conflicts. The clinician teaches the patient to access the underlying vulnerability and the healthy needs that underlie

his narcissistic defense. This is done through the dual process of empathic listening and the coaching of skilled expression of one's authentic feelings and point of view. The patient initially tends both to experience and express vulnerability in the form of anger, criticism, and blame. Empathic listening becomes a way of calming the patient's reflexive reactions and of creating a pause between emotions and the reflexive, harmful behaviors that have resulted from those emotions.

Fourth, empathy training also assists patients in monitoring their emotional reactivity. Patients typically experience that listening empathically and responding within the guidelines for effective expression feels supportive to them. They also begin to discover that when emotions are accurately observed and expressed subjectively with increasing consciousness of how meanings affect feelings, these emotions shift or even vanish quite rapidly. What often perpetuates anger, for example, is the lack of full attention to it on the part of the patient, and to the meanings and desires it reveals. When this attention neither inhibits nor defends the emotion, but instead maintains a compassionate and curious observer stance, change in feelings, meanings, and actions can occur quickly.

Resources

Guerney, B. (1977). *Relationship enhancement: Skills programs for therapy, problem prevention, and enrichment.* San Francisco: Jossey-Bass.

Guerney, B. (1988). *Relationship enhancement manual.* State College, PA: IDEALS.

Impulse Control Training

Impulse control training is an intervention whose goal is to reduce involuntary urges to act. This intervention is usually introduced and demonstrated by the clinician. It is then practiced and applied by the individual. As a result of applying this intervention, the individual increases self-control. This intervention involves three phases: assessment, training, and application. The intervention proceeds in the following fashion.

First, the clinician undertakes an assessment of the pattern of the patient's thoughts and feelings that lead up to self-destructive or maladaptive impulsive behavior. Once this pattern is understood, it is possible for the patient to find other ways to accomplish the same result that have fewer negative effects and are more likely to be adaptive.

Second, the clinician and patient examine the patient's thoughts and feelings leading up to self-destructive or maladaptive impulse behaviors.

For example, the patient keeps a log of thoughts and feelings associated with each impulsive behavior.

Third, the clinician teaches the patient competing responses to impulses by inducing an urge to act impulsively, and then helping the patient to implement strategies to delay acting on that impulse for progressively longer periods of time, which can be cognitive (i.e., counting to 10 before acting or speaking when upset) or muscle relaxation (i.e., progressive relaxation). The most common competing responses are systematic distractions that are either internal or external. Internal distractions are thoughts that are incompatible with the impulses. For example, the patient's self-talk becomes: "This is actually funny, and I'm going to smile instead of fume." External distractions include a change in the environment that focuses the patient's attention. For instance, the patient is prompted to leave the room when a parent is shouting at him and in the past, he has the impulse to hit the parent.

Fourth, the clinician helps the patient practice and supplies feedback until the patient develops a reasonable level of mastery. The clinician teaches the patient to apply internal and/or external distractions to neutralize maladaptive impulses. For example, when the patient is around his father who is drinking, he avoids getting hooked into fighting by conjuring up an image of Charlie Chaplin walking with a drunken limp and telling his father he has to leave to meet a friend.

Finally, because self-destructive impulsive behavior can be particularly problematic, it is essential for the clinician to develop a clear understanding of a patient's motivation for self-destructive behavior by examining the thoughts and feelings leading up to the self-destructive impulses or behavior, and then by asking directly, "What were you trying to accomplish through this action?" Suicide attempts, self-mutilation, and other self-destructive acts can be the product of many different motives: desire to punish others at whom the client is angry, desire to punish oneself or obtain relief from guilt, desire to distract oneself from even more aversive obsessions, and so forth. Once the motivation is understood, it is possible for the patient to find other ways to accomplish the same result that have fewer untoward effects and are more likely to be adaptive. For example, it may be possible to substitute a minimally self-destructive behavior, such as marking oneself with a pen, for a more self-destructive act, such as wrist-slashing. This less destructive act can later be replaced with a more adaptive alternative. Not surprisingly, if the risk of the patient's performing seriously self-destructive acts is high, and the above-described interventions do not prove effective in the limited time available, hospitalization may be needed to allow sufficient time for effective intervention.

Resources

Linehan, M. (1993). *Skill training manual for treating borderline personality disorder*. New York: Guilford.
Turkat, I. (1990). *The personality disorders: A psychological approach to clinical management*. New York: Pergamon Press.

Interpersonal Skills Training

Interpersonal skills refer to a broad range of skills in relating socially and/or intimately with others. These include distress tolerance, emotional regulation, impulse control, active listening, assertiveness, problem solving, friendship skills, negotiation, and conflict resolution. Lower functioning personality disordered individuals may have significant skill deficits, while higher functioning personality disordered individuals tend to have better developed conversational skills. However, to be effective interpersonally requires much more than the capability of producing automatic responses to routine situations. It also requires skills in producing novel responses or a combination of responses when the situation demands. Interpersonal effectiveness is the capacity to appropriately respond assertively, to negotiate reasonably, and to cope effectively with interpersonal conflict. Effectiveness means obtaining the changes one wants, by keeping the relationship and one's self-respect. And, even if higher functioning borderline patients possess adequate interpersonal skills, problems arise in the application of these skills in difficult situations. They may be able to describe effective behavioral sequences when discussing another person encountering a problematic situation but may be totally unable of carrying out a similar behavioral sequence when analyzing their own situation. Usually, the problem is that both belief patterns and uncontrollable affective responses are inhibiting the application of social skills. These patients often prematurely terminate relationships, or their skill deficits in distress tolerance make it difficult to tolerate the fears, anxieties, or frustrations that are typical in conflictual situations. Similarly, problems in impulse control and emotional regulation lead to inability to decrease chronic anger or frustration. Furthermore, skill deficit problem-solving skills make it difficult to turn potential relationship conflicts into positive encounters. In short, interpersonal competence requires most of the other skills described in this chapter as well as others. The intervention proceeds in the following fashion.

First, the clinician must assess the patient's current relational skills and skill deficits. The skills to be assessed include distress tolerance, emotional regulation, impulse control, assertiveness, problem solving, active listening, friendship skills, negotiation, and conflict resolution. Specific skill deficits are noted.

Second, the clinician formulates a plan for dealing with the noted skill deficit(s). If there are global deficits, it might require referral to a group focused on social skills training. Such groups are invaluable in providing social support while patients are learning personal and interpersonal skills.

Third, skill training begins either in an individual- or group-treatment context. Usually the sequence involves modeling of a given skill, and then coaching to achieve increasing levels of mastery. Interventions that involve several modes of practice or enactment seem to be the most efficacious and time efficient. Video demonstration of the skills, role-play practice, and homework exercises are integral features of such an approach. Assuming that a patient who has been referred to a skills training group is also in individual treatment, the clinician assesses and monitors progress.

Fourth, the clinician works together with the patient to arrange for the patient to practice a given skill(s) outside the treatment context. This usually includes initiating conversations with strangers, making friends, making and going on dates. Assessment of the skill level is followed by additional modeling and coaching.

Resources

Liberman, R., De Risis, W., & Mueser, K. (1989). *Social skills training for psychiatric patients*. New York: Pergamon.

Linehan, M. (1993). *Cognitive-behavioral treatment of borderline personality disorder*. New York: Guilford.

Linehan, M. (1993). *Skill training manual for treating borderline personality disorder*. New York: Guilford.

Zimbardo, P. (1977). *Shyness*. New York: Jove.

Problem-Solving Skills Training

Problem-solving skills training is a treatment intervention strategy through which individuals learn to use an effective set of skills to cope with distressing or troublesome personal and interpersonal situations. The goals of this form of social skills training is to assist individuals in identifying problems that cause their distress, to teach them a systematic method of solving problems, and to equip them with a method for approaching future problems. Problem-solving training is often a brief method of intervention that can be used in individual-, couples-, and group-treatment contexts. This is a clinician-initiated intervention than requires some training and

practice by the individual to master this set of skills. This intervention proceeds in the following fashion.

First, the clinician assesses the patient's capacity to solve problems in terms of the five skills involved in problem solving. The five are problem identification, goal setting, generating alternative courses of action, decision making, and implementation of the decided course of action.

Second, the clinician explores with the patient the origin and nature of a specific problematic situation (i.e., problem identification). For instance, the patient notes that she runs out of money about 1 week before receiving her monthly paycheck, because of impulse buying during the first 3 weeks of the month.

Third, the clinician helps the patient to assess the problem, identify causative factors, and set realistic goals. In the above example, impulse buying is identified as the cause, and the goal set is to budget money to last the entire month, and to save 10% in a bank account.

Fourth, the clinician helps the patient to generate alternative courses of action. In terms of the example, alternatives are discussed. One is to develop a 30-day budget, a second is to ask the employer for a biweekly paycheck, and the third is to have an automatic paycheck deposit to a bank account.

Fifth, the clinician helps the patient choose a course of action with regard to its short- and long-range consequences. In this example, the patient decides that setting up a budget is the most realistic short- and long-term course of action.

Sixth, the clinician offers information and supports the patient's efforts to implement the course of action. In this case, the patient agrees to meet with a financial planner and sets up a monthly and annual budget plan, and also opens a savings account.

Resource

Hawton, K., & Kirk, J. (1989). Problem-solving. In K. Hawton, P. Salkovskis, J. Kirk, & D. Clark (Eds.), *Cognitive behavior therapy for psychiatric problems*. Oxford, England: Oxford University Press.

Self-Management Skills

Self-management skills are needed to learn, maintain, and generalize new behaviors and to inhibit or extinguish undesirable behaviors and behavioral changes. In its widest sense, self-management means efforts to control, manage, or otherwise change one's own behavior, thoughts, or emotional responses to events. Thus, the skills of distress tolerance, emotion regulation, impulse control, and anger management can be thought of as self-management skills. More specifically, self-management skills refer to the behavior capabilities that an individual needs to acquire further skills. To the extent that patients are deficient in self-management skills, their ability to acquire other skills is seriously compromised. Patients often need some knowledge of the principles of behavior change to effectively learn self-management skills. For instance, a patient's belief that individuals change complex behavior patterns in a heroic show of willpower sets the stage for an accelerating cycle of failure and self-condemnation. The failure to master a goal becomes additional proof that explanations of failure, such as laziness, lack of motivation, or lack of willpower, are true. The clinician must confront and replace these notions of how individuals change. In short, principles of learning and behavioral control, as well as knowledge about how these principles apply in each individual's case, are important targets in teaching self-management skills. Learning these targeted concepts often involves changes in a patient's belief system. The intervention typically proceeds in the following manner.

First, the clinician assesses the patient's overall level of self-management, as well as specific subskills of goal setting, self-monitoring, environmental control, toleration of limited progress, and relapse prevention, noting skill deficit(s).

Second, the clinician formulates a plan for dealing with the noted skill deficit(s). If there are global deficits, it might require referral to a group focused on social skills training. Such groups are invaluable in providing social support while patients are learning personal and interpersonal skills.

Third, skill training begins either in an individual- or group-treatment context. Usually the sequence involves modeling of a given skill, and then coaching to achieve increasing levels of mastery. Interventions that involve several modes of practice or enactment seem to be the most efficacious and time efficient. Video demonstration of the skills, role-play practice, and homework exercises are integral features of such an approach. Assuming that a patient who has been referred to a skills training group is also in individual treatment, the clinician assesses and monitors progress.

Patients need to learn how to formulate positive goals in place of negative goals, to assess both positive and negative goals realistically, and to examine their life patterns from the point of view of values clarification. Patients typically believe that nothing short of perfection is an acceptable outcome. Behavior change goals are often sweeping in context and clearly exceed the skills the patients may possess. Clinicians will need to teach patients such skills as self-monitoring and environmental monitoring, setting up and evaluating baselines, and evaluating empirical data to determine relationships between antecedent and consequent events and their

own responses. These skills are very similar to the hypothesis-testing skills taught in cognitive therapy.

The belief that a patient can overcome any set of environmental stimuli is based on the assumption that it is possible to function independently of one's environments. Given this belief, it is not surprising that some patients have skill deficits when it comes to using their environments as a means of controlling their own behavior. Nevertheless, some patients are more responsive to transitory environmental cues than others. As a result, the capability to manage environmental surroundings effectively can be particularly crucial. Techniques such as stimulus narrowing, that is, reducing the number of distracting events in the immediate environment, and stimulus avoidance, that is, avoiding events that trigger problematic behaviors, can be targeted to counteract the belief that willpower alone is sufficient.

Some patients respond to a relapse or small failure as an indication that they are total failures and may as well give up. Accordingly, they will develop a self-management plan and then unrealistically expect perfection in adhering to the plan. The issue and focus of relapse prevention is to teach patients to plan realistically for relapse, to develop strategies for accepting the possibility of a slip, and to ameliorate the negative effects of relapse.

Because some patients have limited tolerance for feeling bad, they have difficulties carrying out behavior change action plans that require perseverance. Rather, they will often seek a quick fix that involves setting unreasonably short time limits for relatively complex changes. In other words, they expect instantaneous progress. If it does not occur, they believe they have failed. Therefore, emphasizing the gradual nature of behavior change and tolerance of concomitant negative affect should be a major focus of clinician effort.

Fourth, the clinician works together with the patient to arrange for the patient to practice a given skill or skills outside the treatment context. This usually includes initiating conversations with strangers, making friends, making and going on dates. Assessment of the skill level is followed by additional modeling and coaching.

Resources

Linehan, M. (1993). *Cognitive-behavioral treatment of borderline personality disorder*. New York: Guilford.

Linehan, M. (1993). *Skill training manual for treating borderline personality disorder*. New York: Guilford.

Sensitivity Reduction Training

Sensitivity reduction training is an intervention to neutralize and delimit an individual's vulnerability to criticism, misperception, and suspiciousness. Individuals who habitually misperceive and negatively distort social cues are prone to defensive and acting out behaviors. Instead, this intervention teaches individuals to more accurately attend to, process, and respond more effectively to social cues. This is a clinician-initiated intervention wherein the clinician collaborates with the individual to learn and practice more accurate use of social information. This intervention proceeds in the following fashion.

First, the clinician recognizes that these oversensitivity reactions involve errors and distortions in the course of the information processing. Information processing can be thought of in terms of four components: attending, information processing, responding, and feedback. Subsequently, this intervention is directed to these four components.

Second, the clinician assesses how the individual attends to the full range of social cues. This can be done by reviewing important social interactions of the individual, and critically assessing how the individual attends to pertinent social cues. For instance, an individual reports that as he enters a social gathering, a small group of people look at him and smile, then he hears a whispered comment after which everyone laughs. If the individual selectively attends only to the whispered comment and disregards the other two cues: smiling and laughter, he could misperceive the situation and respond defensively. If the individual is not identifying and attending to such pertinent cues, the clinician focuses training in this area.

Third, the clinician then assesses the accuracy of the individual's interpretation of this social information. Selective attention and misperception can be processed as threatening. Teaching the individual to interpret social cues more accurately is essential. This training can be accomplished with role playing, videotaped feedback, and instruction.

Fourth, the clinician assesses how the patient responds to these cues. Responding refers to the individual's response to the social cues of others ranging spoken words, paralanguage, and overt actions. Responses can range from appropriate and prosocial to inappropriate and harmful. To the extent that the individual is able to accurately attend to and process social cues, the individual is more likely to appropriately respond to the cue. Training is directed at appropriate responding. Although the focus of training is often on verbal responding, at times the individual's tone of voice, facial expression, or hand gesturing needs to be changed to make it less menacing.

Fifth, the clinician assesses how the patient uses the consequences of his or her social behavior, and the extent to which it is appropriate

or maladaptive. Negative feedback can be useful information and the individual needs to learn to use it constructively. Furthermore, with improvement in social behavior, positive consequences should accrue to the individual.

Resource

Turkat, I. (1990). *The personality disorders: A psychological approach to clinical management.* New York: Pergamon Press.

Symptom Management Training

Symptom management training is an intervention strategy for controlling the distressing manifestations (i.e., symptoms) of psychiatric disorders. Although symptoms are of varying types and levels of intensity and duration, patients tend to report symptoms without such differentiation, and unless the clinician clarifies the type and intensity/duration, referrals or needless changes in treatments, such as medication dosage or other medications added, can result in significant untoward effects on the treatment process. Personality disordered patients are more likely to experience low-grade, subclinical symptoms (i.e., persistent symptoms) than acute symptoms. Yet, they are likely to demand increased medication or changes in medication, not realizing that persistent symptoms are rarely responsive to medication. Accordingly, this intervention often requires the use of psychosocial and psychoeducational methods. Symptom management training involves learning such skills as self-monitoring, medication compliance, and relapse prevention. It can be taught in individual or group treatment settings. It is a clinician-initiated intervention that involves mutual collaboration to assess, teach–learn, and practice the requisite skills. This intervention proceeds in the following fashion.

First, the clinician assesses and evaluates the type and nature of symptoms experienced by the patient. Symptoms are of three types: (a) persistent symptoms (i.e., chronic, low-grade symptoms not ameliorated by medication), (b) warning symptoms (i.e., symptoms gradually increasing in intensity that precede an acute episode), and (c) acute symptoms (i.e., the full-blown incapacitating symptoms that often signal acute decompensation). The nature of symptoms includes both their intensity and duration.

Second, the clinician works with the patient to increase his or her awareness and understanding of the types and nature of symptoms and the skills necessary to effectively manage symptoms. The patient is taught the self-monitoring skill of identifying the type of symptom and intensity (i.e., rates and logs on a 5-point scale: 1 = *mild*, 5 = *very severe*), and duration (logs the amount of time in minutes and number of times the symptom types occur each day for 1 week).

Third, an intervention is planned and tailored to the particular type and expression of symptoms experienced by the individual. Accordingly, acute symptoms are usually treated with medication or medication combined with an individual or group psychosocial or psychoeducational treatment. Psychoeductional methods vary from learning activities and formats that include videotapes, role playing, and homework assignments. Because warning symptoms can result from insufficient medication levels, it is useful to raise medication levels or consider adding an additional medication. Because warning symptoms can result from stopping or decreasing medication, it is essential to inquire about medication noncompliance, which may necessitate checking with a caretaker or significant other. On the other hand, persistent symptoms seldom suggest insufficient medication levels or noncompliance. Thus, they do not require changing dosage or drug regimen, but rather psychoeducational methods such as distraction techniques. For example, the individuals with low-level but chronic dysphoria might achieve considerable relief by distracting themselves from the low energy and blue mood by listening to uplifting or energetic music or watching a funny video movie.

Fourth, the patient practices the interventions (i.e., rating and logging symptoms) and distraction techniques for a given time frame and reports the results at the next meeting with the clinician.

Resource

Liberman, R. (1988). *Social and independent living skills: Symptom management module: Trainers manual.* Los Angeles: Rehabilitation Research.

Thought Stopping

Thought stopping is a self-control intervention to block and/or eliminate ruminative or intrusive thought patterns that are unproductive or anxiety-producing. It may also have the effect of increasing the patient's sense of control and reducing distress. This intervention is usually introduced and demonstrated by the clinician. It is then practiced and applied by the individual. As a result of applying this intervention the individual increases his sense of control. The intervention proceeds in the following fashion.

First, the clinician instructs the client on the similarities between normal and obsessive/intrusive thoughts. An agreement is reached to try

to reduce the duration of the intrusive thoughts, thus making them more "normal" and increasing the client's sense of control.

Second, the clinician and client draw up a list of three obsessional thoughts and several specific triggering scenes. Then a list of up to three alternative thoughts (i.e., interesting or relaxing thoughts) is made. For example, a scene from a movie, lying on a sandy beach, or taking a walk through the woods. Each obsessional thought is rated for the discomfort it produces on a scale of 1 to 10 (1 = *lowest*, 10 = *highest*).

Third, the clinician demonstrates how to block obsessional thoughts and substitute an alternative thought. The clinician directs the individual to close his eyes and become relaxed with the instruction to raise a hand when the obsessional thought is first experienced. For example: "Sit back and relax and let your eyes close. I'll mention a specific triggering scene to you, and then describe you experiencing an obsessional thought. As soon as you begin to think the thought, raise your hand, even if I'm only describing the scene." The clinician then describes a typical triggering scene, and as soon as the individual raises a hand, the clinician says "Stop!" loudly. The clinician asks the client whether the obsessional thought was blocked and whether the individual was able to imagine the alternative scene in some detail. The discomfort arising from that obsessional thought is then rated on the 1–10 scale.

Fourth, the clinician then leads the client in practicing thought-stopping with different triggering scenes and alternative thoughts, and the discomfort ratings are recorded. Practice continues until the individual can sufficiently block and replace the obsessional thought.

Fifth, the procedure is modified so that following the clinician's description of the triggering scene and obsessive thought, the client says "Stop" and describes the alternative scene. Practice continues until the individual can sufficiently block and replace the obsessional thought.

Sixth, the clinician gives an intrasession assignment (homework) to the client for 15 minutes of practice a day at times when the client is not distressed by intrusive thoughts. A log is kept with ratings of 1 to 10 made of the distress and vividness evoked by the intrusive thought.

Finally, after a week of practice the clinician prescribes the intervention to be used to dismiss mild to moderately distressing thoughts as they occur. The client is instructed that as his sense of control increases, the thoughts, when they occur, will become less distressing (on the 1–10 scale) until the individual experiences little or no concern about them.

Resource

Hawton, K., Salkovskis, P., Kirk, J., & Clark, D. (Eds.). (1989). *Cognitive behavior therapy for psychiatric problems.* Oxford, England: Oxford University Press.

☐ Summary

Character has been been rediscovered as a basic component of personality and as a key factor in the effective treatment of the personality disorders. To the extent that an individual's temperament dimensions or styles are dysregulated, the individual will express distress or be distressing to others. Higher functioning individuals were socialized and learned self-management and relational skills to regulate such style dimensions as impulsivity, labile affects, and aggressivity during the course of normal child and adolescent development. A hallmark of the early development of personality disordered individuals is deficits in some or many of these coping skills. Both structured psychosocial interventions and medication can be useful in regulating or modulating these style dimensions. This chapter has detailed 15 structured treatment intervention strategies that are useful in modulating affective, behavioral and relational, and cognitive styles.

Reading 15
Ethical Decision Making:
The Person in the Process

Ethical Decision Making:
The Person in the Process

Marian Mattison

Ethical decisions made by social workers are shaped by the decision maker and the process used to resolve ethical dilemmas. Although systematic guidelines for resolving ethical dilemmas offer social workers a logical approach to the decision-making sequence, it is inevitable that discretionary judgments will condition the ultimate choice of action. Social workers are influenced by professional roles, practice experiences, individualized perspectives, personal preferences, motivations, and attitudes. Through reflective self-awareness social workers can recognize their value preferences and be alert to the ways in which these values unknowingly influence the resolution of ethical dilemmas. Understanding which values or ethical principles were given priority from among competing alternatives can inform social workers about their value patterning. This article challenges social workers to view current ethical decisions as linked to other ethical decisions they have made in the past or will make in the future. An approach to developing keener insight into value patterning is presented.

Key words: *ethical decision making; ethical dilemmas; moral dilemmas; values*

It is virtually impossible to pick up a newspaper, magazine, or professional journal today and not find attention being drawn to present controversies about moral or ethical issues. Concern about the morality of professionals focuses on questions of what is to be considered the "right," "correct," or "ethical" position to promote or action to take in a professional capacity. Moral responsibility (the obligation to "act correctly") in actions by professionals is being scrutinized carefully. Increasingly, individual practitioners are being held responsible for their choices of action (Loewenberg & Dolgoff, 1996). The practice of social work is no exception. As social workers struggle with resolving moral dilemmas, pragmatic approaches to ethical decision making must be better linked to daily practice, and the decision makers themselves should be developing insight into how they typically respond to value conflicts. Although moral decision making in any given case involves a concentrated focus on the particular case details at hand, it should also include points of reflection both

CCC Code: 0037-8046/00 $3.00 © 2000
National Association of Social Workers, Inc.

throughout the process and in retrospect, to activate self-knowledge and insight for the social worker. Social workers can benefit from scrutinizing their value decisions to learn, for example, whether they tend to favor following rules or policies over exercising discretionary judgment. In what way is the social worker's decision typically shaped by the worker's role in the agency (direct services practitioner versus administrative role)? Is client self-determination an overriding value, or will the social worker's judgments of right versus wrong direct the ultimate choice of action?

This article attempts to apply the person-in-situation construct to ethical decision making. In addition, it calls for social workers to develop a greater awareness of self throughout the ethical reasoning process. As social workers are engaged in moral decision making, they are urged to be aware of and sensitive to the ways in which their value preferences continuously influence and pervade the process. As ethical dilemmas are resolved, social workers are encouraged to review the decision-making process. This review can provide feedback about individualized patterns of responding to ethical dilemmas. Social workers can then use this feedback to recognize the ways in which they typically respond to value choices in the course of working with clients. A pragmatic approach for gaining greater awareness of one's value preferences is presented. The social work practitioner is encouraged to use reflective self-awareness to make corrections or adjustments to influence future decisions that involve ethical tensions.

Competing Values and Competing Loyalties

Perhaps more than other professions, social work is concerned with values that give direction to its efforts (Noble & King, 1981). "Ethics refers to those rules of conduct that direct us to act in a manner consistent with the values we profess" (Lewis, 1982, p.12), and these rules are embodied in the *Code of Ethics* which "is intended to serve as a guide to the everyday professional conduct of social workers" (NASW, 1996, *Overview*). Although social workers will agree that core values such as client self-determination and the primacy of client interests are

ones to be actualized in practice, translating social workers' values into behavioral acts becomes less certain (Perlman, 1976). When two or more values are activated, it is unlikely that a person can behave in a manner that is equally compatible with each of them (Rokeach, 1973). For example, social workers have long struggled with decisions involving client self-determination (Freedberg, 1989). It is acknowledged that there is no universal application of the concept of self-determination; context and situational preferences lead to exceptions (Rothman, 1989). At what point should client self-determination take precedence over other competing values or obligations that apply? There may be points at which other social work values would be considered more primary than self-determination, in a given situation. Should a social worker honor a pregnant 14-year-old adolescent's right to self-determination, or is there an obligation to disclose the pregnancy to parents or guardians to protect the unborn child? Should an elderly client be returned to an environment that threatens his or her health and safety if he or she so chooses? Clearly there are times when client self-determination should be sacrificed when the social worker believes that the client's chosen course of action is not in the client's "best interests" or threatens the client's safety (Callahan, 1994). The social worker, acting under the obligation of beneficence (the obligation to promote "good" on behalf of clients), may select a course of action that the client opposes. This decision can result in paternalism, "a form of beneficence in which the helping person's concept of harms and benefits differ from those of the client and the helper's interpretation prevails" (Abramson, 1989, p. 102).

The Reality of Discretionary Judgment

Social workers in daily practice make a continuous series of treatment decisions, weighing the relative advantages and disadvantages of various alternatives or strategies. Favorable decisions ultimately are selected on the basis of acceptable practice theory in conjunction with the values of the profession, which, collectively, should guide social workers in their professional capacity. These values, or preferences for what is

362

good, desirable, or ethical, are systematically presented in a code of ethics that "prescribes and explains the obligations for good, right conduct on the part of professional members" (Siporin, 1982, p. 523). Although the new *Code of Ethics* "offers a set of values, principles, and standards to guide the decision making conduct when ethical issues arise, . . . it does not provide a set of rules that prescribe how social workers should act in all situations" (NASW, 1996, p. 2).

How social workers respond to ethical dilemmas depends, in part, on whether the ethical issues are distinguished from the practice issues and how the worker has learned to think about the ethical issues. The expectation that social workers become familiar with "specific ethical standards to guide social workers' conduct and to provide a basis for adjudication" (NASW, 1996, *Overview*) is a foundation for ethical practice. Knowledge of the values, ethical standards, and ethical principles espoused in the *Code* equip the social worker with an appreciation of the complexities of the obligations. Yet the code does not specify which values or principles the social worker should consider primary in cases of competing interests. For this, social workers must be accoutered with a framework or strategy to guide them in determining which principle, value, or obligation to honor foremost when ethical obligations conflict. For example, when a social worker is asked by a 14-year-old adolescent not to disclose her pregnancy to her parents, whose interests should the social worker consider foremost? Is the social worker's primary obligation to the adolescent and her right to self-determination? On what grounds can the disclosure of this confidential information be justified? To what extent might the disclosure of the information be in the adolescent's best interests, in the long run? Is this a circumstance in which the social worker "may limit clients' right to self-determination when, in the social workers' professional judgment, clients' actions or potential actions pose a serious, foreseeable, and imminent risk

How social workers respond to ethical dilemmas depends, in part, on how the worker has learned to think about the ethical issues.

to themselves or others?" (NASW, 1996, p. 7). When the needs of the adolescent, the interests of the unborn child, and those of the family system conflict, how does the social worker determine whose interests should ultimately be served? Although systematic guides for resolving ethical dilemmas offer social workers a logical approach to the decision-making process, to some extent, the use of discretionary judgments is inevitable.

Competing Value Tensions

Decisions regarding ethical questions are not made by social workers in an arbitrary manner; they are grounded in the conditions and factors related to the decision maker, the situational circumstances, and the process itself. Ethical decisions involve not only distinguishing right from wrong, but also addressing the more troubling good/good or bad/bad variety of deliberations. Typically, the more troubling ethical decisions involve choosing from among possible choices of action, each of which offers potential benefits (good/good) or those in which each of the options at hand appears unattractive or undesirable (bad/bad) (Keith-Lucas, 1977). In either case, any option is never entirely satisfying.

Deontological and Teleological Approaches

Delineating the criteria on which moral decisions are made has been argued by philosophers and described in ethical theories throughout time. Two major groups of ethical theories have relevance to social workers in helping recognize and understand the principles on which ethical decisions are based. Although social workers do not normally talk in philosophical terms as they engage in ethical decision making, elements of deontological and teleological thinking operate and influence the decision-making process, whether knowingly or unknowingly. A brief discussion of the deontological and teleological perspectives and consideration of the ways in which each influences ethical choices deepens the discussion of judgments about the rightness and wrongness of professional behaviors.

In the professional training of social workers, a systems perspective highlights the broad understanding of multiple influences and calls for a consideration of the possible consequences that might result from any given intervention. Attention to weighing the potential consequences of proposed actions is central to the teleological school of thought. Decisions for action are made in relation to the consequences that may result; actions that result in greater degrees of good are valued or desired. Subsequently, actions can be justified on the basis of the consequences they create (Loewenberg & Dolgoff, 1996) and the belief that the desired ends will be met, thereby justifying the means.

This focus on consequences, central to the teleological approach, contrasts sharply with the deontological approach, which maintains that fixed moral rules should dictate and define the rightness or wrongness of actions. Deontological thinking is grounded in the belief that actions, in and of themselves, can be determined to be right or wrong, good or bad, regardless of the consequences they produce (Reamer, 1995). From this philosophical perspective, adherence to rules is central. Once formulated, ethical rules should hold under all circumstances (Loewenberg & Dolgoff, 1996). Thus, a social worker would not choose to abide by the rules under some circumstances and disregard them under others. The rules remain in place across all situations, and circumstantial factors do not serve to justify disregard for the rules. A social worker following a deontological approach will differ in the approach to ethical decision-making judgments compared with the social worker who values the weighing of potential consequences. An example will serve to illustrate these points.

Case Example

A 14-year-old adolescent who discloses in confidence that she is pregnant will serve as the reference point. Further investigation reveals that the adolescent intends to keep secret the pregnancy until she is past the legal limit for an abortion. At that point, she believes, her mother and stepfather will throw her out of the house;

this action will enable her to live with her maternal aunt. She asks the social worker to not disclose the pregnancy.

Absolutism versus Relativism

Clearly, every social worker will consider the "standards of care" that direct and guide the choices of action in this case or any other case. The social worker's actions should be consistent with "the way an ordinary, reasonable, and prudent professional would act under the same circumstances" (Reamer, 1994, p. 3). In addition, clinical judgments must be balanced against, and made in light of, legal considerations. With the rise of ethics complaints filed against social workers, the law is becoming an ever-increasing influence on social work practice. Social workers become legally and ethically vulnerable when they are unaware of the legislated responsibilities to which they will be held responsible (Bullis, 1995). For example, in this case the social worker must know the extent to which and under what conditions he or she is obligated to maintain client confidence and under what circumstances disclosure may be warranted. State law may require the practitioner to protect the information shared by the 14 year old. Yet, the social worker may determine that the duty to protect the unborn child outweighs the obligation to protect client confidence. It is not uncommon for social workers who have knowledge of the legal obligation to willfully violate this obligation to serve a perceived "greater good" (Mattison, 1994).

No doubt social workers unilaterally agree that the principles of confidentiality and a respect for a client's right to self-determination are core values to uphold. In this case the rule-oriented (deontological) social worker may feel duty bound to respect the client's right to self-determination. Overriding the obligation to maintain client confidentiality would not be a consideration. If the social worker accepts that the obligations to maintain and protect client confidence and to foster self-determination are central, it would be inherently wrong to violate these under any circumstances. The fact that the client is 14 does not change the imperative to uphold the rules, even if doing so results in harm to the client or client system.

364

For the social worker who views the situation from a relativistic perspective, the focus is on the consequences that may follow. The social worker attempts to balance the risks involved and is concerned with what might result from each of the proposed actions. This worker, with a teleological perspective, weighs and measures the consequences for the adolescent, the unborn child, the family system, the social worker, societal interests, and others potentially affected. Judgments about the correct course of action are made only after a thorough assessment of what might result from each option. Social workers attempt to weight the various obligations to which they are responsible and to evaluate the possible consequences of these actions, ultimately selecting the action that produces the preferred outcomes or benefits.

In the event that a liability case is brought against the social worker, alleging that the social worker failed to carry out duties properly, the social worker must be prepared to justify not only the action selected, but also the process and procedures followed in selecting the action. The client may claim that the disclosure of confidential information was an act of misfeasance, that the social worker performed "a proper act in a way that [was] harmful or injurious" (Barker, 1995, p. 237). Although the court may not go so far as to rule on what action a social worker should have taken, the social worker is responsible for documenting the systematic steps used in arriving at the decision. These steps must reflect the proper professional conduct expected of a professional social worker. For example, where indicated, the social worker must be able to produce documentation that consultation and supervision were sought, in keeping with expected practice guidelines (Reamer, 1994).

Guides for Ethical Decision Making

Ethical decision making in day-to-day practice must never be considered a discrete act or a task that is unremittingly logical or scientific by nature. Although theoretical and technical expertise both steer and direct professional practice, it is clear that there are aspects of social work that require thinking beyond scientific proficiency (Goldstein, 1987). In part, the process of

ethical decision making involves the systematic analysis of the dilemma by the individual decision maker. For this facet of the process, numerous guides offer social workers techniques to systematically analyze ethical dilemmas (Abramson, 1985; Lewis, 1984; Loewenberg & Dolgoff, 1996; Pine, 1987; Reamer, 1990). These analytic tools attempt to move ethical decision making away from the intuitive and toward the cognitive by offering step-by-step approaches to ethical decision making. They are attempts to shift moral decisions made by social workers from the personal and subjective, to treat these decisions with the intellectual rigor afforded other social work decisions (Emmet, 1962). The goal is to build "intellectual moral resources," by ensuring that moral judgments are tied to reason and are supported by an intellectual base (Emmet). Documenting the process and procedures used in making a decision may be critical to justifying a person's action in a court of law (Reamer, 1994). All too often social workers are unfamiliar with the obligations set forth in the code and have little or no training in the systematic analysis of ethical dilemmas (Mattison, 1994).

I have devised a model for analyzing ethical dilemmas (shown in Figure 1). The process begins as the social worker fully explores case details and gathers needed information to understand holistically the client's current circumstance. Social workers must pay attention to ethnic-based traditions and the ways "in which members of various ethnic groups are likely to define and cope with problems" (Schlesinger & Devore, 1995, p. 906). Might the pregnancy be a tradition that is ethnically based? The analysis progresses as the social worker carefully distinguishes the practice aspects of the case from the ethical considerations. In the case of the 14-year-old pregnant adolescent, the practice considerations may involve questions such as "Which treatment modalities should be used?" "Were the limits of confidentiality explicitly reviewed?" "Is the practitioner familiar with empirically based knowledge about the physical, emotional, and financial consequences of adolescent pregnancies?" The ethical components involve questions such as "To what extent should client self-determination be actualized

Figure 1
Framework to Analyze Ethical Dilemmas

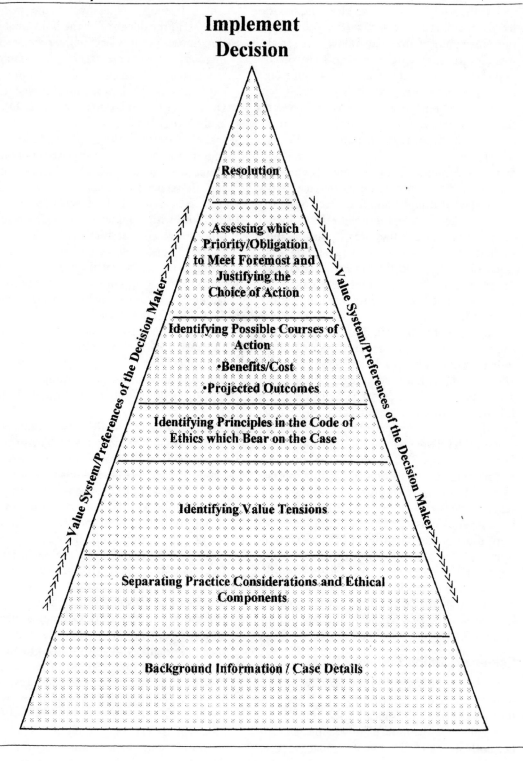

Implement
Decision

Resolution

Assessing which
Priority/Obligation
to Meet Foremost and
Justifying the
Choice of Action

Identifying Possible Courses of
Action
• Benefits/Cost
• Projected Outcomes

Identifying Principles in the Code of
Ethics which Bear on the Case

Identifying Value Tensions

Separating Practice Considerations and Ethical
Components

Background Information / Case Details

Value System/Preferences of the Decision Maker

Value System/Preferences of the Decision Maker

in practice?" "Is a 14-year-old psychologically capable of carrying? Should a 14-year-old carry a child without the supervision of guardians?" "Whose interests should be served foremost, those of the adolescent, those of the unborn child, or those of the family system?"

The analysis continues as the value tensions are identified explicitly. In the adolescent pregnancy case, the value tensions may include the social worker's duty to maintain client confidence versus serving the perceived best interests of the family system; the adolescent's right of self-determination versus the parents' right to know that their daughter is pregnant; the adolescent's right to autonomy versus the health and safety needs of the unborn child; and the legal obligations regarding the protection or disclosure of the confidential information versus the moral obligation to serve "the best interests of the adolescent" (additional value tensions might be identified). In analyzing ethical dilemmas, the social worker must reference the *Code of Ethics* to identify and evaluate which obligations the code addresses and the specific obligations to which the worker is obliged. Next, as part of the ethical assessment, the decision maker projects, weighs, and measures the possible courses of action that seem reasonable and the potential consequences of these. For example, if the social worker were to disclose the information against the expressed wishes of the adolescent, what consequences might result for the adolescent, family members, the maternal aunt, or the social worker? In what ways will the interests of the social worker be affected by a failure to abide by any legal obligations that might bear on the case? The costs and benefits to various choices of actions will differ for each individual involved. After a scrupulous assessment of these obligations, the social worker must select an action. Resolving the ethical dilemma ultimately involves determining which of the competing obligations or values to honor foremost. It is the nature of an ethical dilemma that meet-

> *As part of the ethical assessment, the decision maker projects, weighs, and measures the possible courses of action and the potential consequences of these.*

ing one or more of the obligations comes at the expense of satisfying others. The resolution stage follows; the social worker selects a choice of action based on the outcomes of the assessment and must be prepared to justify the decision. (For a more detailed case example using this model, see McGowan & Mattison, 1998.)

Self-Awareness

Beyond the "scientific" phase, a comprehensive approach to ethical decision making must embrace consideration of the decision maker. The process of decision making is forged by the prejudices and prejudgments brought to the decision-making process by the decision maker (Abramson, 1996). The value system and preferences of the decision maker shape the entire assessment process and influence each step and ultimately the choice of action selected (Figure 1). In the case of the 14-year-old who shares, in confidence, that she is pregnant, the social worker's views on adolescent pregnancy inevitably will factor into the decision making. Weighing the parents' right to know versus the adolescent's right to have her confidentiality protected will be influenced by the social worker's personal and professional experiences. The technical aspects of the ethical decision-making process take shape only as they are applied in practice through the individual lens of the decision maker. Initially, the reasoning process helps the decision maker establish, understand, and organize the complex facts related to the particular situation. Yet there is general agreement in the literature that the ultimate decision for resolving an ethical dilemma lies in the circumstances and the value system or preferences of the decision maker (Keith-Lucas, 1977).

The Person-in-Situation Construct and Ethical Decision Making

We know well, from our understanding of human behavior, the extent to which the context of the environment shapes and defines behavior. It follows, with regard to ethical issues, that social workers themselves are likely to be influenced by their "prior socialization, and developmental stages as well as situational factors, including the immediate organizational or professional context, characteristics of their work roles, and overall organizational culture" (Holland & Kilpatrick, 1991, p. 143). The practitioners' decision making is sensitized by their cultural background and beliefs, which often inadvertently cast judgments on the rightness or wrongness of attitudes and behaviors. Stereotypes and biases, which are not made explicit by the practitioner, undoubtedly will influence professional conduct (Frankena, 1980). A contemporary approach to social work ethics must center "holistically" on the decision maker in the context of the decision-making process, including recognizing and accounting for the cultural perspectives of the client, which may vary widely from those of the social worker. Acknowledging that the client's value orientation may conflict with the professional and personal beliefs held by the social worker can remind the practitioner to consciously consider whose interests are being served. Abramson (1996) called for social workers to be "ethically aware." The challenge is to use ethical self-reflection to learn about oneself as an ethical decision maker. Because it is the character, conscience, personal philosophy, attitudes, and biases of the decision maker that ultimately give rise to the choice of action (Abramson, 1996), we must learn more about our individualized ethical stances.

Individualized Decision-Making Styles

The research demonstrates that social workers indeed develop individualized styles or patterns of responding to moral dilemmas (Holland & Kilpatrick, 1991). Holland and Kilpatrick documented a number of variables associated with individualized decision-making styles. The authors suggested that some social workers adhere more consistently to policies and laws that are relevant to a situation, whereas others emphasize means or outcomes as more essential to selecting a choice of action. Some social workers honor client self-determination over benefi-

cence as a routine value orientation. Clearly, a social worker's organizational role in the agency (direct service versus administrative) strongly influences the priorities that the social worker emphasizes in ethical decision making. Such value patterning must be brought to the conscious awareness of the decision maker. It is the responsibility of the social worker to know how contextual influences such as agency role, judgments about right versus wrong, and principles and philosophies filter unknowingly into the ethical decisions the social worker makes. Because "a person always enters the ethical decision making process in midstream, influenced by his or her past experience . . . the ideal goal is to come to an ethical decision through a personal equilibrium in which emotion and reason are both activated and in accord" (Callahan, 1988, p. 91).

For social workers struggling to resolve ethical dilemmas, there is a lack of information about what constitutes sound professional practice. Reasonable practitioners disagree on what a social worker should do in a given case situation and whether the social worker's actions constitute a violation of the standards of care to which the social worker is held responsible (Reamer, 1994). No where does the profession provide case references or formal opinions about what constitutes appropriate professional conduct. The absence of such practice standards leaves social workers without reference points as they address complex questions regarding professional ethics (Jayaratne, Croxton, & Mattison, 1997), resulting in social workers being left to interpret individually the boundaries of ethical behavior. Practicing social workers voice concerns and ambivalence about what constitutes sound ethical practice and express a desire for such reference points against which to measure the appropriateness of their practice decisions and behaviors (Mattison, 1994).

Developing insight into one's value patterning can be the result of social workers making ethical decisions in daily practice and continuously reflecting on the decision-making sequence as well as the outcomes of the process. Social workers can benefit from viewing ethical decisions as related to other ethical decisions

368

that they have made in the past and will make in the future.

Figure 2 illustrates a decision-making sequence that integrates continuous reflection. Purposeful attention to reflection and self-awareness are essential throughout the ethical decision-making process. As the social worker engages in the process, consideration of his or her value preferences must be in the practitioner's conscious awareness. Thoughtful engagement in ethical decision making involves an assessment of the case details with attention to identifying the ethical tensions. Responding to the ethical dilemma requires that social workers recognize the ethical components and distinguish these from the more familiar practice aspects of their work (Joseph, 1985). How social workers respond to ethical dilemmas is conditioned by their ability to see the value components as separate from the practice aspect of the case details. In this process the social worker isolates ethical precepts to which he or she is obligated. As the process proceeds, detecting the ways in which factors such as the social worker's organizational role, personal values, exceptional client circumstances, and professional obligations influence the choices of action must be considered.

To structure the ethical decision-making process, social workers use an analytic guide (as described in Figure 1) to judge which obligation is more important to honor in a particular case and which value should outweigh the others in importance. Throughout the process, as the choice of action is being selected, justified, and implemented, there is a benefit to social workers reviewing their value preferences in relation to the case. Understanding which values or ethical principles were given priority from among the competing alternatives can inform the social worker about value patterning. This knowledge can be measured against other value choices that the practitioner has made in the past.

After an ethical decision has been made, social workers can benefit by reflecting on their value preferences in the particular case. A practical way for social workers to learn more about their value orientation begins by responding to a series of questions such as those suggested below. As social workers compare their responses from case to case, they should see patterns of responding. This feedback can inform social workers about their individualized approaches to ethical dilemmas.

1. To what extent did my personal values or philosophies influence the preferred choice of action?
   - ❑ I was aware of my personal biases or preferences and attempted to keep these from unduly influencing the outcome.
   - ❑ I had not considered the extent to which my personal values may have influenced the ultimate decision.
2. To what extent did the legal obligation influence my decision in this case?
   - ❑ Not at all
   - ❑ Somewhat
   - ❑ Was a deciding factor in my decision
3. Was I willing to act outside of legal obligations if doing so meant serving the client's best interests?
   - ❑ My legal obligation took precedence over all other obligations.
   - ❑ If the legal obligation does not serve my client's interests, I am not bound to apply the legal rule above other interests.
4. To what extent did adhering to agency policy influence my decision in this case?
   - ❑ Not at all
   - ❑ Somewhat
   - ❑ Was a deciding factor in my decision.
5. If agency policy conflicted with other obligations to the client, was I willing to act outside of agency policy?
   - ❑ My first obligation is to the agency.
   - ❑ Agency policy may not take precedence in all case circumstances.
6. To what extent did my role in the agency influence my choice of action? (Do you believe that your choice of action might be different if you were an administator or direct practice social worker?)
   - ❑ My choice of action was strongly influenced by my agency role.
   - ❑ My choice of action was somewhat influenced by my agency role.
   - ❑ I would have made the same decision regardless of my role in the agency.

Mattison / *Ethical Decision Making: The Person in the Process*

Figure 2
Cycle of Reflection

Engage in Reflection and Self-Awareness

* Be Aware of One's Ethical Preferences
* Develop a Conscious Awareness of One's Value Patterning

Analyze Current Ethical Dilemma

* Begin by Isolating the Ethical Components

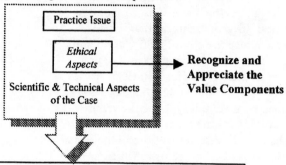

Practice Issue

Ethical Aspects → **Recognize and Appreciate the Value Components**

Scientific & Technical Aspects
of the Case

Continue the Process of Reflection and Self-Awareness

* Acknowledge Which Factors are Influencing the Decision

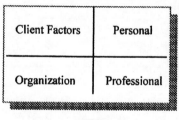

Client Factors	Personal
Organization	Professional

Follow Systematic Steps in the Decision-Making Process/Select a Resolution

* Use an Analytic Guide to Structure the Decision-Making Process

Reflect on the Choice of Action

* Measure the Current Ethical Choice against Others from the Past
* Sharpen and Modify Conscious Awareness of One's Value Patterning

7. If the case involved a conflict between client self-determination and paternalism, which value did I judge to be more essential to honor foremost?
   - ☐ Client self-determination was the overriding value to uphold.
   - ☐ Client self-determination was secondary to my professional judgment regarding what I believed to be the preferred choice of action for the client.
8. In selecting a choice of action in this case, I viewed as more important
   - ☐ evaluating possible costs and benefits to the client and client system for each of the various choices of action.
   - ☐ strict adherence to procedural practices (adherence to laws and policies).

Conclusion

Each ethical decision made in practice can be linked to others by conceptualizing the decisions as related to one another over time. Decision maker bring to the process a proclivity toward selecting choices of action that are in line with their personal preferences, professional roles, commitment to laws and policies, practice experience, motivations, attitudes, and other individualized perspectives. Social workers are challenged to contemplate their value perspectives, which subtly and often unknowingly influence their resolutions of ethical dilemmas. Developing an awareness of value preferences is then used by the social worker to understand better the effect of these values on the resolution of ethical dilemmas. Social workers can be alert to their preferences and can take steps to compensate for and balance the influence of value preferences in future ethical decision making. ■

References

Abramson, M. (1985). The autonomy–paternalism dilemma in social work practice. *Social Casework, 66,* 387–393.

Abramson, M. (1989). Autonomy vs. paternalistic beneficence: Practice strategies. *Social Casework, 70,* 101–105.

Abramson, M. (1996). Reflections on knowing oneself ethically: toward a working framework for social work practice. *Families in Society, 77,* 195–202.

Barker, R. L. (1995). *The social work dictionary* (3rd ed.). Washington, DC: NASW Press.

Bullis, R. (1995). *Clinical social work misconduct: Law, ethics and personal dynamics.* Chicago: Nelson Hall.

Callahan, J. (1988). The role of emotion in ethical decision making. *Hastings Center Report, 18,* 9–14.

Callahan, J. (1994). The ethics of assisted suicide. *Health & Social Work, 19,* 237–244.

Emmet, D. (1962). Ethics and the social worker. *British Journal of Psychiatric Social Work, 6,* 165–172.

Frankena, W. K. (1980). *Thinking about morality.* Ann Arbor: University of Michigan Press.

Freedberg, S. (1989). Self-determination: Historical perspectives and effects on current practice. *Social Work, 34,* 33–38.

Goldstein, H. (1987). The neglected moral link in social work practice. *Social Work, 32,* 181–186.

Holland, T. P., & Kilpatrick, A. C. (1991). Ethical issues in social work: Toward a grounded theory of professional ethics. *Social Work, 36,* 138–144.

Jayaratne, S., Croxton, T., & Mattison, D. (1997). Social work professional standards: An exploratory study. *Social Work, 42,* 187–199.

Joseph, M. V. (1985). A model for ethical decision making in clinical practice. In C. B. Germain (Ed.), *Advances in clinical social work practice* (pp. 207–217). Silver Spring, MD: National Association of Social Workers.

Keith-Lucas, A. (1977). Ethics in social work. In J. B. Turner (Ed.-in-Chief), *Encyclopedia of social work* (17th ed., pp. 350–355). Silver Spring, MD: National Association of Social Workers.

Lewis, H. (1982). *The intellectual base of social work practice.* New York: Haworth Press.

Lewis, H. (1984). Ethical assessment. *Social Casework, 65,* 203–211.

Loewenberg, F., & Dolgoff, R. (1996). *Ethical decisions for social work practice* (5th ed.). New York: F. E. Peacock.

Mattison, M. (1994). *Ethical decision making in social work practice.* Unpublished doctoral dissertation, Columbia University, New York.

McGowan, B. G., & Mattison, M. (1998). Professional values and ethics. In M. Mattaini, C. Lowery, & C. Meyer (Eds.), *The foundations of social work practice* (2nd ed., pp. 43–68). Washington, DC: NASW Press.

National Association of Social Workers. (1996). *Code of ethics.* Washington, DC: Author.

Noble, D., & King, J. (1981). Values: Passing on the torch without burning the runner. *Social Casework, 62,* 579–584.

Perlman, H. H. (1976). Believing and doing: Values in social work education. *Social Casework, 57,* 381–390.

Pine, B. (1987). Strategies for more ethical decision making in child welfare practice. *Child Welfare, 66,* 315–326.

Reamer, F. (1990). *Ethical dilemmas in social service.* New York: Columbia University Press.

Reamer, F. (1994). *Social work malpractice and liability: Strategies for prevention.* New York: Columbia University Press.

Reamer, F. (1995). *Social work values and ethics.* New York: Columbia University Press.

Rokeach, M. (1973). *The nature of human values.* New York: Free Press.

Rothman, J. (1989). Client self-determination: Untangling the knot. *Social Service Review, 63,* 598–612.

Schlesinger, E. G., & Devore, W. (1995). Ethnic-sensitive practice. In R. L. Edwards (Ed.- in-Chief), *Encyclopedia of social work* (19th ed., Vol. 1, pp. 902–908). Washington, DC: NASW Press.

Siporin, M. (1982). Moral philosophy in social work today. *Social Service Review, 56,* 516–538.

Marian Mattison, DSW, ACSW, is chair, Department of Social Work, Providence College, River Avenue, Providence, RI 02918; e-mail: mmattisn@providence.edu.

Original manuscript received January 23, 1998
Final revision received September 21, 1998
Accepted January 19, 1999